THE GAME OF WAR

THE
GAME OF WAR

The Life and Death of Guy Debord

Andrew Hussey

Jonathan Cape
London

Published by Jonathan Cape 2001

2 4 6 8 10 9 7 5 3 1

Copyright © Andrew Hussey 2001

Andrew Hussey has asserted his right under the Copyright, Designs and
Patents Act 1988 to be identified as the author of this work

First published in Great Britain in 2001 by Jonathan Cape
Random House, 20 Vauxhall Bridge Road, London SW1V 2SA

Random House Australia (Pty) Limited
20 Alfred Street, Milsons Point, Sydney,
New South Wales 2061, Australia

Random House New Zealand Limited
18 Poland Road, Glenfield,
Auckland 10, New Zealand

Random House South Africa (Pty) Limited
Endulini, 5A Jubilee Road, Parktown 2193, South Africa

The Random House Group Limited Reg. No. 954009
www.randomhouse.co.uk

A CIP catalogue record for this book
is available from the British Library

ISBN 0-224-04348-X

Papers used by The Random House Group Limited are natural,
recyclable products made from wood grown in sustainable forests;
the manufacturing processes conform to the environmental
regulations of the country of origin

Typeset by Palimpsest Book Production Limited,
Polmont, Stirlingshire
Printed and bound in Great Britain by
Biddles Ltd, Guildford & King's Lynn

To Carmel with love

Contents

List of Illustrations

'Son oeuvre ultime' (*from* L'Humanité, *2 December 1994*).
'The avant-garde dies but never surrenders' (Les Inrockuptibles, *24 September 1997*).
Rue Mazarine, Paris, 1998 (*copyright Éditions Allia*).

Acknowledgements

This book owes a great deal to a good number of people. Two key figures were Alice Debord and Michèle Bernstein who, since I started writing the text, have expressed their firm and absolute wish to disassociate themselves from its contents. Alice Debord wrote to me rather ambiguously to say that she had 'friends who violently regretted calumnies', whilst Michèle Bernstein said that she did not wish to be seen giving her approval in any way to the book. Nonetheless I have reported on meetings and conversations which took place in Paris, Normandy and Salisbury through the course of 1999 and 2000 as part of my research.

In Manosque, Ralph Rumney provided subtle interpretations of key Situationist texts as well as inspiration and alcohol. In Manchester and Scotland, Gavin Bowd was a guiding spirit.

Others who helped shape my views were Jean Baudrillard, David Bellos, Gérard Bérreby, Brigid Berlin, Christophe Bourseiller, Cécile Guilbert, Constant, James Eibisch, Cosey Fanni Tutti, Patrick ffrench, Ronan Fitzsimons, Simon Ford, Lucy Forsyth, 'Gaby', Gérard Guégan, Michel Guet, Chantal Guillaume, Sophie Herszkowiscz, Stewart Home, Michel Houellebecq, Isidore Isou, Anselm Jappe, David Jenkins, Jacqueline de Jong, Irinée D. Lastelle, Jon King, Greil Marcus, John McHale, Patrick Mosconi, Jörgen Nash, Roberto Ohrt, Donald Nicholson-Smith, Sadie Plant, Marcelin Pleynet, Malcolm Pollard, Julian Preece, Jamie Reid, Roland Sabatier, Gianfranco Sanguinetti, Mark E. Smith, Philippe Sollers, Jeremy Stubbs, Raoul Vaneigem, Antony H. Wilson and Alan Woods.

My agent Peter Robinson and my editors Will Sulkin and Jörg Hensgen have each played a crucial role in seeing the text through to completion. I thank also Ghassan, Dawn, Leila and Gabriel Gebara for perspective and John and Doreen Hussey for faith. Patrick and Bessie Regan of Roscommon are also remembered here. And above all I thank Carmel for being herself at all times and in all circumstances.

INTRODUCTION

Le Musée Guy Debord

> Why ask my lineage?
>
> *Iliad*, Canto VI,
> quoted by Guy Debord in *Panegyric*

The hamlet of Champot does not appear on many maps; the granite plateaux of the Auvergne, and, higher up still, the dense and impenetrable woods, make it a hostile place. Despite a meagre influx of disaffected hippies who fled Paris or Lyons in the early 1970s to scratch a living from the poor land, this lonely corner of France has been for years a byword for depopulation and rural wretchedness. Its emptiness and silence are a far cry from Paris, where Guy Debord, writer, film-maker and leader for the course of the 1960s of the notorious revolutionary group the Situationist International, had spent most of his life in arguments and in bars. But it was where he shot himself through the heart during the late afternoon of 30 November 1994.

Debord was remembered by his Auvergnat neighbours – generally considered a clannish and churlish race – as an especially austere figure, even by their tough standards. The last person to speak to Debord was a stonemason from nearby Bellevue-la-Montagne who had been called to his farmhouse to repair wind damage. He heard the facts of Debord's death with an indifferent shrug: 'It wasn't normal the way he hid himself away,' he said. And indeed Debord had spent the better part of a decade in the farmhouse he shared with his companion Alice Becker-Ho, drinking, playing endless war games, and ruminating on the victory of the 'spectacular society' he had predicted and hated.

It was several days before details of Debord's suicide reached Paris. When the news arrived the French media – 'the spectacle' against which Debord had waged such an implacable war – accorded him the status of one of the great thinkers of the age. Philippe Sollers, the most influential and noisy figure on the Parisian intellectual scene, appraised Debord's suicide as a 'post-modern' gesture of defiance; drew a comparison with Antonin Artaud's description of Van Gogh as a 'suicide of society'; and asked young people to make sure 'they heard the sound of the gunshot which killed him and realised its revolutionary significance'.

But Debord's death also stimulated the Parisian appetite for gossip and conspiracy. It was noted that no Parisian journalist had seen Debord's body; and in Bellevue-la-Montagne, villagers recalled that Monsieur Debord had been visited by police only days before his suicide, a visit made doubly sinister by one of Debord's final books in which he asserted that the French secret services had been tracking him since the early 1970s. Adding grist to the rumour mill, two further suicides followed within the week: those of the writer Roger Stéphane and the publisher Gérard Voitey, both intellectuals, both apparently friends of Debord, and all three linked to unresolved mysteries from the 1960s and 1980s.

As the connections were made, the Parisian media world began to ask who had funded Debord, and why. What had prompted the outwardly cheerful Stéphane to kill himself? And who exactly was Voitey – a struggling publisher, or a sinister financier of revolutionary terror? Conspiracy theorists began to talk of terrorism, murder and manipulation: they, like the obituarists in *Le Figaro* and *Libération*, recalled the unsolved murder ten years earlier of Debord's publisher and patron, the mercurial and mysterious Gérard Lebovici. More restrained commentators pointed to Debord's alcoholism, Voitey's financial problems and the despair that overwhelmed Stéphane, and blamed the spiritual and political malaise afflicting Mitterrand's France. On one thing they were agreed: there was a sickness afoot. But was it social, or criminal? In death, as in life, Debord and mystery walked hand in hand.

This was how the death of Debord was reported in France, the UK and the United States, as part detective story and part political thriller. Much to the disgust of former Situationists and friends of Debord, I played a part in this process myself by writing a series of pieces for newspapers and journals in Britain and America which described events in those same sensationalist or ironic terms (for example, I wrote a piece for Julie Burchill's *Modern Review* – then in its own death throes – in which I described Debord as 'a Hegelian Oliver Reed': this had been taken as a grave insult by Parisian friends of Debord). I received angry phone calls and letters and was accused of working for the CIA. However, like everyone else who read the articles in the press, I was still fascinated by Debord's supreme and sovereign act of self-destruction – such an extreme form of social comment, after all.

I further angered ex-Situationists and others by setting up, in January 1996, with the Scots poet Gavin Bowd, a conference dedicated to Guy Debord and the Situationist International at the Haçienda nightclub in Manchester, a place which had been playfully named after a Situationist text and where, at the cusp of the E-fuelled 1980s, Mancunian youth had cast off the shackles of 'the society of the spectacle'. There were serious attempts at sabotage and disruption. Denunciations, pamphlets, poison-pen letters were sent to us and the French Embassy who were financing the conference ('I am a great admirer of Guy Debord,' the French cultural attaché to Manchester had claimed, much to our amazement, when we asked for cash). The conference was described in Paris and Italy as the work of 'imbecile anarchists' and 'a dangerous provocation'. 'We will not forget you,' we were informed in a menacing letter from Paris. 'Your reputation now goes beyond the frontiers of your own country.' My fascination only grew. What was it about this man which incited people to such extremes of emotion?

But that is not why I wanted to write a book about Guy Debord.

I had first heard of Guy Debord and the Situationist International in 1989. That year there was an international exhibition dedicated to the art of the Situationist International which had attracted enormous press attention as it moved between Boston, Paris and London. I had at the same time discovered Situationist texts for myself in the downstairs section of Compendium Books on Camden High Street. I had then just come from Liverpool to London to work as a low-grade researcher for an American news agency, writing about money markets in South America and Spain and undergoing the same squalid humiliations and petty compromises that everybody makes in corporate life at any level. I knew the legend of the Situationists, that they had been the most ferocious participants in the Paris events of May 1968 and that the term 'Situationist' had something to do with the Sex Pistols and punk rock. I also had a vague feeling that they were involved in terrorism in the early 1970s. Certainly, they were extremists if not cranks.

When I first read the Situationists I fell in love immediately and irrevocably with their writings and ideas. With wit, elegance, cruelty and swagger, the Situationists pointed out the obvious: that 'work was a disgrace', 'the concept of leisure was an insult', 'the real economic problem in the first world is not poverty but boredom', 'real life is elsewhere'. The most degrading fact of modern life was that it made everyone a consumer and therefore a serf; we were all victims of a con-trick which gave us the illusion of choice. 'Lack of satisfaction is measured in numbers of cars, fridges, TVs,' they said. 'To be rich today is to possess the greatest number of impoverished objects.' The result of this process, they argued with an imperious sneer and implacable logic, was to 'reduce life to a single choice: suicide or revolution'.

I devoured Raoul Vaneigem's book, *The Revolution of Everyday Life*, hiding it underneath my office desk. 'The economy of daily life is based on a continual exchange of humiliations and aggressive attitudes,' wrote Vaneigem, explaining the imprisonment which everybody can feel in an office in the financial capital of Europe. 'The feeling of humiliation is nothing but the feeling of being an object. Once understood as such, it becomes the basis for a combative lucidity in which the critique of the organisation of life cannot be separated from the immediate inception of the project of living differently.'

The key to understanding this 'combative lucidity' was the notion that the world was not as it seemed. For the Situationists everything you thought, felt, ate, drank, loved and touched in daily life was part of a 'spectacular society', a world of objects, image and unreality, which you could look at but not touch. For the first time in history, they said, human beings were no longer participants in but rather spectators of their own lives. This was the logic of the millenarian nutters who marched down Oxford Street declaring that the end was nigh. Except that when the Situationists, in their passionate heresy, insisted that what you were living was not real life, it made sense: if you looked around carefully enough and saw the cracks and fissures in everyday experience which separated people from each other, you could see that it was all true.

This was also the year that the Berlin Wall was about to fall, revealing for many that history had come to an end in the final victory of Anglo-American liberal democracy. On the Right this moment was a vindication of bourgeois supremacy; the Left took refuge in post-modern, post-Marxist debates which replaced real life with textual theory. The great success two years later was Francis Fukuyama's book *The End of History and the Last Man* which confidently claimed that the future – if, as history dissolved before our eyes, the word could still have any meaning – would belong to the globalising strategies of free-market economies.

When I read Guy Debord's book *The Society of the Spectacle*, written in 1967, I found that he had predicted that this is precisely what we would be told when state Communism collapsed, when the spectre of Communism in the East would be revealed as 'spectacle', an illusion, a chimera. But history, said Debord, did not, could not, end at such a point. Guy Debord said that present conditions in the West could not last for ever either, that they would only last until people realised that they could throw the cheap gifts of the society of the spectacle back in its face. The first step towards this was 'the construction of situations', moments of poetic intensity when 'real life' could be glimpsed.

This was not however really what was meant in the popular application of the term 'Situationism', which in the early 1990s appeared everywhere from the *New Musical Express* to *The Economist*, and seemed to be entering the language in the same way as 'Surrealism' or 'Communism'. The widespread use of the term meant that it was simultaneously losing all of its meaning as it was used to describe activities as diverse as the art terrorism of the K Foundation (although, to be fair, ex-Situationists did enjoy the K Foundation's disruption of the

Turner Prize in 1993 and their final and most devastating gesture of burning a million quid on a Scottish island) or the grim *rock ordinaire* of the Manic Street Preachers, whose lyricist Richey Edwards, addicted to vodka and Philip Larkin, declared himself a fan of Guy Debord shortly before engineering his own disappearance off the Severn Bridge in 1994.

The appeal of 'Situationism' in the early 1990s was for me more political than cultural: more precisely, this was not nineteenth-century Marxism, which argued revolution in the name of classes which obviously no longer existed, but a harder, more vicious and more aristocratic way of challenging the organisation of the world. One famous floating Situationist project in the 1960s involved hurling red dye and a van-load of Asiatic corpses into the Seine to protest against Vietnam. The project only stalled because of logistical problems they encountered whilst trying to hijack a truck carrying Chinese corpses, which had been sold by the Chinese government to a Paris medical school for research. I couldn't help but admire the bravery, resourcefulness, poetry and sheer contempt for the veneer of civilisation which went into planning this assault on all of modern society's sensibilities. The Situationists were chiliasts: they hated modern life and imagined another world, another way of living. They were exciting dangerous friends.

This was the direct opposite of post-modernist philosophy which I met at the dreary meetings of the Socialist Society, a cluster of disaffected Leftists (some of them now stars in the New Labour firmament) who met above a pub in Soho, and who, on fashionable French models, sought to abolish history and politics in favour of 'difference' and fake 'eclecticism'. Nothing ever happened at these meetings, not least of all because, in a half-witted gesture to 'celebrating difference', the chairman of the meetings was a paraplegic and had to spell out his response to questions with Scrabble letters and the aid of a helper. I thought his position was a cruel metaphor for political stasis on the Left outside Labour Party orthodoxies.

In contrast, the glamorous nihilism of the Situationists was powerful, seductive, irresistible. Against the background of the collapsing shibboleths of classical Marxism, it also seemed to have found its historic moment. The Situationists were not afraid of the future and imagined it as a world of endless possibility. 'Ours is the best effort yet towards leaving the twentieth century,' wrote Guy Debord. 'We are only concerned with the moments when life shatters the glaciation of survival,' wrote Raoul Vaneigem. 'Our ideas are already in everybody's heads,' declared the Situationist International. During the 1968 Paris riots, for a brief moment, the Situationists and their friends stood on the barricades amidst the wreckage of the rue Gay-Lussac and believed they would bring down the 'old world'. 'We are not afraid of ruins,' they said.

*　　*　　*

I started writing this book in Paris in 1996. I set out to capture the spirit of 'combative lucidity' which had shaped the pattern of Guy Debord's life. My plan was to trace Debord's itinerary around the bars and streets of the Paris he had loved, through Holland, England, Italy and Spain, where he travelled and occasionally lived, and to speak to people who had known, admired, hated or simply drank with Debord. My aim was to understand the substance of a life which had been lived entirely as a project, an adventure and experiment in the middle of the twentieth century.

One of the first people I spoke to in Paris was the novelist Philippe Sollers, who so loudly declared his allegiance to Debord in *Libération* in the wake of his suicide. When the Situationist International was at its most active in the 1960s, Sollers had been the editor of *Tel Quel*, the journal which had introduced Jacques Derrida, Julia Kristeva (Sollers's wife), Michel Foucault and other avatars of post-modern thought to the wider world. *Tel Quel*'s politics had notoriously veered between orthodox Marxism and, finally and most damagingly, Maoism (I noticed that Chinese prints were still a feature on the walls of Sollers's office). Not a single member of the *Tel Quel* group had ever made the slightest mention of Debord or the Situationist International in the 1960s or any other time. So, I asked Sollers, who was now a regular guest on chat shows on French television describing himself as a 'situationist novelist', what he could have meant by the 'revolutionary significance' of the gunshot which had killed Guy Debord.

'It is a commonplace now, especially in the world of fine art, to talk of artists making life their raw material,' Sollers replied, waving his cigar around his cramped and messy office in the rue Sébastien-Bottin, where he commissioned books for French publishing giant Gallimard and edited his influential journal *L'Infini*. 'They talk of making their lives the site of art, of blurring the distinction between art and life in a way which challenges or disorientates the spectator of art. Guy Debord was however not an artist and he was not interested in challenging or shifting perspectives between art and spectator.'

So why talk about Guy Debord now, at this point in history? 'History does not matter,' Sollers replied. 'When Debord talks of life as a project, it is not art but everyday life which he is pursuing. The construction of situations from which there is no turning back, which is the most concise definition of that dangerous term "situationist", explains not only how Guy Debord lived as he did, but also how he saw life as a game, the rules of which were constantly being defined and redefined by hazard, circumstance or terrain. This is outside history, of course.'

I liked Sollers, he was charming and enjoyed putting on a show, but I didn't trust him. His enemies accused him of being too urbane, too smooth, too suave. He mixed with Jacques Chirac and other political notables on the Right, he was friendly with important people in diplomatic circles and justified his presence at cocktail parties and ambassadorial receptions as 'situationist subversion'. This was obvious nonsense.

As a counterpoint to Sollers's unctuousness and urbanity I went to talk to Michel Houellebecq about Debord's drinking. Houellebecq now has an international reputation as a writer and English translations of his novels have made him a literary superstar in London and New York as well as Paris. In 1996 Houellebecq was still working on his second novel, *Les Particules Élémentaires*, the novel which catapulted him into the literary stratosphere and led to him being alternately described as 'the best French writer since Zola' or 'a Stalinist pornographer' (in truth his style and ideas are much closer to those of Louis-Ferdinand Céline, Jew-baiter, Nazi sympathiser and, for me, the best French writer of the early part of the twentieth century). Houellebecq lived then in a council flat in southeast Paris. He was semi-anorexic and almost permanently drunk, possessed of an acid wit and scabrous vision of the world. We drank hard ourselves and talked about what Debord, who drank persistently and prodigiously, had written about alcohol.

'I am not a Situationist at all: I am nearer to Communism, which is less fashionable now,' said Houellebecq. 'But I admire Debord as a perfect and dedicated drinker.' We talked about how, in the early years of his career as a drinker, Debord was always in pursuit of or just arriving at a perfect point of intoxication which, unlike paid labour or any other servile activity, would reveal 'the true taste of the passage of time'. 'There are those who have got drunk only once,' Debord wrote, quoting Baltasar Gracián, 'but it has lasted them a lifetime.' Drinking was a beautiful poetic game, with its rules and protocols.

Debord devoted pages to describing this notion: 'The hours and their shifting conditions almost always retain a determining role in the necessary renewal of the moments of a spree, and each brings its sensible preferences to bear on the available possibilities. There is what is drunk in the mornings, and for a long while that was beer. In *Cannery Row* a character who one could tell was a connoisseur professes that "there's nothing like that first taste of beer". But I have often needed, at the moment of waking, Russian vodka. There is what is drunk with meals, and in the afternoons that stretch between them. There is wine some nights along with spirits, and after that beer is pleasant – for then beer makes one thirsty. There is what is drunk at the end of the day, at the moment when the day begins anew. It is understood that all this has left me very little time for writing; and that is exactly as it should be: writing should remain a rare thing, since one must have drunk for a long time before finding excellence.' Later on drink diminished him and when Debord, like Orson Welles, grew fat, ill and consumed with boozer's gloom, it played an important role in his destruction. 'All games have risks,' concluded Houellebecq, only just avoiding knocking over his own glass.

Nobody in Paris took the tale of the three mystery suicides of Debord, Voitey and Stéphane seriously. 'It is true that Debord was closely involved with Gérard Voitey. But Gérard was depressed and bankrupt and in shock,' said Christophe Bourseiller in the Café Zegher. 'But I really don't think Debord knew Roger Stéphane at all: that was not his milieu.' Bourseiller came from a well-known theatrical family in Paris and had known Jean Genet, one of Stéphane's closest friends, as a child so I presumed he knew what he was talking about.

Bourseiller had just published his own biography of Debord (this book owes a great deal to Bourseiller and his generosity) and was exhausted with the subject and the attacks that were now being made on him in the press and elsewhere. 'I wrote a book on Debord because I am fascinated by extremes,' he said. This was not the first time that Bourseiller had placed himself in a difficult position by writing a book – after his previous works on Maoists and Trotskyists in France he had received death threats and had a police guard placed on his apartment. Bourseiller hinted that he had not told the whole story ('perhaps that is what you can do as an Englishman'), referring to unsubstantiated far-Right allegiances in Debord's adolescence and other dubious relations. Christophe had just been the target of an attempt at public humiliation on television when, in a live television debate, Gérard Guégan, Debord's great enemy from the 1970s, had gloatingly revealed that he had deliberately given Bourseiller false information. 'For now,' Christophe sighed, 'I have done enough. I am sick of Guy Debord'. He then began to talk about his new project, a study of Throbbing Gristle, Hull's premier industrial art rockers in the 1970s.

In the far posher Café de Flore, Cécile Guilbert, an up-and-coming novelist and intimate of Philippe Sollers and Jean Baudrillard, who had just published her own book on Guy Debord, mused on the significance of these rumours about Debord. 'He obviously loved mystery. I think that was because he saw the world as illusion, mystification. This is why we cannot describe him as an artist or a writer, although he wrote beautiful prose, because he could not take the world on its terms. Literally, there was nothing to write about.' Cécile was beautiful, elegant, fiercely intelligent and part of the Parisian literary world that Debord despised. 'There is no contradiction there,' she said, 'because Debord, like Baudrillard, was also an aristocrat, he had great contempt for the world. Aristocrats are fascinating, don't you think?'

It is true that Debord always behaved and acted with lordly sovereignty. 'I wonder if even one other person has dared to behave like me in this era,' he wondered in one of his final books. Others I spoke to in Paris when I set out to write this book confirmed that Debord always held himself with an elegant and archly ironic disposition. He was variously 'like a Prince', 'a master of despair' (this is how Jean Baudrillard described him to me), 'the most intelligent man I have ever known', 'somebody from another century'. This dark and romantic aspect of his character was indeed as fascinating as his notorious libertinism and his political writings; it is the fact that these are not separate, it may well be argued, which makes Debord such a compelling figure.

He was also famously described as 'chess player, rigorously leading the game whose every move he had foreseen'. His chief obsession was military strategy; his heroes were Clausewitz, Machiavelli and Saint-Just. His tactics were to play life as a game whose rules he alone had invented: his strategy was to restore real meaning to individual experience. This was, argued Guy Debord in the most urgent and convincing way, the essential aspect of existence which had been lost in the twentieth century.

Debord was not the first, nor, as the twentieth-first century begins under the same conditions as the last century, will he be the last to argue this point. This book exists however as an account of a life informed by what an English ex-Situationist has termed Guy Debord's 'chiliastic serenity', that is to say an adventure which, beyond the poetic and political strategies of the Situationist project, seeks to relate history to the future. It is this notion, especially under the present conditions of 'historical absence' determined by post-modern commentators on our times, which best explains Debord's description of himself as 'a remarkable example of what this era did not want'.

Amongst the accusations and criticisms levelled against me (and there have been many) as I have been writing this book is that this biography can only be a 'museum of Situationist ideas'. I would argue that 'Le musée Guy Debord' already exists: the stencilled graffiti of Debord's image which appeared around his haunts on the rue Dauphine and the rue de Buci in the wake of his death are testimony to this. More than this, the cult of Guy Debord in the pages of fashionable and best-selling magazines such as *Les Inrockuptibles* and *Nova* shows no sign of abating: this is where his admirers have installed him as the incarnation of the spirit of revolt of 1968 – the Che Guevara of the 1990s, a figure whose iconic status defines his impotence.

The suicide of Guy Debord affected me because, since 1989, I had admired the fact that his lone and defiant voice was still waging war against what he called 'the forces of spectacular domination'. I did not want to believe that he had been defeated by them. That is why I wrote this book.

Andrew Hussey
Dublin, 2000

PART ONE

Dark Passage

1931–57

Above everything else I am taken by the Revolution. It had to be that way. The wind that blew through the ruin where I was born, the old people who brought me up, the solitude and freedom of my childhood, the scraps of knowledge gleaned from here and there – all that opened my ear to every harmony, my spirit to every illumination. Everything intermingled in a single song, a single dream, a single love: the Revolution.

Louise Michel, *Memoirs of the Red Virgin*, 1898

I was born virtually ruined. I was not properly speaking ignorant of the fact that I should not expect an inheritance, and in the end I did not receive one. I simply did not grant the slightest importance to those rather abstract questions about the future. Thus, throughout the course of my adolescence, if I went slowly but inevitably towards a life of adventure with my eyes open, it can none the less be said that I had my eyes open then on this question, as well as on most others. I could not even think of studying for one of the learned professions that lead to holding down a job, for all of them seemed completely alien to my tastes or contrary to my opinions.

Guy Debord, *Panegyric*

CHAPTER 1

The Lost Domain

1931–45

Guy Debord rarely spoke about his childhood and wrote even less. This was not because his childhood had been especially traumatic or because he had been an unhappy child. Rather it was because, from the moment in his late adolescence when he entered avant-garde circles in Paris, Debord loudly and consistently proclaimed his adherence to the belief, formulated by the Dadaists and Surrealists whom he saw as his true ancestors, that the family was the enemy of liberty. 'Families, I hate you all!' had declared the poet Arthur Rimbaud in a moment of revolutionary insight. Few of Debord's friends or lovers had ever seen anything in Guy's private life or heard him say anything, even in his most loose and drunken moments, which might have contradicted this article of faith. Guy Louis Marie Vincent Ernest Debord was born in Paris on 28 December 1931. This was all the biographical information which was ever given on all of his books and films. He never gave any more details away to anyone but his close associates. He talked about his childhood as if it were something separate from him.

To Jean-Michel Mension, briefly a steadfast drinking companion in Left Bank dives during Debord's first period in Paris in the early 1950s, he would frequently say, 'I never had a childhood.'[1] This much was obviously a pose, typical of the young crowd who had come to bury their provincial origins and reinvent themselves in 1950s Paris. It was also to conceal early hurt and misplaced sense of identity, the result of a constantly changing family set-up, which never quite went away but which was clearly, if rarely, revealed to the girls and women in his life. Above all he could not forgive his mother for either ignoring his needs or, worse still, making him feel as if he didn't exist.

But although he never talked about his family, he was not averse to poetically dissembling about the precise time of his birth, noting that it was also 'at nightfall' (he was born in the early evening) that Hegel's owl of Minerva spreads his wings to announce the arrival of wisdom in the world.[2] It was also a perfect poetic fact, he would often remark to friends, lovers, comrades and others, that Guy Debord, the avatar of negative revolt and deadly enemy of the twentieth century's cult of image and illusion, entered the world as it moved between light and dark. It was therefore no coincidence or surprise that he killed himself at dusk. 'The perfection of suicide,' he wrote for his first film in 1953, 'is the perfection of ambiguity.'

Guy Debord was born in the neglected, almost forgotten quarter of La Mouzaïa, a run-down and homely village only just within the city limits of Paris. Today, La Mouzaïa, with its hidden courtyards and gardens and crumbling villas, is fashionable and an address much sought-after by those working in fashion or the media who want to live in a part of central Paris which, although dominated by grim 1960s tower blocks, still physically resembles the picturesque pre-war Paris of family bistros, winding cobbled streets, accordion music and *guinguettes*. In the 1930s this area had been barely touched by the modern world; indeed it prided itself on its 'provincial' atmosphere. It represented a kind of micro-society, a lost domain which stood apart from the so-called 'new Babylon', a term first used in the nineteenth century to describe the brash new world of commercial Paris.

The quarter of La Mouzaïa descends towards the Parc de Buttes Chaumont which, with its grottoes, artificial lakes and meandering paths, is still one of the strangest open spaces in Paris. Built in the 1860s under the direction of Baron Georges-Eugène Haussmann, the park was intended as an oasis of greenery in the spectacular city of boulevards and passages then under construction. The park had been inspired by the English models which, in London, Liverpool, Glasgow and Dublin, had brought an artificial, sanitised version of the countryside to the city. The overall effect of the Parc de Buttes Chaumont is however rather more sinister than any to be found in the great municipal works of the British Empire. Most notably, in the middle of the park is a sheer and intimidating rock on top of which is a fragile-looking Corinthian temple. The lake below is traversed by a delicate-looking bridge, the so-called Pont des Suicides, which, according to the Surrealist poet Louis Aragon in his book *Le Paysan de Paris*, 'claimed victims even from passers-by who had no intention whatsoever of killing themselves but were suddenly tempted by the abyss'.

Baron Haussmann had built the park as part of his great project to lead a team of architects who, under the orders of Napoleon III, were to make Paris the grandest city in the world. Haussmann's city was built in straight lines which swept remorselessly through the crowded and labyrinthine warrens of the poor and the working classes. In Baudelaire's poem 'Le Cygne' ('The Swan') this process is described as a movement which sweeps the proletariat out of history (this poem is quoted in the final film *Guy Debord, son art et son temps*). It was also noted by contemporary, and more revolutionary, observers that the new layout of the city also meant that troops could move freely from one end of the city to another in time of insurrection.

This latter fact was of central importance for Guy Debord, who came back to Paris in the 1950s. He was at this stage in his career developing the notion of 'psychogeography', making his own emotional maps of the city with all the precision of a military cartographer. He did not often return to the place where he had spent his early childhood on the grounds that Haussmann's development, in the name of progress or modernity, had also meant the eradication of places of symbolic significance, places which had earlier been claimed by history or blood.

The End of the Night

'I was born virtually ruined.' This is one of the few details of what Debord calls 'the date and general conditions' of his early life.[3] But, although in a strict sense it was true that the Debord family fortune had more or less evaporated by the time that Debord came of age, it was not true that the family was either poor or without social status. Guy Debord was in fact born into a well-to-do family who, although they often hovered precariously above a financial abyss, never touched upon any real suffering.

It was true enough that Martial Debord, Guy's father, was not a particularly wealthy man. He was nonetheless sufficiently respectable to be allowed to court Paulette Rossi, a sparkling and vivacious young woman of Italian origin and – for the standards of the times and the place – substantial means. Martial was a hard-working student of pharmacy who had emerged from a modest family background in the Limousin with the laudably bourgeois ambitions of opening his own premises in Paris. He was quiet and well-mannered, with a serious expression which belied a gentle sense of humour and a delight in beautiful young women.

Paulette Rossi came from much more prosperous, albeit much more chaotic, circumstances. The Rossis had come to Paris in the 1920s. They also had a connection with the Limousin, which was where Paulette's mother, Lydie Hélène Fantouiller, had been born on 25 June 1888. Paulette's father, Vicenzo Rossi, had come from humble origins in Naples. Vicenzo had been born on 22 February 1886 to Antonio and Concetta Curci in the slums of the dockside area of Naples. As soon as he was able, he determined to leave Naples, a city where disease and poverty conspired to make life expectancy the lowest in Europe, and like many young men of his generation he headed for the richer towns of northern Italy, eventually finding his way to Paris where he started to make some headway as a budding businessman. He invested in a shoe factory at 63–69 rue Compans, a few yards from the *métro* Boutzaris, overlooking the Parc de Buttes Chaumont, where he concentrated on high-quality, fashionable products. Vicenzo married Lydie in 1910 and Paulette Antoinnette Concetta Rossi was born to the couple on 8 October 1911. By the early 1920s, established in a villa in the courtyard of the factory, which itself housed a variety of artisan workshops, the Rossi family presented to the world a perfect picture of bourgeois domesticity. As business folk they were respected by their middle-class neighbours and held in high esteem by their fellow artisans. They also enjoyed living in a lively and gregarious working-class quarter in which life was lived according to the demands of a local and therefore intimate and human geography.

In the 1920s and 1930s the industrial northeastern part of Paris, comprising Belleville, Ménilmontant, Buttes-Chaumont and La Mouzaïa, was less connected to central Paris than it is now. It was also fiercely working-class as well as home to a floating population of immigrants from Southern and Eastern Europe. Yiddish was the first language spoken around the junction of rue des Couronnes, rue Julien-Lacroix and passage Julien-Lacroix; in the warren of streets and alleyways between boulevard Mortier and rue des Pyrénées, Catalan, Castilian, Portuguese and a variety of Italian dialects were as widely spoken as French. The working life of this district, even as late as the 1930s, was still centred around a *quartier* economy, that is to say it was a close-knit and intimate network of traders and shopkeepers who mixed business and sociability and for whom Paris was a separate place. In this environment the Rossi family played the role of the mild bourgeois, whose social prestige was founded on a paternalistic form of capitalism which depended on class distinction, but who was also an integral part of the pattern of trade in the *quartier*.

The idyll did not last long. On 3 December Vicenzo Rossi, whose health, probably as a legacy of his Neapolitan childhood, had never been strong, took a fever and died within a few days, aged only forty-one. The family was plunged into chaos by this sudden loss. Paulette was only sixteen and her mother, who had come from a traditional Catholic family in Limoges, had abandoned her studies at an early age in preparation for marriage and family. Lydie's courage and determination were remarkable, however, and she propelled herself into taking charge of the business which, from the day she assumed control, began to slide into a slow but apparently unstoppable decline. Like her mother, Lydie had been brought up to disdain work and study in favour of the more feminine practices of familial duty. The death of Vicenzo brought the mother and daughter very close together, however, both in work and in their relationship with each other. Most notably, the death of her husband had made Lydie fiercely protective of her daughter, who was taken to school every day at the age of sixteen, when she was already a deliciously pretty young girl, hand in hand with Lydie who fought off the attentions of sneering and lustful local lads. At the age of twenty, Paulette was pursued by Martial, who had fallen for her brown hair and blue eyes. Despite Lydie's protestations that the young man was only after the money that Vicenzo had left her, the couple were not long in announcing that they were to marry, on 28 March 1931 at the church of Saint-Vincent-de-Paul in the 10th *arrondissement* of Paris.

Martial was an austere and handsome man who delighted in Paulette's youth and beauty and who took a relaxed and generous attitude to family life. He settled into the family home on the rue Compans and, despite Lydie's reservations and her naked hostility towards him, he enjoyed his new married life. He also began planning how to run his own business. Lydie, ever shrewdly prudent of her family's welfare, had bought a pharmacy on the rue des Pyrénées which Martial was to take over as soon as he had passed his exams. At least Paulette would be cared for, she reasoned to herself. When Guy was born, at nightfall on 28 December 1931, Martial took an even greater delight in his beautiful young wife and his new son. The atmosphere in the Rossi-Debord family home was a combination of strict bourgeois values, upheld by Martial with as much conviction as he could muster, and extravagance with which Paulette would playfully contradict her husband's strictures on thrift and hard work. Martial's attempts at imposing some kind of patriarchal order were sabotaged even more effectively by Lydie, who fell hopelessly in love with the new infant and took sole charge of his care. Lydie was now renamed 'Manou' – an affectionate and cosy term – by the young couple and when not hawkishly watching the family business in its slow decline, she devoted herself to doting on young Guy. Normally an anxious person, whose stern expression and dark eyes glowered with nervous energy, she found a release in caring for the adored child.

The 20th *arrondissement* was not only companionable and cosmopolitan but also desperately poor. This was the part of Paris in which Louis-Ferdinand Céline had set his classic novel *Journey to the End of the Night*, a book much favoured by Debord in his adolescence and which was later quoted in his *Mémoires*. Céline had given the fictional name 'Rancy' to the part of Paris in which Debord grew up and Debord immediately recognised, in Céline's account of a cityscape wrecked by capitalism, the décor and the emotional substance of his childhood.

Journey to the End of the Night was published in 1932 and with its virulent pacifism and anti-capitalism quickly established Céline, whose real name was Destouches and who worked as a doctor in Clichy, as a hero of the Left. No less a figure than Leon Trotsky, then resident in the far more salubrious environment of Montparnasse, applauded Céline for his account of the wretched lives of the downtrodden and wrote that Céline 'had walked into great literature as if walking into his own home'.[4] Jean-Paul Sartre and Simone de Beauvoir, then both young and brilliant teachers who had recently graduated from the École normale supérieure, read passages aloud to each other, learned sections by heart and discussed Céline's novel as a premonition of proletarian revolution.

Céline's reputation was soon to be shattered by his pro-Hitler and anti-Jewish writings. Influenced in part by the nineteenth-century racial theories of the Comte de Gobineau, who proposed a pan-German racial aristocracy, and his own personal hatred of Jews, Céline published a series of tracts in the late 1930s which called for an immediate French alignment with Hitler and the elimination of the Jewish race from Europe. However, few contemporaries could match Céline's descriptions of northern Paris, where the vestiges of the ideal nineteenth-century *quartier* life were being visibly corroded by the twentieth century.

The bourgeois status of the Debord family in this environment did not make them immune to its diseases and in the spring of 1936 Martial Debord succumbed to the tuberculosis which had plagued him since youth. By the summer he was dead.

'I hate the lies that have done you so much harm'

Paulette was still only twenty-three when Martial died. Unable to cope with such a catastrophe she asked Manou to step in and run the house and family. It was tacitly agreed between the two women that, after an appropriate period of mourning, it made good sense for Paulette to resume her existence as a young woman, going to dances and being courted by good-looking men, and for Manou to look after the children and the house. If Paulette's good looks attracted a husband then so much the better. Debord often complained in later life that his mother had never been like a real mother. His grandmother, as he would later admit, more than compensated for this absence in his life by treating him as her son and as the most important male in the house.

Paulette threw herself into a hectic social life which soon began to consume much of the meagre fortune which Martial had left her. Despite this apparent frivolity, however, Manou and Paulette were still assiduous Mass-goers and strove to present themselves as respectable in their habits. But their spirituality, like their political conservatism, was more to do with class and keeping up appearances than a reflection of any real, felt emotion or belief.

The arrival of the Second World War did not leave the Debord-Rossi clan indifferent. Their move from Paris to Nice in the autumn of 1939 was however motivated by domestic economic imperatives rather than the European political crisis. Manou had sold the shoe factory in the rue Compans on the grounds that it was time-consuming and too difficult for her to run properly and, looking for an equitable climate and a healthier environment than the one which had killed Vicenzo and Martial, had decided to move to Nice. Guy had by now been diagnosed as asthmatic and Manou was determined not to lose her cherished grandson to the poisoned, tubercular air of northern Paris.

The family arrived in Nice a few weeks after the start of the war, before the real fighting had begun and the mass flight from Paris and the north had turned the south of France into a mass transit camp. The trio settled into an apartment in the smartest quarter in the centre of Nice near the *belle époque* Opera House, and Manou set about the business of providing for the family. Anticipating that the war would bring food shortages, she bought a fruit and vegetable store (she let it out to tenants who refused to pay her in the winter). This turned out to be yet another ruinous financial mistake, although what was left of the dwindling Rossi fortune allowed the family to escape complete disaster and, later on, the hardships of rationing. In the meantime, Paulette was also determined to enjoy herself. She dressed fashionably and, still beautiful, spent a good deal of time on the Promenade des Anglais and other fashionable thoroughfares, courting the attention of well-heeled and stylish young Niçois who affected the Italian practice of the *passegiatta*, strolling through the town at dusk, the young men aping Jean Gabin or Clark Gable, the young women fancying themselves as Betty Grable or Arletty. Paulette did her level best to ignore the political events of the day and rarely mentioned the war to Manou or her children.

But it was impossible to ignore the fact that in the wake of the French collapse of 1940, France had been carved up into zones defined by their relation to the Third Reich. Although it lay outside the immediate sphere of German influence in the Occupied Zone, Nice was, for the duration of the war, a dangerous and sinister place, a long way removed from its former status as one of the most élite playgrounds of pre-war France. The proximity of Nice to Marseilles, until 1942 the only Free Port in France, made it a staging post for refugees, black-marketeers and fugitives who were desperately trying to get out of France.

The Unoccupied Zone was also a focus for the most insidious form of Vichy propaganda. When Pétain made a state visit to Marseilles in 1940 the walls of Nice and Cannes were covered with posters of the Marshal's most infamous maxims: 'The soil tells no lies' and 'I hate the lies that have done you so much harm'. When, however, the demarcation line was suppressed in November 1942, with Cannes ostensibly under Italian control, young Frenchmen were forced to work in German factories in place of military service. Many preferred to join the Maquis and left for the countryside behind Cannes, retreating into the clandestine groups scattered across the hinterland of the Haut Var. The towns and cities of the Riviera in the meantime swarmed with every kind of spy and criminal. The German security forces sought to crush opposition with an iron fist: in the course of a single day, SS squads evacuated and dynamited the oldest quarter of Marseilles, known locally as Le Panier ('The Breadbasket', also a slang word in the 1940s for 'cunt', a not inappropriate nickname given the number of prostitutes in the area), which they had identified as a warren of 'Untermenschen' such as Jews, Communists and Resistance leaders. Twenty thousand people were cleared out of the area, many to the town of Fréjus where they were selected for concentration camps. The first films Debord saw in the ornate Art-Deco cinematographic palaces of wartime Cannes were Vichy propaganda newsreels in which heroic French forces aided the despised 'Boches' who were obviously, even to the ten-year-old Guy Debord, bullies and murderers.

Against this background Paulette fell catastrophically in love again with an Italian driving instructor called Domenico Bignoli, fifteen years her senior and with a wife and family in his home town of Galliate in Piedmont. Paulette, whose appetite for sex was as insatiable as her need for attention, swiftly became pregnant and Guy's half-sister, Michèle Dominique Bignoli, came into the world on 26 August 1940. A brother, Bernard Rossi, was born two years later at Fontainebleu. This time Domenico Bignoli refused to recognise his son, on the grounds that he could not be sure that Paulette, who ignored the German demarcation line and travelled often to the Occupied Zone, did not have another lover or lovers. Given the uncertain climate in his hometown, however, Bignoli thought it prudent to stay with the Rossis for the time being.

The first priority for Manou and Paulette was to ensure that the family was safe. With this in mind, and with Domenico in tow, they set off again in 1942 for the southeastern town of Pau, not far from the Pyrenees. They lodged in the elegant centre of the town and, ignoring the cataclysmic events around them, spent summer days at Sables-d'Olonne and other pleasant spots on the Basque coast. Paulette, flirtatious and seductive as ever, was not long in attracting admirers. Among these was a certain Charles Bernard Prosper Labaste, a notary and native of Pau who had come across Paulette in an official capacity, helping with the family affairs. Labaste was a respected man in Pau. He had recently inherited his uncle's offices in the centre of town and in the short time he had been in charge he had impressed old and valuable clients. He was also reputed to be involved in Resistance activities, a rumour which further enhanced his reputation in the town.

Labaste was sexually intoxicated by Paulette, who seduced him efficiently, effectively and completely. Domenico left within a few short weeks, accepting his fate with sanguine resignation. He was now heartily sick of the capricious Paulette, her wiles and her lovers. His disillusion with Paulette and her fierce mother was absolute. Before he left for Italy Domenico took the eleven-year-old Guy Debord by the shoulders and said to him confidentially, 'I'm entrusting you with Michèle and Bernardo.'

Despite Domenico's gallant retreat, Labaste himself was in an awkward position which threatened his reputation as a man of good standing in Pau. He had been married for over fourteen years and he had two children, fourteen-year-old Bernard and eight-year-old Chantal. Worse still, his wife, Jeanne Elisabeth Marie, was desperately ill, and had been pronounced near to death several times during the past two years. The affair was therefore conducted in secret until 1944, when Jeanne died and it was socially acceptable for Charles to set up openly with the Rossi-Bignoli-Debord family. With the younger children, Paulette moved into Charles's huge living quarters overlooking one of the main squares in Pau. Bernard Bignoli was renamed 'Patrick' to distinguish him from Bernard Labaste, a sign that Charles had decided to treat Paulette's younger children as his own. This, however, was not the case with Guy, who was sent off to live with Manou in a much smaller apartment, on the grounds that Charles's apartment was not large enough for them all. Although Guy loved his grandmother, he never forgave his mother for this betrayal. 'My mother adored making babies,' commented Patrick on this lack of maternal affection. 'The baby no longer interests her when she can't play with it like a doll. This happened when the child was about a year and a half old.'

Debord also found it impossible to love or even like his new stepfather. On one occasion, goaded once too often by an act of minor disobedience, in an attempt to defy Manou and assert his parental authority, Charles had smacked Guy quite hard across the face. The boy did not flinch. From then on, as a tough and defiant older brother, Guy enjoyed a naturally privileged position over the younger members of the family. Michèle in particular looked up to him, although he rarely played games with his siblings, preferring to play solitary war games with his toy soldiers or cutting out pictures of aeroplanes, boats and people which he collected and carefully kept in notebooks. Patrick is able to recall a fleeting enthusiasm for the Tour de France and the occasional trip to watch the Riviera stages of the race, but mostly Guy hated sport or any form of physical exertion, which more often than not provoked an asthma attack. He spent a good deal of time alone, practising the piano, reading adventure stories or devising elaborate campaigns for his growing collection of tin soldiers. Visitors were chased away by Manou who would open the door of her apartment to the troupe of Bignoli-Labaste children to tell them sternly that 'Guy is resting' or 'Guy is working' or 'Guy needs silence'.

The encounter with Maldoror

Guy's sense of his own importance was not helped by Manou, who adored him with a specifically Mediterranean form of child-worship which prized first-born males above all. Manou had disliked all of Paulette's lovers, but had tolerated them. As 'her boy' grew older she confided in him her fears and beliefs about his mother's men. Naturally enough, Guy found it difficult to listen to or respect any form of male authority.

When he began his secondary education at the Lycée in Pau in 1942, entering the *sixième* at the age of eleven, he was not surprisingly a little shy of boys his own age and wary of the boisterous rough and tumble of playground games. His peers at first mistook his timidity for arrogance and his new comrades found it difficult to get to know him on their own terms. Manou did not help matters by insisting on taking him to and from school every day carrying a large knife for his protection (she continued to do this well into his teens at schools in Nice and Cannes).

It was shortly after starting school that Debord first began to fall under the spell of Isidore Ducasse, the legendary *poète maudit* of the nineteenth century who would influence much of Debord's later life. At that time in France, literature was studied, at least until the *troisième* (roughly thirteen or fourteen years of age), in the form of digestible chunks from 'great authors' who were to be admired for their technical mastery rather than their ideas. The 'masters' of French literature were considered to be Racine, Corneille and Molière, who, alongside 'moderns' such as Chateaubriand, Vigny and Hugo, were seen as models of aesthetic virtue and learned by heart. More advanced students were introduced to 'easier' poets such as Baudelaire or Paul Verlaine and some of the more liberal teachers even provoked extra-curricular discussion of Gide or Proust. But effectively literary culture came to a dead stop around 1890.

Debord first came to recognise the name Ducasse not because of the schooling he received in French literature but because, by a remarkable coincidence, Guy first attended Lycée at Pau where the great poet had begun his career in the 1860s. Debord later came across Ducasse in the writings of the Surrealists, but the fact that he had been to the same school as the great poet obviously left a powerful initial impact upon him. Ducasse was the perfect model for an easily bored and somewhat insecure youth. In an account of Ducasse's life found and devoured by Guy, a contemporary of Ducasse, Paul Lespès, described Ducasse at the Lycée as someone who carried himself with 'a disdainful gravity' and who 'considered himself a being apart', alternatively delighting and tormenting Gustave Hinstin, his teacher of poetry and rhetoric.[5] This kind of behaviour was an irresistible example to Guy Debord, who was already deciding to reject all forms of authority but his own.

Ducasse was not a figure whom most schools then or now would hold up to parents or pupils as an example. Most notably, Ducasse became notorious for writings published under the name of Comte de Lautréamont. He was a flamboyant writer, possessed of a sickly eroticism. Most famously, he described his chief poetic ambition as having his sexual and satanic poetry read by fourteen-year-old girls whose minds he would poison with the deadly elixir of poetry.

Even by the decadent standards of late nineteenth-century Paris, Lautréamont's poetry was considered a strong, potentially lethal brew. It was important to the young Debord, however, that Ducasse's life matched his art in both style and content. Most importantly, Ducasse's life was a suitable combination of mystery and drama which culminated in an obscure early death. Ducasse was born of French parents in Montevideo. After Lycée in Pau he went to Paris in 1867 to study at the prestigious École polytechnique, then as now the gateway to the highest appointments of state in France. Ducasse preferred, however, to spend his time drinking absinthe, writing and expounding his genius. He died, probably of drink, a short three years after his arrival in Paris. The few reviews of his work which appeared in the Parisian press after Ducasse's disappearance invariably described its author as quite mad.[6]

For Debord this enigmatic biography was an exemplary account of a literary career given over to the pursuit of an aesthetic philosophy which placed life above art, a pursuit described by the poet himself as 'a perverse idealism'. The exotic pseudonomyn Lautréamont was allegedly taken from *Latréamont* by Eugène Sue, a novelist mainly popular in the 1830s for his extravagant tales of Parisian low life. In *Latréamont* the central character's arrogance drives him to revolt and blasphemy.

Lautréamont's most famous work, *Chants de Maldoror*, is a hallucinatory compendium of erotic, blasphemous, grotesque and grandiose poetic fragments in which Maldoror, a Luciferian figure, cries his hatred of God and his love of the Ocean. Lautréamont's other masterpiece is the unfinished work, *Poésies*, which contains an attack on the style and content of *Maldoror*.

Debord admired this deliberately inconsistent quality in Lautréamont's work, a quality which Lautréamont's near-contemporary Rémy de Gourmont famously described as 'hallucinations used by the will'.[7] The true aim of Lautréamont's poetry was to launch a series of attacks against both his readers and the society which produced them, to 'cretinise' the reader with the poison of his poetic texts, which substitute evil for good, ugly for beautiful, the irrational for the rational, in the name of a dramatised perpetual conflict of the 'all-powerful Self' against the universal Law of 'the Creator'. Lautréamont wrote that his poetry aimed to expose the hypocrisy of all moral structures.

More precisely, in his famous list of similes beginning 'beautiful as . . .', Lautréamont places contradictory or opposing elements together to create a new idea. In this way he is not only undermining the very substance of poetic language, but also revealing a new perspective for both reader and author which opens up a new world of endless possibility, disorientation and metamorphosis. 'Beautiful as the chance meeting on a dissecting table of a sewing machine and an umbrella' and 'beautiful as the congenital malformation of man's sexual organs' read two poetic oppositions favoured by the Surrealists, to whom Lautréamont was a hero and example. 'Beautiful as the trembling hands of alcoholism' read another, much favoured by Debord towards the end of his life.[8]

Debord often supported his ideas by quoting Lautréamont's well-known dictum that 'Plagiarism is necessary. Progress implies it.' Lautréamont meant by this that poetry did not depend on the Romantic notion of the individual genius whose gift has a transcendental meaning for humanity. He argued that 'poetry must be made by all' and that only by insisting upon the negative, evil or perversity can the illusory hierarchical nature of the world be revealed. 'I have seen all my life,' Lautréamont wrote in a text which would go on to have a lingering resonance for Debord, 'men with strong shoulders perform countless stupid deeds, brutalise their kin and pervert souls in all manner of ways. They call the reason for their actions glory. Having seen these spectacles, I have wanted to laugh like many others; but that, o strange imitation!, has been impossible.'[9]

The zone of perdition

As a child, Debord had never really known anything about the family finances, nor really understood the complicated arrangements which meant that the family was so often on the move. He was well aware, however, that as they moved from Paris to Pau, and then, shortly after the Liberation of France, to Cannes, their movements were dictated, at least in part, by lack of money. As Debord approached his middle year at school this fact became particularly important and acute for him. It was explained to him by Charles Labaste that the family fortune, which on the death of Debord's father in 1936 had already dwindled to an insignificant sum, was all gone by the end of the war: he could not expect an inheritance or even the smallest contribution towards an education. Labaste made this cutting fact finally legal by adopting Michèle and Patrick as his own and pointedly leaving Guy outside the family. Manou had always hated Labaste and she took this badly, openly condemning Guy's mother in front of him.

To make things worse Charles Labaste was quite obviously making a financial killing on the Côte d'Azur and spending it freely. Indeed 'la famille Labaste' was quite ostentatiously better off than it had ever been before. The Liberation of France had meant that the rich no longer had to hide their wealth, and chic properties in Cannes and its surrounds soon commanded prices which far outstripped even the wildest dreams of pre-war speculators. Labaste provided an extremely lucrative legal conveyancing service for the well-heeled and fashionable now returning to the Côte from exile or clandestine existence, and his business soon employed over seventy people. The family settled in a chic property on the avenue Isola-Bella, set back in the hills and overlooking the town centre of Cannes. The family even acquired a maid, Anna (Manou continued to direct household chores, mostly just to annoy Labaste), whilst Paulette reinvented herself as the sophisticated and sleek 'Paule', a lady of leisure and means.

Despite this upturn in their fortunes, the financial and emotional well-being of the Debord family had still been undermined by the constant movement across a countryscape mapped by the twin exigencies of Occupation and financial hardship. The frequent changes of scene meant that Guy had, through necessity, grown into something of a solitary adolescent who did not seem to need many friends. His chief pleasures were reading and study, at which he excelled – although by his own admission he was given to periods of 'great laziness', and he gave little outward display to his teachers or his school comrades at the prestigious Lycée Carnot in Cannes of either pleasure or pride in his achievements. He reserved a particular anger and contempt for his mother, who he felt had abandoned him, and he saw no reason why he should try and please anyone else either in school or out of it. 'Guy was very like his mother,' comments Patrick, explaining Guy's ability to disregard the opinions of others. 'He got from her his courage, his foolhardiness.'[10]

Guy was commonly described in school reports as intelligent but uninterested in any work which did not have a literary or historical subject matter. As at least half of the French curriculum of that time was devoted to languages and mathematics, it is of little surprise that Guy had decided almost halfway through his school career that education had little to offer him. He was, however, extremely well-read, often discussing subjects about which his teacher knew little or nothing. He even briefly became a star for winning a radio general knowledge quiz for schoolchildren hosted by the avuncular figure of 'Monsieur Champagne', a retired teacher from the Lycée Condorcet who travelled all over France seeking 'the brightest, the best and the cleverest young people of the time'. A photograph of the period shows a smiling Guy Debord, who had been forced to appear by a bullying form tutor, resplendent in shining white shirt and shorts, on stage with the beaming 'Monsieur Champagne' to receive his prize. His teachers swelled with pride. Manou was beside herself with joy.

Guy's popularity was short-lived, as was his desire to please. As he approached his final exams he grew more defiant of authority and openly ready to challenge it. With a small, intimate group of like-minded rebels, Hervé Falcou, Jacques Fillon and a boy known only as Met, he began to devise games which disrupted the orderly running of the world. One of these was to alter or switch street signs in the centre of Cannes to disorientate people and traffic. On another occasion the group of would-be outlaws broke into the chapel of a convent and, in daring blasphemous imitation of

Maldoror himself, smashed a crucifix. The blasphemy did not worry Guy, or at least not as much as the others, as he had never been religious. The point of the action was to see whether one could live with the responsibility of committing an act of supreme transgression. Guy never showed an ounce of remorse or a flicker of shame.

Guy Debord, lonely but with a fierce resilience and self-belief, grew up determined to leave behind the emotional uncertainties of his early years. He had no desire, however, to pursue the bourgeois aspirations for family and career which were his only inheritance; his own experience of loss and dislocation had already convinced him that such comforts were a fraud. As Debord reached his nineteenth birthday in 1950, it seemed, however, that he could not escape the lingering impact of grim wartime realities. The defining characteristics of French political life in the immediate post-war years were crisis and instability. Successive government coalitions had been careful to avoid leading the country to either revolution or dictatorship. Although the war was over, France was still divided over issues of occupation, collaboration and resistance.

In adulthood Debord recalled very little of his early years in La Mouzaïa, except that this period was the only time in his life when the Debord family, as with France itself, had been truly intact and he did not have to cope with constant change. As such, although he rarely referred to it openly, the lost world of La Mouzaïa took on a totemic significance for him in later life as a kind of ideal world and community. The rest of his youth and adolescence he dismissed as a meaningless prelude to his real education in the bars and dives of Paris. He called this part of his life 'the zone of perdition'.[11]

As he approached his 'majority', Debord was aware that, at best, he could hope for a place at one of the lesser *grandes écoles*. In the bleak economic circumstances of post-war France, even this would be financially difficult, perhaps impossible, for the Debord family. Labaste had told him as much. Worse still was the fact that Guy was well aware that four years of grinding study would do no more than see the young rebel and admirer of Maldoror into a safe place as a minor functionary in the civil service. This fate was made grimmer still by the fact that the rigid structures of the French civil service permitted no mobility or possibility of promotion beyond a rank accorded at appointment. It was to be condemned to a life sentence of mediocrity.

CHAPTER 2

'Umor' and the Suicide Solution

1945–51

The only alternative, it seemed, was a life outside of the constrictions of family and society. Debord found such an existence exemplified in the lives of the literary heroes of his youth. As a child he loved the stories of Robert Louis Stevenson and Jules Verne. However, having started to read Lautréamont in early adolescence, and following in the footsteps of others who also admired the nineteenth-century master of the grotesque, Debord quickly found himself in the company of Alfred Jarry, Léon-Paul Fargue, Guillaume Apollinaire, André Breton and Georges Bataille. Even in provincial Cannes, it was relatively easy to find back copies of avant-garde journals which fired the young Debord's imagination and gave him access to the Parisian world of illuminated wit and radical postures.

In particular Debord admired writers who, like himself, disdained the 'deceitful chatter' of the bourgeois world and who did not accord either meaning or value to a society which seemed so deeply flawed. These writers were, for the most part, anti-heroes and anti-artists who had nothing but contempt for the shibboleths of work, family, politics and art. These were people Debord said that he 'respected more than anyone alive'.[1]

'Joyful terrorists'

Debord found an affinity with the Surrealist movement, a group of artists and writers based in Paris throughout the 1920s and 1930s, and whose ideas on poetry, painting and revolution aimed at a total aesthetic and moral transformation in society. The key to this transformation for the Surrealists, whose leading theorist was the charismatic and imperious André Breton, was to bring together the real (ordinary life, the everyday) and the unreal (dreams, the unconscious) in a convulsive moment of revelation, 'the surreal', which would lead to a world of endless poetic possibilities. Although by the time that Debord began to read Surrealist texts in the 1940s the group had more or less dissolved in a series of acrimonious splits, whilst the word 'surrealism' was already on its way to becoming diluted as a technical term in art history, he was nonetheless fascinated not only by the Surrealist group's iconoclastic energy but also their argument that the distinguishing characteristic of modernity was the fact that reality had been reduced to a series of illusory images.

In the writings of André Breton, Debord read about and admired the style of Jacques Vaché, Breton's early friend and lifelong inspiration. Vaché died in mysterious circumstances, apparently of an opium overdose, and was found naked with another young man in a hotel room in Nantes in 1919. According to Breton, Vaché, who disdained all conventional forms of behaviour in art or life, and whose life was mainly dedicated to the pursuit of 'the cult of myself', incarnated the essential poetic charge of what would become Surrealism. Vaché was a nihilistic wit, a dandy, 'a joyful terrorist' who, in literature, admired only André Gide's anti-hero Lafcadio in the novel *Les Caves du Vatican*, because, as Vaché said, 'he doesn't read and his only products are amusing experiments – such as Murder.'

The style and mystery of Vaché's death were the cornerstones of his legend in Surrealism. According to Breton, Vaché had intended his death as a black joke. In a letter to Breton, Vaché had famously described black humour as a celebration of the irrational which underlined the 'pointlessness of everything'. This form of humour he defined for Breton as 'umor'. Vaché's final act, in which a friend too would be killed by Vaché's 'superb indifference', was the supreme act of 'umor', or, as Vaché put it to Théodore Fraenkel, 'a hilarious trick'.[2]

For the Surrealists, suicide was held to be an especially poetic act of negation. Alongside Jacques Vaché (and, amongst others, Swift, Sade and Poe) in Breton's first pantheon of Surrealist heroes, published in 1924, was the almost forgotten hack historian Alphonse Rabbe, whose book *Album d'un pessimiste*, published in 1835, was a remarkable compendium of gloomy advice on Romantic melancholy. The book included chapters entitled 'A Philosophy of Despair', 'Horror' and 'The Hell of the Accursed'. It was perhaps not entirely accidental that Rabbe himself had suffered terribly in his youth from a disfiguring infection.

It was of great significance for Debord, however, that Surrealist suicides had their origins in aesthetic or political concerns. Although Breton scorned as would-be mystics the young poets of the Grand Jeu group, who, in the late 1920s, would spend much of their time taking drugs, playing Russian roulette and strangling themselves to reach a state of beatific intoxication, the Surrealist group, nonetheless, considered suicide as one of the highest forms of philosophical statement. In the second edition of *La Révolution surréaliste*, published in January 1925, the Surrealist group wrote: 'We live, we die. Where is the function of the will in all that? It seems that one kills oneself as if in a dream. This is not a moral question that we are asking! Is suicide a solution?'[3]

For many members of the Surrealist inner circle the answer to this question was 'yes'. Indeed, the artistic and political activity of the group was, for a long time, haunted by the ghost of Jacques Vaché, whom Breton consistently cited throughout the 1920s and 1930s as an avatar of untrammelled subjectivity. Most prominent as potential suicides in the group were Jacques Rigaut and René Crevel. Rigaut was a handsome and elegant dandy, in the mould of Vaché, who destroyed his own writings and styled himself as an anti-artist. He was a success with women and one of the stars of the Café Certa, the café in passage de l'Opéra where the early Surrealist group established its headquarters. Rigaut was also addicted to drugs and obsessed with his own death and, by the time he met Breton, had made several attempts to kill himself. According to Breton, 'Rigaut, at around the age of twenty, condemned himself to death and waited impatiently, from hour to hour, for ten years, for the perfect moment to put an end to his life.'[4] True to his word, Rigaut finally killed himself with an overdose in November 1929.

In late 1924, René Crevel had introduced the Surrealist group to the process of self-hypnosis. The 'sleeping fits', as they were called, determined the early Surrealist interest in para-psychology and 'automatic writing'. For this, Breton cited Crevel as a Surrealist hero *par excellence*. Crevel was also, however, bisexual, deeply neurotic, and nursed a lifelong contempt for his mother. Crevel's own father had hanged himself when Crevel was a child. His mother had forced the four-year-old child to watch, 'for his own edification', as she excoriated the dangling corpse. Crevel gassed himself in March 1936, after a fruitless struggle to reconcile Breton and the Communist Party. He left a note pinned to his lapel: 'Disgusted. Burn Me!'[5]

'A man of the extremes of suicide'

Above all, Debord was most impressed by those writings in Surrealism, and his other readings, in which it was argued that life should become art. One of Debord's most enduring heroes, whom he also discovered through his reading of the Surrealists, was Arthur Cravan, the English poet, boxer, adventurer and 'probable suicide'. Cravan was born in Lausanne in 1887 as Fabian Avenarius Lloyd. He was by marriage a nephew of Oscar Wilde and arrived in Paris in 1911 where, by virtue of his flamboyance and daring, he established himself as a trilingual wit and leading light on the literary scene. Cravan moved from boxing to literature at the age of thirty, having won title bouts around Europe, and began publishing a journal called *Maintenant*, written entirely by himself, which he sold from a wheelbarrow around boxing booths, *métro* stations and along the boulevard des Italiens and boulevard Montmartre. Cravan transposed his pugilistic style from the boxing ring to the literary arena: he fired pistol shots over the head of a lecture audience in Paris in 1916; he insulted André Gide ('a show-off') and provocatively described the poet Apollinaire as a Jew, whilst suggesting that Apollinaire's mistress, Marie Laurencin, 'needs someone to lift her skirts and stick a fat . . . somewhere to teach her that art isn't just little pose in front of a mirror'.

Cravan fled to Spain during the First World War to escape conscription. He fought a notorious final boxing match in Barcelona with the then world champion Jack Johnson, in the course of which he was alleged to have been blind drunk and begging Johnson not to damage his good looks. The last that was heard of Cravan was a wild and drunken spree of a lecture tour of the United States, in the course of which he was arrested for performing a striptease during a lecture on modern art and 'the New Spirit'. Cravan then travelled to Buenos Aires, Lima and Mexico City on a Russian passport. A body, very blond and very tall, was found washed up on the Mexican side of the border by police in 1920. Cravan's friends in Paris, Zurich and Barcelona assumed that this was Cravan's final performance. 'I am a man of the extremes of suicide,' he had written not long before the corpse was dragged out of the Rio Grande.[6]

The other great influence on Debord during this period was the poetry of Arthur Rimbaud. Debord was particularly inspired by Rimbaud's hallucinatory and fragmented epic of disgust, denial and confession, *A Season in Hell*. He was entranced by the way in which Rimbaud had composed this work during a period of boredom and frustration at his mother's remote farm in Roche in the Ardennes, and saw an immediate parallel with his isolated life in Pau and Cannes. It was of key significance for Debord that the prose poems of *A Season in Hell* describe a world where visionary art, 'a rational disordering of the senses', overwhelms the misery and insufficiency of daily life.

The picaresque life of Rimbaud, who at the age of twenty abandoned literature for action, eventually setting up as a gun-runner in Abyssinia, confirmed the reality of this poetic theory and had great appeal for Debord, who dreamed of a similar escape from his own dreary existence. The poems of *A Season in Hell* are an account of Rimbaud's vagabond existence with his lover, the older and more famous poet Paul Verlaine, whom Rimbaud had seduced away from his wife to the Chinese opium dens of the East End of London, murderous, drunken brawls in Brussels, and eventually prison. This life, it seemed to Debord, incarnated all the qualities of revolt, rage and disgust which he valued.

Rimbaud's life and poetry had the potency of a loaded weapon. As he did with Lautréamont, Debord not only identified with Rimbaud but saw his writings as a programme for living. In particular he admired the arrogant and seditious young poet who, when sickened at the prospect of manual work at his mother's farm at Roche, wrote: 'Work no, never, never, I am on strike. I will never work. I loathe all trades, I hate the homeland, I do not understand the law.'[7]

'Our life is a journey . . .'

As he drew nearer to school-leaving age Debord had also decided, with the same lordly disdain he held for those fools who went swimming at Cannes, that work was a contemptible activity and that he too would launch a permanent general strike against a society whose laws he refused to understand. Debord devoted himself instead to reading, drinking and going to the cinema. He wore expensive casual clothes, ordered freely from the family tailor, silk ties and highly polished Italian shoes. He took to strolling with friends on La Croisette but was equally at home drinking in the sailors' dives of the old town, the hillside warren of streets known as Le Suquet. He styled himself as an intellectual and sartorial dandy and declared his hero to be the 'literary bandit' Lacenaire who, in Marcel Carné's film *Les Enfants du Paradis*, says that as an aesthete he is above all moral law. Most significantly for Debord, Lacenaire sees himself at war with the world and proclaims in a famous self-justifying attack on the world: 'I am not cruel, I am logical. I declared war on society a long time ago.'

Another of Debord's favourite films of the period was *The Dark Passage*, a 1947 vehicle for Humphrey Bogart and Lauren Bacall which tells the story of a convicted murderer who escapes from jail to prove his innocence. Although the film is notoriously mediocre, Debord was impressed by the opening which is an unbroken thirty-minute sequence of narrative tricks and camera angles positioned from the point of the narrator. Debord was intrigued by the way in which this sequence, contrary to the prevailing conventions of cinema, presented a subjective view of the world as the only true reality. Debord was already by this stage a fan of Orson Welles and *Citizen Kane* had made a great impression upon him, both for its narrative flair and political content. *The Dark Passage* was far inferior to *Citizen Kane* but Debord found comfort by seeing the tale of the condemned prisoner who needs to escape to assert justice as a crude parable which explained his own condition as a brilliant young intellectual trammelled by his provincial family and environment.

More importantly, even at this early stage in the development of his ideas, Debord was fascinated by the multiple poetic meanings which he associated with the term 'passage'. It was no accident for Debord that Louis-Ferdinand Céline, whose wartime activities as a Jew-hating polemicist and collaborator did not exclude him from Debord's pantheon of heroes, had spent his early adolescence in near poverty in the passage Choiseul, one of the numerous and mysterious covered arcades of small shops which linked the Parisian *grands boulevards*. Céline gives a scathing account of this early part of his life in his autobiographical novel *Death on the Instalment Plan* in which he rails against the daily humiliations inflicted upon him by commercialism and petty avarice of life in the passage Choiseul. The passage itself is a kind of 'spectacle' in which consumer goods are offered to the gaze of the strolling bystander for entertainment and entrapment. The young narrator, Ferdinand, spends his whole life entombed in the world of the commodity-spectacle, 'fouller than the inside of a prison', tormented by the sight of women, clothes and objects which he cannot possibly own.

Céline had prefaced his novel *Journey to the End of the Night* with a military song, allegedly of the Swiss Guard who were massacred in 1792, which began: 'Our life is a journey in winter and night, we search for a passage where there is no light'. The song had importance for Debord, who quoted it in his *Mémoires*, not only because it was the motif for a novel which presented an entirely negative vision of the world, but also because the 'passage in winter and night' perfectly expressed his intuition that life was a journey without maps. Trapped in his own domestic misery, eager to escape the vulgar commercialism of the Côte d'Azur, Guy Debord, like Ferdinand, desperately desired a passage towards a new world.

CHAPTER 3

The Demolition Expert

1951–2

Debord's first step towards the kind of life led by his literary heroes was his encounter, on 20 April 1951, at the Fourth Cannes Film Festival, in the Vox cinema in the rue d'Antibes, with the Romanian poet Isidore Isou and his disciples who called themselves the Letterists.[1] Debord had just successfully completed his *baccalauréat*, which he had jokily celebrated by sending to his friends a fake Mass card requesting 'fresh flowers only' for his funeral, and was attending the film festival as an onlooker, motivated by idle curiosity rather than any real interest in film or film stars. The subsequent daily meetings with Isou and the Letterists, at a variety of café tables in the town for the duration of the festival, were, however, a revelation.

Debord was impressed, firstly, by the style of the Letterists. They wore the roll-neck sweaters, canvas jeans and desert boots then fashionable with the jazz-addicted Parisian youth, but in such a way as to suggest that they themselves had invented the style. They took over the best tables on the seafront of Cannes and, when waiters and promenading ladies gave them unkind looks, they stared back hard.

Isou himself was a bohemian dandy, who lived in an ever-changing series of cheap hotels in the 5th and 6th *arrondissements*. He was equally at home in the sleaziest dive and the most elegant *terrasses* of Montparnasse and Saint-Germain-des-Prés, which he would trawl for well-heeled *bourgeoises* in search of low-life thrills. He regularly sported silk cravats over his scuffed collars, and his fine oriental cheekbones and delicate features gave him a louche, insolent sensuality which women found hard to resist. The rest of the group, including Gabriel Pomerand, Gil Wolman, Marc O and Maurice Lemaître, drank freely and at every opportunity, and talked loudly of revolutionising art, life, philosophy and politics. They scorned the provinces, the South, Cannes, bad French cinema, Sartre, Merleau-Ponty, the culture industry. Both the 'New Look' of Christian Dior and the films of Jean Renoir they regarded as an insult. Debord and the Letterists spoke the same language: they scorned the art of the day; they placed poetry over politics; they venerated Arthur Cravan, Lautréamont and Rimbaud; above all, they took from these avatars of poetic freedom the central notion that art should not be separated from life. Most importantly for Debord, the meeting with the Letterists at Cannes was his first direct contact with the youngest members of the Parisian avant-garde, 'the milieu of demolition experts'[2] who had the daring to take on André Breton and other respected figures, but who were still young enough to be recognisably contemporaries, comrades and friends. This was of signal importance for Debord, who for all his worldly preening amongst his peers in Cannes was still an unknown provincial, and a somewhat shy and uncertain one at that.

The assault on Notre-Dame

Isou and his friends, in their Paris headquarters (mainly the cafés round the rue du Four and rue du Dragon), had proclaimed themselves the inheritors of the pre-war avant-gardes and declared war on all other forms of non-Letterist art. They had been starting fights on the Paris literary scene for nearly five years. Faithful to central principles defined by Isou, and borrowing from Lautréamont the dictum that poetry must be made by all, the Letterists were dedicated to bringing their art into the street. Gabriel Pomerand would bang a tambourine and read sound poetry aloud to café tables of bemused tourists. A series of recitals of Letterist poetry were given at Le Tabou, the nightclub on the rue Dauphine favoured by Camus, Sartre, Juliette Gréco and other Existentialist luminaries, and where Boris Vian played trumpet. Participants included Serge Berna, Jean-Louis Brau, Bu Bugajer, François Dufrêne, Ghislain de Marbaix and Isou himself. The most serious Letterist activity concerned itself with violent argument and the composition of tracts in a meeting room overlooking place Saint-Michel. In shattered post-war Paris, where debates over the relation between art and politics were informed by violence both in a metaphorical and literal sense, the Letterists saw themselves as conducting a guerrilla war against an obsolete and derelict cultural establishment which refused to relinquish its power.

Most famously, the Letterists had gained brief international notoriety in April 1950 when four of their number, Michel Mourre, Serge Berna, Ghislain de Marbaix and Jean Rullier, had disrupted the Easter Mass at Notre-Dame in Paris by walking up to the central altar where Mourre, disguised as a Dominican monk, read a sermon, written by Letterist poet Serge Berna, declaring 'the Catholic Church as being the running sore on the decomposed body of the West'. As the Swiss Guards, with their swords drawn, rushed the altar, Mourre fulfilled an old Surrealist dream by announcing, in the most important church in France, in Europe, 'the death of God'.

When they saw the ensuing commotion (the original plan had been merely to release red balloons as a prank) the Letterist comrades who were manning a getaway vehicle slipped away. Three of the four Letterists managed to avoid the deadly intentions of the Swiss Guards and were almost grateful to be arrested by the police. With the exception of Mourre, who was charged with impersonating a priest, the group were released without charge. The scandal, however, made headlines around the world. The French press, including the Communist daily *L'Humanité*, unanimously and unequivocally condemned the 'action'. But the remnants of the pre-war avant-garde could not help feeling wistful about the Letterists' attack on the house of God. Even the imperious André Breton felt moved to place the 'action' alongside the activities of such as Antonin Artaud, René Crevel and Paul Éluard, whilst warmly describing the event as being in the Surrealist spirit. 'We welcomed Breton's intervention,' Isou later commented to me. 'But he did not understand that it was he who had to abandon Surrealism to join the Letterists. And that was his big mistake.'[3]

'The destruction of the cinema'

The Cannes Film Festival had been established in the late 1930s as a response to the Venice Festival's tendency to give prizes to films of marked Fascist tendency. By the late 1940s, Cannes was a runaway success which reflected the post-war French love affair with the cinema. Although the *Nouvelle Vague* had yet had to be born, and the French public in the late 1940s was mostly flocking to see Fernandel comedies or rehashes of Colette, in its four years of post-war existence the Cannes Film Festival had come to be regarded as a prestigious and powerful showpiece for French culture in its most official form. The Letterists' express intention at Cannes was to cause enough trouble to get Isou's first film, *Treatise on Slime and Eternity*, shown at the festival. In this way, the Letterists would reveal that the contemporary art of cinema was a lie and that 'the civilisation of the image' which cinema represented in its purest form could be challenged and beaten on its own terms.

In the course of a week of agitation and interruption, the Letterists, including Debord in their number, finally disrupted enough select meetings of high-powered cinema executives to win a screening. In the event, however, only the soundtrack of *Treatise on Slime and Eternity*, an aural collage of guttural sound poetry and random noise, was finally played. Nonetheless, Isou, on the whim of Jean Cocteau, who was irritated and amused in equal measure, was awarded the hastily invented *Prix de l'Avant-Garde*. The film critic of the influential journal *Combat* was astonished and appalled; to him the 1951 winner of the Special Jury Prize, Joseph L. Mankiewicz's *All About*

Eve, and Isou's barbarism had effectively proved that the art of cinema, if not dead, was entering a terminal phase.[4]

This was entirely in keeping with Isou's stated ambition to negate cinema by attacking its textual surface. Isou had indeed preceded the film with 'Le manifeste du cinéma discrépant', a manifesto for a cinema which turns against itself, a cinema in which no connection can be made between sound and image. 'The cinema is too rich. It is obese,' declared Isou. 'I announce the destruction of the cinema.'[5]

Back in Paris, in the wake of his triumph at Cannes, Isou took the further step of advertising the four and a half hours of *Treatise on Slime and Eternity* as featuring the distinguished actor Jean-Louis Barrault and Jean Cocteau, both of whom, needless to say, had nothing to do with it. The film itself features neither story nor characterisation but rather long sections of blank screen; the most significant action seems to be the scratched and flickering quality of the screen. Debord visited Isou in Paris in the summer of 1951 for another screening of the film and, encouraged by the camaraderie and revolutionary fervour of the Letterists, determined to settle there. He mentioned, in the vaguest terms, to his mother that he might pursue studies in Paris and asked her for the 9,000 francs he needed to pay for a room which Isou had found for him. In September, he wrote to Marc O, a Letterist sound poet, and declared Cannes, the so-called Vichy-sur-Mer, 'a town abandoned by God and all creators in general'. In the same letter he boasted that, following Letterist orders to attack the cinema in general, he had 'wrecked the base of support for a cinema club' at a local cinema in Cannes and 'kicked its director out the door'.[6]

The Making of a Name and a Messiah

Isou had his origins in a country and a generation whose experience of war and occupation was at some remove from that of his Letterist comrades. His real name was not the marvellously alliterative Isidore Isou, but the rather more prosaic Jean-Isidore Goldstein and he was born in 1925 in Botosani, a small city in the northern Romanian province of Moldavia which is known to most Romanians as the birthplace of Mihai Eminescu, the greatest Romanian national poet. 'I have never written in Romanian,' Isou explained to me when I put it to him, in April 1999, that he was in the tradition of Eminescu, a poet whose real theme was his identity. 'And that is because I am a Jew from a country which hates Jews.'

Isou was then seventy-eight years old. He had been in bad health for some time and had been unable to walk for some months. He lived in two small rooms at the top of a building on the rue Saint-André-des-Arts. His apartment was no more than fifty yards away from the Beat Hotel in rue Gît-le-cœur where, in the 1950s, William Burroughs and Brion Gysin, who had known and been impressed by Isou, had conducted magical experiments and planned a 'dream machine' which, like the Letterist cinema of Isou and Gil Wolman, would wreck reality and unleash pure subjective vision on the world. There was an unavoidable irony in the fact that in the same street the bookshop Un Regard Moderne had in stock an expensively designed French edition of *The Naked Lunch*, as well as Isou's most recent text, *Introduction to an Imaginary Aesthetic*, written only a few months earlier during the winter of 1999, and published in near-samizdat form by a few Letterist sympathisers who called themselves Cahiers de l'Externité. The fate of avant-garde artists is always unpredictable.

Isou had not left his apartment for two years and received no visitors, apart from a nurse and his friend Roland Sabatier, a film-maker and artist who had tight control over the still active Letterist group in Paris. 'I know that we are only a handful of fanatics', Sabatier told me, after he and a Letterist comrade had subjected me to a fraught interrogation in a council flat in the 13th *arrondissement*, 'but we are the most powerful group of artists in the world.' The questions had been predictable enough: who did I know in Paris? Why did I want to meet Isou? What did I know about Letterists? What did I think of modern art? (The Letterists disliked Gilbert and George and accused the Chapman brothers of pinching their ideas. The Situationists were thieves and fools manipulated by Guy Debord, a weak intelligence and a chancer.) But I had not expected the atmosphere to be so tense, nor the line of questioning so defensive. 'We are not art terrorists,' said Sabatier, calm but grim-faced, as if I had asked him to explain his latest murder, 'but we know that Isou is right. And we know that he is the true genius of the twentieth century.'

Contrary to Situationist black propaganda, Isou was neither a megalomaniac nor a madman. In a baking hot room, which became unbearable as the afternoon lengthened and the heat intensified, with shining intelligence and a self-deprecating wit Isou told me about the war, anti-Semitism, his discovery of *La Révolution surréaliste* in provincial Romania, his meeting and friendship with Giuseppe Ungaretti, his arrival in Paris, his friendship with Debord ('Like a brother. Then an enemy, like a Nazi'). He explained how Letterism had become international Letterism and Situationism. This was a betrayal, he said, the Situationists misunderstood him and he had explained all this in his 1976 novel, named after Kafka *The Inheritor of the Castle*, where he had described the Situationists as 'a reactionary Neo-Nazi group'. Debord himself, as a perverted leader and betrayer, was no better than the blackest Nazi war criminal.

Now Isou forgave them and he saw (it was crucial, Isou said, that I should understand this!) that they were all on the same side after all. This was a remarkably gentle opinion from someone who had been so obviously wounded by a betrayal which was now forty-nine years old but which still cut deep. 'When I first met Guy Debord,' he explained, 'it was clear that he was an extraordinary, remarkable person. He was very intelligent, that was the first thing you knew, and he had a wide culture. I thought he would be a very effective and important Letterist. I do not understand even now, and this a long time on from when I first met him, why he had to attack me in the way he did.'

Isou's patience was all the more remarkable in view of his own story, which explained the vitriol behind the neo-Nazi insult, and as an account of exile and persecution was as familiar as it was disturbing. The Goldsteins had been in Botosani for several generations, at least for as far back as anyone could remember, but found themselves caught up in the wave of anti-Semitism which made Moldavia, and in particular the heavily pro-German provincial towns of Iaşi and Suceava, one of the most dangerous places in Europe to be a Jew outside the immediate influence of the Third Reich. When, in 1941, the Germans occupied Romania, Goldstein immediately joined a resistance unit based on the French model and closely associated with the Communist Party partisans of Gheorghiu-Dej. Clandestine activity suited Goldstein, who was, by his own admission, fearless, clever and brave. He did not care, however, for orders or discipline and, again, by his own admission, found it difficult to justify activity in the name of a collective good. 'Nothing can be learned from wars or revolution,' he declared, 'because they are not for the individual.'

Goldstein and a friend called Harry Pantzer were given the task of sticking up posters and tracts on police and military installations. Sometimes they would try to stick the posters on a policeman's back, an extremely dangerous, possibly fatal activity. Goldstein soon grew bored with resistance activity: 'I think it's more difficult to cross a main street on a day of heavy traffic, taking a piss, with your cock out, with no shame, in front of astonished men and women, as I did one time, than to stick up tracts. The first act demands an amazing self-possession, a total rejection of all conventional baggage, and the second only requires following orders which any cowardly person can do.' Goldstein asked to be involved in sabotage, assassination, the kind of activities he admired in the French and Czech resistance. Unsurprisingly perhaps, his requests were turned down.

In the meantime it was rumoured that Jews in northeastern Romanian towns were being slaughtered to celebrate Hitler's victories (there was indeed a pogrom at Iaşi in June 1941 when 8,000 Jews were massacred by Romanian troops to herald the arrival of the German Einsatzgruppe D in the country). Goldstein himself was forced to work for the Germans. Returning home every evening he was grateful that he was too young to be sent to the East where he was aware that dreadful massacres were happening.

Goldstein survived by a mixture of subterfuge and deception, changing names frequently. In 1945, Goldstein, by now renamed Isidore Isou in homage to his hero Tristan Tzara, avatar of the Parisian avant-garde and also a Romanian Jew whose real name was Sami Rosenstock, joined the many Romanian Jews leaving for Palestine. Isou's passage had been assured by the World Jewish Congress in Geneva, who paid the Romanian government twelve shillings per head. As he was about to board a ship at the Black Sea port of Constanta, however, Isou feared that he would be betrayed and turned over to either Russian or British authorities. He returned to Bucharest and made for Paris. During the war, Isou had already tried and failed to get papers from the wartime ambassador to Romania, the pro-Vichy novelist Paul Morand, who made him 'feel like a turd'. This time, however, despite the dangers of arrest at the Russian demarcation line at Vienna, he travelled through Budapest, Vienna, Livorno (where he briefly contemplated suicide), Milan and finally arrived at Marseilles, where he was arrested as an illegal imigrant. When he left for Paris via the train to Budapest, an uncle made Isou promise that he would write home. Isou could say to his uncle, a religious man, that he no longer spoke Romanian or the Romanian variant of Yiddish even in his interior dialogues with himself: he was instead thinking in French, the language of a country he had never seen.

'God loves everything anti-Yid'

Isou had survived an apocalypse. But he was very much aware that his real identity had been left far behind. Isou belonged to a community of Ashkenazi Jews who, for all their cosmopolitanism and access to the latest texts from inter-war Berlin and Paris, were often dismissed by 'European' Jews as 'Orientals' whose thought tended towards irrationalism and mysticism.

On his arrival in Paris, as a reaction against this, Isou describes the Germans, and by extension the Aryans and Jews of Western Europe, as the mediocre and contemptible products of an ethical and philosophical system which is based on the limited language of Reason rather than the more elliptical and paradoxical language of sacred truth. Isou therefore argues loudly in his autobiography, *The Making of a Name and a Messiah*, for a counter-revolution against the Enlightenment: a 'Judaism on the attack!'[7]

In *Réflexions sur la question juive*, Jean-Paul Sartre advances the argument that although democracy is not concerned with the specific problems of Jews, because it aims at a humanist universality it supersedes local or particular problems of ethnicity or identity. Isou is, however, thoroughly and venomously opposed to Sartre ('You won't have our skin!'), whom he sees as a collaborator with the very rationalist values which have led to the current apocalypse. Isou recalled an encounter with drunken members of Antonescu's Iron Guard whose attentions he deflected on a train from Bucharest to Constanta on the way to Palestine:

> 'Why, yid, do you want to go to Palestine? Don't you like our country anymore?'[. . .] Another: 'Why do you want to stay here yid? Haven't you exhausted the country enough, insect, vampire?'[. . .] He took out a small Bible from his pocket. 'Is the Bible written in Yid talk? There you are, it's in Christian language. That's what God gave to the Christians from Jesus Christ because he loved Christians. God loves Christians and Germans because they are anti-Semites. God loves everything anti-Yid.'[8]

In the declaration, 'God loves everything anti-Yid', Isou found a formula which, unlike Sartre's ill-defined universal Humanism, counter-attacks anti-Semitism in a form which functions as a revolutionary contradiction of social values. Put simply, Isou declares that if God loves all that is anti-Jewish, the Jew, if he is to take his place in the world, must love all that is anti-God. The Jew is therefore, exactly as the anti-Semites would have it, the agent of contamination who undermines all social values. It is through a negative system of reversals based on this formula that Isou can reconcile his first love of revolution with his acquired Judaism.

And through a parallel dialectical reversal, although he never in any of his texts makes reference to other Romanian writers or literary traditions, Isou is able to announce that he is not nor ever will be a French writer. It is this aspect of his work which, according to Isou, most impressed Debord. 'This is how I taught Debord not to be French or literary or philosophical. I taught him how to write and not how to be a writer.' Both Isou and Debord, said Isou in his small room on rue Saint-André-des-Arts, are indeed exact opposites of what is understood by the term 'French writer'. They are both rather writers in French whose primary aim is to negate and undermine the linguistic and cultural system they are functioning within. 'Like Guy Debord, because of my ideas I had to write in the language of all men, that is to say for me all Jews,' explained Isou when I asked him about the early poems about Belsen and Buchenwald which he had written when he first came to Paris, and which he had shown to Guy Debord. 'So I chose French. But only because I hate my own tongue, a provincial dialect which is ugly and which no one understands. You must understand. I do not respect French literature. No, that would be impossible!'[9]

'The only poetry possible'

Isou also claimed, on 19 March 1942, to have discovered the meaning of life. It was this discovery which compelled him to write *Introduction à une nouvelle poésie*, a text composed in Romania and brought to Paris. In this book Isou informs the reader that the first principle of social existence is not the will to survive but the will to create. 'Lettrisme', or Letterism as Isou translated it into English, was a new theory of art, 'the only poetry possible', which would make men like gods. Isou was the self-proclaimed Jewish Messiah who had been brought into the world to give mankind this message.

Isou explained to his disciples, including the young Guy Debord, that the creation of art is fixed by twin principles of 'amplitude' (amplification) and 'ciselant' (chiselling, or paring away) which were diametrically opposed but also interchangeable. If the highest form of art was poetry, then this meant 'ciselant', or reducing, language down to its component parts to create the 'amplitude' of artistic effect. Isou described this process in historical terms with an account of how Baudelaire and Rimbaud had reduced poetry to anecdote, Valéry and Mallarmé had reduced it to symbol and sound, and Tzara and André Breton had reduced it to nothing.

However, unlike Dada, which had much in common with Isou's negative method, the central principles of Letterism are founded upon experience rather than theory. Isou's key notion was that, since Baudelaire's discovery of 'auto-destruction' as an artistic process, all forms of poetry were a lie and sham. True poetry, Isou tells us, is not be found in 'the plasticity of verbal meaning' but in its opposite: the separation of meaning from sound. Letterist poetry aimed therefore at the annihilation of meaning by reducing poetry to its most basic element, the letter. Letterist poets, following Isou's principles, would thus chisel language down to its essential pre-literate sounds which could be depicted as signs on a page.

In this way, the sound poetry produced by Letterists such as Jean Louis Brau, Gil Wolman and François Dufrêne was, according to Isou, the direct experience of poetry's negative. The Letterists were, quite literally, speaking in tongues: in a typical Letterist performance, Isou or Pomerand or Serge Berna would explode into gibberish and noise which could not possibly be tied to meaning. Letterist art, similarly, substituted an art of representation, whether figurative or abstract, with hieroglyphics or signs which had a phonic meaning. These were called 'metagraphics'. In Gabriel Pomerand's 1950 collage, *Saint Ghetto des prêts*, puns, ideograms, cryptic signs, letters from the Hebrew make up a collage which is as much a form of sign language as it is visual art. Gil J.Wolman's 1951 film *L'Anticoncept* applies a Letterist aesthetic to the cinema. The script opposes the film and vice versa: the filmic experience is reduced to experience of nothing or, in Letterist terms, everything.

In this sense Isou's poetry and Letterist theory are both close to the philosophical and poetic method which Giuseppe Ungaretti, whom Isou had met in Rome on his way to Paris, had given to the inter-war movement in Italy which was called 'ermetismo'. The central tenet of this group, often criticised for their obscurity and aestheticism, was that language commands the dignity of a hard-won truth, that indeed language is all that stands between mankind and chaos. In the earlier catastrophe of the First World War, Ungaretti himself had defined revolution as a movement 'which necessarily had to start from the use of words'.

In his poems of the 1930s Ungaretti describes the coming apocalypse of the Second World War as 'a mad disintegration of words'.[10] In the same way the vocabulary and methodology of Isou's theory, the polarities, the diagrams, the destruction of the image and the word all aim at reinventing or reigniting the poetic function which Ungaretti terms 'la parola abusata' ('the deliberate misuse of the word'). Isou's system of Letterism, like 'ermetismo', opposes not only the rationalism of Western thought, which has culminated in the Jewish apocalypse of the Second World War, but also seeks to shatter the conceptual language of rational thinking such as is embodied in the project of the Enlightenment.

For later French philosophers, such as Jacques Derrida (who is himself an Algerian Jew) and others of the 'post-modernist' generation, it would become axiomatic that the universal laws of the Enlightenment were the basis for twentieth-century totalitarianism (it is this perception which under-lies, for example, Derrida's concerted attack on Western 'Logocentrism', the emphasis on language over experience which he identifies as the origin of Western rationalism). Isou's attack on rational thought in the immediate post-war period is however articulated in Letterist poetry with a visceral as well as a philosophical understanding of this fact. Like the exotic oriental Jews of Galatje and Iaşi, whom Isou describes as clustering in the soup-kitchens of post-war Paris, feared by Christians and misunderstood by hypocritical Western Jews, the new poetry defies the logic of the West. The Letterists called this 'the only poetry possible' and Isou put it: 'You couldn't kill five million Jews and go on living as if nothing had happened.'[11]

'Down to the Bone'

The relationship between Debord and Isou was initially like a love affair. Debord admired Isou's flair and unwavering commitment to the extreme cause of Letterism. Debord also believed in Isou's theory of poetry and creation, or at least those aspects of it which corresponded to his own per-ception of himself as an avatar of negative poetic values. Isou's Jewishness, on the other hand, seemed at this stage for Debord to be an irrelevance. This was not to be the case some thirty years on from their initial meeting when Isou, bitter at having a text refused by the publishers Champ Libre under Debord's instructions, accused Debord in print of behaving like 'a neo-Nazi'. Debord's mocking reply to Isou was to accuse him of having 'a system of creation which did not work and which no one had really believed in'.[12] Even from a distance of thirty years or more, Debord felt it was of crucial importance to point out that he had never really been a disciple.

Nonetheless, when he came up to Paris from Cannes, Debord settled easily into the room which Isou had found for him at the hôtel de la Faculté on the rue Racine, which lay halfway up the boulevard Saint-Michel, at the crossroads of Latin Quarter bohemia and the sophistication of Saint-Germain-des-Prés. The tiny room was not particularly cheap at 9,000 francs a month, but it had a small balcony which overlooked the rue Racine at the point where it met boulevard Saint-Michel and which allowed Guy to spend long hours smoking, watching the movement of the streets. There were no facilities for cooking and washing was despatched on a weekly basis to Manou in Cannes. He wrote to his mother, telling her that he was to enrol in law at the Sorbonne, which gave him both a social security number and the right (which he rarely exercised) to use the various university restaurants scattered around the Left Bank.

In the meantime he eked out the small monthly sum which she sent him by adopting the time-honoured lifestyle of a poor Left Bank student. He ate at the student canteen on the nearby rue de l'École de Médecine and frequented student dives, smoking black tobacco and drinking mainly wine or beer. Books and journals were either borrowed or stolen, or simply read on the spot in bookstores friendly to students, bohemians and idlers.

Despite his family's concern about his future, Debord made no effort at the university beyond enrolment. Nonetheless, he was hardly averse to drinking in student bars or chatting up the prettier girl students who took their coffee in the cafés around the main building on place de la Sorbonne. His seduction technique was, however, to say the least, unconventional. One wild and stormy evening in early October it had rained so hard that the quais of the Seine had been flooded. Debord had been drinking freely and carelessly and, overcome by the storm and the alcohol, had decided to stretch himself out in the gutter of the rue Cujas, a narrow street alongside the Sorbonne, to let the rain wash over him. On seeing this curious spectacle, Barbara Rosenthal, a student at the Sorbonne, had lowered herself to help the obviously drunken but elegantly dressed young man, worriedly whispering, 'If you stay lying here like that, you'll end up drowned.' 'Then why don't you come with me, and we'll die together?' was the response from Guy. Barbara was entranced by the romantic young fool and she quickly became Guy's first Parisian girlfriend.

Drinking and girls were not his exclusive interests. He had, by dint of his participation in the Letterists' most daredevil activities in Cannes, as well as by his general demeanour as an intransigent and fearless would-be poet inspired by Lautréamont, convinced Isou that he was a worthy comrade in the Letterist adventure. Debord had been in Paris less than a month when

Marc O invited him to contribute to a new Letterist journal *Ion*, whose first issue was to be dedicated to the cinema. Although Isou had announced the death of cinema, this did not mean that the Letterists should miss a chance to kick its corpse.

This first and only issue of *Ion*, edited by Marc O under his real name of Marc-Gilbert Guillaumin, was published in April 1952. It consisted of articles and manifestos which, faithful to the Dadaist origins of Letterism, called unanimously for the destruction not only of art, but also of civilisation.

In an essay by Serge Berna, published in the journal under the title 'Down to the Bone', the Letterist aesthetic is explained as a violation of the physical constraints of art. This, says Berna, is a crucial shift from a positive to a negative value which is a movement, or experience, that breaks down the barrier between artist and spectator. It is a reversal wherein the spectactor becomes an artist and the artist a spectator. In this way, Isou goes on to argue in 'Aesthetics of Cinema' (the opening essay of *Ion*), the destruction of the cinema will herald a new civilisation of vision rather than image.

Debord's contributions to *Ion* were both in keeping with Letterist ambitions to re-invent art as method as well as process, and also faithful to ideas which Debord had been developing during his days as a clever and bored *lycéen* in Cannes, devouring Rimbaud and Lautréamont, and admiring the lives of Cravan and Vaché.

He contributed to *Ion* two written texts, 'Prolegomena for all Future Cinema' and an outline scenario for a Letterist film which, in the manner of Isou's 'cinéma discrépant', sought to separate meaning and image. The first of these was distinguished by the clarity of its style and the singularity of its purpose. 'The decomposition of the cinema' wrote Debord, would simply be a prelude to 'displacement of the values of creation toward the spectator'.[13] Debord here articulates, for the first time, the promise made by Rimbaud and Lautréamont, and exemplified by Cravan and Vaché, that life is equivalent to art. Encouraged by Marc O and Isou himself, Debord planned a film which, in line with the Letterist principles of paring down language to pre-literate sounds, would 'destroy the cinema' by breaking it down to its constitutive elements.

Debord's other contribution to *Ion* is a photograph taken in June 1951 to mark the completion of the *baccalauréat* which he had celebrated with the fake funeral Mass card. In this photo, the young Debord, wearing a sports jacket and a polo shirt, the most stylish clothes of the period, leans back against a wall, slightly away from the camera, and holds a self-possessed, expectant expression. Unlike the other Letterist self-portraits which appear in *Ion* – Serge Berna staring blankly into the camera, Gabriel Pomerand playing enigmatically in front of a backdrop of triangular shapes, François Dufrêne pouting in movie-star style, Gil Wolman as thinker and poet – Debord's photograph stands out as an action as well as a pose.

Most importantly, borrowing the technique of using purposely damaged film from Marc O and Isou, Debord had reshot the original photograph to blur and destroy the image. 'Destruction was my Béatrice,' explained Debord much later, quoting Mallarmé to justify his love affair with the negative principles of creation expounded by Isidore Isou.[14]

CHAPTER 4

Like a Pack of Bastard Dogs

1952

In the late 1940s and early 1950s Paris was still a mythical place. Despite the physical devastation of war, it was visibly the city whose brothels, dance-halls and bars had been photographed by Georges Brassaï and eulogised by Henry Miller during the furious collision of hedonism and impending catastrophe which characterised the 1930s. The post-war city was captured on film by a young photographer, Robert Doisneau, who was inspired by Brassaï. Doisneau had a keen eye for the poetry of everyday life and his photographs of the battered suburbs of Paris, in spite of the dirty, twisted streets and drab hoardings and shops, are also still-life portraits of a world full of possibilities. In the same way, a new generation, Boris Vian, Lola Mouloudji and Juliette Gréco, inspired by Jacques Prévert and Charles Trénet, eulogised the city, and all its post-war *tristesse*, in print and song. Although, since the Liberation, ordinary life for most Parisians had been characterised by shortages and material misery, it was still possible, if you were young enough or feckless enough, to live cheaply, drink copiously and stumble in the warm glow of an alcoholic haze through streets still free from the dead hand of gentrification.

At the heart of Paris was Les Halles, still then a fiercely working-class area. As the location of the main Parisian food markets, Les Halles had a long tradition as the 'stomach of Paris'. It was equally renowned, and loved by Parisians, for the drinking and prostitution which went on in the magical, splendid chaos of markets and bars which fanned out in concentric circles towards the *quartier* of Montorgueil Saint-Denis, beyond the rue Saint-Martin or Strasbourg Saint-Denis towards the Gare du Nord. This was the Paris, beloved of Debord, which had resisted Baron Haussmann's attempts to rationalise the city in the nineteenth century and which was still made up of the dream architecture of covered arcades, labyrinths and passages which led nowhere.

It was, however, Saint-Germain-des-Prés, the chic epicentre of the Left Bank, which was the site of the real cultural explosion in post-war Paris. The chief reason put forward for Saint-Germain's post-war ascendance was usually attributed to the influence of economic and political factors. An influx of displaced persons, often backed with black-market capital, had created a wave of nightclub owners, restaurateurs and other entrepreneurs eager to turn a fast buck and keen to cash in on the new cult of youth. The Left Bank renaissance, however, was also the clear product of the artistic traditions of the area. Students from the Sorbonne, academics, politicians, publishers and gallery owners were all equally keen, in the post-war climate of re-awakening, to establish the primacy of cultural egalitarianism by taking an apéritif on the most fashionable *terrasses* and thereby asserting the democracy of the café table.

The cultural explosion of Saint-Germain-des-Prés was one of the first manifestations of post-war pop culture. To this extent, it had as much to do with style as philosophical content. For young people who flocked to the area, the so-called *Germano-pratins* in the *argot* of the day, the mainly unisex clothes were predominantly black and casual. For males, *la canadienne* – a heavy felt coat designed for harsh Canadian winters – and the 'Montycoat', or duffel coat, were permissible in winter. Girls wore fringes and ballet shoes. Both sexes wore polo necks. The soundtrack to the cultural, sexual and political activity of the Left Bank was jazz, the music of those oppressed and enslaved by American capitalist culture. The most common style, famously adopted by its finest Parisian exponent, Claude Luter and his band Les Lorientais, was usually the traditional New Orleans idiom perfected by Louis Armstrong. By the early 1950s, however, there could be heard the first strains of hard, metallic bebop played, more often than not, by Black American expatriates in imitation of Dizzy Gillespie, who was a frequent and much lauded visitor to Paris, or Charlie Parker, whose first experiments in atonality and free-form rhythm were the epitome of Parisian cool.

'Saint-Germain-des-Prés is a ghetto. Everyone there wears a yellow star above his heart,' Gabriel Pomerand wrote at the beginning of *Saint Ghetto des prêts*, his 1950 Letterist metagraphic, subtitled a 'grimoire' or 'book of spells'. 'Saint-Germain-des-Prés', he also wrote, 'is a mirror of heaven.' In the cold winters after the Liberation, however, it seemed to many that the existentialist lifestyle was not merely hedonism but presaged a darker, more vicious form of nihilism.

The Tribe

Debord had not been long in Paris before he discovered that the true headquarters of the avant-garde was not to be found on the boulevard Saint-Germain but rather at the infamous Chez Moineau, 22 rue du Four. Moineau's was not more than four hundred yards away from the fashionable cafés where Camus, Sartre and their followers had made their headquarters, but a world away in terms of atmosphere, with a clientèle of deserters, drug addicts, petty criminals, runaway youth and hardcore boozers.

Moineau's had survived the Occupation more or less intact. As the rest of Saint-Germain-des-Prés set about smartening itself up to fit in with post-war notions of glamour, it had remained obstinately a down-at-heel *troquet du coin*, or local dive, which belonged to another, more faded era. *La mère* Moineau served up notoriously revolting but cheap meals at all hours whilst *le père* Moineau tolerated all forms of excess except the public consumption of ether (not for reasons of moral health: he couldn't stand the smell). Drunkenness was the norm: customers who passed out or who vomited on the floor the previous night were welcomed back without comment or reproach.

Debord found a kind of home here amongst a small group of young people who had dedicated their lives to doing nothing in a grand style. Ralph Rumney, for example, was a painter, trained at the Halifax College of Art, who had fled his native Yorkshire for Paris to avoid a prison sentence for dodging conscription. 'When I first met Guy in Moineau's I was famously idle, a runaway, a professional layabout, not even then an artist. I considered Guy, for a short time, as my best friend, certainly a kindred spirit,' Rumney said to me in a slow accent which blurred public school intonation with unmistakably Northern vowels. 'Guy Debord was a pioneer, in drinking, in art, in thought. But the real question I thought then, and I think it is even more important now, is how did he become "Guy Debord", this figure whose comportment, style and politics were absolutely, unassailably, intact from the moment I knew him.'

I first met Rumney in May 1998 in Manosque, a sleepy and thoroughly bourgeois town in Haute Provence, known in France – if at all – as the scene of the bucolic novels of Jean Giono. I had first spoken with Rumney two years previously to invite him to Manchester to speak at the Haçienda conference. He promised a video and a talk but, deciding at the last minute not to appear at a 'Situationist wake', he had telephoned me in Manchester to berate me drunkenly for over two hours for betraying his ideals (I didn't mention the £200 cheque which he had been sent for travelling expenses). Somehow, from that conversation and others in its wake, a friendship developed and I had grown used to a growling, inevitably drunken but always lucid presence on the line from Provence on a weekly basis, discussing politics, art, philosophy and cricket in equally measured tones.

Rumney was now sixty-five years old and bedridden, thin, elegant and fiercely bearded, living on a diet of powerful, filterless French cigarettes and a ceaseless stream of excellent local wine. He was frank, almost heroic, about his alcoholism ('the Prozac of the artist') and, serving me a large locally-distilled pastis which tasted cleanly of freshly cut herbs, he explained to me the origins and motivation behind the Polaroid shots of naked female torsos which covered the walls of the room and which were part of a series entitled 'The Map is Not the Territory'. 'I consider them to be abstract, geometrical patterns,' he said. 'This is still Situationist work. I am still a Situationist artist.' We talked about his friendship in the Paris of the 1950s with William Burroughs and Brion Gysin ('I didn't know they knew Isou,' he said. 'I knew Brion very well, a magician, a mystic, a true Surrealist, I think'). From the windows of the apartment, you could see only the hill of Mont d'Or or a labyrinth of old streets and passageways, shuttered flats and playing children. There were no advertising hoardings, cars, buses, banks, shops or any bits of twentieth-century paraphernalia to be seen. We could have been anywhere in Europe in the Middle Ages.

I had spent the previous evening in Marseilles, drinking Jameson's whiskey and, in a hotel room overlooking the Vieux Port, watching a television debate on the legacy of May 68. It was almost thirty years to the day since the most violent street-fighting had taken place. 'Those cunts know nothing,' said Ralph, as I explained the arguments of Daniel Cohn-Bendit and other wheezing bores who had been wheeled out to explain the revolution. Ralph himself had most recently been in Marseilles a few weeks before when, enfeebled and suffering from lack of drink, he had been locked in police cells for apparently having frequented 'a known Corsican terrorist' (in reality a former girlfriend on the run). 'I have no time for people who talk about revolution and who don't run risks, or know danger. The police know who the real revolutionaries are, obviously. They have to, it's their job.'

Rumney's life had been predicated on danger. His career, as he put it, had begun when he encountered the writings of Karl Marx and André Breton as an adolescent in Halifax public library. Inspired by his readings of the Surrealists, Rumney had gone on to order from the hapless and innocent librarian the complete works of the Marquis de Sade, not realising that at that time any student of the works of the 'Divine Marquis' needed dispensation from the Archbishop of Canterbury. Rumney's father, a local parson, was outraged to receive a letter from the Bishop of Leeds enquiring after the moral health of his son and even more outraged to find that his son was a pervert. To add insult to injury, Rumney was also subsequently dismissed from his local Communist party for a lack of moral rectitude. Aged eighteen, and already with a semi-criminal past, Rumney washed up in Chez Moineau, via a brief escapade in Sicily, in the early spring of 1952. He quickly became an intimate of Debord and a firm friend of Gil Wolman. 'We weren't just friends, we were also committed, we were like a sect, a tribe. We thought, quite seriously, that we could change the world. Perhaps we have done, although not in the way we intended.'

Other young artists who passed through Le Mabillon, Chez Moineau and The Old Navy (the chief headquarters of English-speaking expatriates) included the young Dutch artist Karel Appel, who lived with his wife Tony Sluiter on the rue Santeuil. Appel was often to be found in the company of his friend and compatriot, the artist Corneille Guillaume van Beverloo, and his wife Hennie Riemens. In Amsterdam, Appel and Corneille had initiated, with the architect and painter Constant, also then in Paris for a year, the Nederlandse Experimentel Groep. This was a coalition of artists who sought to sustain the promises of the revolutionary avant-garde by marrying the urgency of the language of Surrealism with the most brutalist forms of Expressionist painting. The Nederlandse Experimentel Groep was also linked to CoBra, an alliance of artists from Copenhagen, Brussels and Amsterdam whose maxim was 'in a barbarian age, to paint like a barbarian'.[1]

Other more unstable leading players in the nightly theatre of Chez Moineau included Jean-Michel Mension, who came from a solid Communist family but who, at the age of eighteen, had abandoned the orthodox Marxism of his family for a headlong flight into alcohol and oblivion. Mension and Debord were, for a short time in the cold winter of 1951 and 1952, firm friends who shared a common love of drinking to suicidal extremes. Mension was awed by Debord's capacity. He once watched Debord drink more than twenty beers with rum chasers at the Rhûmerie Martiniquaise on boulevard Saint-Germain without betraying any sign of drunkenness. The pair would regularly settle down in the late afternoon on the steps of the cour de Rohan, a tiny passage between boulevard Saint-Germain and rue Saint-André-des-Arts, and each drink a litre of white wine and then a litre of red wine before moving on to Moineau's or wherever the group was moving towards that evening. 'That was the beginning of our friendship; it was sealed there, if you like,' recalled Mension. 'There was a little staircase and we sat on the steps and gave speeches, we put the world to rights drinking one or two litres each. That was like an apéritif, and then we would go off to Moineau's.'[2]

Other leading figures in the group included Pierre Feuillette who was half-French and half-Mexican, although brought up in Morocco. Pierre was notoriously ruthless and it was rumoured that he had had half of his ear torn off in a knife-fight (it was actually bitten off by a girlfriend, 'la petite Édith', who was carrying his child). He was also the group's principal *kif* supplier and because he 'spoke American' functioned as the group's ambassador in the anglophile Old Navy. Feuillette's best friends were Fred and Mohamed Dahou. Another friend of Pierre Feuillette was Mel, an Austrian Jew in Paris on a GI Bill and would-be writer, who returned to New York to follow the jazz scene before finally killing himself with an overdose in a bath in Venice (he later became a character in Alexander Trocchi's *Cain's Book*).

Vali Meyers, an enigmatic and dazzling red-haired Australian beauty, was Feuillette's occasional lover ('He was my number one. Mean as they come and tough,' she said, recalling her youth when she was a lost and sick junkie in Paris in 1980)[3] and a constant presence in the group. Vali lived mainly in the Hôtel d'Alsace Lorraine on rue des Canettes, near place Saint-Sulpice. The concierge, Céleste Albaret, boasted that she had worked for Marcel Proust and that her husband had once been Proust's chauffeur. Vali described Céleste as an angel, mainly because she tolerated her opium addiction and did not mind the visits from Vali's bohemian friends, dealers and lovers.

Vali was notoriously seductive (Ralph Rumney wolfishly recalled three nights in a row in a hotel on the rue de Seine as an unforgettable sexual revelation) and her charms had even entranced the crew-cut Georges Plimpton, then one of the rather strait-laced young Americans gathered around the *Paris Review*, which, it was rumoured, had been recently established with money from the CIA. Plimpton, who was not a regular at Chez Moineau or any other of the Letterist haunts, would describe Vali as 'the strange one, my favourite jewel'.[4]

Other no less eccentric denizens included Ivan Chtcheglov, an early close friend of Debord. Chtcheglov was the son of a Russian refugee family in the 16th *arrondissement*. His parents were old and he had been brought up in a dark flat which might well have been the setting for a Dostoyevsky short story ('His background was what you might describe as "very Samovar",' said Michèle Bernstein, who knew him well). He would later suffer from schizophrenia and even now publicly teetered on the near side of madness, but in such a way as to charm his audience with hallucinatory tales which made him resemble a young Surrealist or the young Rimbaud.

Henry de Béarn, scion of an old and noble family from the Catalan Pyrenees, plotted with Chtcheglov to blow up the Eiffel Tower because its reflected light shone into their shared attic room and kept them awake at night. The pair were arrested in possession of dynamite (pinched from a neighbouring building site) on their way to plant the bomb, having boasted too loudly and unwisely to their audience at Le Mabillon. The adventure, however, made them heroes at Chez Moineau, where revolution was not simply a matter of rehearsal or theoretical debates.[5]

The Youth Front

The disaffected youth who met and drank at Moineau's had a political meaning for Debord. In 1948, the centenary of famous insurrections and the most politically unstable year in France since the war, the Letterists had plastered the walls of the Left Bank with posters which announced that '12,000 youths will take to the streets to make the Letterist revolution'. Most importantly for Debord, it was one of the most attractive features of the Letterist crusade that, in making his revolution, Isou claimed to have discovered youth as a new social category and proclaimed them as the new revolutionary class.

Youth, announced Isou in a tract widely circulated in Moineau's, and entitled *Traité d'économie nucléaire: le soulèvement de la jeunesse* ('Treatise on Nuclear Economy: Youth Insurrection'), was excluded from the economy because it had no exchange value: without employment, family, capital, youths were not people but 'luxury items' or 'utensils'. Isidore Isou's call for a Letterist revolution had been based on the Letterist principles of negation which demanded that all cultural activity be reduced to its most essential elements. In the same way that the Letterist programme, beginning in a critique of art, had called for films without images, stories without words, poetry without meaning, Isou's call for an insurrection was for a negation of all political activity.

> Every politician defends the interests of one or other specifically defined 'mass', while subjugating it to the surging force which is our youth – and those who manipulate the masses deny the suffering of youth as such. Their argument is this: 'While the proletarian or the bourgeois' – the economic agent – 'remains definitively within his condition and finds himself obliged to defend his interests, youth is only a passing, fluctuating state. One is only young for x number of years.'
>
> This assertion is false. Neither the proletarian nor the bourgeois remains definitively within this condition. Both die. They leave their place for another: death.
>
> Any reform must begin with millions of 'pre-agents' who collectively comprise the 'sickness of society'.[6]

This is the argument extended in the Letterist pamphlet, *Front de la jeunesse* ('The Youth Front'), edited by Maurice Lemaître but written by Isou, which called for young people, defined as outsiders by the economy, to refuse to take their allotted future economic position in society. Revolution would be made, argued Isou, by all those who realised that youth was an economic construct and nothing to do with age. This made youth, or at least the economic definition of 'youth', the new proletariat, the new revolutionary class. All those who, through age, boredom, drunkenness, alienation, found themselves excluded from the economic life of society were, in fact, harbingers of freedom from family, work, money. As soon as the new class realised this and unleashed their revolutionary potential, the constructs of state, government and finance would melt away. 'We will call young any individual, no matter what his age, who does not yet coincide with his function,' wrote Isou, 'who struggles to attain the realm of activity he truly desires, who fights to achieve a career in terms of a situation and a form of work other than which was planned for him . . . Those who know and love their places, whether proletarians or capitalists, are passive, because they don't want to compromise themselves by appearing in the streets. They have goods and children to protect. The young, who have nothing to lose, are the attack. They are the adventure!'[7]

The 'Youth Insurrection' imagined by Isou was not, however, simply a manifesto but also a call to arms. In early 1950, a band of 'Letterist youth' – in reality, no more than a gang of *voyous* (hooligans), students, young drunks and petty criminals rounded up from the less salubrious drinking dives of the Latin Quarter by Marc O, Maurice Lemaître and Serge Berna – led an 'action' against a Catholic orphanage in the chic Parisian suburb of Auteuil. Éliane Papaï, friend and comrade of the Letterists, and Debord's latest Parisian lover, had been in and out of Auteuil ever since she could remember; her latest incarceration was all the provocation the Letterists needed to launch an attack.

Once in Auteuil they hurled abuse and bricks at the staff and provoked a small-scale riot in the courtyard of the building. The police arrived, heads were broken and many 'Letterist youth' hauled off for a kicking in the cells. Isou was not directly involved but his point had been proved: 'So long as youth suffers in slavery, or is super-exploited by the seniority system, it will hurl itself into all the warlike follies and all the banalities which are permitted it as a compensation for its own non-existence.'[8]

The youth who attacked the orphanage at Auteuil as a symbolic force of control were rioting out of boredom rather than material privation, asserting their refusal to be assimilated into a pre-ordained economic order. By throwing a brick, spitting in the face of authority, committing a crime, getting hopelessly drunk, drifting pointlessly between bars, they were able to short-circuit the 'circuit of exchange' which controlled their lives. 'Let youth cease to serve as a commodity,' preached Isou. The new proletariat, above all, Isou said, must be able to accept nothing as given and deny all social forms of order. They were outsiders who were determined to stay on the outside.

Love on the Left Bank

Newspaper reports of 'doomed youth' and licentious 'existentialist' behaviour, as well as a long-nurtured sense of adventure, had inspired the ambitious young Dutch photographer Ed van der Elsken to travel from Amsterdam to Paris. Van der Elsken hoped to establish a career for himself as a photo-journalist, selling photos to *Samedi Soir*, *Le Figaro*, Dutch newspapapers and the syndicated US foreign bureaux in Paris. As a regular (and sometimes spectacular) drinker and participant in activities at Chez Moineau, he had also found himself, almost by accident, a chronicler of Parisian low life with an inside view. He had arrived in late 1950 (he tells the story of arriving with his rucksack weighed down with uneaten sandwiches which his mother had given him in Amsterdam as insurance against anticipated food shortages in Paris) and found on the Left Bank a world which was as exciting as he had guessed it would be, and which, indeed, dramatically surpassed anything which newspaper reports might have prepared him for. What he found exciting was that the group he encountered – rootless, without papers, nationality, ambition, money, employment – drifted from hotel to hotel, from bar to café, with the sense that they were living in their own movie set. They were actors in their own lives who had turned their backs on a world which they neither valued nor understood.[9]

Van der Elsken was especially impressed by the way in which the community which floated between Chez Moineau, The Old Navy and Le Mabillon seemed to form a coherent whole which had no need of external reference points. Having started by photographing, in imitation of Georges Brassaï, the familiar Paris interior landscapes of whores and their pimps at La Pergola nightclub, dancers dressing for a show at the nightclub La Rose Rouge and drunken *clochards* on the quais, van der Elsken turned his attention and his camera on those around him. The group at Chez Moineau were the same age as the ambitious young photographer, who did, after all, have to earn a living with his press work, but they seemed to have dropped from another planet.

Van der Elsken had a premonition that this existence would not last long and he began to concentrate on photographing the inhabitants of this seemingly doomed, lost world, in the way that someone might seek to preserve a dying species. His first idea was to make a photo-novel, 'Love on the Left Bank'. This book, which consisted largely of photos of Fred, Vali, Pierre Feuillette and other luminaries, was meant to be both narrative and documentary account of the romance of this obscure, bohemian, parallel universe. Van der Elsken staged his photographs by filming into one of the mirrors in the café so that conversations, arguments, a couple kissing, men and women drinking and eating, a young man who has taken an overdose and who is slumped over his table in front of a glass of wine, are all moments which exist in real space and time. The effect is of events, incidents, which take place beyond the immediate gaze of the viewer in an intimate place where symbolism meets real life.

In a favourite photograph of van der Elsken, Vali, the most 'flamboyant symbol of the group', is framed against a wall wet with rain in a back alley near Saint-Germain-des-Prés. She is wearing canvas slacks, ballet shoes and a long, loose sweater. Her long red hair is dark in the camera's eye; her face is thin and diamond-shaped. She pouts, looking away from the camera, and her eyes, blackened with kohl, stare into the middle distance. Her expression is urgent, nervous, indifferent. Above Vali, on the wall, there is the scrawled legend 'grêve' ('strike') which in the photo is truncated by the camera's eye to 'rêve' ('dream'); the political and the oneiric are beautifully blurred in the photographic juxtaposition.

It was the privilege of the group at Chez Moineau that, in the words of Vali, 'we lived like a pack of bastard dogs'. By this Vali meant, quite simply, that much of their time was spent avoiding police raids, living without papers, scrounging money, chasing drugs. However, in the photographs taken by van der Elsken, as he himself puts it, the description takes on a more powerful resonance: the youth of Chez Moineau were vagabonds who were 'passive, dark, melancholy'; they had nothing of the fey allure of the gilded youth who fluttered around Sartre at Café de Flore or Les Deux Magots; their faces were tight, impassive, frozen in space and time. They were, he says, a future generation whose youth had marked them for ever.

Bomb culture

Guy Debord was extremely protective of the closed world of Chez Moineau. He never mentioned in his letters home the nature of the crowd he had fallen in with and was careful to describe his activities in the most circumspect manner. Having abandoned Cannes, family and, as he saw it then, all prospect of making a respectable way in the world, the cloistered environment of the Letterist headquarters at Chez Moineau provided Debord with the language and style of negation.

Although, at least at first, he resented van der Elsken's invasion, which he saw as a violation of the codes of secrecy, discretion or anonymity which effectively sealed off the group from the outside world, Debord came to admire the photographs of the hidden society of Chez Moineau and The Old Navy. The restless nature of their existence was what made them unique adventurers in a society that was organised around the controlling principles of work, home and duty, and it was this that van der Elsken captured in his photographs.

According to Ralph Rumney, Debord was also, even at this early stage, cultivating the qualities of decisiveness and intransigence which marked him out as the intellectual leader of this group of renegades. One of the earliest victims of these aspects of Debord's nature was François Dufrêne, the Letterist sound poet who had considered Debord a good friend. After a disagreement in Chez Moineau (Rumney forgets what about) Debord swore to Dufrêne that he would never speak to him again. Dufrêne was mortified the following day on the boulevard Saint-Germain when Debord crossed his path, stared him dead in the eye, and cut him dead. Debord never did speak to Dufrêne again.[10]

Although Debord and the other regulars at Chez Moineau had initially been amused by the attention given by the French and then the international press to youth activities on the Left Bank, they were soon bored and disgusted by the way in which the spontaneous life of the Left Bank had become a staple of lifestyle magazine articles. It seemed that French newspapers and magazines were as delighted and fascinated by 'Existentialism' as they had been by the launch of Christian Dior's 'New Look' in 1947 when, despite the grim post-war atmosphere, it had re-established Paris as the capital of the fashion world.

It was also remembered at Chez Moineau, however, that when Dior's models had first appeared, they had been attacked in the streets by working-class Parisian women furious at such extravagance when they were suffering such hardship. So, when lurid articles appeared in *les torchons*, the popular press, featuring Juliette Gréco, Anne-Marie Cazalis, Marc Doelnitz and other leading lights of the Left Bank sulking, pouting, kissing in a variety of nightclub poses, Debord, Berna and Marc O planned a counter-attack in the form of a film or a riot, or both at the same time. The succession of sensationalist stories in *Samedi Soir* and *Le Parisien* about free-living *décadents* who gave their lives to jazz and late nights had to be matched by an 'action' which would demonstrate that youth was a revolutionary moment and not a lifestyle choice.

Not far from Chez Moineau, there was a famous government information poster which warned that 'L'alcool tue lentement' (Alcohol kills slowly). The poster had not been up for twenty-four hours when, on Debord's instructions, a raiding party from Chez Moineau had scrawled over it: 'On s'en fout. On a le temps' ('We don't give a fuck. We've got the time'). This was not simply a joke: for the Letterists, the key principles of creation were inextricably linked to those of auto-destruction.

The nihilistic mood was captured by a reporter on *Samedi Soir* who described the feckless 'existentialist' Left Bank youth as 'drinking, dancing and loving their lives away in cellars until the atom bomb, which they all perversely long for, drops on Paris'.

CHAPTER 5

Howling in Favour of Sade

1952–3

'It is sometimes surprising to discover the atmosphere of hate and malediction that has constantly surrounded me, and as much as possible, kept me hidden,' Debord wrote in 1989. 'Some think that it is because of the grave responsibility that has often been attributed to me for the origins of the May 1968 revolt. I think rather that it is what I did in 1952 that has been disliked for so long.'[1]

The most important sequence of events for Debord in 1952 began with a mini-riot and a personal failure in the south of France. In April, a Letterist commando team, with Debord in their number, set out again for the Film Festival at Cannes with three films, *L'Anticoncept* by Gil Wolman, *La Barque de la vie courante* ('Navigating Modern Life') by Jean-Louis Brau and *Le Tambour du jugement dernier* ('The Drum of the Last Judgement') by François Dufrêne. The festival organisers were by now well informed in advance about the Letterist hooligans and managed to defuse potentially difficult situations by refusing entry to those Letterists who had been recognised from the previous year, or who had not been able to pass themselves off as journalists or film producers.

Incensed by this, a group of twenty or so Letterist sympathisers, on the orders of Marc O, attacked the press office where tickets were being handed out. The struggle was violent: one of the Letterists, the tiny wife of Marc O who was nicknamed La Poucette ('Hop of my Thumb') on account of her diminutive stature, had, on Marc O's orders, flung herself at the unfortunate press attaché, a young girl named Christiane Rochefort (ironically, within a few years, Christiane would be famous for her novel of bored suburban youth, *Les petits enfants du siècle*. Later still, an unrepentant 68er, she would become a friend of Guy Debord in his final years.) Terrified but angry at the unprovoked attack by the obviously mad La Poucette and her cohorts, Christiane grappled with the enraged Letterists and shrieked for the police.

The Letterists were kicked out and, despite their best efforts to disrupt performances, the press, who decided that they had seen all this the year before, maintained a bored silence in the face of their provocations. This media *omertà* provoked further Letterist disgust, which was aired at café *terrasses* across the town. The big films that year at Cannes were *Viva Zapata!* by Elia Kazan and Orson Welles's *Othello*. The only film which won anything like Letterist approval was André Cayatte's *Nous sommes tous des assassins* ('We're all killers').

Letterist anger had also been fuelled by the fact that in April the French government had seen fit to ban Gil Wolman's film *L'Anticoncept*. Wolman had aimed with this film to stretch the Letterist negation of art to the limit by making a film which would provoke a physical reaction from the public. He had done this at the première of *L'Anticoncept*, which took place on 11 February 1952 at the Avant-Garde Film Club at the Musée de l'homme, by projecting an alternate sequence of black and white circles onto a barrage balloon. Seventy minutes of this visual torture was accompanied by a text which Wolman read aloud as a featureless drone. The text, faithful to Isou's principle of chiselling meaning down into sound, began with a meaningless babble which slowly and hypnotically took on a mysterious meaning for those who had come armed with hash, ether or booze.[2]

The French censorship board, the Commission de contrôle des films, was uncertain about the meaning of *L'Anticoncept* but was fairly sure that anything which brought together such a drunk or drugged rabble from the Latin Quarter was not in the best interests of the Republic. They therefore took great exception to Wolman's adventure in raw sound and vision and Wolman and the Letterists bizarrely found themselves listed alongside American-made primitive porn classics such as *Behind the Green Door*, *The Dirty Girls* and *A Bedroom Fantasy*, as well as Italian-made fascist propaganda (*The Death of Mussolini* and *Second Bureau of the SS*, for example) and other corrupting or politically subversive material. The assault on the Film Festival had been a doomed attempt to right this wrong.

A mother's love

The return to the Côte was also a personal failure for Guy Debord who, after a few days of causing trouble in Cannes, had decided to take advantage of the trip to visit his mother and Manou. The family had moved yet again, to an apartment on the Croisette, the seafront promenade and most prestigious address in this luxurious town. Labaste had also been sexually abandoned. Paule in her slightly plump if glamorous middle age had lost none of her lustre or appetite for men and had not wasted any time in seducing the interior designer who had come to fashion the new Debord-Labaste residence. A photograph taken in the spring of 1952 shows Guy and his mother on the balcony of the apartment. He is smartly and conventionally dressed in jacket and tie, a long way from his new Parisian milieu. Paule is elegant in pearls and a haute couture dress. Guy is smiling frankly and dutifully at the camera. Paule has only the shadow of a smile and her gaze is elsewhere, absent in the distance.

Guy returned to Paris by the end of April, hurt but unsurprised by his mother's indifference to him. He immersed himself in the Left Bank world of endless late-night drinking sprees, drinking harder than ever before. Unlike Cannes, this was a city where he had a real place, where he was known for who he really was and where he belonged. The Left Bank of Paris had always seemed to him a magical site. Now it really was home. He passed his time walking the streets between Censier-Daubenton and rue de Rennes, discovering bars and exploring the subterranean nightlife. 'I found myself at home with the lowest form of company,' he wrote, recalling this early period. 'It was in Paris, then a city so beautiful that many people preferred to be poor there than to be rich somewhere else.'[3]

However, the world beyond the Left Bank was turning fast in 1952. On the political front, France was a long way from recovering anything like a semblance of stability. The government, led by the vacillating Antoine Pinay, fought hard and without noticeable success to quell a wave of mainly Communist-inspired strikes around the country. In late May, the potential for serious civil unrest was unleashed at a demonstration against General Ridgway, the former American Commander-in-Chief in Korea, who had allegedly been responsible for bacteriological warfare. The march had been banned, but with Communist organisation thousands poured onto the streets to register their disgust. They met concerted police violence; a North African was killed by a police bullet, hundreds more were arrested and battered in police cells as suspected 'Reds'. In a fit of Cold War paranoia, the police arrested Communist leader Jacques Duclos as a spy on the grounds that officers, checking Duclos' parked car, had found two pigeons which might well have been transporting vital secrets to the Soviets.

This was farce, but, in the reactions of the government to the threat from the French Communist Party and the extreme Left, there were also elements of melodrama and the potential for tragedy. Most particularly, the cultural and literary life of the mainstream Left in France in the early 1950s was characterised by an ambivalent relation to the powerplay between the Soviet Union and the United States which demonstrated not only how little, in political terms at least, France had developed since the disaster of the war, but how far she had to travel before taking her rightful place as a major nation and economic power.

It was also in the early 1950s that France, in cultural and literary terms, seemed to be taking her first tentative steps away from the shadow of the Occupation and the polarised demands of either American corporate capitalist culture or Stalinism. In philosophy Louis Althusser, who was beginning his re-reading of Marx at the École normale supériere, offered to his students (who would include the young Michel Foucault and Jacques Derrida) a vision of a new society which, faithful to the late Marx, emphasised that revolution would emerge from a 'scientific' analysis of society and class structures. This reading of Marx would not only come to shape the ideological imagination of large sections of the French Communist Party, but also, for Debord and those who would become Situationists, remove Marxist theory from the proletariat it had theorised as subject.

In straightforward political terms, the early part of the 1950s was charac-terised by a somewhat schizophrenic approach to debates about art and revolution. Whilst it was accepted that the iconoclasm of Dada and Sur-realism had given the post-war avant-gardes their literary and political direction and impetus, they were also pre-war antiques which, in the face of the sciences of interpretation, loosely assembled under the banner of 'Structuralism', which were now asserting themselves as the new intellectual forces on the Left Bank, were no more than the faded reminders of the failed promises of pre-war utopianism.

Debord's own activity for the larger part of 1952 stood in direct contra-diction to the prevailing winds of change. It seemed to him, in the first instance, that Letterism had served its purpose. It seemed moreover that, with the possible exception of Wolman, only he amongst his comrades could see this. It was time to seize the moment.

'. . . something really dirty'

It was imperative first of all to make a break with Isou and his followers. In a political and cultural climate which had abrogated itself from the demands of the revolutionary avant-garde in favour of the pseudo-sorcery of the new science of 'Structuralism', it was necessary. Secondly, it was necessary to reinforce the teaching of the Surrealists and their Dadaist antecedents: that revolution emerges out of poetry as well as economics. It was this principle which was to be the guiding theory behind Debord's first action in the public arena, the screening of his first film, *Howling in Favour of Sade*, on 30 June 1952, during a session held by the Avant-Garde Film Club in Saint-Germain-des-Prés.

This was the film which Debord had promised and planned in his first article for *Ion*. In the article 'Prolegomena to Any Future Cinema', Debord had argued for an imaginary film which would overcome, or supersede, the conventions of mainstream cinema. The future film would also, he promised, overcome or overwhelm *cinéma discrépant*, the Letterist shattering of cinematic representation into its supposedly unbreakable components, by defying the paradox at the heart of Letterist creation: that representation is a betrayal of the act of creation. Debord misquoted Breton: 'I have destroyed the cinema, because it is easier than shooting passers-by.'[4]

The title of *Howling in Favour of Sade* may, similarly, have been a misquotation; the renegade Surrealist writer Georges Bataille had originally given his early essay on Dalí, 'Le jeu lugubre' ('The Lugubrious Game'), the title 'Howling in Favour of Dalí'. In this essay Bataille had argued that darkness, as it was understood by the Gnostic theologians, was not a metaphor but an active living principle. Blindness was, in artistic terms, as important as vision. The highest work of art was one which was able to represent, in literal as well as metaphorical language, a vision of negativity.[5]

The screening of *Howling in Favour of Sade* was an event which matched this principle. In the distinguished tradition of avant-garde art riots especially beloved of the Dadaists and the Surrealists, there was a considerable degree of planning and prankish anarchy about the screening. Michèle Bernstein, a young student at the Sorbonne who had recently joined the group at Moineau's, and Debord had hidden themselves on a balcony with bags of flour. Serge Berna, who had started the evening by pretending to be a professor giving a learned discourse on the importance of Guy-Ernest Debord in the history of the cinema, told the audience that if they waited to the end of the film, which was a full and final twenty minutes of silence, there was 'something really dirty'. Bernstein, who claimed to have a voice which could break glass, loosed a piercing scream, literally howling in favour of Sade.

The visual content of *Howling in Favour of Sade* consisted of a movement between a black and white screen. The screen contained no content at all but only twenty or so minutes of flickering nothingness. When the screen was black there was silence. During the moments of scratchy, white blurred screen, for the first part of the film there was a soundtrack, read in a monotone by Gil Wolman, Serge Berna, Barbara Rosenthal and Guy Debord. The four voices began by playing off each other in ironic, sometimes vicious counterpoint;

Voice 1: The film by Guy-Ernest Debord, Howling in Favour of Sade . . .

Voice 2: Howling in Favour of Sade is dedicated to Gil J Wolman

Voice 3: Article 15. When a person shall have ceased to appear at his place of abode or home address for four years, and about whom there has been no news whatsoever, the interested parties shall be able to petition the lower court in order that his or her absence be declared.

Voice 1: Love is only worthwhile in a pre-revolutionary period.

Voice 2: None of them love you, you liar! Art begins, grows and disappears because frustrated men bypass the world of official expression and the festivals of its poverty.

Voice 4 (young girl): Did you sleep with Françoise?
Voice 1: What a time! Memorandum for a history of the cinema:
    1902 – Journey to the Moon
    1920 – The Cabinet of Dr Caligari
    1924 – Entr'acte
    1926 – Battleship, Potemkin
    1928 – Un Chien Andalou
    1931 – City Lights
    1931 – Birth of Guy-Ernest Debord
    1952 – The Anti-Concept. Howling in Favour of Sade.[6]

This opening of the film, like the deliberately destroyed photograph published in *Ion*, is as much autobiography as auto-destructive art. In the legal article from the French Civil Code, read by Serge Berna, for example, Debord is signalling not only his absence from society but also his position as, in literal terms, a displaced person without home, family, identity: an unanchored subject. It is also a personal reference to the way in which he felt disconnected from his mother and family on returing to Paris from Cannes. The technique of inserting a personal detail, impossible for an impersonal audience to know, into the body of a text would become a hallmark technique of Debord's art.

Similarly, the insertion of Debord's birth into the history of the cinema is not merely an arch joke, but also a totemic act. His existence is falsely fixed into the history of cinema, the history of twentieth-century represent-ational art, in the same way that Isou, in *The Making of a Name and a Messiah*, identifies himself completely with his system of creation. In this way, the individual existence of the subject negates history, time and chance.

Serge Berna goes on to mock Isou's 'revolts [which] become conformism'. Barbara Rosenthal then makes sexual gossip; there are asides about the Letterist attacks on Auteuil ('The little skivers all had glorious futures in the school and college systems') and Notre-Dame ('several cathedrals have been erected to the memory of Serge Berna'); quotes from John Ford's *Rio Grande*, the great Hollywood success of 1952, and Saint-Just ('Happiness is a new idea in Europe').

At the close of the opening section, Debord reads a sentence which seems to define this moment and the rest of his life: 'The art of the future will be the construction of situations, or nothing.' This first screening of *Howling in Favour of Sade* broke up, as Debord had anticipated, into something between a walk-out and a brawl. This, however, was not unusual by any of the standards of the day. What was more surprising was the reaction that the film had provoked in its audience; boredom and fury had met in an audience which had first been hypnotised and then duped by a film that, as Debord had hoped, demonstrated the limits of representational art in its most extreme form.

'The cold interstellar space'

Yet there was also a dreadful pathos in this first film. Amidst the detritus of political and cultural changes of 1952, Debord himself had been most moved that year by the suicide of the twelve-year-old radio starlet Madeleine Reineri. Reineri, under the pseudonym Pirouette, presented a programme called *Happy Thursdays* on Radio Alpes-Grenoble. She had deliberately thrown herself into the Isère river which flows through Grenoble on a Friday afternoon, having left her satchel on the bank. Her death shocked a generation raised on the notion that youth was an endless adventure.

All forms of suicide fascinated Debord. It was, after all, according to Debord's literary heroes, the simplest and most beautiful act of all.

There was, however, in the death of this young girl, who had been a star of the glittering, consumerist myths of the New France, an emblematic meaning. Suicide was an absolute form of negation: 'The cold interstellar space, thousands of degrees below freezing point of absolute zero Fahrenheit or Centigrade; the first indicators of dawn approaching,' read Gil Wolman. 'The hurried passage of Jacques Vaché through the clouds of war, that catastrophic haste which destroyed him; the rude lashing of Arthur Cravan, himself swallowed up in the Bay of Mexico.' 'My little sister, look at the state we're in,' read Debord. 'The Isère and misery go on. We are powerless. The perfection of suicide is ambiguity.'[7]

Not for the last time, Debord's signature note to his work was the imprimatur of his own death and the bleak margins of his own existence. *Howling in Favour of Sade* ended with a quotation from Marcel Carné's *Les Visiteurs du soir* ('The Evening Visitors'): 'Nous vivons des enfants perdus, nos aventures incomplètes.' ('We live as lost children, our adventures incomplete.')[8] This film by Carné was conceived originally as a political allegory in which the Devil visits the earth to abolish the possibility of love; the Devil was, obvious to the eyes of the wartime audience of *Les Visiteurs du soir* as well as the audience of *Howling in Favour of Sade*, an allegorical representation of Hitler. The 'lost children' was an allusion not only to how the popular press reported the doomed youth of Saint-Germain-des-Prés, but also to the youth of Auteuil. It was originally, however, used in *Les Visiteurs du soir* as a coded reference, borrowed from army slang, to the youths sent out on dangerous missions across the no man's land between the trenches. It was a military metaphor which signalled that *Howling in Favour of Sade* was as much a form of attack or assault as it was an abstract work of art.

But why howl in favour of Sade? In 1952, The 'Divine Marquis'' reputation was at the centre of much bitter debate. An important section of the intelligentsia, including Sartre, Simone de Beauvoir and Camus, saw Sade not merely as the patron saint of revolution but, in Raymond Queneau's words, as 'a hallucinatory precursor of the world ruled by the Gestapo, its tortures, its camps'. Queneau was writing about Sade in 1945, six months after the liberation of Buchenwald, Dachau and Ravensbrück. 'All who embraced the Marquis' ideas to one degree or another must now envision, without hypocrisy, the reality of the death camps, with their horrors no longer confined within a man's head but practised by thousands of fanatics. Disagreeable as it may be, philosophies end in charnel houses.'[9]

Imitating the voice of a young girl, Barbara Rosenthal initiated the fifth 'white section' of the film with the question: 'But no one's talking about Sade in this film.' One of the central points of the film was, however, that everyone was talking about Sade outside the cinema; his nightmares or dreams had been the everyday substance of life during the war. And now, in the post-war climate of recrimination and self-hate, French writers and thinkers had seized upon the philosophy of the Marquis as cause and origin of their own disaster.

For Debord, however, Sade was still the patron saint of revolution, revered by the Surrealists as a proto-Communist militant, materialist philosopher and neophyte libertine terrorist. Man Ray's famous portrait of Sade, against the background of the Bastille in flames, encapsulated the idea of the Marquis as the very emblem of revolutionary excess. 'O that worthy couple, Sade and Robespierre!' wrote the journalist and Gothic novelist Jules Janin.[10] For Janin, writing in 1834, Sade was the friend of the Terror who became its prey. For the Surrealists, however, it was Sade's necessary acceptance of evil and disaster which established him as a member of the Surrealist pantheon: 'Sade is surrealist in his sadism,' wrote Breton in the *Premier manifeste*.[11]

As Debord knew from his reading, Sade's political philosophy was so dispersed, elliptical and fraught with paradox that it escaped all attempts at practical analysis. Most importantly, for Debord Sade attempted all attempts at reduction. To howl in favour of Sade was, therefore, to howl for a return to the absolute promises made by the avant-gardes in the first part of the century. It was to howl for the return of Arthur Rimbaud, Lautréamont, Alfred Jarry, Arthur Cravan, Jacques Vaché. It was also to howl over the corpse of little Madeleine Reineri, drowned and bloated, floating face down in the Isère.

'For us, the young and beautiful, the only end to suffering is revolution'

The reaction to *L'Anticoncept* and *Howling in Favour of Sade* brought Wolman and Debord closer together as artists and as conspirators. Wolman's film had been banned by the government censor; Debord's film had effectively been banned by the viewing public. Both of them saw themselves as leading commando raids on the cultural establishment. Isou, who had condoned Debord's work and participated in *Howling in Favour of Sade*, was now regarded as an irrelevant megalomaniac. As Wolman and Debord prepared to cast him aside, he was to become the first victim of the guerrilla war announced by Debord in *Sade*.

Wolman and Debord decided to take their conversations one step further and turn their ideas into a movement. They secretly founded the Letterist International (LI) in July 1952. They explained their ideas, through the course of the summer, to Jean-Michel Mension, Michèle Bernstein, Éliane Papaï, Pierre-Joël Berlé, Jean-Louis Brau and other members of 'the tribe' who lived on the periphery of conventional existence and who, thereby, seemed to incarnate the spirit of 'the extreme Left wing' of the Letterist movement and who were either too drunk, too drugged or too lazy to follow 'the cult of Isou-worship'.

In the company mostly of Mension, Berlé, Berna and Wolman, Debord spent the summer months in a blur of poeticised drunken sprees across Paris. The group would drift across Les Halles, north to Aubervilliers, or to République and the Canal Saint-Martin, or down the rue Xavier-Privas, a street where few white Frenchmen would dare to venture, but where hashish or *kif* could be bought from the Algerians at prices which 'defied all competition'.[12] The reckless mood of that summer was typified by an incident on a hot evening at a shared apartment on the rue Saint-Martin. When, after a night of drinking at Chez Moineau, most of the crowd had drifted off into sleep or drunken unconsciousness, two of the company, still awake and bored, decided to turn on the gas for a 'hilarious trick' in the style of Jacques Vaché. It was only the fact that Debord was smoking hash on the balcony and was able to raise the alarm that averted a catastrophe.[13]

However, the work of the LI, as Debord and Wolman envisaged it, was less concerned with such 'hilarious tricks' than a direct engagement with the enemy forces of work, money, duty. Both Wolman and Debord, in their respective films, had defined the enemy as representational art which, as the direct product of an economic order which substituted morality for truth, was bound to be false. The weakness of the enemy, the capitalist economic model, was its inability to control subjective needs and responses: 'Order reigns but it doesn't govern,' was a key axiom for Debord. As *L' Anticoncept* and *Howling in Favour of Sade* had demonstrated, a breach in the enemy's defences, as Debord described it, was bound to emerge out of 'a science of situations'.

The Letterist International undertook its first 'action' on 29 October 1952. The occasion was a press conference called by Charlie Chaplin at the Ritz Hotel in Paris. Chaplin was on the French leg of a world tour and had called the conference to thank the French government for awarding him the Légion d'Honneur. Having been denounced in the United States, then in its most McCarthyite phase, Chaplin had come to Europe to promote his latest film, *Limelight*, and found himself banned from re-entering the United States, branded as a 'subversive' and Communist 'fellow-traveller'. He was therefore delighted to find himself fêted by the British public and Elizabeth II, the young Queen of England. On his arrival in Paris 'Charlot' found himself the darling of the French press and a cultural hero to the Anti-American Left. In the clamour outside the Ritz, as Chaplin was deafened by the cheers and applause of an adoring crowd, Serge Berna and Guy Debord charged and blocked the entrance to the hotel, as Gil Wolman and Jean-Louis Brau darted through the police line, shrieking insults at Chaplin and throwing pamphlets over the heads of the crowd.

The pamphlet, signed by Berna, Brau, Wolman and Debord, was entitled 'NO MORE FLAT FEET!' Its main charge against Chaplin was that his films were a form of 'emotional blackmail' and his sentimental worldview robbed the oppressed of the urge to rebel. For this, he was compared to Stavisky, the French arch-villain of the 1930s whose high-finance swindles had caused riots in the streets of Paris, and described as a 'fascist insect'. In Chaplin's famous rattan cane, a world-famous emblem of the good-natured hobo down on his luck, the Letterist International claimed to see 'the nightstick of a cop'. Poverty, however, was no joke: 'For us, the young and beautiful,' screamed the pamphlet of the Letterist dissenters, 'the only end to suffering is revolution.'[14]

An hour or so after the 'action', Isou, not quite understanding the nature of the Letterist International, had applauded the actions of the group and commended them as exemplary cultural commandos to his followers in Chez Moineau. His tone swiftly changed, however, when he realised that the group were a breakaway faction led by Debord and Wolman, and that the real purpose of this assault was not only to relive the hours of international scandal and glory which had attended the assault on Notre-Dame, but also to destabilise his position as leader and chief tactician.

Chaplin left France within a few days, like most of the French press and public no more than mildly bemused by the event. However, in a series of tracts and pamphlets distributed in the cafés of Saint-Germain-des-Prés an internecine war raged between the two splintered factions of the Letterist movement. Isou, together with Gabriel Pomerand and Maurice Lemaître, somewhat unwittingly opened hostilities by writing to the newspaper *Combat* to point out that in its coverage of the event it had wrongly attributed the hooliganism to the Letterists. Those who had called themselves Letterists were 'extreme and confused in content'; Isou then declared that the Letterists unequivocally associated themselves with the 'homage given to Chaplin by the entire populace'.

Wolman and Debord were in Belgium, where they had travelled to show Isou's *Treatise* . . . at a cinema in Brussels. The purpose of the trip was to make contact with Wolman's friends and mentors who still held the Surrealist faith intact. These included the poets Marcel Mariën and Paul Nougé who were planning to set up a journal which would continue the pre-war revolutionary tradition of Surrealism as a social movement as well as a creative method. Mariën and Nougé, veteran surrealists and revolutionaries, were supported in their venture by the poet Louis Scutenaire, who saw his principal contribution to the Belgian Surrealist movement as acting as an ambassador between Brussels and Paris. Scutenaire was also a poet of great talent, with a gift for startling and evocative language. Mariën, Nougé and Scutenaire planned a journal which served as a direct link back to the early days and hopes of Breton's *Premier manifeste, La Révolution surréaliste* and *Le Surréalisme au service de la révolution*, texts which set forth a programme for change founded on aesthetic violence as well as utopian promise.

At this stage, Letterist activity in Paris was almost exclusively controlled by Isou and his chief lieutenants, Pomerand and Lemaître. This meant that not only did the execution of collective tasks need to be shaped by the principles of Isou's 'system', which he alone could change or modify, but that even individual activities, such as the construction of a metagraphic collage or the composition of a poem, had to be judged by the shifting criteria defined by Isou. Worse than this, Isou had not only placed himself in antagonistic opposition to pre-war Surrealism in its entirety, but was clearly heading in the direction of mysticism. The ultimate aim of Letterist activity was now to replace God as the central creative agent in the universe; with this solipsistic approach, the Letterist group seemed to be taking on all the attributes of a cult with 'Le Dieu-Isou' as its godhead.

In Belgium, Debord had been impressed by the intransigence and determination of the Belgian Surrealists, as well as their commitment to the reinstatement of radical subjectivity as the cornerstone of Surrealist activity. Debord had been particularly convinced by the argument that avant-garde activity was not simply a question of forming a critique of contemporary conditions but that, as in the earliest days of Dada or Surrealism, the language of the avant-garde could shape the structures of social change. The Letterist retreat into mysticism and 'Isou-worship' was an abdication of this responsibility. In conversation with Wolman in Brussels, Debord resolved to model his future activity on the exemplary extremism of the Belgian Surrealists.

On reading Isou's remarks in *Combat*, Debord saw his opportunity and, on his return to Paris, fired off a stinging reply to Isou in a tract called 'Death of a Fellow-Traveller'. In this text he accused Isou of mendacity and disinformation; 'we have so little passion for literary types and their tactics,' he wrote scathingly, 'that the incident is almost forgotten. It's really as if Jean-Isidore Isou was nothing to us.'[15] Like François Dufrêne, who was unaware of his only and original crime, Isou was thus effectively excommunicated and shut off from history. 'I was not frightened of Debord,' Isou told me. 'But I was shocked, I was stunned. It was a betrayal which I could not possibly have anticipated. It was something which was executed with military precision, and which was as cold and brutal as all military actions.'[16]

'. . . passion, if not the terror'

Some months later, on 7 December 1952, Serge Berna, Gil Wolman, Jean-Louis Brau, Ivan Chtcheglov and another seven hooligans, drunks, poets and drifters from Chez Moineau, including Guy Debord, met in Aubervilliers, a run-down, working-class district in the north of Paris immortalised in Jacques Prévert's song, an ode to the urban dispossessed, which began 'gentils enfants d'Aubervilliers' ('Lovely children of Aubervilliers'). This was the first congress of the Letterist International.

Up to this point, aside from the 'action' against Charlie Chaplin, the LI had confined its activities to printing and distributing pamphlets and tracts denouncing Isou and reprinting the correspondence between the Isou and Debord factions. This, however, was the beginning of a new phase of activity: the LI was about to launch itself as a revolutionary organisation. But the programme agreed by the members had more in common with a publisher's copyright disclaimer than a programme for a rapid cultural and political transformation. Its key point was article 4: 'Extreme circumspection in the presentation of works that could engage the LI and the expulsion *ipso facto* of whoever publishes a commercial book under his name.'

In the second bulletin of the Letterist International, however, the group revealed itself as a revolutionary group. This was revolution in the true Sadean sense of unleashed, unlimited subjectivity, a vision of negativity delineated by Bataille and defined in *Howling in Favour of Sade*: 'All black, eyes closed to the excess of disaster,' read Debord from the text of his first film,

> letterist provocation serves to pass the time. revolutionary thought is nowhere else. we pursue our little uproar in the realm of literature. and lacking anything better, naturally it's to manifest ourselves that we write manifestos. offhandedness is a beautiful thing. but our desires were perishable and deceiving. youth is systematic, as they say. weeks multiply in a straight line. our encounters are by chance and our precarious contacts are led astray behind the fragile defence of words. the world turns as if nothing

ever was. all said the human condition doesn't please us. we dismissed isou who believed in the utility of leaving traces. there are no nihilists, there are only weaklings. almost everything is forbidden us, the diversion of minors and the use of drugs are pursued like all our gestures to fill the void. several of our comrades are in prison for theft. we rise up against the pain inflicted on those whose conscience insists that one must absolutely never work. we refuse to discuss it. human relations should be based on passion. if not, the terror.[17]

The congress at Aubervilliers was where the revolution was defined in its first phase. 'Passion and terror' struck the authentic Sadean note. This was also a revolution predicated on real, lived experience as much as Marxist theory.

Most importantly, the transformation was to be the product of poetry as well as dialectical contradiction. Accordingly, when every member of the Letterist International had signed a copy of the group's programme, one copy was sealed into a bottle and thrown into the canal.

The group then proceeded to a Spanish café, Chez Paco, which was renowned in the *quartier* as a place where you could hear all the regional accents of Spain (the place would later become a favourite haunt of the Spanish novelist Juan Goytisolo who claimed to prefer it to Franco's Spain). They chose the area mainly because Jean-Louis Brau's father, Communist deputy mayor of the district, had a large house there where the Letterist comrades could sleep. In Chez Paco, having taken their seats 'at the banquet of the life', the Letterist International then got drunk on litres of strong, rough Spanish red wine.

CHAPTER 6

Playtime

1953–4

The first principles of the Letterist International were a mixture of Isou's Letterist anti-art theory and a concerted attack on Isou himself. The document called for the overcoming of art and the adoption of the principle of exclusion for any member of the group selling a work of art.

This in itself was hardly a coherent programme, let alone a call to arms. However, using their social charms and the promise of no small amount of alcohol, the 'groupuscule' of Debord, Brau, Berna and Wolman found no trouble in recruiting to their side not only intellectuals like Michèle Bernstein but also Patrick Straram and Jean-Michel Mension, whose chief interest in forming the 'dissident Left-wing' of the Letterist movement was motivated more by a taste for drink and anarchy than by politics or philosophy. Genuine delinquents like Fred and Éliane stood at the edges of the group offering physical and moral, if not intellectual, support.

In the small enclosed world of Chez Moineau, the break with Isou soon took on the dimensions of a full-scale war. Before the row with the Letterist International Isou, who never drank alcohol, had already been a rare and infrequent visitor to Chez Moineau, preferring to observe and control developments from the fringes of the protean society which occupied the rue du Four. After the break, Isou kept well away, preferring his habitual haunts, La Petite Source on the boulevard Saint-Germain and cafés on the place de la Croix Rouge, knowing full well that if he had come to Chez Moineau, even if he avoided a physical conflict with Mension or Fred, he would have been jeered at or even thrown out by the rest of the crowd.

Although Isou, in public at least, acted as if the break had not really happened, he was in fact dismayed by this unexpected betrayal which not only undermined his previously unshakeable and narcissistic self-belief but which also seemed to contain a poisonous personal attack. In private, Isou confided to his closest lieutenants, Gabriel Pomerand and Maurice Lemaître, that he had been deeply hurt by Debord, whom he had brought to the heart of avant-garde Paris from provincial Cannes and whose career and itinerary he had nurtured with fraternal care. Isou was indeed deeply, almost fatally, wounded by Debord's unexpected manoeuvre. Although the Letterist crusade continued throughout the 1950s and 1960s, Isou found himself an increasingly marginalised figure and his subsequent career a long retreat into the poetic solipsism which he had originally sought to overwhelm through the Letterist revolution, the universal application of his 'system of creation'. During the events of May 1968, former Letterists reported Isou's enthusiasm for a revolution 'he had created but which also ignored him'. Isou himself was amongst the first to run to the barricades, where he found himself a forgotten figure. In the occupied Sorbonne he was shunned by his erstwhile Letterist comrades who were now members of the Situationist International.[1]

The immediate impact of the break with Isou was that despite his lack of physical presence and his slightly withdrawn, aloof manner, Debord had established himself as the intellectual leader of the group in Chez Moineau. 'With Guy there was this sense of finding an answer, to go further then mere rebellion, and that is what was exciting,' explained Jean-Michel Mension.[2]

Although the conversation around the tables and the bars in the café generally revolved around who was sleeping with whom and other drunken intrigues, Debord, in founding the Letterist International, had also signalled an intellectual framework which could include mavericks such as Éliane and Fred and which set its face dead against the 'older generation' of Pomerand, Lemaître and Isou himself. In an early bulletin drawn up by Debord, the Letterist International declared itself ready for 'the war for freedom which is waged with anger'. In the acrimonious break with Isou, who had seen in Debord a future leader if not a prophet of the Letterist cause, the opening shots of this war had been fired with both spleen and venom. It was no small irony, however, that the shots had been fired against an enemy, Isou, who had been taken completely by surprise and whose intentions had always been honourable.

The Consul

During his first few years in Paris, Ralph Rumney described himself as both uncharacteristically shy and tongue-tied. Often this was because he was drunk. Upon his arrival in Paris Rumney had been quickly nicknamed 'the Consul' by the crowd at Chez Moineau who, like much of Left Bank Paris, had been very impressed by Malcolm Lowry's alcoholic epic *Under the Volcano*. Rumney did not necessarily drink more than anyone else at Chez Moineau, but as a tall and thin Englishman with little French, a taste for quoting chunks of poetry and a propensity for keeling over after too much red wine, the innocent Rumney was seized upon by Debord and others as their own version of Lowry's doomed hero, Geoffrey Firmin, an exile and outsider in 1930s Mexico, whose life unravels in front of him through the course of a single drunken day. *Under the Volcano* had recently been translated into French by Maurice Nadeau who serialised it in *Combat* and helped Lowry publish the work under the prestigious imprint of Club Français du Livre, a subsidiary of Buchet-Chastel-Corréa (this imprint had already published Henry Miller in French and would later publish Guy Debord). Nadeau was then mainly known as the most authoritative historian of the Surrealist movement, but it was not because of Nadeau's reputation as a subtle and discerning critic that Lowry became a hero of the French avant-garde. *Under the Volcano* scorched through the dense undergrowth of literary Paris and quickly became an essential reference point for all those who considered Faulkner and Joyce out of date and the French novel, represented by Sartre, Aragon or Malraux, in terminal decline. Only the black American writers, Richard Wright and James Baldwin, who had easily settled into Left Bank life and an exile which only enhanced their prestige in the United States, enjoyed a more fashionable status than Lowry who, disappointed by his book's failure in the United States, declared the French translation a masterpiece.[3]

Rumney, with his public school education and provincial background, had much in common with the young Malcolm Lowry, whose good looks, cockiness and wit were the legend of pre-war Soho pubs long before his superb talent was drowned in alcohol. Like Lowry, Rumney was given to drinking sessions which would last days and during which he would impress his new-found comrades with his elegant, relaxed charm and innate good manners which would prevail even in the stickiest, most drunken situations. Rumney's only real problem was that he didn't speak French.

Fortunately for Rumney the banter at the bar of Chez Moineau was far from high-flown, revolving mainly around sexual gossip and drunken escapades, and he quickly acquired a *patois* which allowed him to join in drinking parties or pick up girls. There was little talk of politics and even less of literature or art. These subjects, Rumney recalls, were reserved for intimate, if modest, dinners with Debord, Bernstein and Berna, the self-appointed intellectuals of the group. 'I was allowed to speak, which was an important thing. But Guy was someone who was really quite insecure about his own education and he would be quiet or sarcastic if you talked about something he didn't know about.'[4]

Conversation was nonetheless dominated by Debord, who, although quietly spoken, even at this early stage demonstrated a gift for controlling and manipulating a social situation. Debord was shy about his lack of formal education and tended to fall silent if the conversation turned to authors or thinkers he had not encountered in his own reading. He professed relentless scorn for the courses which Michèle Bernstein was following at the Sorbonne, and which she soon abandoned, but he nevertheless kept abreast of the theories and ideas then current.

Rumney remembers these dinners as consisting largely of long monologues in French, conducted at a high theoretical level, which he would nod along to and occasionally season with a feeble 'oui' or 'non' (Michèle Bernstein challenges Rumney's account, claiming that there was little or no intellectual contact between Debord and Rumney until their meeting at Cosio d'Arroscia in 1957).

Even so, despite his position as the youngest and apparently most intellectually naive member of the group, it was Ralph Rumney who claimed that in early 1952 he introduced Debord to Johan Huizinga's classic text *Homo Ludens*. Although this book had been widely available in German and English translation, as well as in Huizinga's native Dutch, since 1938, the book had only recently been translated into French and was not easily available even on the Left Bank. Rumney had encountered the book in London, where it was a key text for the Independent Group, a group of mainly British artists centred around the Institute for Contemporary Arts (ICA). Debord was notably offhand, even recalcitrant, when others suggested books that he might not have heard of. However, inspired by Rumney's account of Huizinga's argument for a society where play was more important than work, Debord quickly acquired a copy and found in it confirmation of many of the key ideas which he had been developing since he had first read Rimbaud and Lautréamont at school in Cannes. '*Homo Ludens* was obviously a turning point for Guy,' says Rumney. 'But although I introduced it to him, I can claim no responsibility for what he did with it.'[5]

War games

Johan Huizinga was primarily a social scientist, which meant that his first concern was with the study of social relations as they were mediated through political and social development. From his home university in Leiden, where he was Rector, he sought to examine the notion that play was as much a social phenomenon as a biological function. During the Nazi Occupation, he distinguished himself by expelling from the University of Leiden a German-speaking *lektor* who had been distributing anti-Semitic propaganda. This earned Huizinga a short spell in a prison camp before a period of internal exile during which he died. Huizinga's ideas on the relation between play and seriousness in the development of human culture and community, although severely tested by the rigours of occupation and war, were nonetheless fundamentally opposed to all forms of rationalism. Most importantly, at least for the Independent Group in London, Huizinga's argument that all great culture emerged from play rather than planning was a counter-balance to the rationalism which characterised the development of post-war aesthetic theory in architecture and urban planning.

Huizinga's main thesis was that the instinct for play preceded the instinct for culture and that, in fact, all forms of cultural expression emerge from this original 'ludic' instinct. In some ways this thesis echoed the Surrealist pursuit of the irrational, the surreal, which Debord had found most attractive in his early readings of André Breton. Debord's concern as a fledgeling poet had been how to introduce poetry into daily life, indeed it is this quality which had drawn him to Isou and the Letterists, and, following on from this, how to overcome the alienated and alienating patterns of ordinary existence through the pursuit of untrammelled subjectivity. In Huizinga, Debord found arguments to support not only the notion that the 'ludic' instinct preceded the instinct to build or make, that *Homo ludens* was at least equal or even superior to *Homo faber*, but also that the two modes of existence were in fact in opposition.

It was this opposition which was for Debord the fundamental insight of Huizinga's thesis. Most importantly, according to Huizinga, spontaneity, play and festival were not only essential to daily life but also transformative agents which allowed otherwise passive individuals insight into the stultifying nature of boring, 'non-ludic' life. This observation had a revolutionary significance for Debord, who was intrigued by the suggestion that games or spontaneous play could be experimental forms of new behaviour. For Rumney and the Independent Group in London, Huizinga's arguments had provided a blueprint for a new form of architecture which would be designed around human desire as much as human need; for Debord, Huizinga provided a vocabulary for thinking about future forms of social behaviour which anticipated 'situations' which could reveal the totality of everyday existence.

In the central chapter of *Homo Ludens*, entitled 'Game and War', Huizinga compares the oldest and most noble forms of warfare, mainly the classical tradition which persists into the late medieval period as well as Muslim or Japanese tradition, with the atrocious and degrading spectacle of modern, total warfare which is subordinate to the demands of technology and a global economy. Modern war, says Huizinga, has become separate from the ancient notion of combat as a game as well as struggle and is therefore less human. In modern warfare, he writes, there are no rules. There is, therefore, no real sense in which modern warfare can be made equivalent to the delicate and complex codes which governed battles and wars in the pre-modern world. Most importantly, at least for Debord, Huizinga argues that the codes which informed earlier ritualised forms of combat were not only an articulated language which expressed the true political conflicts of a given period but also formed a matrix of signs and symbols which had a real and authentic value for the individual. The flags and banners of the medieval tournament or the battle-songs and poems of Spain during the wars of the counter-reformation were not only an expression of collective cultural meaning which connected with individual subjects, but also the true emblems of the meaning of history.[6]

'If you believe you have genius'

In 1953, when Debord first encountered Huizinga, these notions were far from being refined into a theory of action; indeed he barely understood them. Rumney recalls that Debord feigned either disinterest or scepticism when he described to him the discussions which the Independent Group had had in London and how the group most closely linked to the ICA had tried to apply Huizinga's theories directly to architecture. The vocabulary of the Letterist International, however, very quickly began to betray a familarity with both the form and content of Huizinga's ideas and in particular the notion of the individual, pure subject or 'Genius' as the motor of history. Debord caught this notion in a small sticker he designed for the Letterist International and which was distributed in the cafés, bars and restaurants of the *quartier* towards the end of 1953.

Si vous vous croyez

DU GENIE

ou si vous estimez posséder seulement

UNE INTELLIGENCE BRILLANTE

adressez-vous à l'internationale lettriste

édité par l'IL, 32, rue de la montagne-saint-geneviève, paris 5e

If you believe you have

GENIUS

or have merely

A BRILLIANT INTELLIGENCE

write to the Letterist International

published by the LI, 32, rue de la montagne-saint-geneviève, paris 5e[7]

The term *génie* in French means not only 'genius' in all the same senses as English but also has a military meaning. More specifically, from the mid-eighteenth century onwards it has been used in French to designate all forms of military activity which involve the construction, or destruction, of roads, bridges, railways, communications. As the Letterist International was about to embark on its first phase of concentrated activity in the form of the journal *Potlatch* and the operations of Letterist commando groups who would 'conduct researches around the city', it was no coincidence that this particular military metaphor was used in propaganda to attract the bored youth of the city to the ranks of the LI. This was first expressed by Debord in his principal artistic action of 1953, the ludic graffiti 'Ne Travaillez Jamais!' ('Never Work!'), borrowed from Rimbaud and scrawled in chalk on a wall of the rue de Mazarine where it meets the rue de Seine. This announcement of a 'general strike against modern life' was photographed by a tourist who, much to Debord's disgust, was entranced. (Debord would have no doubt been further disgusted to find that in May 1998 somebody had written in homage to the Situationists, in exactly the same hand and on exactly the same spot, 'N'écrivez jamais', 'Never write!').

Gangland

The Letterist International went on to produce a flurry of publications through the course of 1953 and 1954. Most of these were in the form of tracts or posters. These included polemics against the cinema, and calls for the police to stop harassing Letterist comrades, such as Pierre-Joël Berlé who had found himself arrested after drunkenly stumbling into the catacombs.

They would even later include what seemed to be straightforward publicity, designed by Debord, for a new bar, L'Homme de Main, on the rue de Jussieu. According to Jean-Michel Mension, L'Homme de Main was 'a kind of dark chaos, where you never arrived sober, which you couldn't even find when you were sober'.[8] It soon became a favoured haunt of those members of the Left Bank crowd who wanted to drink until the early hours and who were becoming ever more bored with the increasingly tourist-infested clubs of Saint-Germain, which in the second half of the 1950s, when L'Homme de Main was at its height, was already turning into a parody of itself.

The bar was owned by Ghislain de Marbaix who, despite the noble cast of his name, enjoyed passing himself off as a louche gangster in the style of his cinema heroes Jean Gabin and George Raft. Marbaix had also been on the edges of the Letterist scene since the late 1940s although his interest in the Letterists had more to do with an attraction to the free-living girls who attached themselves to the group than with a desire to transform daily life. Although he had been drinking at Le Mabillon at the time, hesitating to join in the adventure, Ghislain had been arrested in the wake of the Notre-Dame scandal of 1950. A photograph of Ghislain – dark eyes, thin, angular features and a gaunt, sneering expression – had even appeared in the pages of *Combat* in the wake of the incident, photographed alongside Michel Mourre in his Dominican disguise, and Serge Berna in the police headquarters of Saint-Gervais. The reader was invited by the *Combat* journalist to decide whether the trio were 'three mental cases, three hooligans or three heroes'.

Ghislain was not a regular at Chez Moineau nor a regular member of the anarchic drinking group which centred around Mension, Fred and Brau. He was known to the group, rather, as a hard man who indulged in their eccentricities but played no part in the activities. Mension remembers him as someone who would spread legends around himself: 'He was a physical brute, incredibly strong when he had been drinking . . . Legend has it that he had broken a lad's arm when he was just arm-wrestling him. A lot of people said that he had killed someone, beaten them to death with his fists, but I think he was the one who started that story.'[9]

Debord was very quickly attracted to Ghislain, who was never seen in the company of his legendary African wife (known as 'The Countess') and who spoke in the sub-Raymond Chandler language of French detective novels. Ghislain was open about his activities as a pimp but was secretive about other dealings in a way that suggested that he was a far more prominent figure than he really was. Nonetheless, with his physical strength, appetite for drink and volatile temper, Ghislain was a genuinely dangerous friend.

As he had done earlier with his Arab friend Midou, whom he had courted and enchanted in Moineau's, Debord adopted Ghislain as a bodyguard. Debord admired Ghislain because he had something of the romantic adventurer or buccaneer about him. Debord enjoyed also Ghislain's reputation as a violent man and an outlaw. This contact with a world of physical force and aggression, for Debord at the time, was equally important as the philosophical discussions he had within his own milieu. No less important, at least from the point of view of his friends, was the way in which the quietly spoken Debord would detach himself from a conversation with a group of his peers at Chez Moineau to huddle at the bar with Ghislain. No one knew what they were talking about.

Ghislain's bar was not quite a brothel and not quite an ordinary bar. No one was quite sure where the money had come from and few dared to ask. Its most well-known habitué was Marise, nicknamed La Tatouée ('the tattooed one': the tattoo was a small rose on her behind), who in the afternoons plied her trade to the office workers of the 8th *arrondissement* at rue Vignon, next to the Madeleine church. It was suspected that Ghislain had physically forced Marise into prostitution, but few dared to ask him how she had embarked upon her career. According to Michèle Bernstein, Marise had taken the decision to prostitute herself on the grounds that all work was prostitution anyway and boasted that she was one of the few working whores in Paris to have a thorough knowledge of Dostoyevsky and Nietzsche or read *Finnegans Wake* on the job.

Marise and Ghislain lived together for a short while and then Ghislain disappeared. When they were drunk after midnight the crowd at Chez

Moineau continued to frequent L'Homme de Main, where Marise still held court. There was a rumour that Ghislain had been shot and, as in all the best traditions of French cinematic gangsterism, his body thrown into the Canal Saint-Martin. Even Marise said that she hadn't really known what he was involved in. Somebody said that Ghislain had been working as a bodyguard for people mixed up in the seamier side of politics, people who had been dealing with the darker edges of Gaullism, something to do with Indochina. Others said that he was involved with the Algerian drug trade in the 11th *arrondissement*. Whatever happened, once he had disappeared, Ghislain never came back.

If Debord was shocked or saddened by Ghislain's disappearance he did not show this emotion to even his closest associates at Chez Moineau. Debord saw Ghislain as an adventurer and his untimely end was the inevitable risk of such a dangerous life; although such a death was not necessarily to be expected, it was not to be lamented. Debord indeed was proud to have been in the company of the man and it would have been a betrayal of Ghislain's style to have worried over him.

Ghislain's death also changed the status of the poster which Debord had designed for the bar's opening night. The Letterist International detested publicity and advertising in all its forms. The 'publicity-hungry' Isou had condemned himself in the eyes of the Letterist International by claiming that art could be sold and put to commercial use without necessarily tainting the artist. However, when Ghislain asked Debord to produce a poster for his bar Debord said immediately that he would be glad to do it and within days produced a design which Ghislain reproduced and had pasted up across the Left Bank for the opening night.

In the wake of Ghislain's disappearance, Debord justified this, however, by saying that this was not advertising, but an invitation. L'Homme de Main was a secret place, an environment which you could only find by chance and whose pleasures were random and furtive. The poster did not sell the bar any more than the bar sold the poster; they were simply signposts towards a world of adventure. The poster for L'Homme de Main is not, however, a masterpiece in miniature but rather a run-of-the-mill flyposter. Above and around an image of an atomic explosion, there is the simple legend, a deformed quotation from Right-wing ideologue Charles Maurras: 'France alone has a bar like L'Homme de Main, 31 rue de Jussieu'.

CHAPTER 7

Who is Potlatch?

1954–5

The Letterist International loudly proclaimed themselves indifferent to the shifting sands of mainstream politics. It was noted, however, even in the Café de la Contrescarpe, the new base of the international Letterists in the Latin Quarter, that the summer of 1954 seemed to mark a brief interlude of optimism in what many commentators on the Right and Left saw as the apparently doomed history of the Fourth Republic, the uneasy coalition of opposing parliamentary forces which had been brought together to stave off revolution or dictatorship (both of which had seemed very close at hand in the chaos of the immediate post-war period).

The history of the Fourth Republic was far from glorious. It was characterised by crisis and ministerial instability (there were twenty-six governments between 1944 and 1958). This was in large part the result of an electoral system which was constructed around divided parties, an overwhelmingly powerful parliament and a weak executive, making it impossible for any one party or group to fulfil a mandate or carry out any coherent programme of action. The Fourth Republic reached one of its many crisis points at the end of 1953 when, as Vincent Auriol came to the end of his seven-year presidential term, it became clear that there was no one who commanded either the authority or support to succeed him. The veteran parliamentarian Édouard Herriot, then eighty-one years old, was discussed as the future President of the Republic but refused to stand on health grounds. The most important position in France was handed by default to the thoroughly mediocre René Coty, a businessman from Le Havre who was a compromise candidate. Auriol could not disguise his distaste for his successor when he received him on Boxing Day 1953.

Against this background of disintegration and bad faith in the system itself, there was concerted American pressure through the course of 1954 to resolve France's internal and external problems. In mid-June, the vacillating government of Joseph Laniel had collapsed over its inability to deal effectively with the crisis in Indo-China and handle the new domestic pressures made by the demands of the fragile post-war economy.

Laniel's administration had been succeeded by the new government of Pierre Mendès France, Laniel's main tormentor in the National Assembly, who called for a spirit of national renewal. Mendès France was loudly applauded by the French public and foreign, mainly American, observers alike. PMF, as he came to be known, was thus tacitly awarded a summer of grace by press and public to solve France's problems. PMF's status as the would-be saviour was heightened when he was allegedly nicknamed 'Superman' by the American Secretary of State John Foster Dulles. On the back of this simple-minded approbation, Mendès France claimed that he would 'liquidate' France's problems. 'Mendèsisme', so PMF's supporters claimed, would at least herald a new era of growth and reconciliation for the Republic.

Neither proved true: the beginnings of open rebellion in Algeria and rising discontent in Metropolitan France (mostly orchestrated by *Poujadists*, the followers of Pierre Poujade, a *petit bourgeois* demagogue who used the rhetoric of the Left to argue against world markets and to defend essentially conservative French interests) would eventually bring Mendès France crashing down in 1956 and the Republic face to face with its impotence in a rapidly changing world of global politics. This much had been clearly predicted, the denizens of Café de la Contrescarpe were informed by Guy Debord, not by the press of the Right or the Left, but by the Letterist International, who affirmed that not only did they understand the development of modern politics better than anyone alive but that they didn't care about it either.

The most committed publication in the world

So it was that four days after the investiture of Pierre Mendès France as premier, on 22 June 1954, a cheaply duplicated pamphlet of four pages of brilliant, megalomaniac dissidence was mailed to fifty addresses across Paris. Some were selected at random from the phone book, others chosen because they would be annoyed at receiving such a pamphlet, and others because they might like it. The pamphlet was called *Potlatch* and subtitled 'The Bulletin of Information of the French group of the Letterist International'. The writers of *Potlatch*, fiercely separate from the outer world of 'Mendèsisme', constitutional politics and American foreign policy, and ironically detached from the mediocre imperative to build 'a new post-war society', magisterially declared themselves to be working for the 'collective and conscious establishment of a new civilisation'.[1]

The *Potlatch* addressees, aside from those picked out from the phone book, were told that they had been individually selected by the Letterist International (addressees included André Breton and Raymond Queneau, for example, but not Jean-Paul Sartre). The only other way to get hold of a copy of *Potlatch* was to ask an International Letterist for a copy or be handed a sheet of papers at a café table on the place de la Contrescarpe, rue du Four, rue de Rennes or rue du Dragon. Under no circumstances could *Potlatch* be bought or sold. It was simply a gift.

Potlatch described itself to its new readership, with no discernible shred of irony, as the most committed publication in the world. Its declared intention was to provide a running international Letterist commentary on the movement of history and the world. This, it seemed to some observers, was not so much a joke as a threat. It would appear every Tuesday.

The political content of *Potlatch* was utterly uncompromising and insistent in its thesis that the world must be wrecked in order for it to be rebuilt. All forms of rebellion, subversion and defiance were to encouraged. In this first issue, in 'Make them swallow their chewing gum', a text signed by André-Frank Conord, Mohamed Dahou, Guy-Ernest Debord, Jacques Fillon, Patrick Straram and Gil J. Wolman, the Letterists called for a civil war in Guatemala as a prelude to global war against the United States. The International Letterists called for volunteers from all over Europe, based on the model of the International Brigades of the Spanish Civil War, to join the fight. The expropiation of the United Fruit Company had led John Foster Dulles to warn of the dangers of Communism and describe the otherwise moderate Guatemalan government as 'forces of evil'. Dulles, wrote the Letterist International, was setting off on the Crusades. 'Arm the workers' was the response of the International Letterists. The tone was alternately cool and contemptuous or witty, even innocent. John Foster Dulles, like a character from a Tintin comic strip, was nicknamed Foster Rocket Dulles. This did not mean, however, that Dulles any more than any other enemy could escape the revolutionary justice of the Letterist International.[2]

The Letterist International mixed the global with the local: other texts eschewed contemporary affairs and called for the return of myth to modern society, described a Letterist art exhibition under the mysterious rubric 'The Dark Passage', or gave clues on how to organise a psychogeographical game: 'Choose the season and the hour. Bring together the most able people, records and the most agreeable forms of alcohol. The lighting and the conversation will have to be obviously fortuitous, like the weather outside or your memories. Send results to the editorial team.'[3]

Although the editor-in-chief of the bulletin was named as André-Frank Conord, it was Debord who contributed the longest and most politically outraged piece to this first edition of *Potlatch*. In future issues, Debord would go on to develop a style which was as acid as it was intransigent, writing about Jacques Vaché, Arthur Cravan, China, theories of war, Spain. In this opening statement of intent, 'All the Water in the Sea Couldn't . . .', Debord presented the news of the week: the killing of a rebel leader in Kenya, the killing of anarchists in Madrid, the moral and physical rottenness of some French novelists and intellectuals. In this first piece, however, Debord's primary target was an 'appel à la jeunesse' ('call to youth') published in May in *L'Express*, the news magazine which was the chief organ of propaganda for Pierre Mendès France. *L'Express* called for the youth of France to forget the sterile divisions of the past, Left, Right, secular, clerical, and to place its faith in the future, science and modernity. Debord's appalled response to this call for a new France of vigorous new technocrats was to describe how the attempted suicide of two young lovers had led to their incarceration on the grounds of 'moral responsibility'.

Only months earlier, Debord had boasted to friends at Moineau's that he himself had tried to kill himself by strangulation and had subsequently spent two weeks in a sanatorium. (The truth was far less glamorous: Manou, having noticed Guy coughing up blood during one of his rare visits home to Cannes, had insisted on him spending two weeks in a TB sanatorium for fear that he had inherited the disease which killed his father. Doctors insisted that the blood was caused by smoking and drinking too much: it was, however, too good an opportunity not to be made into a glamorous tale of self-destruction by Debord.) Like the rioting of the rebellious 'orphans' of Auteuil, or the 'youth uprising' planned by Isou, the suicide of Madeleine Reineri or the innumerable daily provocations of Mension or Fred, the suicide pact was a sovereign and complete form of negation, an absolute refusal of society. What right could society have to judge and punish such a poetic form of revolt? It proved only that the professionals of art, philosophy and politics, Albert Camus, François Mauriac and Mendès France, were all ridiculous liars or mythomaniacs. 'What these gentlemen lack,' wrote Guy-Ernest Debord, recalling Louis de Saint-Just and spinning the clock back from 1954 to 1794, 'is the Terror!'[4]

Potlatch was incoherent, fanatical, confusing, wildly allusive, often incomprehensible and absolutely sure of its opinions. The cheaply mimeographed sheets were drawn up on a weekly basis for at least nine issues and meticulously typed up on a rented machine by Michèle Bernstein ('For Guy, typing was women's work. He never changed his mind on this,' she commented later). It was an enduring game played amongst the inner circle of those who claimed to speak the secret language of the International Letterists, that no one was really sure if they knew who or what *Potlatch* was or is. The Letterist International enjoyed this fact and in *Potlatch* 14, when *Potlatch* had become a monthly, they threw out the puzzle to the readership. 'Who is Potlatch?' they asked in a brief piece subtitled 'a small homage to the American people'. The International Letterists offered their readers three choices:

1. A Soviet spy, the main accomplice of the Rosenbergs, discovered in 1952 by the FBI?

2. A practice of giving a sumptuary gift, calling for other gifts in response, which would have been the foundation of an economic system in pre-Colombian America?

3. A term devoid of all meaning, invented by the Letterists as a title for one of their publications?[5]

Answers were promised in the next issue of the journal.

Oedipal skirmishes

In the same issue of *Potlatch*, the Letterist International, led by Debord, expressed their delight in the angry response of André Breton to the Letterist International's plans to disrupt, with Surrealist support, the centenary celebrations of Rimbaud. Initially, Breton had been more than ready to sanction Surrealist involvement in the Letterist commando action. Although Breton's earlier meetings with Isou in 1947 and 1948 had been fruitless and even acrimonious, with the younger man refusing to defer to his former idol, Breton had been impressed enough by subsequent Letterist activity to allow the group to invoke the Surrealists as their peers. The stumbling block for the joint action had been the Leninist phraseology introduced by Debord into the planned joint tract justifying the action. Breton himself had composed a response to the Letterist International's actions, which he circulated secretly around the Surrealist group. The Letterist International learned of this from a sympathiser close to Breton (Debord and Wolman would often meet up with younger Surrealists such as Gérard Legrand in the Storyville on rue de la Huchette, one of the first French discothèques, where the plush leather armchairs and music of Charlie Parker provided a more elegant atmosphere than that of Debord's usual haunts). Wolman and Debord managed to collar a hapless signatory of Breton's document near place de la Sorbonne and threatened to give him a severe hiding if he did not produce the text accusing the Letterists of misunderstanding Lenin and Surrealism. It was handed over and reproduced, to Debord's glee, in *Potlatch* 14.

With Debord's encouragement, Gil Wolman also fired off a denunciatory pamphlet on Breton, depicting him as the inept managing director of a disintegrating business: 'Breton, these days it's bankruptcy. Your enterprise has been in the red for too long, and it's surely not your associates who can get you out of it. They don't even know how to behave themselves at table. You're not being served as well as before.'[6] Since the end of the war it had been increasingly difficult for Breton to maintain the authority he had once had over the now fragmented and tired force which constituted the Surrealist movement. The argument with the Letterists, minor as it was, was further proof of this fact to those around Breton who suspected that he was becoming tired of his position as the sole leader of Surrealism. For Debord, more pertinently, it was a chance to exhibit the filial disloyalty which had been a central part of his activity ever since he had moved from Cannes to Paris.

Such fractious encounters had, however, only served to heighten Debord's faith in the original Surrealist project. Having dispatched the middle-aged Breton as a weary and confused ex-revolutionary, Debord nonetheless exhorted respect for the pre-war avant-garde in *Potlatch*: 'We send our comrades off to read *La Révolution surréaliste*, which during the first quarter of this century, was an intelligent and honourable undertaking.'[7] Debord's condescending tone was doubly provocative, given that *La Révolution surréaliste*, which had been a stylish and expensive publication funded by gallery owners and publishers and which had an immediate international reputation, bore no comparison with the scruffy tracts handed out by the International Letterists in the bars of the *quartier*.

The great game

Both publications did have in common, however, a steely poise and a passion for subversion which was informed by a mythic pantheon of heroes. In Breton's famous *Manifesto of Surrealism* of 1924, the figurehead of Surrealism, then at his most powerful and dynamic, drew up a list of friends and figures from the past who gave Surrealism an imaginative pedigree. These included then unknowns, such as Louis Aragon, Benjamin Péret and Robert Desnos, as well as Sade ('Surrealist in sadism'), Poe ('Surrealist in adventure'), Swift ('in malice'), Baudelaire ('in morality'), Rimbaud ('in the way he lived') and Jacques Vaché ('Surrealist in me').

In *Potlatch* 2, Debord, in imitation of Breton, drew up a list of heroes in 'psychogeography', a term used to denote the effect of the individual subject on his or her environment. These included Poe ('psychogeographical in landscape'), Vaché ('in his manner of dressing') and even Breton himself ('naively psychogeographical in his encounters'). There were, however, two more significant figures. Madeleine Reineri, the teenage radio star whose suicide had been cited in *Howling in Favour of Sade* as a beautiful and elegant act of negation, was described as 'psychogeographical in suicide'. Louis de Saint-Just, according to Debord, was 'psychogeographical in politics'. Debord explained in a footnote that 'the Terror is a change of scene'.

It was Saint-Just's formula 'Happiness is a New Idea in Europe' which also best defined the revolutionary activity of the International Letterists. By literally doing nothing, by devoting themselves only to the pursuit of useless activity, drinking, talking, walking around Paris, the Letterist International had found the opposite of what society needed and demanded from its 'worker-slaves'. In this way, they had found a world which they described in the language of Charles Fourier, the nineteenth-century businessman and social philosopher who had been another, earlier adventurer in the potential of riotous imagination, as 'full of the free play of passions'. Freedom, argued the International Letterists, could only be found on the other side of this society of 'continuous work' and 'the obligatory degradations of stadiums or television programmes'. The grand game imagined by Debord was one in which work dissolved into play and spread, like Saint-Just's vision of a continual revolutionary war. This would take the form of a ceaseless, unstoppable chain of situations.

> More than one to whom adventures happen, the adventurer is one who makes them happen.
>
> The construction of situations will be the continuous realisation of a great game, a game the players have chosen to play: a shifting of settings and conflicts to kill off the characters in a tragedy in twenty-four hours.[8]

Those who would go on to become International Situationists later referred to *Potlatch* as 'pre-Situationist', meaning that the journal was a kind of laboratory where experimental games could be played out under controlled conditions determined by the floating committee of the Letterist International. The term 'Situationist' had not yet been coined but, as Debord's texts in *Potlatch* made clear, the play-tactics of the LI were already fully formed strategies for combating a world which had replaced real experience with empty representations of that experience.

None of these games made any sense beyond the closed world of the Letterist sect. This was inevitable: as an exercise in experimental heresy *Potlatch* could only make sense as a dreamed version of an unlimited future. This was one of the crucial keys to the meaning of *Potlatch*: a study in the theory and practice of revolution informed by radical desire.

'Solar economics'

The original meaning of 'potlatch', as it was explained in *Potlatch* 15 to those readers who had not guessed its real significance in the preceding issue, was 'a sumptuary gift'. What Debord did not try to explain was where this term had come from and why the LI had applied it in this way. 'Potlatch' was a term that had entered the French language via the anthropologist Marcel Mauss who had encountered the word in his study of the economic activity of the American Indian tribes of British Columbia and Alaska. In his 1925 book *The Gift*, Mauss, disciple and nephew of Émile Durkheim the father of modern sociology, described the auto-destruction of the 'potlatch' as the defining feature of tribes which placed honour and community above the mutable laws of exchange value.

The word described a strange game, made illegal by the United States authorities at the end of the nineteenth century on the insistence of white observers of American Indian habits. The reason for this was that the game of 'potlatch' fundamentally destabilised the economic systems of organisation on which white traders depended. What happened was that two or more tribes would arrange to meet to exchange a series of gifts which had to be of increasingly higher value. In this way, as the exchange-value of the gifts increased to impossible proportions, the giving of sea-canoes, hunting rights, the burning of a village, the game took on a sacred aspect, finally becoming a series of sacrifices which offered no way back to the original exchange-value system. In this sense, the 'potlatch' was the 'construction of a situation' from which there was no turning back; a game of pure negation. In his autobiographical book *Potlatch*, George Clutesi, a native of Vancouver Island, gave an eye-witness account of the last known potlatch of the twentieth century in British Columbia. His description of the life of the tribe during the festival of potlatch had curious echoes of the life of the tribe at Chez Moineau.

> They lived from one day to the next, they accepted all things as they came. They spoke slowly, they took much time before uttering, before replying, before expressing an opinion. When it was necessary to journey in their canoes to far-off places, they paddled because it took more time. The thick black hair upon their heads stayed blacker, longer, and did not shed and fall off.
>
> Ah yes, to those people, time meant little, if considered at all, yet time was never on their hands. They never sat idle for the sake of sitting idle. When the artisan sat doing nothing for hours, for days, he was really planning, formulating, or wrestling with a problem in his mind. Indeed, he made no start on any project until all the details had already been completed in his mind, so at times he sat for days ostensibly doing nothing.[9]

The term 'potlatch' had also famously been used by the writer and critic Georges Bataille, first of all during the seminars of the Collège de sociologie and then in the writings on mysticism and economics he published during and shortly after the war.[10] When *Potlatch* first appeared in the bars and on the streets of Paris, Bataille was a distinguished and influential figure, editor of the respected journal *Critique*, whose long rivalry with André Breton had established him and his circle as a rallying point for dissident Surrealists. Bataille, who combined a diligent career as a librarian at the Bibliothèque nationale with a thirst for excess and violence in philosophy and politics, also had a reputation as an eroticist. Bataille's fictional writings were notorious for their blasphemous and sadistic content; Bataille's own personal life was alleged to match anything found in his fictions.

Most bizarrely, a rumour circulated that during the 1930s, under the aegis of the semi-secret society called 'Acéphale', Bataille, in imitation of the Aztec ceremonies which fascinated him, had either committed or wanted to commit a human sacrifice. Those who had attended the rites and ceremonies of Acéphale further fuelled rumours by remaining mysteriously silent on the matter; others, such as Bataille's friends Michel Leiris or Roger Caillois who did not take part in the activities of Acéphale, condemned the project as misguided. Bataille's lover during the 1930s, Colette Peignot (known as 'Laure'), was also Bataille's collaborator during the Acéphale adventure. The notoriety of the Acéphale project was heightened by the fact that Laure had a well-known appetite for exotic varieties of sexual sadism (she was, for example, famously reported to have eaten her own shit during an encounter with the Berlin doctor, Edouard Trautner, author of *God, Cocaine and Present Time*).[11]

Debord admired Bataille's most pornographic works, reserving particular admiration for the violent erotic parables *The Story of the Eye* and *Madame Edwarda*. However, for all their libertarian instincts, the International Letterists, including Debord, could be remarkably prudish in terms of sexual morality. According to Michèle Bernstein, the International Letterists were all, or nearly all, 'children of good families who practised good manners and morality'. Although Debord would later espouse a free-thinking attitude to sexual morality in practice as well as theory, at this stage in his career he was content to express his would-be libertinism in a certain sartorial flamboyance (Mension remembers being shocked at finding Debord at home in the rue Racine wearing a bourgeois dressing gown and slippers: this, Mension later concluded, was Debord's '*dandysme*' at work).[12]

In his writings on the 'potlatch', Bataille developed a theory of economic exchange which entirely matched the Letterist International's negative reading of capitalist economics. More precisely, Bataille was fascinated by the way in which the destructive nature of the 'potlatch' was also a type of total economic war in the form of a sacrifice. Bataille distinguished between commercial activity as the reproduction of a society's values, and social activity which aimed at going beyond the limits of what civilisation defined as the law or limit. He argued that in those societies which circulated wealth through the practice of 'potlatch' the mercantile instinct had been overcome by the more powerful and ineradicable urge to destroy, to overcome the useful and utilitarian, in a festival which defined the gods. The highest and most destructive form of economic activity, according to Bataille, was therefore to give a gift which could not be returned. This was, in the language of the Mexican Indians whose sacrifices to the sun Bataille admired as a simultaneous affirmation and destruction of a society, an economy built on waste and destruction as collective forces: 'solar economics'.[13]

Anti-matter

In *Potlatch* 5, Debord insisted that the Letterist International reprint an article taken from *Combat* which gave news of the recent discovery by an American physicist of the anti-proton:

THE CATHARS WERE RIGHT

Washington 9th July – All the American press have today published photos of the physicist Marcel Schein, Professor at the University of Chicago, of his blackboard and of his 'anti-proton', a mysterious particle of cosmic matter which was detected last winter by a weather balloon 30 kilometres above Texas.

This would be in fact one of the greatest discoveries of modern science. The anti-proton, which has been sought after for many years by physicists all over the world, would be the opposite of the proton.

The proton is the nucleus of the hydrogen atom, and, in consequence, constitutes the basic element of all terrestrial matter. A proton and an anti-proton which meet are fated to mutual destruction. Thus the anti-proton will be capable of annihilating all matter composed of protons. In essence, this will be 'anti-matter'. Nevertheless, it appears impossible for them to combine with enough force to destroy the planet. (*Combat*, 10 July 1954)[14]

Little is known about the origins of the heretics who first appeared in southern France in the twelfth century and were variously described as Catharist, Albigensian and neo-Manichaean. What is known is taken mostly from the records of interrogations by the Inquisition held in the Bibliothèque nationale, the Vatican Library and the archives of Carcassonne and Toulouse, and from these accounts it is clear that the Cathars, as they called themselves, believed that they alone had access to the Kingdom of God. They taught that the world was ruled not by God but by Satan, the Demiurge or Monster of Chaos, and that the Church of Rome, which involved itself with money and politics, was the work of the Demiurge. The term 'Cathar' comes from the Greek word *katharos* meaning 'unpolluted' and the Cathars, retreating to the remote hamlets and villages of Concorezzo in northern Italy in the face of a crusade mounted against them, referred to themselves also as 'perfecti', the perfect ones. Above all, the Cathars taught that when the world fell, as it surely would, it would be theirs and theirs alone.

The Letterist International despised religion and were always wary of mysticism or occultism. Debord in particular had been scathing, both in private and in print, about the alleged mystical tendencies of Isou and his 'disciples'. Breton, who had seemingly abandoned politics, as the fracas over the Rimbaud centenary had shown, in favour of the pursuit of 'magical thinking', which would find expression in his text *Arcananum 17*, was no better. The Cathar heresy appealed to Debord therefore not as an esoteric doctrine but as a negation of the organising forces of the twelfth-century world, Church, money and land. In the same way the Letterist International, a loose and obscure collection of young alcoholics, drifters, deserters, misfits, bad poets, petty thieves and hooligans, were bound together by their collective belief in a dualism which set the world of light – the world of night-time Left Bank Paris – against the world of darkness – the world of work, everyday boredom and commodity exchange. It was an easy comparison to make for Debord who, according to Michèle Bernstein's own account, had already begun to conceive of the subterranean world of Chez Moineau in mythic terms. The headline, 'THE CATHARS WERE RIGHT', for the piece on the anti-proton was then a good Debordian joke, elusive, allusive and fraught with meaning in the same space. Most obviously, like the anti-proton, the elementary particles which floated from bar to café and back across the *quartier*, from place Saint-Sulpice to the place de la Contrescarpe by way of rue du Xavier-Privas, in pursuit of drink, sex, play, avoiding boredom and work, were the 'anti-matter of society'. The joke, however, was also a powerful metaphor. The Letterists were like the Cathars because they stood against ordered society and disrupted it by deliberately turning its first principles inside out. The Cathars had taught that the world, 'rotten with sin', would collapse under its own weight and that changes, revolutionary changes, would be brought by the 'perfecti' turning away from the 'unreal world'.

As Debord signals in 'THE CATHARS WERE RIGHT', the LI were not just the descendants or the heirs to the prophesies of the Cathars, but also their resurrected contemporaries who enacted and lived out their hermetic techniques of negation. Most importantly, like the original heretics who denied that the passage of time proved the meaning of the world, the LI negated the substance of modern society by refusing to allow the language of modern life into their vocabulary. Their activities, reckless, wild, destructive, were conceived separately from the world around them.

In this the Letterist International itself constituted the most literal application of the term 'potlatch'; 'potlatch' is the highest form of game. It is also the living moment of poetry, a moment which breaks down or reverses conventional chronological patterns. Most significantly, the object or gift which the Letterist International gave functioned symbolically between the giver, the International Letterists, and the receiver. The relationship between the two constitutes the third term – the gift is also a catalyst of the future in the form of a crystallisation of desire. 'Don't collect *Potlatch*!' ran a line at the end of the journal's second year. 'Time is working against you!'

CHAPTER 8

Paris without Spectacle

1954–5

It was of crucial significance to the Letterist International that the demands which they made were not only political but aesthetic. More specifically, politics emerged directly out of a preoccupation with reintegrating an aesthetic system into daily life. A consistent obsession in the texts of *Potlatch* was therefore with the LI's everyday experience of cities in general and the city of Paris in particular.

In the first instance this translated itself into a concern with maps and their various possible meanings. Early articles in *Potlatch* introduced readers to key terms which were developed out of this fascination with cities. These were *psychogéographie* ('psychogeography'), *situations* ('situations'), *urbanisme unitaire* ('unitary urbanism') and *dérive* ('drift'). Each of these terms was connected to Debord's notion, borrowed from the Surrealists, that cities existed as sites in which arbitrary separations between work and leisure or the private and public could be overcome in a poetic totality. Under Debord's direction, the Letterist International thus began to devote a great deal of energy to developing techniques of 'psychogeography', a way of reinventing the city according to one's own personal mythology and experience. No one can now remember who first used the term 'psychogeography' in conversation, or when it was first used. Debord first used it in print in his article 'Introduction à une géographie urbaine' in a 1955 edition of *Les Lèvres nues*. The central argument of the article was that Haussmann's Paris was 'a city built by an idiot, full of sound and fury and signifying nothing'.[1] The practice of 'psychogeographical' techniques was a way of restoring meaning to the city. Debord attributed the term 'psychogeography' to an 'illiterate Kabyle', who used the term to describe the random actions of the International Letterists in 1953. Michèle Bernstein gave credence to this unlikely coinage with her account of how she and Guy would frequent a certain restaurant on the rue Xavier-Privas to eat couscous and smoke *kif* which was sent in homely parcels to exiled Algerians in the *quartier*. One evening they had come across a particularly stoned Kabyle who had taken Guy on a night-time stroll through the Jardin des Plantes comparing each plant he came across with the elegance of the cannabis plant. 'That experience and charming misuse of the French language,' she said, 'is what lies at the origins of psychogeography. Guy was stoned, and so was I, and we had invented in this experience a new way of thinking about and seeing the city.'

Debord had also been inspired, however, at least according to Patrick Labaste, by a popular novel by Jean-Paul Clébert called *Paris insolite* ('Strange Paris'). This book, which enjoyed great success in the early part of the 1950s, was a loose narrative which drew together accounts of random wanderings across the city. Even more intriguingly it seemed that one of the characters in the book had been based on Jean-Claude Guilbert, a well-known character at Moineau's, famous for his roles as a part-time actor and for his heroic capacity for drink (Guilbert was also briefly the lover of Michèle Bernstein).

Whatever the origins of the word, the developing techniques of psychogeography were clearly borrowed not only from the Surrealists, but also from Baudelaire, whose poetry was seen as the first modern poetry of the city, and De Quincey, whose intoxicated wanderings around Manchester and London were, for Debord, the purest example of the perfect collision between poetry, space and architecture which created a 'situation'. The International Letterists practised 'psychogeography' by wandering around the city ignoring the products of capitalism and religion (at one point the LI had a rule never to use the word *saint* when referring to street names) and pursuing a fascination with dreamscapes or forgotten corners of the city, sites wrecked and ignored by history. The key to this method was the prime importance of real, lived experience. In January 1954, the International Letterists received a questionnaire from the poetry journal *La Carte d'après* which asked, 'What meaning do you give the word poetry?' The collective response, signed by Debord and others, was 'Poetry is in the form of cities. We are going to build cities which startle you. The new beauty will be in the form of SITUATION, that is to say temporary and lived.'

Drifting

The most important 'psychogeographical' technique was the practice of *dérive*, or 'drift', in the course of which members of the LI would float across Paris in the pursuit of anarchy, play, poetry: 'Paris without spectacle'.[2] Their favoured places were those which, like the rue du Xavier-Privas, square des Missions Étrangères or the Canal Saint-Martin, moved observers, such as Michèle Bernstein (who first introduced the term *dérive* in an article in *Potlatch* praising the role of the taxi in pointless journeys)[3] to 'salutary states of awe, melancholy, joy or terror'.[4]

The origins of the *dérive* were also simply an extension of the drunken practices of the Letterist International and their cohorts at Moineau's, whose own map of the city was marked by bars and cafés. The first *dérives* around Paris were motivated by the pursuit of pleasure rather than theory. The group would walk to rue de Chalon behind the Gare de Lyon, then the site of a burgeoning Chinese community, to eat cheap food, or they would *dérive* to Saint-Paul in the Marais, then still predominantly a working-class or Jewish district, to eat salted anchovies which would give them an unslakeable thirst for beer. Further north, much favoured by Debord, was the Spanish quarter of Aubervilliers, where the Letterist International had drawn up its protocols. This quarter had a multitude of working-class bars and *bistrots*, mainly founded by Republican exiles and survivors of the Spanish Civil War. Faithful to the practices of Spanish alcoholic extremism, and much to the delight of the International Letterists, it was considered dishonourable to arrive sober at these dives, or to leave anything less than dead drunk.

The theory of the *dérive* was developed out of the experience of being intoxicated and 'lost' in the city. The first real *dérives* were inspired by the railwaymen's strike in the summer of 1953, when hitch-hiking around Paris and its suburbs became the only viable form of transport. After a regular visit to the Gare de Lyon to hurl abuse at those waiting for trains or breaking the strike, Guy Debord, Jean-Michel Mension, Éliane Papaï and her latest friend Linda, would get in the first car to stop and head off wherever the car happened to be heading. After fifteen minutes or so, Debord would ask the driver to stop at the nearest *bistrot*, where he would buy bottles of wine for the group. These would be drunk before the group headed off again in an entirely random manner.[5]

There was, then, initially nothing poetic about the *dérive*. A forced march to a restaurant in the Chinese quarter in the 13th *arrondissement* had its heroic qualities, but, as Jean-Michel Mension puts it, this was mainly because it was tiring to walk, 'particularly when you're drunk and distances are obviously longer because you don't walk straight'.[6] The *dérive*, on the other hand, as theorised by Bernstein and Debord in the pages of *Potlatch*, became a practice which disordered and disoriented the subject in the city. In this way it revealed for Debord, as did the earlier experiments in sound poetry of Isou and the original Letterists, the collision between poetry and its opposite. The *dérive*, most importantly, was an exercise in spatial projection, a rediscovery of the city as a labyrinth. Like Surrealist poetry, it was also a collective practice which separated objects from their functions. As a fundamentallly poetic game it revealed its opposite in an urban topography of fragmentation and dispersal; above all it made the city into an adventure.

'The hacienda must be built'

As an essential strategy in the guerrilla war the Letterist International had declared on the city, the group had its own points of retreat. These included, most notably, l'allée du Seminaire, a quiet spot at the head of the rue Bonaparte where it was possible to smoke or drink in relative intimacy. Another favoured spot was the square du Vert-Galant, the small islet which juts out into the Seine at the end of Île de la Cité. This small, tree-lined triangular stern of the island, named 'Vert-Galant', meaning a 'lusty noble', is named for Henri IV's sexual conquests. For the Letterist International and their friends it was also an enclosed green space surrounded by water which allowed them to withdraw from the city, to smoke hash, daydream, make love. Mension once fell in the Seine, but still saw the place as an almost sacred spot. Michèle had famously gone swimming in the Seine after midnight, despite gashing her foot on broken glass, earning herself a short stay in hospital, and described the island as a magical place. 'We were completely free there. The city of Paris was our playground and we were invulnerable.' Debord and Éliane loved it: it was a place where the police never came looking for schoolgirls on the run or their drunken associates. The square also marked a frontier between the free life of the Left Bank and the exigencies of commercialism and commerce on the Right Bank.

These points of retreat were also concrete examples of what the LI meant by *urbanisme unitaire* ('unitary urbanism'). This was later defined in *L'Internationale situationiste* (the *Situationist International*) as 'the theory of the combined use of arts and techniques for the integral construction of a milieu in dynamic relation with experiments in behaviour'.[7] In practice, at this early stage in the development of what would become Situationist theory, this meant blurring the distinction between meaning and function in the decor of the city. At one point the International Letterists urged in *Potlatch* that the *métro* should be open to pedestrians, that pharmacists should sell cigars and that streetlighting should have an on–off switch.[8] In this way, 'unitary urbanism' was the corollary of another technique currently being developed by the Letterist International and which they called *détournement*. Literally translated from the French this term means 'diversion' or 'rerouting'. It also carries nuances which are closer to terms such as 'hijacking', 'kidnapping', 'corruption' and 'theft'. This appealed to the International Letterists as a way of describing their game of attacking art by plagiarising and stealing 'pre-existing aesthetic elements' to make a new work entirely disconnected from the original.

The practice of 'unitary urbanism' sought to *détourne* the city in a similar way. The theory was encoded in an essay written for the Letterist International by Ivan Chtcheglov in 1953, the same Chtcheglov who had tried to blow up the Eiffel Tower because its lights, reflected into his apartment, were disturbing his sleep (although according to Mension both occupants of the flat were usually so drunk that 'they could have slept with the Eiffel Tower on top of them'). In this essay, 'Formulary for a New

Urbanism', Chtcheglov argued for a 'symbolic urbanism', that is to say a city whose shape was determined by the subjective vision of those who live in it or who journey through it, rather than by the artificial demands of work, capital, leisure.

Inspired by his favourite painter, Giorgio de Chirico, whose 'metaphysical paintings' distort space and perspective to the point of obliteration, Chtcheglov described the new city as encapsulating those qualities of desire and dream which are only awakened by experience of the uncanny or unknown. He termed the ideal site of this experience 'the hacienda', declaring that although 'you will never see the hacienda', 'the hacienda must be built'. It was this enigmatic phrase which, thirty years later, inspired Rob Gretton and Anthony H. Wilson, managers of Joy Division and New Order, to name their Manchester nightclub The Haçienda: the club's late 1980s reputation as a haven for drug-fuelled excess was partly a vindication of this choice of name.[9]

Chtcheglov was greatly admired by Debord, who listened with rapt attention at the bar to his accounts of his 'continuous drifts' through Paris. Sometimes Chtcheglov would find it impossible to stay in one place for more than a few minutes and would wander through the city for days in a kind of trance, hallucinating from fatigue and lack of food, in pursuit of 'the hacienda'. Chtcheglov's language was deeply influenced by his readings of esoteric or occultist literature. He was particularly fond of quoting the Hermetic philosopher Raymond Abellio and, like Antonin Artaud, the once brilliant Surrealist actor, poet and painter whose public mental disintegration shocked and fascinated the post-war literary élite, he claimed that his actions were being controlled by Tibetan Lamas. Artaud had once famously stormed into Les Deux Magots and proclaimed that the incessant masturbation of Tibetan mystics was draining him of his life blood. Although Debord at this stage was set solidly against any form of 'occultism' or 'Surrealism', he perceived in Chtcheglov a culture and an intelligence which gave his tales of psychic vagabondage a real poetic worth. Although Chtcheglov was excluded from the International Letterist group in the series of purges which took place through the course of 1954, his ideas on 'unitary urbanism' were important enough for him to be later made a founding member of the SI and his 1953 text to be published in the first edition of the *Situationist International*.

Chtcheglov didn't usually drink as much as the other members of the group, but when he did he veered towards a dangerous excess which unnerved even the hardest boozers of Moineau's. One afternoon in late June 1954, after a row with his wife, Chtcheglov became violently drunk and smashed up the bar of Les Cinq Billards, a café on the rue Mouffetard favoured by the Letterists for its liberal 'drink now pay later' policy. His wife Stella, much despised by the International Letterists, called the police who had Chtcheglov incarcerated in a mental hospital. He was immediately diagnosed as schizophrenic and subjected to the range of insulin comas and electro-shock treatment which then passed for therapy. Guy and Michèle visited him but found his condition so upsetting – he was dribbling and muttering in a confused way – that they could not go back. Chtcheglov had played the crucial role of 'voyant' or 'seer' in the poetic games of the Letterists and his mental collapse was terrifying for all who knew him. The last that was heard of him was that he ended up at La Borde, an experimental clinic where the 'post-Freudian' ideas of Jacques Lacan held sway and where Félix Guattari, the co-author with Gilles Deleuze of *The Anti-Oedipus*, practised. Nobody knows now whether Chtcheglov is still alive or dead.

'Lost young hoodlum girls'

In August 1954 Debord married Michèle Bernstein. Debord described himself as 'always attracted to foreign women' and evidently Michèle, part French and part Russian Jew, was sufficiently exotic to interest him. Michèle, by her own admission, however, was not initially attracted to Debord, having known him reasonably well since 1952. But within a short space of time her 'interesting friend' had become her lover and husband without her being quite sure what had happened.

'I married a genius,' she said, laughing out loud at the absurdity of the statement. 'I never thought of him as a genius, but I know that other people did, and perhaps Guy thought of himself as one as well. Who knows? But I did love him, and I am sorry he is not here with us now. I think that suicide is, well, you know, it was the best way for him to leave. It was a noble act.'

We were sitting in the front room of Michèle's fine Jacobean house in Salisbury (a short step away from Ted Heath's current residence and local pub). An open fire blazed and I was drinking whisky whilst Michèle drank wine and, wrapping herself in a fine woollen shawl, told me about her love for Guy Debord. She was heavier than I had imagined and she also used a walking stick with a redoubtable *grande dame* elegance, but her eyes still flashed as they had done in the thirty-year-old photos I had seen.

Michèle couldn't remember the first time she had met her future husband, except that he was sharply dressed, with elegant manners. Invariably accompanied by Gil Wolman, Debord would regularly prowl the early-evening *terrasses* of the Left Bank where, alongside Wolman, he became something of an accomplished *dragueur* or pick-up artist. 'He tried to pick me up at the café in front of the Sorbonne,' Michèle recalled. 'He says that I shook my cigarette and I said something disparaging. He sent to find me later in another *bistrot*, Le Carrefour. I finally arrived in Moineau with Jean-Michel Mension, whom I told I wasn't a student. Guy was at the *comptoir*: I was then with him at the screening of *Howling in Favour of Sade*, but we were not in love. I thought he was very interesting. When we fell in love we acted in a way that was *bien élevé* ('well brought up'), and we married. I don't know why we did it. In that time even people like Wolman married. It was something serious.'

The idea of marriage had originally been suggested to Guy and Michèle by Jean-Michel Mension during a long and alcoholic afternoon in late July 1954 when, according to Mension, all three of them, like most young people of their age, had been toying with the notion as a playful abstraction. 'Suddenly, it occurred to me that they were made for each other,' said Mension. 'I said that they should get married and that it was something that made sense. They said "fine". And Guy took another drink . . . I can see him clearly now, with a slight smile, looking a little bit crafty.'[10]

The marriage was a civil service held in the *mairie* of the 6th *arrondissement*, attended by a handful of regulars from Chez Moineau, who went on to subdued celebrations in a couscous restaurant in the rue Galande. Michèle's parents in Le Havre and Debord's family in Cannes were not invited and indeed were only told about the wedding much later. The couple were nonetheless conventional enough to settle into a kind of domesticity in Debord's rooms at the hotel on the rue Racine shortly after the wedding. Debord's bourgeois manners, which had so shocked Mension and which he had reported back to the the other more hard-line members of the Moineau crowd, were obviously amenable to Michèle's own middle-class standards.

Although Michèle had been loosely involved with the crowd at Moineau and the Letterist International since 1952, she was not officially assimiliated into the inner circle until 1954 when, signing herself Michèle-Ivich Bernstein, she contributed a brief statement of intent to *Potlatch* 3. 'There are people called "Letterists" like those who are called "Jacobins" or "Cordeliers",' she wrote cryptically.[11] Although renowned for her cleverness, Michèle was also for a long time the object of suspicion for those who disliked her patrician manners and detected snobbery beneath the revolutionary rhetoric. Certainly Michèle lived well, supplementing the income paid to her by her father with a series of part-time jobs. It was difficult, however, for even the most vehemently 'anti-work' members of the tribe to complain about this apparent betrayal of principle when she was able to buy them restorative *petits rouges* on grim hung-over weekday mornings in Chez Moineau. 'They had to pretend to like me then,' was her comment.

By styling herself 'Ivich' in the pages of *Potlatch*, Michèle was making a reference to her origins as a Russian Jew. In the imagination of the males who clustered at the bar of the various Left Bank cafés she frequented, she was also comparable herself to the character 'Ivich' in *The Age of Reason*, the second volume of Jean-Paul Sartre's trilogy *The Roads to Freedom* (she denies that this was her intention). In this novel, set during 1938, Ivich is a beautiful, feckless and ultimately doomed young student at the Sorbonne who embarks on a love affair with the vacillating middle-aged intellectual Mathieu. For Mathieu, Ivich represents, with her *hauteur* and sulky indolence, all the fire and sexual promise of youth and an ideal of poetic action. She is as unattainable to Mathieu, however, as the political vigour which drives his peers and contemporaries to the battlefront in Spain. She is therefore a symbol of frustration and impotence as much as of freedom and poetry. Like Sartre's Ivich, Michèle could in this way trap men with her style rather than her looks.

At one point Michèle so closely resembled Sartre's 'Ivich' that she was almost unbearable: according to Mension she was almost always, in the space of the same conversation, an *emmerdeuse* ('a pain in the arse') and the soul of sweetness itself. André-Frank Conord, who was himself briefly in love with Michèle, noted this quality and in *Potlatch* 6 played up to Michèle's fantasy in a piece entitled 'The Delimitation of Myth' in which he made 'Ivich' an exalted avatar of poetic caprice: 'sometimes noticed, sometimes adored, never understood'.[12] In the same piece, Conord also made a cryptic allusion to Debord's forthcoming marriage to Michèle, referring to Debord as a poor substitute for himself. It was no surprise, therefore, that by the end of August Conord, who had not realised the depth of Michèle's attachment to Debord, found himself permanently excluded from the Letterist International and reviled as 'a neo-buddhist, evangelist and neo-spiritualist'.[13]

As Conord also found out, if Michèle, like 'Ivich', was in equal measure cool, intelligent and sharp, she could also be vituperative, hot-tempered and passionate; these were the qualities which made her sufficiently 'foreign' to attract Debord. These same qualities also applied in abundance to Éliane Papaï who was Debord's only serious girlfriend before Michèle. Although there was never any shortage of available and willing companions in the protean sexual world of the Left Bank, and despite the fact that Debord enjoyed the sexual favours on offer, he was also a romantic who enjoyed the drama of love affairs. He used the word 'love' often and seriously, especially with Éliane who was foreign and wild, two qualities which were irresistible to Debord.

Éliane's father was Hungarian and her mother, who died of cancer at a young age, Spanish. In the imagination of the Left Bank crowd it was this mixed parentage which accounted for the 'volcanic' aspect of Éliane's character. There was also, however, Éliane's hatred of all forms of social hierarchy. Shortly after the death of her mother, Éliane's father had married a governess in the service of a Romanian general who owned a distinguished house in the 16th *arrondissement*, the richest and most élite part of Paris. Éliane thought it demeaning that her father had been obliged to abandon his original trade as a master glazier to work as an odd-job man in the house of a rich bourgeois. She also missed the busy streets of the working-class district of the 11th *arrondissement* where she had been brought up.

From her early teens onwards, Éliane was a runaway. The first time she had run away, fleeing the 16th *arrondissement* for the 11th, she had been picked up by the police and thrown in the reform school at Chevilly-Larue. When her father came to pick her up, the police refused to release her on the grounds that she was a criminal delinquent. Éliane took matters into her own hands and escaped, making for the bars and dives of the *quartier latin*. She was picked up again during a routine police raid and, most humiliatingly, forced to pursue her studies at a convent in the 16th *arrondissement*. Debord met and fell in love with Éliane as she was smoking hash in Moineau's, on the run for the second time.

Éliane was uncontrollable in both her behaviour and conversation. Unlike Michèle who, even when embracing the most outrageous ideas, still preserved an air of gentility and elegance, Éliane was liable to fly into extravagant rages, drunken tantrums or laugh hysterically at the slightest provocation. Stories abounded of Éliane. One drunken midnight she kicked the owner of the Mabillon in the balls, much to the delight of the waiters, and she was reported to have danced a naked flamenco in a dive on the Right Bank. When she was picked up by the police, along with a crowd of others, for pissing in a doorway on the rue des Ciseaux at two o'clock in the morning, she howled, 'Never ever would I piss in front of men!' To the disbelieving eyes of the police, she hitched up her skirts and urinated in front of them, earning herself a record of two fines for public drunkenness in the same quarter of an hour.[14]

It had been assumed by most of the crowd at Moineau's that Debord's affair with Éliane had been entirely casual. Jean-Michel Mension discovered the opposite after making love to Éliane one drunken evening in the apartment of Raymond Hains, a mutual friend and would-be film-maker who lived in the rue Delambre. 'I found out that Guy had a very pure vision of eternal love, perfect love, a vision impossible to live out in the rotten world where we live, and I learned that in fact Guy and Éliane had separated on a phrase, on something which opposed all that.'

Éliane had a special significance for Debord. Although later married to Jean-Louis Brau and accused with him of 'falsification' by the Situationist International in the wake of the events of 1968, she was also recalled by Debord as an essential moment in his early life. In *Panegyric*, she is described as one of those *jeunes voyelles perdues* ('lost hoodlum girls') whose wayward and unpredictable violence makes them, like Villon's female accomplices, such 'good company'. Éliane's image is also reproduced in Debord's *Oeuvres cinématographiques complètes* as an emblem of irrecuperable revolutionary desire. This picture is included in *Panégyrique tome second* together with a fragment from François de Motteville, a favourite memoirist of Debord whose texts bear witness to the tensions of pre-revolutionary France. The text reads: 'A private person that those who write history will never know, or will never find worthy of mention. Yet it is this private person which makes it known whether we deserve honour or blame.'

Éliane incarnated for Debord 'all hatred of the world, all fear of the world, all violence'.[15] The image of her which is used and reused by Debord is a key reference point for the most extreme aspects of what would become Situationist thinking, a cipher for revolutionary intransigence in its purest and most poetic form. The demands which Éliane's gaze in this photograph make upon the viewer are those of Max Stirner's ideal anarchist who wages a perpetual and amoral conflict, 'the war of each against all'. It could even be said that as the passionate embodiment of revolutionary promise, like Ivan Chtcheglov in Debord's imagination she effectively contributed as least as much to the origins of the Situationist adventure as Michèle Bernstein.

A dangerous vocation

Debord's marriage also coincided with yet another change of venue and change of personnel in his life. Although it was difficult to extricate himself completely from the habits and associates he had formed at Moineau's, the succession of purges in the Letterist International which Debord had launched through the course of 1954 had made social life awkward in his favoured haunt. Mension, who had been one of the first to be excluded on the grounds that he was 'purely of decorative value', explained that more than anything else this created problems of protocol: 'If we were in a group of six including Guy I would not speak to him and I would pay a round for five and he would pay for himself. He of course reciprocated.'[16] Obviously, as the purges continued, this sort of behaviour became more frequent and harder to sustain.

It was Debord's idea to decamp to the bar Le Tonneau d'Or, also known as Chez Charlot, at 32 rue Montagne-Sainte-Geneviève (the *Sainte* part of the street address was obviously excluded from all International Letterist communications). This new address was not only at some remove from tourists and troublesome, possibly even violent, encounters at Moineau's or thereabouts, but also nearer to the 13th *arrondissement* and fired Debord's imagination for further exploratory manoeuvres in this area of decaying working-class communities and new immigrants. The move to Chez Charlot, no less importantly, signalled that it was now Guy and Michèle who were calling the shots in the Letterist International.

In the *Potlatch* 'special summer holiday issue' of 13 August 1954 there was news of an empty bus which had crashed into Chez Charlot, 'notoriously used by the Letterist International'. Four drinkers were injured but by 'a lucky chance there were in the bar none of the Letterists who were usually stationed there at that hour'. This might not have been an assassination attempt, but it was great fun to imagine that the Letterists could attract enough hatred to force them to move camp.

PART TWO

The Modern Art of Revolution

1957–61

I wanted to show the bourgeoisie that henceforth their pleasures would not be untouched, that their insolent triumphs would be disturbed, that their golden calf would rock violently on its pedestal until the final shock that would cast it down in filth and blood.

Émile Henry, 1893

This, I should say, is the essential myth of modern life: that the city has become a free field of signs and exhibits, a marketable mass of images, an area in which the old separations have broken down for good. The modern, to repeat the myth once more, is the marginal; it is ambiguity, it is a mixture of classes and classifications, it is anomie and improvisation, it is the reign of generalised illusion.

T. J. Clark, *The Painting of Modern Life*

Disperse, fragments of art critics, critics of fragments of art. The Situationist International is now organising the unitary artistic activity of the future. You have nothing more to say.

The Situationist International will leave no place for you. We will starve you out.

Action in Belgium against the international assembly of art critics, *Situationist International* 1958

CHAPTER 9

The Wreckers of Civilisation

1956–7

Throughout 1955 and 1956, Debord effectively took charge of *Potlatch*, replacing Conord as editor with Mohamed Dahou, nicknamed 'Midhou'. Midhou was not interested in politics or literature but worshipped Debord, accompanying him for a period as a semi-official bodyguard. Both Michèle Bernstein and Debord thought it an excellent joke, as well as a useful ploy, to install the most feckless and least literate member of their gang as its apparent intellectual leader. 'Read Marx and Dahou!' exhorted Michèle to *Potlatch*'s baffled but curious public.[1]

In the same period Debord published an important series of articles in the Belgian journal *Les Lèvres nues*. This was the journal that Marcel Mariën and Paul Nougé had been planning when Debord and Wolman had visited them in early 1952 as they were conspiring to break with Isou and set up the Letterist International. The journal was well-produced and stylish, firmly in the Surrealist tradition of creating provocative images out of random 'found' materials. Issue number 4 had on the front cover two naked men in an embrace, a single fig leaf touching both sets of genitals. On the back cover, there was a cluster of joky magazine advertisements – 'For a quicker death, drink Coca-Cola!', 'Martini, the apéritif of queers!'[2]

Literary communism

This was the favoured Letterist tactic of *détournement* at work. *Détournement* was not just a joke but also an artistic tool which had a direct political impact. Amongst the varied meanings of the term in French was 'rerouting' or 're-contextualisation', meaning that objects, signs, words placed out of their real context revealed new meanings. This was the point made on the front cover of issue number 8 of *Les Lèvres nues*, which showed a map of France that had been 'detourned' so that Algerian cities had replaced the French ones.[3] This image was a perfect visual *détournement*: the slogan 'Algérie Française' ('Algeria is French'), the rallying cry of all good Gaullist French patriots in the 1950s, had been neatly reversed into its opposite,

'France Algérienne' ('France is Algerian'). In one swift, neatly executed reversal, Debord had shown how the technique of *détournement* had the power to shock and stimulate.

The potential of this technique was further examined in an article, 'Détournement and how to use it', written by Debord and Wolman (announced as Aragon and André Breton on the cover). It was especially important, they explained, that *détournement* had its origins in poetry and poetic technique. More particularly, Lautréamont's famous *détournement* of the moral philosophy of Pascal and Vauvenargues in his 'Poésies' not only turned the ethics of these avatars of intellectual honesty upside down, but also, by exposing the impotence of these 'philosophical frauds', revealed the limits of the whole French tradition of rational thought.[4]

For a variety of reasons, the revolutionary meaning of two of Lautréamont's most famous maxims, 'Plagiarism is necessary. Progress demands it' and 'Poetry must be made by all', had been underestimated or misconstrued even by those, such as the Surrealists, who had professed admiration for the author of *The Cantos of Maldoror*. The insufficiency of Surrealism was again cruelly stressed by Debord in 1956, when he sent out fake invitations to a lecture at the Hôtel Lutétia, 'Surrealism's eternal youth', on the occasion of André Breton's sixtieth birthday. If applied to all areas of collective cultural experience, the cinema, the visual arts, everyday life, *détournement* could become not merely a form of parody, but a way of giving real subjective meaning to the world. This was the beginning, wrote Debord, of 'literary communism', a way of thinking and writing which aimed at total freedom.[5] Debord and Wolman described how the secret societies of ancient China would give hidden meanings to the most mundane activities by giving words new 'detourned' meanings. 'The need for a secret language,' they argued, again following Huizinga, 'is indistinguishable from the tendency to play.' And it was play, the creation of situations from which there was no turning back, which would turn the world on its head.

In his other pieces for *Les Lèvres nues* Debord extended this point by demonstrating how the practice of the *dérive* or 'drift' was a concrete example of how the life of the city could be disrupted or negated by a small group of people who chose to defy its controlling structures. By 'drifting' aimlessly around the modern city of Paris, which had evidently been designed as a capitalist work-camp, Debord and his comrades were able to imagine a new civilisation in which play had replaced work and poetry, made by all, was the true controlling principle of daily life. The paintings of de Chirico and Claude Lorrain, in which architecture had a magical dream quality, were cited by Debord as representations of what this city might look like. The practice of 'psychogeography' not only described present activity in the International Letterist camp, but also, more importantly, would come to be recognised as the first new art of the future.

The two accounts of 'continuous drift' in Paris which accompanied the analytical piece 'Theory of the Drift' present Debord and the other Letterists as undercover agents involved in clandestine operations. In the first of these, Debord and a comrade spend several days drinking continuously at a bar in the rue Xavier-Privas, getting involved with a mysterious West Indian who hinted at voodoo powers, before, on New Year's Eve and Debord's birthday, drinking at the bar in the middle of a stand-off between the bar-owner and a band of Algerian gangsters from Pigalle. Once dead drunk, without knowing how or why they got there, they stumble into a row being conducted in Yiddish in the rue Vieille-du-Temple. The account ends with a suitably film-noirish account of the Letterist pair being followed by sinister figures in black hats, whom they dodged by slipping down the passages and stairwells of Île de la Cité, before finding their way home to the safety of 'Le Continent Contrescarpe'.

In the second account, Wolman and Debord set off like nineteenth-century explorers to discover a new route from the Left Bank to the 'beautiful and tragic' *quartier* of Aubervilliers. On the way, they were delighted to encounter a charcuterie owned by a certain A. Breton in the 11th *arrondissement*, before abandoning operations and the search for the Northwest Passage out of Paris in the aptly named Taverne des Révoltés, a Spanish bar already well known to the Letterists. This was, Debord insisted, only a preliminary operation. 'One day we'll build cities for drifting,' he asserted.[6] In the meantime it was to create living poetry out of existing conditions.

Situationists

It was notable that in all of his pieces for *Les Lèvres nues*, Debord was using the term 'Situationist' with confidence, as if it were understood with ease by his comrades and readers. However, this was not the case. Michèle Bernstein first heard Debord use the term around 1955, and when she asked what it might mean and where Debord might have first heard it she was met with a confusing explanation which 'might have had something to do with Sartre, or which might have had nothing to do with Sartre' (Sartre had recently published a series of influential essays under the rubric *Situations*).

It was not Debord who had coined the term 'Situationist' but most probably the Amsterdam architect Constant who, in a slim volume published in 1953, *Pour une architecture de situation*, had argued that existing buildings provided identical interior spaces for wildly different internal uses: architecture should seek to create spaces for specific 'situations' and build quite different shapes for sleeping, eating, working, daydreaming. When I asked him about the history of the term 'Situationist', like everybody else I had spoken to about this subject, Constant claimed that the origins of the term were obscure.[7] Constant was already known to the International Letterists as one of the Dutch group of artists who infrequently visited Moineau's and other Left Bank haunts. More importantly, Constant had also been a leading light in the Nederlandse Experimentel Groep and CoBra. He was therefore well versed not only in architectural theory, but also in painting. Most crucially, he applied to architecture the same demands that he made of art. 'Life demands creation,' he wrote in 1949, 'and beauty is life!'[8]

Forbidden territory

This period was fertile for encounters and friendships. In late 1955 Guy and Michèle were introduced to a young Spanish writer, Juan Goytisolo, on his second trip to Paris. On the first trip he had arrived from Barcelona, then still under Franco's iron heel, with an idealised adoration for the city which had not diminished despite loneliness, hunger and spartan student accommodation on the rue St-Jacques. Goytisolo was a reader of Genet and Bataille and in Barcelona he had consistently sought out the low life around the Barri Xines, the dark and labyrinthine streets at the bottom end of the Ramblas which had held a magnetic attraction for the French writers.

On this second trip to Paris, Goytisolo was not quite so dazzled by the cafés and boulevards and would-be writers he met at The Old Navy and Le Mabillon. He now had his first novel behind him (published in Argentina), and had been disappointed not to win Spain's premier literary prize, the Premio Nadal. More confident and more demanding, he now craved what he called 'an open, untrammelled culture', a vision of the city which explosed its innards and did not flinch from the appalling, the uncanny and the fascinating.

He found this culture, at least in part, in the company of Guy Debord and Michèle Bernstein who were the ideal guides for his imagined city. Goytisolo remembered their friendship in *Coto Vedado* ('Forbidden Territory'), his autobiography written in 1985 in Marrakesh, when he had established a world-wide reputation as Spain's leading literary figure and, from his exile in Morocco, had been the sharpest critic of what Spain was and had become. Goytisolo's portrait of the 'two young, very young' intellectuals provides both an insight into their charismatic style and tastes and prefigures some of his own literary themes:

> Guy Debord and his companion at the time, Michèle Bernstein, lived in a hotel on the rue de Racine adjacent to the boulevard Saint-Michel and published a journal called Potlatch, organ of their tiny Situationist International. Bitter, implacable enemies of the whole literary establish-ment – enveloped in internecine quarrels and ferocious splits that at times

humorously mimicked Breton's terrorist language and the Stalinist trials –
they possessed an all-embracing curiosity and an acute demystifying vision of
things. Their admiration for the Palais Idéal du Facteur Cheval [the bizarre
edifice of stones, broken glass and seashells which a local postman, Ferdinand
Cheval, had built for no apparent reason in his hometown, Saumane, also
the scene of the Marquis de Sade's youthful crimes] and delight in visiting
places and settings as far away as possible from the tourist routes and
famous monuments and vistas matched my developing taste and provided
an intellectual justification that it lacked. In their healthy, consistent contempt
for everything bourgeois and well-off, Debord and his friend used to visit the
Arab cafés that were then located in the rue Mouffetard and the back-streets
of Maubert-Mutualité next to the Seine and one day they took me by bus
from the Gare de l'Est to the proletarian suburb of Aubervilliers and a dive
frequented by old Spanish Republican exiles, whose walls and owner I think
were filmed by Carné and Prévert in their beautiful film on the poor children
in the district. The subtle dovetailing of their tastes and mine, strengthened
with the passage of time, conferred a baptismal, initiating value on that first
tour with them around districts that I would soon assiduously trawl on my own:
that compact, aged, broken-down Paris, shot through by canals, viaducts,
railways, and rusty underground arches, which from Belleville to Barbès is
crowded in a perspective like an illustration of an 'Industrial Landscape' from
an old, dog-eared children's picture encyclopedia. The harmonious, elegant,
cosmopolitan metropolis that dazzled me on my first visit – the famous second
home of all artists, so lauded by the 'lost generation' and their Latin American
followers – would gradually lose its primitive attraction at the expense of a
bastard halogenous urban environment, polluted and fertilised by the clash
and interweaving of so many cultures and societies. When it was already dark
I crossed the rue d'Aubervilliers with Debord and his companion and walked
along the giant meccano-like boulevard de la Chapelle, far from thinking
that one day the mere idea of crossing the Seine to meet someone in the
intellectual districts of the Left Bank where I then lived would seem as remote
and unappealing, say, as going on safari in Kenya: my almost animal longing
for the Sentier and its continuous creative improvisation would later not allow
me any other excursions except to those luxuriant, teeming areas where I truly
found my feet, guided by my initiator's prophetic instincts.[9]

Goytisolo is now recognised, within Spain and in the wider world, as a
writer whose primary aim is to dissolve the boundaries and frontiers which
mark out 'otherness' in cultures and places. His long exile in Morocco
marks his moral revulsion and disgust at a territory which he described as
'filthy Stepmother, country of masters and slaves'. It is curious to reflect
that it was apparently Guy Debord and Michèle Bernstein and their culture
of 'continuous, creative improvisation' who were the initiators of this crucial

theme of exile and conscious, deliberate rootlessness in Goytisolo's work.

By the same token, Goytisolo was a fascinating companion for the Letterist intellectuals. Debord still nursed grievous memories of a summer holiday spent in Barcelona two years previously, where a combination of too much cheap alcohol and the dour Francoist cultural climate had laid him low for some weeks with an unnamed fever. (His doctor advised abstinence from all alcohol. Debord blamed Franco for this curse.) But apart from that Debord had already begun his long love affair with Spain and all things Spanish which, nurtured by the drink and talk in the Republican cafés of Aubervilliers, would become a major motif in his work. Goytisolo, witty, stylish, observant and with a powerful thirst for alcohol, did not disappoint him. Goytisolo was also at this period struggling somewhat with his homosexuality and presented a sexually ambiguous, probably bisexual, appearence. Guy and Michèle were only beginning to explore their full sexual potential, but this ambiguity was already appealing to them.

Indeed the relationship became so close at one stage that Goytisolo was invited, in the select company of Guy, Michèle, Guy's schoolfriend Jacques Fillon and his wife Véra, on a trip to the Désert de Retz, the strange, dream-like garden outside Paris at Croissy-sur-Seine, which was built in the eighteenth century as a monument to the aspirations of the human race and which was much loved by the Surrealists. But Goytisolo was also ambitious. He had already been cultivated by Elena La Souchère, the influential Spain correspondent for *France-Observateur*, and he was writing anonymous articles about Spain which were making an impact. His career would shortly bring him close to powerful figures on the literary Left such as Maurice Nadeau, Marguerite Duras, Dionys Mascolo and even Albert Camus. For the time being it was enough that Guy and Michèle noticed that the young Spaniard was more at home on the *terrasse* of Les Deux Magots and Café de Flore than in the Left Bank dives favoured by the Letterist International. For this, and for no other apparent reason, Guy and Michèle refused any more communication with him and referred to him in conversation punningly and contemptuously as 'Goyti-salaud' ('Goyti-the-bastard').

The ambiguous sexuality which had so obviously been an important part of Goytisolo's charm for Guy and Michèle was also an important factor in the appeal of Michèle Mochot, an elfin-faced young girl who fell immediately in love with the glamorous pair at a dinner party arranged by a mutual friend, Jean-Marie Bourgoignie. Michèle came from the same bourgeois background as Guy and Michèle ('My family always had servants in the house,' she said. 'It was one of the things which we all had in common').[10] Guy and Michèle Mochot slept together a few days after their first meeting. They would wander the streets of Paris together, drinking, talking, trying to get lost in the labyrinth. 'I was his secret garden. We never talked about politics. I helped him rest. We were like two children, incapable of thinking of ourselves as adults.'[11] The relationship was developed under the watchful eye of Michèle Bernstein who, far from showing any signs of jealousy, would pay for taxis, meals and drinks.

It was not without significance that both Debord and Bernstein were at this stage passionately enthusiastic about *Les Liaisons dangereuses*, the classic eighteenth-century novel of pitiless sexual intrigue by Pierre Choderlos de Laclos. In this novel, the cynical libertine Valmont delights in a remorseless series of seductions which drive his victims to death or a convent. He recounts his adventures in letters to the even more sinister Madame de Merteuil, his accomplice and confidante, who drives him to greater and greater crimes. The characters in Michèle's Bernstein's first novel, *Tous les chevaux du roi*, were obviously modelled on Valmont and Madame de Merteuil. Michèle Mochot was enormously attracted by Guy's aristocratic nonchalance and the way in which he played the libertine dandy. 'Guy was courageous in his dislikes because he was indifferent to most people and things. He would say things like "gaiety is vulgar".' Guy and Michèle Bernstein had decided that, in sexual relations as in society, total freedom was an absolute value. Total freedom involved the deliberate creation of scenarios or situations which crossed literal or metaphorical boundaries. According to Michèle Bernstein, their sexual life was 'another game'. With Michèle Mochot, the game was to be of long duration: she remained in close, intimate contact with Guy Debord until 1984.

Politics was as important in friendship as sex. It was in 1954 that Debord first came into contact with the Danish painter Asger Jörgensen. Jörgensen was already into his forties and an established figure on the European avant-garde scene, one of the most energetic members of CoBra, and a fine and widely exhibited painter whose work betrayed the twin influences of Paul Klee and Joan Miró. Jörgensen, who had by now renamed himself Jorn, was also a Marxist and in his own journal *Helhesten* ('the horse of hell'), which he founded in 1941, had published articles on primitive art, children's art, jazz and popular psychology. Jorn devoured the copies of *Potlatch* which Enrico Baj loaned him, sought out Debord and declared himself greatly impressed by the younger man. 'Since the end of the war,' wrote Jorn, almost immediately after meeting Debord, 'I have met no one else but Guy Debord who, unaware of the other problems which could attract his attention, concentrates himself exclusively, with a maniacal passion and a capacity which comes from that, on the task of correcting the rules of the human game according to the new given conditions of our time.'[12]

Most significantly for Debord, Jorn was also the founder and leading figure of the International Movement for an Imaginist Bauhaus (IMIB), a group which sought a middle way between 'the rational art' of the Bauhaus group in Germany and the 'idealism' of French Surrealist theory.

In September 1955, the IMIB had set up what they called 'an experimental laboratory' in the Italian semi-rural idylls of Albisola and Alba. Here, Giuseppe Pinot-Gallizio and his son Piergiorgio began researching the possibilities of 'industrial painting', painting which fought back against the mediocrity of modern life by turning the weapons of commodity culture back against modern industrial society. Other artists included Enrico Baj and Sergio Dangelo (former members of CoBra who had established the Milan-based Movimento Arte Nucleare), the architect Ettore Sottsass and future Situationists Piero Simondo (who had studied in Turin under Felice Casorati), his wife Elena Verrone and Walter Olmo.[13]

Debord, who professed a dislike of paintings and painters, was impressed by Jorn's style and his fierce polemical manner (an exception was made for those like Ralph Rumney or Yves Klein who judged painting to be a dead form). He even accorded a grudging respect to Jorn's paintings and those of other CoBra artists which seemed to Debord to represent a deliberately violent and brutal form of political desire. Jorn's 1954 text *Image et Forme* was partially reprinted in *Potlatch* 15, whilst Jorn and Debord, excited by each other's daring and intransigence, began planning collaborative projects almost straight away. In June 1956 the Parisian Letterists participated in a collective action with representatives of *Les Lèvres nues*, the Movement for Nuclear Art (which included Jorn and Enrico Baj in their number) and a group of independent artists and critics (including Herbert Read) in the form of a tract against an exhibition in Brussels on industrial art. Some two months later, under Jorn's direction, in the small town of Alba there took place the rather grandiosely named World Congress of Artists which would announce the first steps towards the foundation of the Situationist International.

Now the SI!

The Situationist International was founded in 1957 on 27 July in a bar in the tiny hamlet of Cosio d'Arroscia in the province of Imperia, a remote spot still high enough in the Ligurian Alps to make it a full day's journey from the nearest town.

Cosio was the birthplace of Piero Simondo, who kept a house on the edge of the village and whose idea it was to meet there for a week. The winding covered streets, which smell of wood smoke even in high summer, the open squares which surprise and bedazzle the visitor, the shadow of the mountains, made it a perfect psychogeographical site; it remains an inaccessible and beautiful spot, untouched by tourism or urbanisation.

The meeting brought together eight representatives of three previously unknown and deliberately mysterious groups. The largest of these was the IMIB, led by Jorn. The Letterist International was represented by

Guy Debord and Michèle Bernstein, and the London Psychogeographical Committee by its only known member, Ralph Rumney. Rumney took photographs of the meeting at Cosio which portray the delegates in various symbolic sites around the village; the most famous of these photos shows the group, with Debord and Michèle at the centre, staring down into the camera from the edge of a height, in front of a crumbling house.

The groundwork for the meeting had been laid in September, when Gil Wolman had visited Alba, representing the Letterist International at 'The First Conference of Free Artists', convened by Jorn and Pinot-Gallizio in the name of the IMIB. The Parisians and the Italian-based group established a common platform which made the pursuit of 'the construction of situations', otherwise known as 'unitary urbanism', their primary preoccupation as artists, a move which particularly pleased Constant who had by now abandoned painting for architectural theory. A further meeting in December strengthened the links established at Alba and an exhibition of 'pre-Situationist art' was organised at the Taptoe Gallery in Brussels by the indefatigable Jorn.

Wolman, in the meantime, had been permanently excluded from the Letterist International, despite his hard work, on the grounds that he had been living 'a ridiculous lifestyle, cruelly underlined by ideas which became every day more stupid and narrowminded'. His exclusion was reported in *Potlatch* in the form of an obituary, 'Wolman had an important role in the organisation of the Letterist Left-wing in 1952, then in the foundation of the LI. Author of "megapneumic" poems, a theory of "cinematochronicity" and a film, he was Letterist delegate at the congress of Alba in September 1956. He was twenty-seven years old.' Wolman was not the first to be thrown out, but he was the most important member of the Letterist International to be abandoned as the group asserted itself as the new force, the Situationist International.

Although there was serious work to be done at Cosio the atmosphere was also festive. The villagers ensured an endless flow of rough local wine which within two days of constant drinking had turned the tongues of the Parisian delegation purple. Ralph Rumney was accompanied by his girlfriend Pegeen Guggenheim who, having known such luminaries as Max Ernst and Giacometti, could not conceal her disappointment at discovering that the much-vaunted Situationist International was no more than a group of obscure bohemians. Her boredom is clearly visible in a photo of her and Debord at a café table taken by Ralph. Debord was taken by her haughtiness.

Ralph tried his hand at cooking a meal for the villagers and his Situationist comrades, drunkenly strangling an emaciated chicken before plunging it, half-plucked, into a boiling pot. 'Ralph Rumney a fait un coq étique' ('Ralph Rumney has cooked a skinny chicken') quickly became the chorus of an invented song strummed by Piero Simondo on a battered guitar. 'It was great fun, a hilarious party,' said Michèle more than forty years later.[14]

According to Piero Simondo, Debord was already behaving like a leader, although Jorn was still the most senior and influential member of the group. 'Debord drank a great deal,' recalled Simondo, forty years later and now Professor of Audiovisual Art at the University of Turin, 'but it was also Debord who reminded us that what we were trying to achieve was political as well as aesthetic. In fact, that our aesthetic philosophy came out of our political positions.' It was Debord's idea, says Simondo, to name the new organisation the Situationist International, pre-empting Jorn's suggestion that the Letterist International, as the smaller group, should be subsumed into the Imaginist Bauhaus.[15]

Having won his first real contest in power-politics, Debord went on to insist to the delegates at Cosio that what had really brought these disparate groups together was the common belief that contemporary avant-garde movements had all reneged on the original promise of revolution. The Situationist project aimed at reinstating revolution, he said, not as a metaphor but as a real experience, at the heart of the avant-garde programme. 'There has been a notable progression from Futurism through Dadaism and Surrealism to the movements formed after 1945,' Debord told the delegates in Cosio, warning of the difficulties ahead and identifying the failure of previous avant-gardes as a failure of nerve. 'At each of these stages one discovers the same totalistic will for change; and the same crumbling away when the inability to change the world profoundly enough seems to lead to a defensive withdrawal.'[16] Situationist strategy, Debord argued, would be in contrast an endless, ever-changing series of offensive actions, 'situations without a future', which would confuse and wrongfoot the enemy.

'We will wreck this world,' the Situationists then declared in an early manifesto which was pitiless and absolute. 'It is simply a question of courage.'

CHAPTER 10

The Art of the Future

1957–8

The keynote text which Debord had delivered at Cosio was entitled 'Report on the construction of situations and on the conditions of the organisation and action of the Situationist International.' This report ran to some twenty pages and was the longest and most complete text which Debord would write until he started work on *The Society of the Spectacle* in the mid-1960s. The composition of the report had taken Debord almost a year, with sections being read and discussed with Wolman and Bernstein. When Debord finally read the text aloud in Cosio, it was clear, according to Ralph Rumney, that Debord's thinking was in many ways theoretically complete.[1]

The central question which Debord asked in the report was how could a real transformation in the nature and quality of human life be brought about given that present social conditions – the rise of the consumer society, the development of a homogenised global culture – actively worked against creative expression and the possibility of individual freedom. Debord addressed this question by first of all considering the failure of previous avant-garde movements. The Italian Futurist movement, led by the poet and novelist Filippo Tommaso Marinetti, was admired by Debord for its ambition to discard and overcome all outmoded forms of cultural activity (the Futurists advocated, amongst other things, the destruction of museums and the rejection of rules of language in poetry). However, this apparently revolutionary movement was profoundly reactionary, cutting artists away from history in favour of a falsely aristocratic sophistication. In this way, Futurism pandered to bourgeois optimism about technical progress and it was inevitable, as history had demonstrated, that the cult of the 'machine aesthetic', Filippo Marinetti's celebrated formula for poetry, would dissolve into bourgeois nationalism and finally Mussolini's brand of Fascism (Marinetti did indeed end his days as a propagandist for 'il Duce').

Dadaism, or at least the variant of it which had emerged from the notorious Cabaret Voltaire, founded in Zurich in 1916 by a motley collection of dissident poets, artists and mystic which included Tristan Tzara, Marcel Janco, Emmy Hennings, Richard Huelsenbeck, Hugo Ball and Hans Arp, had proved more robust. This was essential, concluded Debord, because the Dadaist movement had been absolutely negative: disgusted by the butchery of the machine civilisation which had created the First World War, the Dadaists declared themselves implacably opposed to their time and situation. This negative force, said Debord, had left its imprint on all future avant-gardes, the most important of which was Surrealism. Debord was sceptical about the prestige which the Surrealists accorded to the unconscious, and it was a mistake, he concluded, to see the unconscious as a revolutionary principle in history. The melting away of the Romanian Surrealist group in the 1930s (whose history Debord had learned from Isidore Isou) when faced with the political realities of the period was only one example of this error. It had been the historic fault of the Parisian Surrealist group, the centre of the movement, to have perpetuated this mistake. But, like the Dadaists before them, the Surrealists had confronted modern society with the irrational, the negative, and even if they had not won a victory in this engagement, they had nonetheless exposed the hypocrisies and lies upon which modern life was based.

It was the task of the Situationist International, Debord urged, to carry on with this engagement and, if necessary, to extend this conflict to all forms of human activity. This meant, in the first instance, the development of 'a new science of situations' which would emerge from endless, experimental behaviour. Debord had now made the term 'situation' his own. He would later define it as a precise moment in life, 'concretely and deliberately constructed'. This moment of passionate, realised intensity was revolutionary because it had the potential to disrupt and transform the mediocre nature of everyday life; the practices of 'dérive', 'psychogeography' and 'détournement' were proof of this. Most importantly, the 'constructed situation', which was a moment of pure subjectivity, also had the potential to subvert the hypnotising power of the 'spectacle', another term which Debord was now using confidently as a metaphor for the way in which the forces of state, capital and media denied the individual control or participation in his or her daily life. Hitherto, this term had been used by Debord and the Situationists mainly to describe the false representation of life which took the form of the urban spectacle of consumerism and capital. It was now taking on a fuller political force as a way of describing how modern life reduced individuals to a state of passivity in which they lost all sense of full human potential and became spectators of their own lives.

Although the language of 'The report on the construction of situations . . .' was clearly modelled on French classical prose of the seventeenth century, it was also strikingly faithful to the conceptual language of both Marx and Hegel. Debord admitted the fact that he had at this stage read very little Marx. One reason for this was that there was at this stage no reliable version of his complete works in French; Debord also confessed himself temperamentally unsuited to either studying indigestible translations or, worst fate of all, learning German. But he had understood enough in his readings of pre-war Communists allied to Surrealism, such as Boris Souvarine and Jean Bernier, to be able to use Marxist concepts such as 'super-structure' and 'historical materialism' with fluency. Despite his well-advertised contempt for the French Communist Party, Debord had also been impressed by PCF-sponsored translations of Marx's pamphlets, including most notably Marx's text on the Paris Commune, *Civil War in France*, in which Marx had defended the martyrs of the Paris Commune as the most conspicuous heroes of the revolutionary classes.

Debord's reading of Hegel was in some ways closer to the original source than his understanding of Marx. The reason for this was that during the period of Debord's earliest intellectual development, Hegelian studies were in the ascendant in France. Like many of his generation Debord had first encountered Hegel via the work of Jean Hyppolite, then a professor at the Collège de France, who would influence a future generation of thinkers, including Michel Foucault and Jacques Derrida (the work of both men is largely conceived either as an attack on or disengagement from Hyppolite's version of Hegel). Hyppolite's magisterial study of *The Phenomenology of Mind* appeared in 1947 and appealed to Debord by insisting that Hegel was the avatar of a tradition of philosophical thought which 'answers a double demand: that for rigour in analysis, and that for direct contact with lived experience.' Through his reading of Bataille and the Surrealists, Debord had also come across another version of Hegelian philosophy, the so-called 'terrorist Hegel' whose thought had been propounded by the Russian émigré philosopher Alexandre Kojève at the École de hautes études in the 1930s. His lectures had electrified a generation which was really coming to Hegel in French for the first time. (Kojève's lectures were attended by, amongst others, André Breton, Georges Bataille, Pierre Klossowski and Jean-Paul Sartre. They were collected and edited by Raymond Queneau in 1947 and are considered a crucial influence on post-war existentialism.) Kojève taught that Hegel was essentially a political thinker and that his true importance was as a theorist of revolution. Kojève isolated negation as the central lesson of Hegel's philosophy: negativity, he argued, was not only essential to the triadic movement of the Hegelian dialectic from thesis to antithesis to synthesis, but was also an active contradiction, 'negativity without use', an absolute form of revolt. As Debord was formulating the concept of 'spectacle', it was of central importance that this term was not only a metaphor for modern life, but also, in a lesson learned from Kojève, that the formulation of a concept in entirely negative terms was also a dialectical weapon. This indeed is the conclusion of 'The report on the construction of situations . . .' which proposes a strategy of total negation, which begins with the negation of art ('there will be no painters but at most Situationists who engage in painting amongst other activities') and continues through to the negation of everyday experience in favour of passion and poetry: 'What changes our way of seeing the streets is more important than what changes our way of seeing painting.'[2]

First excommunications

This was even more clearly defined in an internal document, 'Remarks on the concept of experimental art', circulated in the autumn of 1957 and conceived partly as an attack on Walter Olmo and Piero Simondo, the artists whose support and comradeship had been so vital at Cosio. Debord accused Olmo of 'naive simplification' in his conception of art as separate from the everyday; Simondo, although perhaps a genius, for his part was accused of 'lack of methodological understanding'. In their idealism, the Italians were 'enemies of reality' and 'anti-experimental'; the art of the future would be, in contrast, an art of negation.

This early attack on those who, only four months earlier, had celebrated the foundation of the Situationist International at Cosio was unsurprising to those who had known Debord in Paris and had lived through the splits and schisms with Isou, Mension and the rest of the Letterist International. To the Italians, whose friendship with Debord was new and whose generosity and hospitality was as authentic as they were innocent, it came as a shock. Walter Olmo, whose subsequent career as an artist took him towards a form of abstract expessionism, was genuinely appalled; he now claims to remember nothing of Cosio and can only speak of Debord with contempt as a vicious manipulator. Piero Simondo and Elena Verrone (soon to become Piero's wife) were less shocked by Debord's attack than by the way he had accepted their hospitality (it was after all at their suggestion and at their house that the Cosio conference had taken place) and lured the first members of the Situationist International into believing that they were an unbreakable and dedicated group: Simondo saw this less as a betrayal than as a preliminary exercise in manipulation, as if Debord were rehearsing the purges and power shifts which would later move the group endlessly forward towards an ever more hard and pure position. To their disgust and disappointment Verrone, Olmo and Simondo were officially ejected from the Situationist International in January 1958.

It was one of the extraordinary characteristics of someone who talked so much about passion and lived experience that Debord refused to take any account of the human cost of his actions, or if he did he did not reveal this to anyone. Worse still, Debord even seemed to delight in his power, often giving frivolous or meaningless reasons for excommunicating people (to be thrown out of the SI was also to be disallowed from communicating with any present member). Even Michèle Bernstein, who knew him better than anyone else in this period, was at a loss to explain him to the others. 'The worst of all was Gil Wolman,' she said, 'who truly loved Debord and supported him through everything in the first years.'

The expulsion of Gil Wolman was not only a baffling and emotional event for Gil himself, but signalled to other members of the group that from now on in Debord's eyes no one was indispensable. On the final afternoon at Cosio Ralph Rumney had made a speech declaring that 'if this project of overturning the world is going to work we have to be absolutely fanatical and dedicated to our purpose.' When later, over drinks and general congratulations, Rumney had questioned Wolman's absence from the activities at Cosio, remarking that Wolman had always been the most faithful and hardworking member of the Letterist International, both Debord and Bernstein made a point of refusing to justify their actions. Bernstein later explained this by saying that she herself had not really known why Guy had taken against Wolman but thought she should follow Guy even if it was all still a mystery to her ('Recently Wolman has been behaving like he did in 1954 and 1955,' Debord wrote cryptically to Midhou in August 1957).[3]

According to Ralph Rumney (about whom Guy was already expressing doubts to Elena and Piero) the real reason for Wolman's exclusion was that he had recently married Violette, who had already given birth to their first child. 'Gil was delighted that his wife had had a baby and he had spent time looking after it and talking fatherhood when he should have been dedicating himself to the work of the avant-garde. Guy, and Michèle for that matter, had an absolute horror of domesticity and babies in particular. They were trying to experiment with new ways of living, which for Guy meant total sexual freedom. Wolman's happy family life could not be tolerated.'[4] Within twelve months of the Cosio conference, Rumney would find himself excluded in similarly cruel and mysterious circumstances, having married in Venice Pegeen Guggenheim, the troubled alcoholic daughter of the heiress and art collector Peggy Guggenheim, and, worst of all, having committed the crime of having a private family life. The *Daily Express* had been more enthusiastic than Guy Debord about Rumney's marriage and had published a lengthy celebratory piece in its society column under the rubric 'Vicar's son marries millionairess!'; back in Halifax, Rumney *père* had been less delighted by the news.

The urgency which characterised the first wave of excommunications had also been, at least in part, determined by the fact that for a brief moment it looked as if the very existence of the leadership of the Situationist International had been threatened by a stronger, external force. Despite Debord's best attempts to preserve his nominal position as a student of law, after seven years, the University had had enough of his phantom presence and revoked his status. He was now looking at a call-up which might even be, worst fate of all, to Algeria. The emergency was avoided on the grounds of physical (genuine asthma and myopia) and mental (an invented 'neurotic anguish') disability. Even better, Debord gained a reputation as an expert draft-dodger to whom comrades could turn if and when the call-up came.

A leap into the void

Not only had 1957 been a year characterised by the development of theories, rows and expulsions. It was also the beginning of a flirtation with the creation of art which went hand in hand with theorising its destruction. Amongst the few artists to whom Debord accorded respect during this period was Yves Klein, a native of Nice who was then establishing an international reputation as one of the most interesting and daring exponents of the post-war avant-garde. Most notable was Klein's belief that art was something that had to be overcome in the name of the realisation of human potential. This involved awakening the spectator's response to time and space. Klein became mostly known for his invention of a colour of his own, International Klein Blue (IKB), which was, according to Klein, 'the colour of revolution'. He began to paint in monochrome, assigning colours specific meanings (gold, for example, was the colour of alchemical change). Above all, like the International Letterists, Klein believed that artistic activity could overcome all physical limitations. Klein's most impressive works, such as 'A leap into the void', were therefore parallel to the Situationists' concerns with making lived experience, even negative experience, more important than art. It was not without significance that Klein was an expert at judo which for him represented a form of activity that was higher than art. Klein's premature death from a heart attack in 1962 may well have been the result of his strenous efforts to live out these principles.

Klein had known about Debord and Bernstein since 1952 when he had been in the audience for *Howling in Favour of Sade* and been impressed by the film's negative magnetism. Since then he had followed the activities of the International Letterists and the origins of the Situationist International (in 1956 he had even collaborated with Jorn, Rumney and Wallace Ting). In April 1957, Klein was at the peak of his powers. He had two exhibitions which would shortly run concurrently in Paris, as well as work on display in Düsseldorf, Milan and London. It was at this time that he invited Guy Debord and Michèle Bernstein to his studio on the rue Campagne-Première for a drink and to ask if Debord would write the introduction to the catalogue for his forthcoming exhibitions. Although admirers of his work, both Debord and Bernstein were suspicious and scornful of Klein's esoteric beliefs (he had been interested in Rosicrucianism since 1947 and had, more recently, been elected into one of the movement's most elitist sects). Debord demurred at Klein's request. Klein, in the spirit of the 'potlatch', asked Debord to take any of the paintings on view in the room as a mark of good faith. Rather than take any of the large (and expensive) paintings available and with his usual nonchalance in the face of any transaction which involved money, Debord chose a miniature piece, explaining to the baffled Klein that it fitted best of all into his duffel-coat pocket.

However, art was important to Debord during this early period of the Situationist International. A short trip to Denmark in the company of Asger Jorn in the early part of the year had given Debord the impetus to begin a series of collaborations with the Danish painter which brought together several important strands of Debord's thought on poetry, play and the city. The first of these, *Fin de Copenhague* ('End of Copenhagen'), was printed in a limited edition of 200 in May 1957 in Copenhagen. The work consisted of a volume of thirty-three pages: like other attempts at experimental writings composed by Debord and Jorn at this point, these 'may be read in any direction, and [in which] the reciprocal relationships between phrases are invariably incomplete'.

Each page, upon which Jorn had splashed lurid yellows, greens and reds in monotype, was made up of images and phrases from newspapers and magazines. These images were mostly drawn from articles or advertisements that celebrated leisure and the consumer society. 'What do *you* want?' asked an advertising blurb 'hijacked' by Jorn and Debord, and set against a red and blue background in the then fashionable style of a Jackson Pollock 'action' painting: 'Better and cheaper food? Lots of new clothes? A dream home with all the latest comforts and labour-saving devices? A new car . . . a motor launch . . . a light aircraft of your own? Whatever you want, it's coming your way, plus greater leisure for enjoying it all. With electronics, automation and nuclear energy we are entering the new Industrial Revolution which will supply your every need, easily . . . quickly . . . cheaply . . . abundantly.' Another text, set against an Islamic green, proclaimed: 'There's no whiteness' and 'Long live Free Algeria!' Other texts sneeringly celebrated the joys of alcohol: 'When asked if he would like a Dubonnet before dinner, my uncle replies that he would like a Dubonnet before anything.' There were several defaced maps of Denmark and Copenhagen, and in particular a map of the then rundown quarter of Christianshavn. On the final page readers were exhorted to 'Tell us in not more than 250 words why your girl is the sweetest girl in town.' The misspelt address for Debord and Jorn (both of them had a very approximate command of English) was the 'Psychogeografical comitee of London (especially Debord and Jorn) c/o Institute of Contemporary Arts 17–18, Dover Street London W1.'[5]

Debord claimed that *Fin de Copenhague* had been created in a bad-tempered and drunken afternoon after a raid which he and Jorn had made on a Copenhagen news-stand. They had stolen newspapers and magazines, cut them up and reassembled them in order to announce the forthcoming

death of the city, 'The End of Copenhagen'. They did this by showing
how advertising, the degrading language of the 'spectacle which purported
to reflect the wishes and dreams of the city's inhabitants', was a debased
currency and a lie. Only through the practice of *détournement*, which put
the language of commerce to a more revolutionary use, could poetry and
real desire be restored to their proper place at the centre of human activity. It
was the practice of *détournement* which constituted the transformative power
of poetry : 'And there you are, your life is transformed!' explained Debord,
adding a coda to the hijacked advertising text, 'WORDS TAKE ON A NEW
SENSE!'

The *Architectural Review*, in a remarkably prescient contemporary review
of *Fin de Copenhague*, praised Jorn and Debord for pronouncing 'the end of
Copenhagen' and for revealing the city, any modern city in the capitalist
world, as 'the seat of ancestral boredom'. The reviewer, obviously an eager
early fan of Situationist iconoclasm, anticipated a future assault by Asger
Jorn (clearly seen as the leading figure in the collaboration, much to
Debord's chagrin) upon the substance as well as the style of modern life.
Fin de Copenhague was, however, far from being the first use in art of the
language of advertising. The appropriation and deliberate misuse of such
language was a tradition which stretched back before the Futurists and
the Dadaists to Baudelaire, Jules Janin and even Balzac. In recent times,
however, the art world had seized upon the ubiquity and the hollowness
of such language and images to approach problems of representation in an
ironic way. A notable example of this tendency had been Richard Hamilton's
famous collage for the Independent Group in London, 'Just What Is It That
Makes Today's Homes So Different, So Appealing . . . ?', which depicted
a variety of images taken from advertising, from comics and the cinema in
ironic counterpoint. In this work, as in the later Pop Art of Andy Warhol
or Robert Rauschenberg, Hamilton's artistic use of iconic language was
as much a celebration as a critique. For Debord and Jorn, in contrast,
the consumer spectacle was something which had to be entirely negated.
Fin de Copenhague was intended as an attack on the spectacle, not just a
commentary or critical observation.

The second important piece which Debord undertook with Jorn was a
screenprint published in May 1957 and entitled *The Naked City: illustration
de l'hypothèse des plaques tournantes en psychogéographie*.[6] This piece focused
more precisely on the theme of the city, a central theme for the nascent
Situationists as it was for the Letterist International, and addressed problems
and theories of architecture and urbanism.

The title of this piece had been 'kidnapped' from a famous American
documentary of 1948 which portrayed hard-boiled cops at work in New
York City. This film is particularly distinguished for the camerawork in
its opening shots which swoop across the cityscape of New York at night,

focusing on incidental details before returning to the broad cinematic sweep of panoramic vision. In their own version of *The Naked City*, Debord and Jorn sketched a fragmented picture of Paris which borrows the technique of the film and presents a bird's-eye view of the city. Debord and Jorn had begun by reading maps of Paris made by those who had tried to order and control the capital, including a 'scientific' survey from 1652, a plan from 1739 and the *Plan de Paris* of 1956: on Jorn's instructions, all were cut up and reassembled according to the dictates of 'objective chance' to make a disordered work which, Jorn insisted, would tell Debord 'what the city felt like'. Unlike the camera in the original *Naked City*, which zooms in to focus on parts of the city pullulating with life, the two Situationists use the aerial perspective achieved through the 'cut-up' technique to commemorate a Paris which is about to disappear for good. *The Naked City* is a map which has been *détourné* and it is intended to function as the negative reflection of de Gaulle's programme, the so-called 'reconquest of Paris', which decanted the working classes from Saint-Lazare, Gare du Nord, and place de la République to the new suburbs, the 'neo-Corbusian barracks' of Sarcelles. It is a map of a city which is being emptied of human activity and which is in the process of becoming a dead site, a city without a *telos*.

Across this map, which runs roughly from the Gare de Lyon, on the right, to a line marked by the Palais Royal and the Jardins du Luxembourg on the left, there is a movement, moreover, which designates sites that are absent – rue Sauvage, Halle aux Vins, rue Xavier-Privas. The Situationists protested at the destruction of these places which they identified as having magical or poetic significance and which were therefore essential to the metaphorical meaning of the city. Many of these sites would disappear shortly after the map was drawn.

Debord and Jorn's psychogeographical map was also an attempt to capture the movement of the city in time without freezing it into spectacle. It was therefore necessarily fluid, continuous and opposed to the static language and principles of conventional map-making. It was a map of real, lived experience rather than 'spectacular' activity.

CHAPTER 11

A Civil War in France

1958

Immmediately after his return to Paris from Cosio, despite his uncertainties about his Italian colleagues, Debord's priority was to establish the newly formed Situationist International as a firmer presence on the French intellectual scene. His first task was to establish in the eyes of his comrades that *Potlatch* had now outlived its usefulness. The difficulty here was that the journal still enjoyed a notoriety which far exceeded its resources and readership. Much to Debord's disgust, the journal had been collected and placed amidst other radical publications on the shelves of La Joie de Lire, a radical Leftist bookshop on the rue Saint-Sévérin, owned and run by Francis Maspéro and Jeanne Bercier (the unfortunate Maspéro, a well-meaning intellectual with Trotskyist leanings who founded, amongst other activities, the journal *Partisans*, was later a target for Situationist abuse when the term *maspérisation* became a favourite term in the Situationist lexicon to denote falsification or lies). Aware of the impact that *Potlatch* was still making, Debord was reluctant to finish with the journal altogether and so planned to diminish its importance by relegating it to the status of an internal document circulated within the closed ranks of the Situationist International.

The Letterist International had over the past five years behaved in a sufficiently obnoxious manner to have their members not only known to the leading lights of the Left Bank, but also to be banned from several bars and known to the police. The gendarmerie made no clear distinction between those purely 'decorative' members of the LI, such as Éliane and Jean-Michel, whose persistent drunkenness, street-fighting and petty larceny was quite separate from the 'theoretical activities' of Debord, Bernstein *et al*. This again was a notoriety which had been hard fought for and was to be cherished, and it was initially with reluctance that the LI itself was relegated to a 'pre-Situationist' footnote in the history of the revolution. This was a necessary prelude, 'one step back' as Debord put it, to the forthcoming struggle. In a final contribution to *Potlatch*, Debord returned to Sade to announce a call to arms in the name of the Situationist cause, detourning the Divine Marquis's famously incendiary polemic hurled at his French revolutionary admirers, 'Another effort if you want to be revolutionaries!' as 'Another effort if you want to be Situationists!' The message of the piece was clear: from now on there was to be 'no useless indulgence'.[1]

To signal that he himself had broken irrevocably with his past, in the spring of 1958 Debord gave away to his friends copies of a book entitled *Mémoires*, which he had conceived whilst staying with his family at the luxurious villa San Lorenzo in Cannes and which he had composed in another collaboration with Asger Jorn. The text purported to give an account of Debord's inner life from June 1952 to September 1953 during the break with Isou and the foundation of the Letterist International. Like *Fin de Copenhague*, the text consisted of 'detourned' quotations chosen by Debord and collages and splashes of ink and paint organised by Jorn. The effect was, however, both more intimate and enigmatic than *Fin de Copenhague*. Most of the quotations from authors such as Bossuet, Céline and Saint-Just had a personal resonance for Debord. The text echoed the 1954 text *La valeur éducative* which, although finally published in *Potlatch*, had been intended as a radio programme. There were even moments of sexual tenderness in the central two pages where Debord evokes his first great love Éliane ('show me your papers . . . marijuana . . . naked on the bed . . . I saw her at night and admired her'). The central purpose of the book was to express the negative tensions which would drive Debord towards the foundation of the Situationist International. He declared that his intention was to speak 'the beautiful language of the century'.[2] Accordingly, on Jorn's advice, Debord called the book an 'anti-livre' and had it bound in sandpaper so that it destroyed any other book it might be placed next to on the bookshelf.

The Invisible Insurrection of a Million Minds

Debord also cited the London showing of his 1952 film *Howling in Favour of Sade* as an example of what he meant by successful Situationist action. The film had been taken to the ICA in June 1957 by Debord himself in the company of the Scots writer Alexander Trocchi. Debord had first met Trocchi, a charismatic and brilliant graduate from Glasgow University, in 1954. Trocchi was writing pornographic hack novels for Maurice Girodias' Olympia Press (Trocchi was also not averse to acting out the more baroque scenes) and was also the editor of the small but influential review *Merlin* (its first issues included A. J. Ayer, Samuel Beckett and Paul Bowles amongst its contributors). Amongst those who sold *Merlin* on the streets of the Left Bank were the young Colin Wilson and the Scottish poet Kenneth White.[3]

Having fallen under the spell of the Letterist International shortly after meeting Debord in 1954, on Debord's strict instructions Trocchi broke all contact with his former friends, abolished *Merlin* and set about promoting the revolutionary avant-garde. By the end of 1957 he was addicted to heroin (he had been using the drug seriously since leaving Glasgow in the early 1950s before deciding 'to make a career of it') and wandering the Californian coast. Debord admired Trocchi as an adventurer and thinker and in particular his text *Invisible Insurrection of a Million Minds* which sets out a programme for revolution by stealth and provocation. He wrote warm letters from Paris congratulating Trocchi on taking the revolution as far away as Mexico, although declining enigmatically an invitation to visit the United States (Debord never did visit America nor showed any interest in doing so).[4]

Trocchi was a friend of the Situationists and a fellow traveller rather than a fully-fledged adept of Situationist practice. The trip to London was no more than an experiment but it was an experiment which had provoked interesting results. The film had predictably been met with a confused and angry reaction from a British audience whose notion of the French avant-garde was the rather more comfortable world of the so-called 'new novelists' Alain Robbe-Grillet and Claude Simon (both of whom were then riding high on a tide of literary fashionability and were suitably excoriated by Debord as weak-minded and timid representatives of what he termed 'cultural decomposition'). However, although many members of the audience were furious at having been cheated, no one dared ask the mysterious 'Situationists' for their money back. One man threatened to resign from the ICA and another complained that he and his wife had come all the way from Wimbledon and had paid for a babysitter. The commotion reached the queue for the second showing of the film who were made all the more eager to see it by the protests of those leaving. Nobody really believed that a film could be a complete blank, and the air was charged with further excitement and anticipation.

This was, in Debord's terms, a most perfect demonstration of the innate passivity of all audiences. It confirmed his view that the first aim of the Situationist should not be to make works of art but to produce works and writings which actively accelerated the process of 'cultural decomposition'. In this way the Situationists were laying the ground for the establishment of the 'new word', the new civilisation which had been envisaged at Cosio.

A further giant step towards this aim was to be achieved firstly by the foundation and publication of a Situationist journal which would provide a site for theoretical experiment as well as a forum for what the former members of the Letterist International were now confidently calling in the pages of *Potlatch* 'Situationist critical theory'. Debord had been impressed not only by the content of *Les Lèvres nues*, but also by the high quality of its production values, which allowed its contributors to play more freely with images, ideas and graphics. Debord's collaborations with Jorn had only deepened Debord's vision of the impact which his ideas would have when allied with a sufficiently intelligent and disciplined approach to colour and image. There was a long tradition in French avant-garde circles of marrying image to word for a subversive purpose. Debord was particularly enthusiastic not only about Breton's *La Révolution surréaliste* and *Minotaure*, which had both been financed by wealthy art collectors, but also Bataille's *Documents* and *Acéphale*, both of which brought together the most transgressive currents in thought and art in a way which, even some twenty years later, infused readers with a sense of poetry, adventure and dread. This would also be the aim of the new journal of the SI.

Cultural revolution

The metal-board jacket of the first issue of the journal *L'Internationale situationniste* ('Situationist International'), which finally appeared in June 1958, was a brilliant gold. The journal would thereafter appear twice a year until 1961, when its sporadic appearance would be compensated for by larger text and denser, more analytical articles. The contents of the first issue were a series of articles, just as incandescent as the journal's cover, attacking modern art and advertising, the limitations of orthodox Marxism, the cinema, the consumer society, psychoanalysis, in short all forms of cultural activity which replaced real, lived experience with metaphors and made people passive spectators of their everyday lives.

An article by Asger Jorn brilliantly attacked a society which accorded 'leisure' its highest social value and thereby, with the nodding complicity of managers, experts and sociologists, 'tried to sneak their way to a fully automated society' in which the individual, exhausted by work and dazed by pleasure, had lost any sense of himself as a unique subject. The Situationists followed on from the original Surrealist group, argued Jorn, unlike their heirs who descended into 'vaudeville' (the opening editorial piece of the journal was an attack on Surrealism) and would throw all their strength into fighting a society which wiped out true human desire in the name of production, abundance, boredom.[5] In the same vein, the SI published Ivan's Chtcheglov's poetic meditation on the city, 'Formulary for a new urbanism', in which the doomed psychogeographer, here mysteriously renamed Gilles Ivain by the SI, articulated his separation from the modern would with the formula, 'Sire, I am from another country.'[6]

Debord himself compiled a series of theses on the coming 'Cultural Revolution' (the term was yet to take on its full Maoist meaning) which declared a war of secession to be fought by the Situationists against 'the world of decomposition'. The aim of the Situationists, he wrote, was 'immediate participation in a passionate abundance of life'.[7] For the theory and practice of this form of action, unlike orthodox Marxist theory which aimed at freedom as an abstraction (Debord quoted the Communist thinker Dionys Mascolo as proof of this assertion), the Situationists saw that the weapons for the future struggle were already at hand. The assault on art, the 'détourning' of everyday life, the pursuit of the dizzying perspectives of high altitude which was the aim of Situationist activity, were not promises but already existing techniques. Debord praised Henri Lefebvre who, alone among his Marxist peers, realised that only by hastening the cultural decomposition of the present world could true revolutionary action be possible.

This first issue of the *Situationist International* also intended to introduce Situationist ideas and terminology to a wider audience beyond the closed circle of what seemed to many outsiders to be a sect. Accordingly, the journal gave a series of definitions of what it meant to be a Situationist. These definitions would become touchstones for all future activity, eventually taking on the status of statutes or articles which could be cited against the enemies of the Situationist International as well as its own members, who could be instantaneously expelled for failing to grasp the full significance of a given term.

DEFINITIONS

Constructed situation: moment in life concretely and deliberately constructed by co-organisation of a unitary environment and an interplay of events.

Situationist: concerning the theory or the praxis of constructing situations. Someone who constructs situations. A member of the Situationist International.

Situationism: meaningless coinage by adventitious derivation from above. Situationism does not exist; it would imply a doctrinal interpretation of existing facts. Obviously the notion 'situationism' is invented by anti-situationists.

Psychogeography: study of the precise effects of the geographical milieu, whether consciously arranged or not, and its direct influences on the affective behaviour of individuals.

Psychogeographic: concerning psychogeography. That which demonstrates the direct action of the geographical milieu on behaviour.

Psychogeographer: one who studies and communicates psychogeographic reality.

Dérive: experiential behavioural mode linked to the conditions of urban society: technique for passing rapidly through varied environments. Also used, more specifically, to denote a period of continuous practice of this research.

Unitary urbanism: theory of the concomitant use of arts and techniques contributing to the integrated construction of a milieu in dynamic relation to behavioural experience.

Détournement: used as an abbreviation of the formulation; 'détournement (de/re-contextualisation) of pre-existing aesthetic elements' (c.f. ready-mades).

Integration of artefacts (past or present) in an enhanced construction of the milieu. In this sense there can be no situationist painting or music, only a situationist use of these means. In a more primitive usage, *détournement* within passé cultural constructs is a propaganda technique which emphasises the obsolescence and devaluation of such constructs.

Culture: reflection and harbinger of the means available for the organisation of daily life at a given moment in history; aggregate of the premisses and mores by which a group reacts on the living conditions which its economy affords. (This definition is applicable solely in terms of the creation of values and does not apply to their dissemination.)

Décomposition: process by which traditional cultural values auto-destruct, as the means of shaping nature evolve, making possible and necessitating more advanced cultural constructs. There is a distinction between the active phase of decomposition, actual demolition of outmoded superstucture – which ceased towards 1930 – and a new phase of repetition which is currently dominant. Delay in moving from decomposition to new constructs is linked to delay in the revolutionary liquidation of capitalism.[8]

It was Debord alone who had finally codified these terms, long familiar to members of the Letterist International. These definitions were meant as a warning as well as an explanation to outsiders. Most important was the definition of 'Situationism', which was a term used only by 'anti-Situationists'. In the first instance, it was clear enough that Situationist practice, *détournement, dérive*, the constructed situation, were activities which denied the possibility of any fixed theory of 'Situationism'. Secondly, here Debord guarded against the process whereby the word which designated an avant-garde movement, such as 'Surrealism', entered the language, became a doctrine, then a technique and lost all of its polemical, revolutionary force. This had happened to 'Surrealism' and was happening now to 'Existentialism'. Art and artistic movements in the modern world were, Debord insisted, either an impossibility or a lie.

This was because modern civilisation, argued all the Situationist writers, was based on a con-trick. Instead of living a life according to the principles of subjective desire, each individual was persuaded or conditioned (there was only a slight negligible difference between these two terms) into accepting the mediocre comforts of modern society. This was the process by which life was turned into an empty vessel, a 'spectacle', and it was the coercive power of this 'spectacle' which had to be opposed and fought in the most urgent terms. Glamour shots of bikini-clad sex kittens, images of commodified desire who were preening themselves or pouting *à la Bardot*, were placed alongside Situationist writings which were in equal measure imperious, sarcastic, aristocratic and contemptuous.

Venice

They were also fiercely sectarian. In an article which was entirely incomprehensible to outsiders, 'Venice has conquered Ralph Rumney', Ralph Rumney was publicly thrown out of the group and denounced as a 'young man, full of life and promises, who is lost and dissolved in our many memories'.[9] Rumney had apparently been slightly late in delivering a 'psychogeographical report' on Venice, where he was briefly based at the time, and had been expelled for this minor crime. In a thoroughly legalistic manner Jorn and Debord had sent ultimatums and deadlines to Rumney from Paris. The article, although unsigned, was written by Debord, and the tone was catty (Debord, who was aware of Rumney's somewhat conventional background as a parson's son, made a glancing reference to this in the remark 'Rumney has just disappeared and his father has not yet set off to look for him').

The real reason for Rumney's expulsion was mysterious but something to do, Rumney suspected, with his recent marriage to Pegeen Guggenheim and the birth of their son Sandro (now an art dealer in New York). As the expulsion of Wolman had demonstrated, Debord's horror of domesticity could very quickly be translated into ruthless political action. Rumney also suspected that the reason went deeper. Debord was also very jealous and saw Rumney as a rival. This was partly rivalry of a sexual nature. There had been a certain amount of flirtation between Rumney, Pegeen, Michèle Bernstein and others at Cosio and at other venues. Debord, who fancied himself as a '*drageur*', was, according to Rumney, clearly unhappy with this and showed it by sarcastically berating Bernstein.[10]

More than this, Rumney was now firmly and comfortably ensconced in the bohemian milieu of Venice where he was busily cultivating an image as an international playboy artist. He became a friend of Alan Ansen, beat poet and an intimate of William Burroughs, whom he stalked with his camera to make a collage called 'A Psychogeographical Map of Venice' and whose flat on the top floor of a *palazzo* in the via delle Carozze was an occasional base. Burroughs came to Venice on a flying visit, abstaining from heroin and drinking heavily, impressing Rumney with both his capacity and intelligence.

Burroughs and Ansen were both invited, through Rumney, to a cocktail party at Peggy Guggenheim's *palazzo* Venier dei Leoni, which was opposite the Prefettura. Peggy Guggenheim, who disapproved of her daughter's marriage to the apparently feckless artist Rumney, had had an extravagant career which had taken her from Jazz-Age Paris, through friendships with

James Joyce, Samuel Beckett, Marcel Duchamp and marriage to Max Ernst, to a reputation as one of the great art patrons of the twentieth century. She revelled in her Venetian nickname of the last *dogaressa* ('the last countess') and her *palazzo* on the Grand Canal was now both a living museum of twentieth-century art and an obligatory stop-over for the international cultural élite. Paintings by distinguished artists hung in the bathrooms, alongside drying clothes. Brancusi's *Two Birds* was in the garden and a Calder mobile in the entrance hall, hung too low, often smacked the unwary or drunken guest in the face. A six-foot-high bronze of a horse and rider by Marino Marini overlooked the canal, with the rider's arms oustretched and the horse's cock proudly erect (Peggy had asked the artist to make the member screwable so that it could be taken off on holy days when nuns visited the town hall opposite the *palazzo*).

Peggy was, however, less than impressed by the antics of Rumney's new friends. When Ansen told Burroughs that it was usual to kiss Peggy's hand on introduction, Burroughs remarked, 'I will be glad to kiss her cunt if that is offered.' This was overheard and reported to Peggy, who thereafter did her best to keep a suitable distance from the louche company kept by Rumney. Peggy was also somewhat prudish on matters homosexual and expressed revulsion at the playful locker-room activities of Burroughs and Ansen, who vied for the attentions of the best-looking Venetian boys (Ansen was eventually expelled from Italy on the grounds of 'corrupting minors').[11]

Back in Paris, Debord loudly claimed that he was not in the slightest bit interested in the activities of high-life international trash. Others detected an asperity in his tone which belied a certain jealousy of Rumney's easy access to high-life finance. More particularly, even at this stage, Debord was clearly interested in the possibility of having his life and work funded by a patron. This apparent dependence could be philosophically justified because, as Debord read it, it was a Renaissance model of artistic activity which placed art, politics and philosophy on a more intimate and human footing and therefore entirely separate from the twentieth-century model that dealt in art as commodity. Secondly, it was a well-known commonplace that, as Machiavelli pointed out, contrary to appearance, such a relationship gave ultimate power to the artist and not the patron. The work of the Florentine artists of the early Italian Renaissance, who worked directly under the patronage of the Medicis but whose art was universal and spoke eternal truths, was clear proof of this fact. Debord was already reading at this stage not only Machiavelli's *The Prince* but also *The Discourses*, as well as Castiglione's *The Book of the Courtier* which, along with the Bible and *The Prince*, the Holy Roman Emperor Charles V had famously kept by his bed. These books would accordingly become guiding works for Debord in later years.

Debord was clearly unhappy about Rumney's position. The young

Englishman was never a rival for political or artistic leadership, and indeed was second only to Wolman as Debord's most faithful and disciplined disciple. Rumney also provided an important conduit to London, where the SI was making its first impact on avant-garde circles, modelling their activities on De Quincey and William Blake, using London as a site for 'psychogeographical' research. Even as early as 1955, the Letterist International had protested to *The Times* in French-accented English, and in the pages of *Potlatch*, at the possible destruction of London's Chinatown: 'Sir, [. . .] We protest against such moral ideas in town-planning, ideas which must obviously make England more boring than it has in recent years become,' they wrote imperiously. 'The only pageants you have left are a coronation from time to time, an occasional royal marriage which seldom bears fruit; nothing else. The disappearance of pretty girls of good family especially will become rarer and rarer after the razing of Limehouse. Do you honestly believe that a gentleman can amuse himself in Soho? . . . Anyway, it is inconvenient that this Chinese quarter of London should be destroyed before we have the opportunity to visit it and carry out certain psychogeographical experiments which we are undertaking.'[12] It was however intolerable that Rumney should be more socially, financially and artistically advanced than Debord. It was this point which explained the headline of the text, 'Venice defeated Ralph Rumney', in which Debord cast out one of his most dedicated allies.

Revolutionary justice

Such arguments were either incomprehensible or irrelevant to the first readers of the *Internationale situationniste*. However, with its elegant design and aristocratic tone, for many older and sophisticated readers on the Left Bank, it more than matched the pre-war cleverness of *La Révolution surréaliste* or *Documents* in style. The *Internationale situationniste* was also relentlessly political. Following Lefebvre, who was then developing his theses on 'moments' which transformed everyday life in debate and conversation with Debord, the SI sought to develop a critique which placed the unlimited possibilities of ordinary existence at the heart of its programme.[13] It promised a vision of a future society in which aesthetic, 'poetic' values were as least as important as principles of general economy or theories of labour. As an antidote to these alienating social processes of modern capitalism, the Situationist International offered 'a revolutionary game' in which 'constructed situations', moments of poetic intensity which had the potential to disrupt and transform everyday life, were the most effective weapons of attack as well as the defining principles of the ever-changing critique which was Situationist theory.

It was a mystery for many where the money for the journal, which unlike

Potlatch was by no means cheap or easy to produce, had come from. Henri Lefebvre, who was immediately impressed by this first issue, had asked Debord this question and also wondered how Debord himself managed to get by without work or any other paid income. 'I live off my wits,' was the enigmatic reply.

In truth, the money for the the journal, as well as for Debord's lifestyle, which was by no means austere even at this stage, came from a variety of sources. These included Debord's family and wealthy friends or relatives of other Situationists who were persuaded to give financial support to a 'revolutionary artistic project'. In line with Debord's thoughts on the power-relationship of patronage as one which swung towards the artist, he had no moral qualms about this. Michèle Bernstein, however, had always worked in some way, even if only to occupy herself ('I do not have Guy's power to do nothing for a long period,' she said. 'For him it was a great negative force. For me it was boring'). She told Henri Lefebvre that she had managed to acquire an unsteady but lucrative income by writing horoscopes for horses which were then published in racing magazines. She determined the date of birth of the horses and did their horoscopes in order to predict the outcome of the race (she later claimed ruefully never to have made any money from her own predictions).

However, despite the utopian promises of an artistic revolution, and the rackety lifestyle and finances which belied these statements, there was also an impressively practical side to the SI which did not shy away from engagement with present realities. The most important of these, for Debord, the SI and the rest of their generation, was the Algerian war, 'the war without a name' which had been festering since an insurrection launched in Algeria by the National Liberation Front (FLN) in 1954 had forced the French government's hand and precipitated military intervention. Having lost the territories of Indo-China, Tunisia and Morocco, the government of Mendès France was determined not to go down in history as the government which gave away the last French colonies. The problem was made even more complicated by the presence in Algeria of a French settler population, *les pieds noirs* or 'black-feet', so-called because their polished black shoes marked them out from native Algerians. This population called upon the French government to refuse all concession to the Algerian side. Although the Left-wing consensus was against the actions of the French government, even some of the most intellectually distinguished members of the Left were confused as to where they finally stood on Algeria. Albert Camus, himself a *pied noir*, famously told students in Stockholm in December 1957, on being awarded the Nobel Prize, 'I believe in justice, but I would defend my mother before justice.'

By the time that the first edition of *L'Internationale situationniste* was ready for publication, the Algerian war had become an inescapable and shameful fact of French life. Particularly in the capital, where riots in the streets and the use of Algerian informers in the communities of Barbès and Belleville had created a near-war mentality, there was a palpable tension in the air. The concluding, unsigned article 'A Civil War in France' was written by Debord in the wake of revelations of the systematic use of torture by French forces in Algeria and growing disquiet in France itself over the Algerian crisis (the article had been inspired by the mass demonstrations against the war in Paris in May 1958). The Situationists were far from being the only group on the French Left who saw that the French response to the struggle for independence in Algeria also posed a threat to the functioning of democracy at home. Most notably, only months before, the Communist Henri Alleg, editor of *Alger républicain*, had had his book *La Question*, an account of torture at the hand of French paratroopers, clumsily banned by the French government. But it was with a rare prescience that the Situationists also saw that the Algerian war laid bare divisions in French society which were simply class-based. Debord blamed the French Communist Party and the Trade Union Congress, the CGT, for the continuation of the war by not calling the working class to a general strike. 'There has not been any reaction from the working class,' wrote Debord in disgust, railing against the weakness of democratic systems to defend themselves under duress. 'We have fallen into a state of political absence from the bourgeoisie and the proletariat where pronunciamentos decide power.'[14] Most importantly, to even the most casual reader of *L'Internationale situationniste*, this article demonstrated in the clearest terms that for this new grouping of the avant-garde, the term 'revolution' was not used as a metaphor but understood as a real, lived experience.

CHAPTER 12

Scandals and Supreme Tricks

1958–9

The first issue of *L'Internationale situationniste* did not exactly set the world on fire despite the aims of its first editors (the issue had been put together by Debord and Bernstein; G. E. Debord, as he still styled himself in print, was named as 'Director'). The journal was printed in a small run of some two hundred copies and distribution was limited to half a dozen sympathetic bookshops on the Left Bank. The initial reception from the journal's first readers was, however, generally enthusiastic. (The journal's reception in Cannes was less sympathetic: with grandmotherly pride Manou had sent a copy of the first issue to a family friend, a certain Professor Debré, professor of paediatrics and father of the politician Michel Debré, to gauge reaction to what Guy was doing in the world. The professor's reaction, which horrified Manou, was that this was very intelligent but rather too strong for his tastes.)

Amongst the journal's other first readers was André Breton, for whom Debord still had a grudging respect as well as a complicated sense of filial duty. Breton expressed enthusiastic approval and interest in Situationist texts for their anti-capitalist, anti-Stalinist politics and the message that art had uses beyond the world of art galleries and museums. In a recently founded Surrealist newsletter called *Bief: Jonction surréaliste* (edited by the art critic Gérard Legrand who had also co-written *L'Art magique* with André Breton), Benjamin Péret, the veteran Surrealist, notorious drinker and confidante of Breton, wrote of a 'so-called Situationist International who think they are doing something new by creating misunderstanding and confusion'.[1] Péret's tone was not disapproving but his benign, almost fatherly approval was received with contempt by Debord who, less tolerant of Breton's acolytes, acidly dismissed Péret as a 'disgusting fool'.[2]

Another early reader of the Situationists' first publications was Philippe Sollers, then twenty-one years old and a budding star of the French literary scene. Sollers was from Bordeaux and had arrived in Paris with a prodigious reputation as a young writer and thinker. His first novel, *Une curieuse solitude*, had won high praise from François Mauriac, the Right-leaning fiercely Catholic *éminence grise* of the French novel who disregarded Soller's Left-wing opinions, claiming he knew a novelist when he saw one. Sollers had also intrigued André Breton, less for his writing than for his manners and style which, precocious, impudent, imperious and elegant, were obviously closely modelled on those of the old Surrealist master himself. Despite his youth Sollers thought nothing, for example, of engaging the now elderly Georges Bataille in conversation at a café in the rue Bonaparte and casually drawing André Breton, Bataille's former arch-enemy who happened to be passing in the street, into the discussion.[3] Inevitably, Sollers was at this stage making his first moves towards establishing the avant-garde group which would call itself *Tel Quel*. This group was in fact established in 1960 by Sollers and would bring together such luminaries as Roland Barthes, Julia Kristeva, Jacques Derrida and Gérard Genette. Sollers declared himself 'enormously excited and delighted' by early Situationist writings which were met with indifference by the rest of his coterie. Debord was able to say nothing good about him, his circle and his interests. Sollers was a charismatic and gregarious character, well-connected and easy to be with. However, his few overtures towards Debord were met with blank hostility from Debord and those around him.[4]

Few others outside of the closed circuit of international connections which made up the Situationists' network expressed interest or astonishment at what the Situationists produced. This had to be remedied. In the spring of 1957, Debord and Michèle had moved from their rooms in the hotel on the rue Racine to a new flat in the rue Saint-Martin. Although technically on the bourgeois Right Bank it was still in walking distance from the Left Bank, as well as lying adjacent to their beloved Les Halles and almost at the heart of the Marais, which was then a crumbling working-class slum, a fascinating labyrinth of psychogeographical possibilities, rather than the gay, media culture ghetto it has since become. Henri Lefebvre, soon to be a frequent visitor, described the flat as 'unbearably dark, but always tidy and busy' and Michèle and Guy as 'dedicated to constant thought, constant activity'.[5]

In this atmosphere, Debord determined to extend the SI's sphere of influence across Europe, even the world. The months after the publication of the first issue of *L'Internationale situationniste* saw him travelling incessantly, from Milan to Amsterdam, from Munich to Brussels and then to London, establishing collaborations with artists and writers in those cities. A German section of the Situationist International had been established early in 1958, publishing a pamphlet *Nervenruh! Keine Experimente* ('Calm down! No experiments') under Jorn and Debord's direction. It advocated attacks on such less obvious enemies of the Situationists as current culture heroes Dylan Thomas, Jackson Pollock and James Dean as well as promoting the SI as 'the spectre haunting the world'.

'We demand kitsch, filth, original mud, chaos'

The third international conference of the SI took place in Munich in April 1959. One of the main aims of the SI at this point was to extend its influence outside France and the Scandinavian countries. The conference was the ideal starting point for this manoeuvre. It followed from this that, after long days and nights of drinking across the city's cafés and bars (the main headquarters was the café Herzogstand, a well-known bohemian haunt on Munich's main drag), the German avant-garde movement Groupe SPUR, named after the German word for 'track' or 'trace', of which Jorn was also a member, registered its affiliation to the Situationist International and produced a manifesto which had a more specifically German bias.

The SPUR group had emerged from the wreckage of the pre-war German avant-gardes to embrace Dada, Surrealism and the 'post-Expressionist' work of CoBra. Conscious of the need to shake off the immediate past and aware that the present divided nature of Germany only served to confirm Western capitalist opinion that the Marxist spirit of opposition was dead, the SPUR group set their faces against both East and West with a declaration of intent that called for a 'spiritual revolution' which could be arrived at through the abolition of art. Besides Jorn, the group comprised Helmut Sturm, Heimrad Prem and Hans-Peter Zimmer who identified themselves as painters who 'painted for the new world'. (At the time of writing members of the original SPUR group are all now dead, mainly from drugs or suicide, or in prison.)

They declared themselves for a new aesthetic which defined itself against the 'decomposed ideal of beauty of the old world'. The new aesthetic was to be 'kitsch', a German word which had the first meaning of inauthentic but was now also a description of all that seemed to be fake or artificial in the modern consumer society. This was expressed in the SPUR manifesto as a threat as well as a promise: 'The tired generation, the angry generation, everything is buried. Now it is the turn of the kitsch generation. WE DEMAND KITSCH, FILTH, ORIGINAL MUD, CHAOS. Art is the shitheap where kitsch is staking its claim. Kitsch is the daughter of art: the daughter is young and sweet-smelling, the mother an old woman who stinks. We want just one thing: to spread kitsch around.'[6] As the conference closed and the Situationists caught the train back to Paris, a tract was distributed at Munich's museums, galleries and bookshops entitled 'A cultural putsch has happened while you were sleeping!' Further scandals, assaults on the cultural establishment, were promised in line with Situationist strategy.

The first real scandalous offensive action of the SPUR group, as reported in this tract, had been an attack on a Professor Bense, philosopher, mathematician and Leftist militant at the University of Munich. The attack took the form of a lecture which the SPUR group announced would take place at the Museum of Ethnology in Munich to open an exhibition of 'Extremist-Realist' paintings. Instead of the distinguished radical professor himself, the audience was slightly bemused as they filed in to find the podium occupied by a green suitcase. A tape recorder hidden inside the suitcase was switched on and a voice claiming to be Bense explained that although urgent business compelled him to be in Zurich, history had demanded that he also give this important talk on the 'new art of the future' here in Munich, albeit in cybernetic form. The audience settled down, and the green suitcase gave a cough, prefacing a learned disquisition which veered between German, Latin, French and garbled quotations from Marx and Hegel. The suitcase announced that it would also give a talk 'in Hegelian'. The *Süddeutsche Zeitung* reported that although this new technique of giving a talk had its problems (the sound quality was not at its best apparently), the professor's rhetorical skill was such that the Munich intelligentsia could hardly stop themselves from giving him a rousing reception. Bense was furious, the Munich public humiliated whilst, much to Debord's glee, the term 'Situationismus' entered the German language for the first time.[7]

'Scumbag intelligentsia'

In Italy, the Situationists organised exhibitions of 'industrial art' in Milan and Turin, the industrial heartland of Northern Italy, at which Giuseppe Pinot-Gallizio, one of the few survivors of Cosio, exhibited a variety of 'art machines', producing long rolls of prints as a parody of the mass production of images as commodities. Michèle Bernstein published a text in Turin, 'Elogio di Pinot-Gallizio', praising Pinot-Gallizio for pre-empting capitalist logic, and eulogised these new developments in the history of the civilisation of the image, lauding Pinot-Galizzio's deconstruction of the creative myth. A photograph in the second issue of *L'Internationale situationniste* showed Pinot-Gallizio at work, in a laboratory surrounded by test tubes and bunsen burners, evidently concocting the art of the new civilisation. Pinot-Gallizio himself was pleased with the exhibitions, writing to Enrico Baj that he thought that only the Situationists offered him the opportunity to extend himself fully beyond the limits of Surrealism, which 'no longer frightened people'.[8] He declared that the 'industrial paintings' had been a success although he and the Situationists had not quite realised their ambitious plans to paint the *autostrada* outside Milan, the fashionable thoroughfare the via Montenapoleone, and the 'arse of any woman with a squint'. The only draw-back, Pinot-Gallizio wearily confessed, was that writing for *L'Internationale situationniste* also attracted the attention of the French and Italian police who were obviously already becoming familiar with the activities and friends of a certain Guy Debord of the rue Montagne-Sainte-Geneviève, Paris.[9]

Debord's nascent reputation with the police as an agitator and manipulator of people and events was further enhanced in Italy by the inevitable scandal which accompanied Pinot-Gallizio's exhibition and which now seemed to be becoming a trademark of Situationist activity. At the end of June 1958 an obscure young Milanese painter, Nunzio van Guglielimi, had slightly damaged a painting by Raphael, *The Coronation of the Virgin*, by sticking a small handwritten poster – 'Long live the Italian Revolution! Down with the government of the Church!' – on the painting's protective glass. Guglielimi had been arrested on the spot, declared mad, and without any form of trial or judicial process was thrown into a mental hospital for an indeterminate period.

The 'Italian section' of the Situationist International (the Italian nomenclature was rather notional as the group was still obviously led and organised by Jorn and Debord) immediately leapt into action. On 4 July they produced a pamphlet, 'Difendete la libertà ovunque' ('Defend Freedom Everywhere') in defence of Guglielimi. Local printers, fearful of police action and perhaps even heavier pressure from devout local worthies with Mafia connections, refused to print the tract which claimed that 'Guglielimi's action had expressed the opinion of a great many Italians'. The tract was finally published by a sympathetic printer, who preferred to remain anonymous in case of retaliation. The text was handed out in the colonnades around La Scala opera house and Piazza del Duomo by the 'Italian section' (Debord, Pinot-Gallizio, Jorn) along with Maurice Wyckaert, the representative of the 'Belgian section'. In a most provocative and foolhardy gesture they even braved a hostile crowd of Mass-goers on their way to prayer in the surroundings of Il Duomo, Milan's main cathedral. The Situationists were lucky to escape a good hiding from the *carabinieri*, who lost the fleeing Situationists in the cathedral's backstreets (they later regrouped in a nearby bar for restorative drinks), and the enraged Milanese faithful who could hardly be expected to approve sentiments such as 'Freedom is in the destruction of all idols!'

In a further confusing move, which was against public opinion as well as being entirely unrelated to Situationist agitation, Guglielimi was declared sane and released on 19 July. To the disgust of the Situationists, amongst many others who were less concerned with art than the due process of law, Guglielimi's release had been privately negotiated only on the humiliating grounds that he accepted to be photographed praying on his knees in contrition before Raphael's painting. The photograph was indeed duly taken and widely circulated across the world. This stupefying twist to the Guglielimi affair, which as a violation of civil rights had been shocking enough, gave the Milan scandal further weight as an offensive action against the cultural establishment.

Most importantly, this 'revolting image' served to confirm Debord's powerful argument that art, politics and religion were not only inseparable in a society which placed power-structures out of the reach of the ordinary individual, but were also active agents of oppression. This argument was hardly original; all avant-garde movements of the twentieth century, from Dada through Futurism and Surrealism, had indeed been forced into recognising this fact. What had changed at this point in the century, Debord pointed out, was that the potential for 'falsification' on the part of the society which controlled art, image and feeling was becoming unlimited. Details were of crucial significance: a photograph of the painting had been retouched to make it look as if Guglielimi had damaged the painting beyond repair, whereas in fact damage had been minimal. Worse than this, the offending Guglielimi pamphlet had been blurred and made unreadable in the photographs in the Italian press and therefore lost its revolutionary meaning. This 'falsification' was final proof, if any were needed, that the forces of media, state and Church were indeed in active conspiracy against the work of the avant-garde. The incident was therefore 'instructive', wrote Debord in the second issue of *L'Internationale situationniste*, before launching a vituperative attack on the 'scumbag intelligentsia of Italy'.[10]

'A love story that ended badly, very badly'

When Debord came to denounce Simondo, Olmo and Verrone in late 1957 it was by implication that the collaborations with Jorn could be held up as ideal forms of Situationist artistic activity. The Italians had disappointed not only because they apparently failed to commit themselves wholeheartedly to the programme of total negation which Debord had outlined in 'The Report on the Construction of Situations . . .' but also because they had failed to understand that Situationists did not *make* art, but, as Jorn and Debord had done, *use* it. This was, at least, the account which Debord gave to Bernstein and Jorn at the SI conference (really a meeting in a bar) in January 1958. They were joined by a new member, Abdelhafid Khatib, an Algerian who was not interested in art and whose main contribution for the moment was a good supply of smokable *kif* (quality was not always consistent in those days according to a number of regular smokers of the period).

It was also, most importantly, at this time that Debord first came into contact with Henri Lefebvre. Lefebvre was an inveterate drinker, seducer of women and Surrealist sympathiser as well as the leading academic Marxist philosopher of the day. Their paths crossed in 1958 when Evelyne Chastel, a student friend of Michèle Bernstein, became the lover of the great man. Drinks, talk and mutal empathy flowed.

At the time of his first meetings with Debord, Lefevbre was about to be pushed out of the French Communist Party to which he had held allegiance for thirty years. The main reason for this was because Lefebvre had, through

German colleagues, gained access to and finally published a translation of Khrushchev's 'secret' report on Stalinist crimes to the 20th Party Congress of 1956. The French Communist Party, then re-entering a Stalinist phase, refused to accept the documents as genuine and slandered Lefebvre, who had been setting up opposition groups within the PCF, as a 'gauchiste', a 'Leftist deviationist'.

This was the culminating point of a political career which Lefebvre had begun as a student in the 1920s in reaction against the philosophy of Henri Bergson, which led him to embrace Dada, then Surrealism, before finally joining the Party in 1928. He had contacts with Breton and Aragon during this period and made a lifetime friend of Tristan Tzara. He began his professional career in 1927 as a schoolmaster at a *lycée* in the Ardèche region before taking up a position at Montargis, which was much nearer to Paris. His career was interrupted by the war, during which he fled Paris and involved himself in resistance activity, first in Marseilles and then the Pyrenees. He was later appointed to a Chair of Sociology at the University of Strasbourg (it was not unrelated that the University of Strasbourg was later to be the scene of much Situationist-inspired disorder) where he took positions against the structuralism of Louis Althusser and the Marxist humanism of Sartre and Merleau-Ponty. Above all, Lefebvre insisted, following Marx, the material conditions of social existence were the key to practical rather than theoretical transformation.

Lefebvre's Marxism was largely informed by his reading of the early Marx and in particular the 'Economic and Philosophic Manuscripts of 1844'. Although Lefebvre had been considered one of the most brilliant Marxist philosophers of his generation by the Party, he was far from being shattered by his exclusion. Holding firm to his commitment to the 'young, true Marx', as one commentator has put it, 'he did not leave the party by the right door but by the left'.[11]

Lefebvre devoted himself therefore to encouraging and working with radical groups and artists following his lead, and rejected the dead language of classical French Marxism in favour of revolutionary action. Lefebvre had made his reputation in 1947 with publication of his *Critique of Everyday Life*, in which, taking the early Marx as his model, he saw the problem of alienation as one which could only be solved through social means, that is to say at the level of ordinary everyday experience which had to be raised to the level of poetry.[12] Only in this way, by seeing revolution as 'a totality of interests', could the true revolutionary aim of living life 'as a project' be achieved. Lefebvre extended these concepts in *The Sum and the Rest*, a book he was writing when he first met Guy Debord, in which he explained how 'moments', transitory but definitive emotions (horror, disgust, joy, surprise and so on), could reveal to any individual the revolutionary potential of everyday life.[13] History itself had been made up of these 'moments', the Paris Commune chief among them, which had laid bare the mechanics of history and shown people how to take charge of their own lives. Lefebvre was essentially a Romantic, a fact that appealed to Debord, but one who applied his passionate aestheticism in an intellectually rigorous manner. This latter aspect of Lefebvre's thinking was of course to Debord an exemplary form of behaviour.

In practice, this meant for Lefebvre not only engaging in debates and discussions about revolutionary activity but also participating in ways of life which ranged from the merely unconventional (it was considered a daring action for an unmarried couple to live together) to the wildly experimental. The Situationists, with their taste for all-night drinking sessions (Lefebvre remembered Mescal and Tequila as a particularly deadly favourite of the Malcolm Lowry-obsessed Debord), refusal to work and endless speculation on play as the guiding theory of revolution, had an immediate appeal for Lefebvre.

When Debord met Lefebvre, the older man was fascinated by a project, the Situationist International, which, as Debord explained to him, aimed at a 'totality', a revolution which made no separation between aesthetic and political experience but rather sought their fusion in a 'constructed situation'.

From this encounter onwards, much of Lefebvre's work would be either in reaction to or in debate with Guy Debord. Debord briefly put himself in the position of a pupil attending Lefebvre's lectures in the company of Jean Baudrillard and Henry Raymond. Lefebvre later described his relationship with Debord as 'a delicate subject, one I care deeply about. It touches me in some ways very intimately. In the end it was a love story that ended badly, very badly. There are love stories that begin well and end badly. And this was one of them.'[14]

'You have just heard Guy Debord, spokesman for the Situationist International'

The use of scandal as a polemical weapon was the defining feature of a debate on the future of Surrealism organised by Noël Arnaud, the future biographer of Alfred Jarry. The Situationists had been invited to participate largely through the agencies of Henri Lefebvre, whose recent anti-Stalinist positions and debates with the Communist Party had made him an even more credible and influential figure in Surrealist circles. Lefebvre, who was laid up with influenza on the evening of the debate, was however unaware of the fact that Debord saw this debate as an opportunity to make clear his position of filial disloyalty towards the Surrealists and to express even more precisely what he saw as an inadequate response from the Surrealists, the so-called 'extreme wing of modernity', towards the immediate political problem of Algeria.

The debate began with a confused introduction from Jean Schuster, a former member of the Communist Party who had fallen under Surrealism's spell as an eighteen-year-old at an exhibition in 1947. Since then Schuster, under Breton's patronage, had gone on to assume minor responsibilities within the Surrealist group, editing tracts, organising the distribution of pamphlets and announcing meetings. Most recently, Schuster, with the Communist writer Dionys Mascolo who had come under heavy fire in the first issue of *L'Internationale situationniste*, had founded an anti-Gaullist journal, *Le 14 juillet*. Although Debord was undoubtedly at some remove in political terms from this neo-Surrealist and Communist fellow-traveller, who was roughly the same age and who had the confidence of the likes of André Breton and Maurice Blanchot (soon afterwards Schuster convinced Blanchot to help with a questionnaire on de Gaulle which was sent to a hundred prominent intellectuals), there was also more than a hint of personal enmity in Debord's dismissal of this inexperienced youth who 'had shown that he could not think, could not write, could not speak', and when faced with a noisy crowd at a public debate, had shown that 'he could not even shout'.[15] When he managed to make himself heard, according to Debord, Arnaud simply bleated a litany of 'obscene declarations of mysticism and Christianity' (obviously a disparaging reference to the interests Surrealism had lately shown in occultism as demonstrated in the journal *Médium*).

Debord's own contribution to the debate took the form of a pre-recorded statement which, like the spoof speech delivered by the German Situationists in Munich, was deliberately made confusing for its public, in this case by Mohamed Dahou who had obliged Debord by genially strumming his guitar and smoking hash as Debord was making his original recording. Debord, for once without his entourage of thugs and delinquent Situationists, refused to take the stage, indeed declared himself absent. Following Situationist orders, Schuster switched on the tape recorder. The result sounded like a garbled and incoherent musical interlude, interrupted by snatches of discourse read by Debord in a flat monotone which, when meaning could be discerned, only served to enrage further the assembled representatives of the Surrealist group.

> Surrealism is obviously still alive. Those who founded it are still not dead. New people, of an increasingly mediocre character it is true, have now become part of it. Surrealism is known to the general public as the extreme form of modernism and, on the other hand, it has become the object of academic scrutiny. It is indeed one of those things which lives alongside us, like Catholicism and General de Gaulle.[. . .] Surrealism today is perfectly boring and reactionary. . . . Surrealist dreams correspond to bourgeois impotence,

artistic nostalgia and to the refusal to envisage the liberating use of the technical means of our time. From the control over such means, concrete collective experimentation with new environments and forms of behaviour there is correspondingly the beginning of a cultural revolution outside of which there can be no authentic revolutionary culture. It is in this direction that my comrades of the Situationist International are heading.

The speech was then interrupted for several minutes by loud and vigorous pre-recorded applause which further angered and baffled the Surrealists. Then the tape began again, in the dry tones of a radio announcer: 'You have just heard Guy Debord, spokesman for the Situationist International. This talk was offered to you by the "Cercle Ouvert".' And then finally a chirpy female voice: 'And don't forget! Your most urgent problem is to fight dictatorship in France!' The Surrealists, including Isou in their number, walked out, tossing a copy of *L'Internationale situationniste*, to which someone had taken a match, like a flaming rag towards the stage.

The incident was written up by Debord in a venomous and sarcastic tone in issue 2 of the *L'International situationniste*, which appeared in November 1958, under the rubric 'Supreme trick played on the defenders of Surrealism in Paris provides a revelation of their real value'. The piece was accompanied by two photographs. The first, entitled 'Independence of Algeria', was of a young woman apparently on trial. The photo was accompanied by a poem by the Surrealist poet Paul Éluard in homage to Violette Nozières, who had become a heroine of the Surrealist movement in the 1930s by poisoning her own father who had been sexually abusing her.[16] The fact that Nozières' mother, as well as crowds of well-to-do Parisians, was pictured in the newspapers literally screaming for the death penalty had only further incited the Surrealists. Éluard's poem in praise of Nozières, 'one day there will be no more fathers, in the gardens of youth', obviously had a dual meaning. In the first instance, it was clear that the paternal relation between France and Algeria was an abusive one and should be ended in the same way Violette Nozières had put an end to her father. In the same way, the image signalled another final fracture in Debord's relationship with Breton and Surrealism. Being disgusted with Breton's disciples only made it easier for Debord to turn his fire on Breton himself, who as the symbolic father had to be destroyed.

The second photograph illustrated how pleased Debord was with the success of this latest scandal. It closed the 'Supreme trick' article and showed Debord himself in heroic mode, his face turned upwards, cropped hair worn with a fringe in the 'Roman style' (predating the Beatles' adventures with such radical haircuts in Hamburg by three or so years), a large cigar in his hand, and wearing a duffel coat, the fashionable trademark of the Left Bank bohemian dandy. The photo was accompanied by a maxim from

La Rochefoucauld which set out Debord's version of himself at this stage: 'What stops us from giving ourselves to one single vice is that we have many.'[17]

CHAPTER 13

Psychogeographers at Work

1958–9

During the course of the late 1950s Debord had travelled to and come to know a variety of European cities. He was most frequently a visitor to London, Copenhagen, Munich, Milan and Brussels where he 'wandered extensively' and 'appreciated everything that deserved it'.[1] Debord sought out in his travels those aspects of city life which corroborated his own ideas on the city as a place which should be constructed according to the dictates of poetry and individual desire. In Paris he particularly appreciated alcohol, food, conversation and the fact that even amidst the confusion and hubbub of a great metropolis life could be lived on the intimate level of the *quartier*, a space in which every individual had their own place and function. He would stroll the streets slowly, taking drinks at any bar which seemed worth the trouble, chatting to a multiplicity of characters, sometimes offering his own views on life, art and politics and other times simply joining in with gossip or listening to idle chat. Days would drift endlessly by in this way, a continual series of encounters, ideas, sensations. Never having undertaken any paid employment in his life (still much to his mother and Manou's discomfiture in Cannes), Debord put the maxim 'Never Work!' to its most literal application and found that it opened up a new world of possibilities.

The project of the Situationist International, as Debord conceived it, was to create the Utopian society in the here and now; the Situationist International was a revolutionary micro-society whose rules and codes of conduct were in constant evolution, whose very way of life was at the heart of their programme. In the city of Paris, in his own personal kingdom, Debord was the very opposite of the harsh and dour theoretician which he was later perceived to be: rather, like François Villon, the outlaw poet of the late Middle Ages he sometimes compared himself to, in love with all he saw, Guy Debord 'took it all in his favour'.

Debord reserved a particular relish for the uncommon detail of a city, which could be architectural, a strange or historically significant building, or artistic, an unusual statue or square. More often this was best expressed or understood in alcoholic terms: 'The catalogue on this subject could be vast,' he mused. 'There were beers of England, where mild and bitter were mixed in pints; the big schooners of Munich; and the Irish; and the most classical, the Czech beer of Pilsen; and the admirable baroquism of the Gueuze around Brussels, when it had its distinct flavour in each artisanal brasserie and did not travel well.'[2]

Alcohol was the transformative agent which released subjectivity and objective chance into the city. Alcohol, which had been for the Letterist International the magical elixir which transformed *dérives* into epic poetic adventures in the labyrinth, was also now established as a central part of Debord's life. He prided himself on never passing a day without drinking, usually until most of the party with him had succumbed to drunkenness. Michèle Bernstein said that, 'Guy was never really drunk, no one who met him would have known that he had been drinking much at all. When everybody was collapsing around him, he was intellectually and physically self-posessed. He liked drunks, even admired them, but he was not one of them. It was a question of style.'

Certainly, Debord showed no physical signs of dependency at this stage and was able to flaunt his drinking as a mark of unrepentant bohemianism. Unlike his hero Malcolm Lowry, who by Debord's age in 1960 had already been battered by two serious nervous breakdowns before beginning his finest literary work, Debord was psychically robust and claimed that alcohol played a necessary role in determining his character and behaviour. The effects of alcohol disrupted the controlling forces of work and duty, releasing at the café table or zinc bar the ludic and the poetic elements which Debord held to be humanity's most important qualities. Most importantly, alcohol distorted the passage of time, either compressing or elongating it according to the individual perspective of the drunken subject. This, for Debord, gave the fullest poetic or magical meaning to what Baudelaire had meant in his call for poets to 'Get Drunk! At All times and For Ever!'

Methods and aims

It made sense then that, at the end of 1958, the Situationists thought of opening their own bar. The original idea came from Michèle Bernstein, who was then working as a secretary at the Éditions de Navarre publishing house in order to finance the activities of the Situationist International. One of Michèle's closest friends at the time was a singer called Florencie who, having just been fired from a regular job at the Mont Blanc, dreamt of opening a bar. Inspired by Florencie's idea, Michèle put the idea to her father who without hesitation advanced the substantial sum of 200,000 old francs.

Guy and Michèle undertook the pleasurable task of wandering across the night-time Left Bank in search of suitable premises, finally settling on a bar on the rue Descartes, at an angle with rue de la Montagne Sainte-Genevieve and nestling into the hill rising towards the Panthéon. They named the bar 'La Méthode' in homage to Descartes, although they had seriously toyed for a long time with 'Au non ferme et résolu' ('the firm and resolute no') in sarcastic homage to de Gaulle.

An old pal from Moineau's, Jacques Harbutte, also known as Baratin ('sweet talk'), promised to paint the place up (although the job was not quite finished by the time the bar opened on 10 November). Pinot-Gallizio contributed 'industrial artworks' which pleased Debord because in the candlelit gloom no one was quite sure what they were. An orange flyer announced that Florencie, lately of Le Mont Blanc and Le Bistrot-Moineau, would sing there every night (Debord mooted the idea of inviting Michèle Mochot, now living in Cagnes-sur-Mer and singing in a local cabaret under the name Michèle Brehat, up to dress all in white and sing as 'the unknown singer'; Florencie refused the notion on the grounds that Michèle was a terrible singer). All in all, with a hard-boozing clientele of Situationist and Letterist pals and others attracted by the novelty, it was hard not to pronounce the venture an unmitigated success. 'The Method is a smash-hit in the new quarter of Paris,' Guy wrote to Pinot-Gallizio. 'We're thinking of doing something else twenty metres further on.'[3]

'First, like everyone, I appreciated the effect of slight drunkenness,' wrote Debord much later in life, in one of his most beautiful passages eulogising the pure 'potlatch' of alcohol. 'Then very soon, I grew to like what lies beyond violent drunkenness, when one has passed that stage: a magnificent and terrible peace, the true taste of the passage of time. Although in the first decades I may have allowed only slight indications to appear once or twice a week, it is a fact that I have been continuously drunk for periods of several months; and the rest of the time I still drank a lot.'[4] In La Méthode Guy Debord held court and presided over renegades from Moineau's and Le Tonneau d'Or with a princely swagger, giving way to his love of talk and his notion of an addiction to alcohol as a form of aesthetic practice which defied the bourgeois world. He imagined himself as Maldoror, Villon and Malcolm Lowry rolled into one supremely witty and poetic form.

Inevitably, however, after a dispute with the bar's previous owner, inept handling of the bar and cash register, and a row with staff, the adventure was over within a few weeks. Michèle conceded financial defeat and went back to her job as a secretary, whilst Guy quietly abandoned the project, referring darkly in a letter to Pinot-Gallizio that the demise of the bar 'had caused a lot of agitation in the new intellectual area of Paris'. The bar was never referred to again.

Amsterdam

During this period the city of Amsterdam had gained a special significance and exerted a peculiar fascination over Debord, as a place to drink, talk and create. When he first came to know Amsterdam, in the company of his friend and Situationist comrade Constant in the late 1950s, the city was still recovering from the wreckage of the war. Although the old centre of Amsterdam had been left more or less untouched by the Allied bombing raids, which had concentrated their attentions on the docks and outlying industrial zone, the city was poor and shabby. Well into the 1950s, handcarts loaded with black cardboard coffins carrying the bodies of the poor, dead from disease or hypothermia, were a daily sight on the narrow streets of the medieval centre, an area which then as now traverses the red-light district between Warmoesstraat and Nieuwmarkt, as well as in the bomb-scarred landscape of the Jodenhoek, the Jewish quarter which had been almost entirely emptied of its population and been left to the city's human detritus, whores, drunks, drifters, before its reconstruction could be planned. This was also the city which Albert Camus had chosen as the site of his 1956 allegory of punishment and redemption *The Fall*, because the concentric circles formed by the canals resembled the circles of hell in Dante's *Inferno*, of which the ninth and final circle is reserved for moral traitors such as Camus' hero Jean-Baptiste Clamence, whom we first meet drinking in a dive on the sleazy waterfront area known as the Zeedijk. It was here that Debord would wander, sometimes in the company of Constant or Armando, another Dutch artist friend, and sometimes alone, fuelling his drifting with endless white wine or occasionally a *kopstoot*, the Amsterdammers' favoured combination of a short measure of beer with a jenever chaser.

Debord was also fascinated by the Jodenhoek, now empty and desolate, a landscape of wrecked buildings occasionally pillaged by hard-up Amsterdammers for fuel and building materials. Even the name of the area, the Jodenhoek or 'Jewish quarter', was disappearing from history as Amsterdammers, in a whirl of guilt, shame and forgetting, stopped referring to the area by its original name as they literally dismantled its buildings. The area was soon to be scheduled for reconstruction and a metro built to connect the Old Centre with the dead modernist suburbs of Bijlmermeer, then designated by planners as the main dormitory suburb for the future citizens of Amsterdam. Aware that the site would soon pass away into the past, Debord was particularly intrigued by the exposed interiors of the wrecked buildings in Jodenhoek which he saw as revealing myriad secret, forgotten histories. The exposed innards of buildings, in their intricacy and intimacy, also functioned as a metaphor for the way in which architecure concealed but could not control individual subjective experience. In this way, for Debord, the destroyed Jewish quarter was the negative reflection of aims of the modern architecture which, following Le Corbusier, sought to provide 'machines for living' and thereby 'living machines'.

Debord would also wander through the area known as 'The Old South' or 'De Pijp' ('The Pipe'), a name which came from the way in which the tall and austere nineteenth-century tenements which absorbed and concealed the most variegated and densely packed population in the city – a population which was made up of Surinamese and other immigrants as well as a traditionally radical working-class community – formed long and labyrinthine lines of passage. It was here, during one of his first trips to the city to see Constant and Armando, that Debord planned an ambitious exhibition of Situationist work which would spread across the city, 'detourning' the commercial centre around Damrak and Rokin and including *dérives* through psychogeographically significant parts of the city such as the Jodenhoek and The Old South.

In part Debord's affection for Amsterdam was the result of his warm and well-established friendships with Constant, Armando and other expatriate Dutch artists who had frequented the Left Bank dives favoured by the Letterist International in the early 1950s. Drinking, talking with a genera-tion of artists who were some ten or more years older than him, and who, like Asger Jorn, had direct experience of war and occupation, Debord was already well disposed towards the city and its citizens before he had even set foot there. In turn, these Dutch artists, inspired by the pre-war writings of the Surrealists, excited by the possibilities of the post-war Existentialist movement, had come to Paris in search of experimental forms of art and self-expression. They had not been disappointed in the loose, floating communities which drifted through day and night from café to bar across the city. It was only a matter of time before the Letterist International and Guy Debord, as the publishers of *Potlatch* and highly visible participants in the night-time mêlée of the Latin Quarter and Saint-Germain-des-Prés, would come to the attention of the Dutch bohemians and impress them by their strident calls for the reinvention of daily life. The later alliance between the Situationists and former members of the CoBra movement was an intellectual union, but it had been forged in part as a result of these friendships.

Cities in history

Jacqueline de Jong first met Debord when she was a young assistant curator at Amsterdam's Stedelijk Museum. 'He was very arrogant,' she recalled. 'I can see him now entering the bar, always first at the bar, pushing his way forward to get a drink with his fat belly. He was like a little arrogant plum pudding.'

This 'plum pudding' had been introduced to Jacqueline as the 'brilliant individual' who led 'the most potent revolutionary force in the world', the Situationist International, who were tentatively pursuing funds to launch an exhibition across the city. Jacqueline de Jong had been given the job of helping them to organise the adventure. 'I didn't know what to do,' she said, cackling hoarsely and sexily over a beer and a cigar in the Café Krum, one of Amsterdam's finest and most hospitable bars. 'They told me that it was the beginning of a revolution, that they were taking over Amsterdam and then the world. They were also very funny, drinking always and laughing.'

But despite the laughter, warmth and the charm, Jacqueline was also immediately struck by what she called the 'double nature' of Debord's personality. 'Guy was a double,' she said. 'Guy was very witty, very funny, very intelligent. But he was also Jesuitical in his manner, very strict in his ideas, very arrogant and superior. He had a particular dislike of painters, especially young ones, because he had decided art was dead and that was that. I remember that we drank a lot, and I was better able to support the drink then than I am now. And I remember walking with him in Paris, when I first came to see him there, and we wandered around his *quartier*, visiting café after café. He had to show me this, all of it in the greatest detail, he said, because this was his ambience, it was the ideal ambience of a city. He took a very detailed interest in what was happening in his *quartier* because this was his universe, his ideal place.' There was also sexual intrigue and jealousy involved. 'One of the first times I met Debord, he was with Jorn and Armando, was at the Stedelijk Museum, and they had come to discuss plans with us. Jorn came in first, leaving the others to drink beer in a café, and when he met me he fell in love with me. This was how he put it. I was quite pretty then, I suppose, a well brought-up girl, and he came out with me on his arm and ignored the other Situationists in the café. Debord came over and said, "What's going on, why are you not sitting with us?" and Asger explained that he had fallen in love and would return to the Situationist philosophy in a short time. But from then on it was never easy with Debord, although I became very quickly a Situationist. I stayed with Debord and Michèle in Paris and became very committed. But there were always young girls around them, and I suppose I was one of them.'[5]

In the early summer of 2000, Jacqueline de Jong was still a beautiful woman who exuded a febrile sexuality. It was easy to see what had attracted Debord to her. The attraction was not reciprocated: 'I could not think of doing anything with Debord. Not just because I was with Asger, but no, he was not for me. There were always games but I didn't play them. When he threw out Constant, or when Constant left, Guy said to me, "Here, you can take the Netherlands, the Dutch Situationists can be led by you," but it was flattery and nothing else. When I really did take control and started up my own journal, *Situationist Times*, he didn't like it and I was out and that was that. Everybody clever, I thought, from Constant to everybody else was being thrown out. But I wouldn't let him throw me out. Amsterdam was my parish, my city, and he had no right to annex it, to make it a historical conquest. He could remind you of Napoleon like that.'

When Constant first met Debord in Paris in the early 1950s, he was in the process of turning away from painting towards urbanism and architectural theory. During the period of their first meetings, Constant was preoccupied by the devastation of war and was working on a series of what he termed 'war paintings', works which aimed at giving some sort of contextual meaning to the physical destruction he had witnessed during the war. Constant felt keenly that painting was an insufficient medium for such a project, that it lacked what he was beginning to term a 'total experience', that it did not touch or affect ordinary existence in any real way.

I met Constant in the early summer of 2000 in a bar called Scheierstoren ('Tower of Tears'), a circular tower dating from 1480 and overlooking the harbour of Amsterdam. The name had apparently been given to it on account of the weeping women who had waved their husbands off from here. It was also from here that Henry Hudson had set off to negotiate the Northwest Passage to the East Indies and 'found' the Hudson river instead. Against a background of screeching traffic, Constant, a tall and elegant man of eighty accompanied by his miniature dog Tigus, settled himself onto the terrace and ordered a glass of white wine. 'I like to drink in the morning,' he said (it was 11 a.m.), 'and then through the afternoon. It is the best way of working, the best way to be always aware and be awake.'

During his first conversations with Guy Debord, Constant said, he sensed that although it was clear that Debord seemed to lack the qualities of an artist, aesthetic sense or the abillity to think in image and colours, as a thinker he was lucid, intelligent and, more often than not, unsettlingly precise in his conclusions: 'I think he was a genius, of course.' Most importantly, for Constant, these conclusions confirmed his suspicions that art was dead, it belonged to the 'old civilisation', and that the image was a form of falsification of experience. The present day demanded new forms of expression, 'situations' which revealed the future and its possibilities. Having acquired the term 'situations', Constant and Debord, in Paris and then in Amsterdam, began to codify and transform this vocabulary into a conceptual language which would carry the weight of their respective ideas in practical terms.

Later on that day, I drank more wine with Constant in the elegant front room of his house, overlooking a still and melancholy canal. We were only yards from the industrialised eroticism of the red-light district but, as was the case with other Situationists, we could have been sitting in another century. Constant recalled first visits to Debord's tiny apartment on the rue Saint-Martin and their dreams of creating a future city for the end of the century. 'We wanted to build a new world, using the wreckage of this one,' he said. 'We wandered through Amsterdam, drinking white wine and other things, never truly drunk, but always talking, pursuing a way, a passage we had not yet taken.'

There also were long, seemingly endless drinking sessions in Paris at the Café Curieux, an appositely named location on the rue Réaumur whose drinking population did indeed seem to be made up of a higher than normal percentage of oddities and eccentrics. Like De Jong, as their friendship developed, Constant was struck by the 'double' nature of Debord's personality, which swung in the space of an hour over a bottle of wine from high theoretical seriousness to booze-fuelled bonhomie. 'Debord was good company,' Constant says. 'I remember a lot of alcohol, a lot of talk. The conversation was also intelligent and always informed by free and independent thinking. But you were also aware that Guy developed his thinking in an entirely independent way from whatever you said. He was charming and serious, pleasant. But although it was possible to work with Debord, and this is what I did, he could be intransigent and you were not a friend but someone who was not serious. I made a portrait of Guy in his later years, because then he was not like he was when he was younger. The side which was too serious, too hard, had taken over.'[6]

Constant and Debord collaborated first of all on a theoretical statement, the 'Amsterdam Declaration', which was published in the second issue of *L'Internationale situationniste* and which laid out the first principles of Situationist arguments on architecture and urbanism. 'Architecture is the simplest means of articulating reality, of engendering dreams,' Chtcheglov had written for the Letterist International.[7] 'Architecture must advance by taking emotionally moving situations, rather than moving forms, as the material it works with,' Debord had declared to his new comrades at Cosio, building on Chtcheglov's arguments to imagine 'a new, free architecture'.[8] In the 'Amsterdam Declaration' they loftily announced: 'A constructed situation is a way of approaching unitary urbanism, and unitary urbanism is the indispensable basis for the development of situations, as a game and as a serious way of building a freer society.'[9]

There would later be serious, irreconcilable differences between them, and even at this stage Constant was clearly more interested in spatial geometry than the dialectics of revolution ('Architecture is not revolution, although can be revolutionary,' he later explained). In the 'Amsterdam Declaration', however, Debord imagined with Constant a Utopian city based on the principles of 'unitary urbanism', the term which they now both applied to an imaginary city designed to encourage the free play of its citizens. 'Unitary urbanism' meant above all that social and aesthetic could not be separated on the level of everyday life; instead of being organised, designed and controlled by the needs and demands of commerce, industry, the circulation of traffic and the movement of workers from workplace to home and back again, 'unitary urbanism' sought to make the city a free space, open for play, anarchy, danger, passion.

New Babylon

It was significant that the term 'unitary urbanism', although coined by Debord, had its origins in the 'unitary architecture' imagined by the nineteenth-century utopian socialist Charles Fourier. Fourier, whose career as a businessman, journalist and thinker traversed the French Revolution and its aftermath, combined social philosophy, economics and a millenarian view of the world, seeing the universe as destined to last for 80,000 years and following a curve from chaos to harmony and back again. In the period of harmony, Fourier wrote that the sea would become as sweet as lemonade, the North Pole as mild as the Riviera, and that the world would be geometrically balanced, with 37 million poets as good as Homer, 37 million scientists as important as Newton ('These are approximate numbers, and no less than four husbands for each woman,' Fourier conceded after being challenged about the precision of his figures). Most significantly, Fourier had put his ideas into practice with the establishment of an early form of Communist society at Condé-sur-Vesgre, near Rambouillet not far from Paris. These were ideal, mainly agricultural, communities of ten families, called *phalanges*, who were to live in harmony in a set of buildings called a *phalanstère*, a coinage which brought together *phalange* (a phalanx, or combat formation of soldiers in antiquity) and *monastère* ('monastery'). The idea behind the *phalanstère* was to dissolve what Fourier saw as an artificial distinction between the individual body, the family and the self, and the social body, the collective authority of the group and system. Fourier advocated the abolition of money and free love, with men working for passion rather than money (he was not above applying to Rothschild for money to finance his ventures, however).[10]

Although Debord disdained Fourier's naïve perfectionism, he was nonetheless interested in the careful terms in which Fourier had laid out his pre-Marxist project. It was self-evident to Debord that any future architectural and urban theory of the passions must refer back to Fourier. It was in the Utopian spirit of Fourièrisme therefore that Constant began work on a project called 'New Babylon'. For Constant the working out of this project was to extend over several years and in many ways become his 'masterwork'. Certainly, Constant's later activities over the next two decades as a leading member of the 'Provos' (an Amsterdammer abbreviation of *provocative*, 'provocation'), the Dutch radical group which did much to transform the centre of Amsterdam into the headquarters of the international underground in the 1960s, stemmed from his early collaboration with Debord. The famous 'white bicycle plan', which aimed at banning all cars in the city in favour of 20,000 white bicycles for the free use of the public, and the many Provo-inspired 'happenings' in the centre of Amsterdam were all related in some way to the Situationist dream city called 'New Babylon'.

This was a city in which town planning was abolished in favour of the 'continuous drift', a perpetual movement between spaces which reflected and recast the whole spectrum of human emotions. Chtcheglov had imagined a city with a 'Happy Quarter', 'Bizarre Quarter', 'Historical Quarter', 'Noble and Tragic Quarter' and so on: Chtcheglov's dream architecture was constructed out of labyrinths, covered passageways, mazes, ramparts, stairways which led nowhere. Accordingly, Constant made models and maquettes of a city in an endlessly fluid series of spaces or 'sectors', a 'floating city' defined by the imperatives of need or desire. A 'hanging sector' was suspended over the movement of traffic and commodities, allowing free circulation beyond even the most rational forms of modernist architecture; a 'yellow sector' and 'red sector' were 'ever-changing, mobile spaces' which changed according to the emotions of those who filled the space. 'New Babylon' could not of course be fully realised, even Constant himself admitted as much. Its function rather was to provoke meditation or reflection on the possibilities of everyday life. Although Debord was soon to deliver harsh words on Constant and dismiss 'New Babylon' as merely 'pre-Situationist', for the time being the collaboration represented for Debord a concrete form of visionary thinking and a major leap forward from the Utopian reverie of the Letterist International.[11]

Making and unmaking films

Although Amsterdam was an important psychogeographical site for Debord, a useful and fascinating laboratory for Situationist experiment, and Brussels and Milan the perfect venues for scandal and provocation, it was still Paris, the world capital of revolutions, which, despite the poisonous atmosphere, stirred the deepest emotions. This was confirmed by Debord's next two ventures into film, *On the passage of a small group across a rather brief moment of time* and *Critique of Separation* which, although funded by the Dansk-Fransk Experimentalfilmskompagni, a Danish cultural enterprise financed by the mercurial and by now quite wealthy Jorn, concentrated exclusively on the small triangular zone of the Left Bank of Paris where Debord and his intimates spent most of their time.

Neither of these two twenty-minute black and white pieces was strictly speaking a 'Situationist' film according to Debord who, before an audience of Situationists, later described them as experiments rather than fully realised projects. Debord himself shot very few of the images, preferring to control the editing process and take responsibility for the selection and insertion at correct intervals of the 'detourned' images which made up most of the content of *On the passage* . . .

What both films had in common was an elegiac view of a Paris which seemed to be about to disappear. The opening scenes in *On the passage* . . . take place in Paris in 1952. We are shown Saint-Germain-des-Prés, the Latin Quarter, prisons, police vans flitting across the screen, images of Éliane Papaï *truqueuse* ('lousy little cheat'). We hear recordings of the debates in French and German at the Situationist conference in Munich. There are three voices, Guy Debord with Jean Harnois and Claude Brabant (neither of whom had any further contact with the Situationist International). The central theme is that all we see, hear, feel, know, will fade away before our eyes. Long sections of *On the passage* . . . focus on Les Halles and its surrounding streets of crumbling eighteenth-century buildings. 'The details are already lost in the dust of time,' intones Debord. 'Who was afraid of life, afraid of night, afraid of being taken, afraid of being kept?'

Critique of Separation begins as a miniature love story set on the Left Bank, with Debord, in leather jacket and black shirt, persuading the elfin Catherine Rittener (a would-be actress who again had no further contact with the Situationist International) to walk away from a café with him towards a wider world of adventure. The narrative then collapses into incoherence, screentime is wasted, there are 'detourned' Hollywood sequences of actors in medieval costume, riots in the Congo, shots of Krushchev, de Gaulle, Franco, Eisenhower. There are two separate forms of history, Debord tells us, the personal and subjective world of love, friendship, and the outward, spectacular world of frozen gestures and power. The relationship between the two worlds is fraught. 'It's always far away,' says Debord, referring to spectacular history. 'It makes us disappointed in ourselves.'

The opening scenes of the film, with its slow panning and elliptical movement, are like shots from an early film by Jean-Luc Godard. The aim was, as it was for Godard, François Truffaut and Alain Resnais, the most notable young turks at the forefront of the 'New Wave' in French cinema, to capture something of the textures and surfaces of real life. For Debord, real life meant the real life of the city. The 'separation' of the film's title also refers to the sudden separation between the poetic and the modern, the subject and the spectacle, which was the defining characteristic of modern life. It was this point of separation which Situationist psychogeographers tried to overcome by destabilising the 'spectactular' organisation of the city. Debord was right to assert that neither *On the passage* . . . nor *Critique of Separation* were Situationist films because neither of them actively sought to dissolve this point of separation.

What they did capture, like *Mémoires*, was a mood of elegiac despair and a sense that a unique and individual world of intimate human relations was already receding into the past. Like snapshots of a closed forgotten world, they evoke melancholy and regret in the spectator. This was to become a central theme as, at the cusp of the 1960s, Debord decided to cast off friends, enemies and ideas from the dying decade and prepare the Situationist International for its most radical phase in which it would insert its disruptive critique into history in the most violent manner.

CHAPTER 14

Socialism and Barbarism

1960–1

From 1960 onwards, the French capital began to feel the full force of the rapidly worsening crisis in Algeria. In September 1959 the new president de Gaulle famously announced that the only course open to a 'great nation' like France was to offer self-determination to the Algerian people. In January 1960 de Gaulle recalled to Paris the notorious General Massu, the commander of the 10th Paratrooper Division, who had been accused of torture ('Your Gestapo in Algeria!' screamed one typical headline in *France-Soir*) on the grounds that he had attacked the government policy of self-determination. Incensed by this, thousands of *pied noir* extremists declared a general strike across the country, poured onto the streets of Algiers and for seven days openly took on the French government, their erstwhile protectors, in what became known as 'the week of the barricades'. Inevitably, the violence spilled over onto the mainland, its momentum quickened by the terrorist campaign launched by the Organisation de l'Armée Secrète (OAS), which declared war on liberals and Left-wing sympathisers (they famously planned to assassinate de Gaulle himself).

The atmosphere in Paris was poisonous. On 17 October 1961, tens of thousands of Algerians marched through the centre of Paris in favour of a negotiated peace in the troubled province. The march had barely begun when the police charged, killing two Algerians, wounding sixty-nine and making hundreds of indiscriminate arrests. As the marchers were made to leave Paris, flowing towards the Pont de Neuilly in northwestern Paris, police outflanked the protesters, trapping them with their backs to the Seine. The police waded in, clubbing Algerians and throwing obviously injured or unconscious victims into the river. When almost two hundred bodies were found over the coming months by ordinary Parisians, the police, on the orders of the Paris Prefect of Police, Maurice Papon (who was charged in the 1990s with crimes against humanity for his wartime involvement in the deportation of Jews), denied all knowledge or involvement. The violence did not stop there. A demonstration against OAS terrorism organised by trade unions and Left parties on 8 February 1962 was intercepted by police at the *métro* station Charonne as demonstrators made their way back down the rue de Charonne from the demonstration's climax in place de la Bastille. Hundreds were injured and eight people were killed, all trade union members and seven of them Communists. Half a million attended the funerals. The police again denied any responsibility.

Against this developing background, Debord began to reconsider the extent to which debates about art could really be justified in the name of the Situationist project. The question of the relation between politics and culture was, in the light of the impending catastrophe in France, to be debated with more urgency than ever before.

'The Situationists, whose judges you perhaps imagine yourselves to be, will one day judge you. We are waiting for you at the turning'

The headquarters of Situationist activity was in 1959 and 1960 occasionally and temporarily based in Brussels rather than Paris, partly because Asger Jorn was there and could pay for long, boozy sessions in the Hôtel Canterbury where he was living, and also because the machinations and manoeuvrings of day-to-day politics in Paris were, in Michèle Bernstein's words, 'insignificant rubbish, the stuff of nightmares'. In March 1959 Debord had given an interview to RTBF (Radiotélévision belge), explaining the nature of Situationist activity and the importance of industrial art. Notwithstanding this rare foray into the public domain, Debord was concerned that the Situationists should maintain their aloof distance from the 'spectacle', a term which had appeared for the first time in *L'Internationale situationniste* of December 1959.

The fourth conference of the Situationist International was also held outside France, in London. The 'secret' venue for the conference was the hostel of the British Sailors' Society in the East End, chosen both for the ludic significance of its name (the Situationists cherished nautical metaphors, seeing themselves as 'navigating' a passage towards an unknown destination) and because it was cheap.

Debord was by this stage no stranger to London which he had visited alone and in the company of Alexander Trocchi who, in thrall to the 'magical' aspects of Situationist psychogeographical method, described Debord as 'a man who could discover a city'.[1] Like his drug-addicted friend, Debord had been inspired by Thomas de Quincey, who in *Confessions of an English Opium Eater* pursued his lover Ann 'across the immense labyrinth of the streets of London', scrutinising the night sky of stars, mapping his route like a sailor, searching for the 'north-west passage' which would reveal the full mystery of the city to him. Trocchi recalled that time and distance did not matter to Debord in his quest for poetic sites, which were inevitably areas of London abandoned by history and capital, such as the ruined areas of Limehouse or

Wapping, and which moved Debord to quote R. L. Stevenson, De Quincey or the young Marx.

The substance of the debates in London was unremarkable, extending the themes of international solidarity expounded in Munich and again focusing on what the pressure points were in society which were most vulnerable to Situationist attack (these themes were further emphasised in several articles in the fourth issue of *L'Internationale situationniste*, along with yet another sweeping assault on the wretched Isou who by now was thoroughly sick of Debord and the Situationist International). Most notable was the drawing up of a pamphlet in English, 'Hands Off Alexander Trocchi', in defence of the unfortunate Scot who had been arrested in New York in possession of heroin. Trocchi was at this stage no longer a fellow-traveller but a fully fledged member of the Situationist International. He had been notoriously indiscreet about his drug use in Paris, where indifference and ignorance made for a tolerant atmosphere. New York was different; the holding cells at Lexington were full of sick junkies who all too often died or committed suicide in the face of official distaste for their deviant habits. When halted by police officers on his frequent sorties to the Bronx to buy heroin, Trocchi would go into an act as a Calvinist preacher whose zeal and Scots accent were normally enough to foil the New York City flatfoots. He had however fallen foul of the law and ended up facing deportation, thus bringing to an end the American chapter of his project of 'systematic nihilism'. Back in London, the Situationist International declared that 'taking drugs was of no significance' and called upon the British cultural establishment to petition for Trocchi's pardon on the grounds that he 'is beyond all doubt England's most intelligent creative artist today'.[2]

On 28 September, the Situationists had been invited to talk at the ICA, where many of their ideas had aroused a sympathetic curiosity in the wake of a second showing of *Howling in Favour of Sade* which had taken place there earlier that year. Jorn declined the invitation in favour of a dinner with his agent. The responsibility for the talk therefore fell solely to Debord, whose English was poor and who did not want to be seen in a bad light. The talk was scheduled to start at 8 p.m. but at 9 p.m. the Situationists were still in the bar of the ICA, locked in furious semi-drunken debate about the quality of the translation of the text to be read out. The director of the ICA, the rather stern Dorothy Morland, asked Guy Atkins, the art critic who was acting as interpreter and minder for the group, to tell Guy Debord that if he wasn't ready in five minutes then the talk would be called off. Aware that if he delivered such an ultimatum Debord was likely to storm off anyway, Atkins diplomatically suggested to Debord that the ICA director wanted the text of the talk to be as authentic as possible and that the audience was quite prepared to wait. At this Debord collected his papers and with the other Situationists marched off to the podium in the main hall.

The opening part of the talk was given by Maurice Wyckaert, who was quite drunk and, having explained that 'Situationism' doesn't exist, continued in a continental Hegelian jargon which was largely incomprehensible to the expectant audience. He finished aggressively, with a threat: 'The Situationists, whose judges you perhaps imagine yourselves to be, will one day judge you. We are waiting for you at the turning.' He then staggered into the audience. There was a silence as people realised that the talk had finished. Finally, nervously, a question was asked. 'Can you explain exactly what Situationism is all about?' a man asked in cultured tones. Wyckaert looked severe; Debord's features darkened as he finally spoke. 'We're not here to answer questions from stupid cunts,' he said quietly. And with that the Situationist delegation filed out. The whole event had of course been most carefully stage-managed and on the way back to Paris was declared a great success.[3]

Algeria

According to Henri Lefebvre it was at this stage in their evolution that the Situationist International began to most closely resemble a sect or 'micro-society' with Debord at their head. Jacqueline de Jong's description of Debord as 'a kind of Jesuit priest' was now particularly apt and did not seem to her or others close to Guy a particularly healthy state of affairs. Even close fellow-travellers such as Lefebvre were careful to keep their distance. 'I was never part of the group,' said Lefebvre. 'I could have been, but I was careful since I knew Guy Debord's character and the way he had of imitating André Breton, by expelling everyone to get at a pure and hard little core [. . . .] There were some outer groupuscules, satellite groups which is where I was [. . . .] It's rubbish. It was really about keeping oneself in a pure state, like a crystal. Debord's dogmatism was exactly like Breton's. And what's more it was dogma without a dogma, since the theory of creating situations, of the creation of situations, disappeared very quickly, leaving behind only the critique of the existing world, which is where it all started with the *Critique of Everyday Life*.'[4] Whenever the conversation turned towards a critique of the existing world of politics and everyday business, Debord would quietly restate the principle that the primary task of the avant-garde was to pre-empt and animate a new civilisation, and that all else was pure commodity. And so political commentary, in conversation as well as in the pages of *L'Internationale situationniste*, would be kept to a bare minimum.

Algeria was different. It was impossible to preserve any detached stance in the face of the violence which was about to explode over the next two years in the streets of Paris. The Algerian crisis provoked a variety of reactions amongst the Situationists themselves, most of whom found it difficult to reconcile their stated position of distance and indifference towards official government with the actual struggle taking place on the streets of Algiers and Paris. This was not yet, however, a revolutionary struggle: in the eyes of the Situationists, too many reactionary traditional Leftist forces were involved for this to be possible. The Situationists thrived on the atmosphere of conspiracy and counter-conspiracy which the crisis had brought to the streets of Paris: they formulated a response to the increasing violence, arguing that the importance of the Algerian crisis was to expose the weakness of all contemporary Left-wing groupings and reveal their lack of revolutionary will. It was also clear that words were not enough. There was therefore a tacit consensus in the group which did not debar Situationists from actively becoming involved in political action, which meant collaboration with other groups.

The first and most important of these actions was Debord and Bernstein's signature on the second edition of the so-called 'Manifesto of the 121', a document dated 1 September 1960 and signed by 121 non-Communist intellectuals. The text was also known as 'The Declaration of the Right to Insubordination in the Algerian War' and, amongst other things, called upon the army to disobey orders to shoot Algerians. The first edition of the manifesto was published as a direct reaction to the French government's arrest of the philosophy teacher Francis Jeanson and other members of a small group, the so-called *réseau Jeanson* ('Jeanson network'), which had allegedly been handling funds for the FLN in Paris.

The text of this document was largely the work of Jean Schuster and Dionys Mascolo, both of whom Debord had so recently and so mercilessly reviled in print. Schuster had also not forgotten the 'cybernetic attack' launched on him by Debord at the previous year's meeting on the future of Surrealism. The text had been further revised by Gérard Legrand and André Breton, who obviously saw the document as reminiscent of the Surrealists' famous 1925 protest against the Rif War, 'Revolution Now and Forever', which praised Lenin's 'immediate disarmament' and called upon French soldiers to desert. The document included the signatures of Breton and every French Surrealist, as well as Jean-Paul Sartre and Simone de Beauvoir, the writers Maurice Blanchot, Michel Leiris, Marguerite Duras, Nathalie Sarraute, Alain Robbe-Grillet, the painter André Masson and film directors Alain Resnais and Claude Lanzmann. Despite its prestigious signatories, no paper or magazine would touch the document, refusing to print it on the grounds that it was unpatriotic or liable to provoke violent retaliation. This had some justification: the OAS was then moving towards the climax of a terror campaign which specifically targeted intellectuals. These included the likes of the Liberal-Left political scientist Maurice Duverger, who had a lecture at the Sorbonne interrupted by the crack of an explosion from a neighbouring street. Duverger finished his lecture and returned home to find that it was his own flat which had been reduced to smoking ruins by the OAS. Dionys Mascolo ran off two thousand copies of the document which he sent out as a personal letter to influential figures, whilst Sartre's *Les Temps modernes* published two blank pages and an explanation that the printer had refused to touch the manifesto. The tract was also handed out by protesters who blocked railway lines and boarded trains taking soldiers to the southern ports and Algeria.[5]

Official response to the manifesto was severe. Within a month twenty-nine of the signatories had been arrested on a variety of trumped-up charges, all those working as actors or performers had found themselves without work and unofficially blacklisted, and the Surrealist Jehan Mayoux was suspended from his teaching job. It was as a direct result of this manifesto that Guy Debord and Michèle Bernstein, previously well known to the local gendarmerie of the Latin Quarter as members of a cohort of drunken or drugged Left Bank layabouts, now found that they attracted the more serious attentions of the intelligence services as well as police officers whose first interest was in counter-attacking political subversion. Debord was himself taken away and interrogated on 21 November, declaring that he was not scared and would not be intimidated by authoritarian mediocrities. Although no legal proceedings followed, he was now a marked man.

Negationists and Situationists

The Algerian crisis also led the Situationists to some dubious contacts from the non-aligned Left which was apparently their own side. On 27 October Debord first came into contact with a certain Pierre Guillaume, who was then nineteen years old and living in his parents' flat near the Panthéon. Guillaume was a member of the groupuscule Socialisme ou Barbarie, a coalition of anti-Stalinist intellectuals who sought a 'third way' beyond the orthodox Marxism of the French Communist Party. Guillaume had been asked by the leaders of the group to sound out Guy Debord as a potential recruit. Guillaume had telephoned Debord, having acquired the number from a mutual friend, Daniel Blanchard, and asked Debord to meet him for a drink. Blanchard had been friendly with Debord for some months and they had even collaborated on a pamphlet, 'Preliminaries Towards Defining a Unity Revolutionary Programme', which argued in strict Situationist terms for 'a social totality', that is to say a revolution which aimed not at overturning present bureaucratic structures or hierarchical class division, but rather at dissolving them in a 'leap forward' to the new horizon of free thought and play. When Blanchard left Paris for his military service he entrusted the responsibility of maintaining contact with and possibly recruiting Debord to Pierre Guillaume. Guillaume set out to do this with a vengeance, having himself been recruited in the same way by Jean-François Lyotard, then a young philosophy teacher at the Sorbonne and a leading light in Socialisme ou Barbarie.

Guillaume and Debord first met in a bar near the Panthéon on their way to a demonstration against the war which started from the Mutualité. The meeting was amicable enough, drinks and pleasantries were exchanged, and despite losing each other in the ensuing mêlée of scuffles and police charges at Mutualité, it was not long before they met again and a cordial relationship was established. 'It was not long after this first meeting and memorable demonstration,' recalled Guillaume, 'through a coincidence which wasn't really a coincidence, I met Guy Debord with Michèle Bernstein on the *terrasse* of a small café which has now long since gone from the boulevard Saint-Germain, near the rue Saint-Guillaume. They had just visited an art exhibition which was being held on the rue du Pré-aux-clercs in the wine cellar of an apartment building. It turned out that this building belonged to the family of a childhood friend whom I hadn't seen for many years. I had just come across him with great pleasure. Like me, he had just 'come up' to Paris from the provinces to finish his studies. I had been invited to this exhibition and I had thought that the invitation had been sent to me by this friend. In fact it had been sent to me by Debord and the Situationists. When I met Guy Debord and Michèle Bernstein at the café *terrasse*, I had already been to the exhibition the night before, but I didn't know that they had some kind of relationship with this artist, aside from the fact that they had just come out of the exhibition, which explained why they were there, apparently waiting for me.'[6]

Over drinks, Guillaume explained to the Situationist pair that he was indifferent to artistic activity, which he considered a form of decadence and a sign of capitalist society's decomposition. This opinion had been confirmed for Guillaume by the way in which the artist whose exhibition they had visited had painted an apparently blasphemous image of Christ; this was ridiculous and boring, he said, only in a society where religion still had a residual value could blasphemy have any meaning. The Situationist couple couldn't have agreed more. The friendship was cemented and the trio saw more and more of each other, either in the *quartier* Saint-Germain, or more often at Debord's new drinking headquarters, the Cinq Billards near place de la Contrescarpe (an erstwhile haunt of the International Letterists). It was as a direct result of this friendship, according to Guillaume, that over the next year or so Debord began to frequent meetings of Socialisme ou Barbarie, attending debates held at the café Le Tambour and editorial meetings at the group's headquarters at Bastille, as well as contributing ideas to the group's newsletter *Pouvoir ouvrier* ('Worker Power'). Debord was clearly breaking the cardinal principles of the Situationist International, which excluded members for even speaking to members of another group. There was however much in the theoretical content of Socialisme ou Barbarie, the group and the journal, which attracted Debord.

Socialisme ou Barbarie had been founded in Paris in 1949. The two leaders of the group were Cornelius Castoriadis and Claude Lefort. The group had been founded as an attempt to build on Trotsky's description of the Soviet Union as a worker's state which had been 'deformed' by the rise of a bureaucratic hierarchy, 'a parasitic stratum'. For the members of Socialisme ou Barbarie, the Soviet Union, with its class system and systematised exploitation of labour, was 'worse than feudalism' and only a mirror image of its capitalist counterpart, the United States. Until their demise in 1965, despite internal divisions, they argued consistently that the way forward lay in neither a planned economy nor the accumulation of capital, but rather a concrete and visible improvement in the quality of daily life which would be marked by creativity, harmony between man and nature, meaningful work, and the end of alienated activity.

This clearly resembled many of the ideas which Debord was himself currently developing in the pages of *L'Internationale situationniste* and which were reaching a genuinely international audience that had been anticipating a truly new revolutionary theory. For Guillaume, however, it was also clear that many Situationist ideas reaching this audience were coming from Socialisme ou Barbarie. 'I couldn't say when Guy Debord actually joined the group, but on the 20 December there were serious strikes in Belgium. After the strikes in East Germany in 1953, and especially the extraordinary uprising in Hungary in 1956, where the workers' councils played a leading role, we had no doubt that the Stalinist regimes would collapse and we were waiting for the awakening which would allow us to "hang Maurice Thorez [leader of the French Communist Party] with the guts of Benoît Frachon [leader of the CGT trade union]" . . . I am sure of that date when Debord resigned. It was on the evening of 22 May 1961, during a three-day international conference . . . Debord participated in the debate and then announced his resignation to Chaulieu, Castoriadis, then Lyotard and then to everybody. Chaulieu tried to stop him leaving. Debord listened without saying a word. Then he said, "Yes, but I don't feel up to the task" and also "It must be very tiring organising a revolutionary organisation". He came to the next meeting at Le Tambour and paid his dues, said that he thought that it was a good thing that the group existed, that he had learned a lot, and then disappeared.'

Debord was intrigued by the group's belief that autonomy, on an individual and a collective level, was the key to massive social change. This is indeed the guiding notion behind most of the pieces in *L'Internationale situationniste* in the period 1960 to 1961, a period during which Debord first began contemplating moving the group's activity from an 'artistic phase' to a more 'political phase'. The challenge of the Algerian crisis had provided a way into political engagement; the problem now was how to continue this engagement according to the theory of situations, the paradoxical theory which Lefebvre described as a 'dogma without dogma'.

Negations

It was not the fact that Guillaume was involved with Socialisme ou Barbarie which made him such a dangerous acquaintance. Indeed it was not until Debord was nearing the end of his life that the full extent of Guillaume's duplicity became known. Guillaume is known in some Parisian circles as a notorious liar and manipulator ('a Neo-Nazi anarchist traitor', according to Philippe Sollers). He is even more notorious now as the owner of La Vieille Taupe bookshop (named 'The Old Mole' after Marx's famous description of 'the old mole' of revolution; the shop, which was on the rue des Fossés de Saint-Jacques, is now closed) and publishing house which specialised in 'revisionist' or 'negationist' works of history, that is to say works which, either in the name of the anarchist Left or the neo-Nazi Right, deny or denounce the death camps as Jewish propaganda. The most famous of the books sponsored by Guillaume was published in 1980 and called *Mémoire en Défense – contre ceux qui m'accusent de falsifier l'histoire. La question des chambres à gaz* ('Testimony in defence: Against those who accuse me of falsifying history. The question of the gas chambers'). It was written by Robert Faurisson, lecturer in French literature at the University of Lyons II, who specialised in 'demystifying' texts. Most bizarrely, this book was prefaced by Noam Chomsky, whom Guillaume had inveigled into writing a plea for freedom of expression. Since then, Guillaume has published a prodigious number of books, pamphlets and tracts, claiming the mantle of Paul Rassinier, a former socialist and *résistant* who was deported to Buchenwald during the war and who in the 1950s 'crossed the line' from 'rouge' to 'brun' and became the author of a series of rabidly anti-Semitic texts which are cornerstones of contemporary 'negationist' thinking. In 1989, Guillaume appropriated Debord to the 'negationist' cause, citing sections of Debord's work *Commentaries on the Society of the Spectacle* in his publication *Annales d'histoire révisionniste* ('Annals of revisionist history') in support of his notion that the Nazi death camps never existed and on 'the central role of Auschwitz in the spectacle'. Guillaume not only quoted two unnamed former Situationists as offering 'discreet support' for these ideas, but also argued that because Debord never attacked La Vieille Taupe, nor Faurisson, nor any other 'revisionist' text, that Debord tacitly supported the 'revisionist' cause.

When Debord was safely dead in 1997, Guillaume published *Les Mythes fondateurs de la politique israélienne* ('The founding myths of Israeli politics') by Roger Garaudy, the veteran Marxist philosopher turned 'islamiste' (also 'a crappy Stalinist', according to Debord). The book was immediately banned and Guillaume and Garaudy brought to trial in Paris for 'incitement to racial hatred' and 'complicity in crimes against humanity'. I noticed in Paris that the trial attracted a curious hotchpotch of onlookers in the public gallery from across the 'rouge–brun' spectrum: pro-Palestinian militants (the book was a best-seller in the Arab world), well-known activists from far-Left groups (some of them hiding their faces in scarves), the curious public and – objects of fascination to journalists present – the monstrous and distinguished 'négationnistes' Robert Faurisson and Henri Roques. Most bizarrely, as he made his case for Garaudy's thesis of the 'false myths of a martyrology of deported Jewish slaves',[7] Guillaume cited Debord's 1989 text *Commentaries on the Society of the Spectacle* and thereby called on the late Guy Debord, the implacable enemy of falsified history, as chief witness in the case for the defence (the trial rumbled on until 1998 when Guillaume and Garaudy were found guilty as charged and fined a substantial sum).[8]

It is of course impossible to know from this distance whether Debord was, as Guillaume claims, a fully paid-up member of Socialisme ou Barbarie or simply a fellow-traveller. Lefort, Castoriadis and Lyotard are now all dead whilst other members offer wildly conflicting accounts. What is sure is that Debord did see in Socialisme ou Barbarie interesting and useful parallels to Situationist activity – the collaboration with Canjuers is only one example of this – but also that Debord under no circumstances would have accepted the discipline of another organisation. He did not accept Lefebvre's authority for a minute, although for a while he admired him a great deal, and there is no reason to believe that lesser lights such as Castoriadis or Lyotard would have inspired anything like the same admiration. Conversely, there is no real tangible presence of Situationist ideas which can be detected in any of Socialisme ou Barbarie's writings during or after the time that Debord sought to build a common plat-form with Canjuers, and an even less discernible presence in the later writings of Jean-François Lyotard which, focusing on mainly theoretical questions of space, identity and meaning, are all now well established in the post-modern canon. The final suggestion made by Guillaume, that Debord might have supported 'negationist' texts, is both laughable and desperate. In his lifetime, according to those who knew him best, Debord did not denounce Guillaume because he didn't think it was worth doing so. On a more personal level, Michèle Bernstein, as the descendant of *émigré* Russian Jews, had taught Debord a few hard lessons about anti-Semitism.

More precisely, in the early part of the 1960s the Algerian crisis had polarised French society, and the Situationists were not immune from these tensions, their consequences and the dangerous friendships which were made in the heat of battle. What the Situationists had learned, from their brief flirtation with other groups and their involvement in street demonstrations and other protests, was that it was more necessary than ever before to spend the coming years defining and refining what it meant to be a 'Situationist'.

PART THREE

Attack by Fire!

1962–72

In fire attacks, one must respond to the changing situation. When fire breaks out in the enemy camp, immediately co-ordinate your action from without. But if the enemy troops remain calm, bide your time and do not attack at once. When the fire reaches its height, follow up if you can. If you cannot do so, wait. If you can raise fires outside the enemy camp, it is not necessary to wait until they are started inside. Set fires at suitable times.

Sun Tzu, The Art of War

Where there was fire, we brought gasoline.

Guy Debord

CHAPTER 15

No Dialogue with Cunts

1961–2

As 1961 drew to a close, Debord was growing visibly impatient with the content of *L'Internationale situationniste* and those who formed the hard core around the journal. The organisation was now run by a 'Central Council' which consisted usually of the current editorial board of the journal and which met sporadically in any number of European locations. The job of the 'Central Council' was to define and enforce a 'general line' which all Situationists were forced to respect and adopt. Anybody could in theory become a member of the Central Council as long as they were committed Situationists. As yet, however, Debord had failed to recognise a sufficient level of commitment in all but his small retinue of most trusted comrades and it was evident that the Situationist International, if it did not change or harden its position, would be no more than just another artistic, and therefore worthless, avant-garde.

There had nonetheless been worthwhile efforts in 1961 and 1962. Most notably in late May Debord had given a lecture to a research group convened by Henri Lefebvre under the auspices of the prestigious Centre nationale de la recherche scientifique. The title of the lecture, 'Perspectives on conscious modifications in daily life', was pompous and academic enough to please Lefebvre's research students. The content was however an undiluted call to arms in the name of a revolutionary transformation. 'Everything depends,' Debord argued, 'on the extent to which you dare to ask this question: how do you live? How are you satisfied? Not satisfied? This must be asked without for a minute letting yourself be intimidated by the various adverts which are aimed at persuading you that you are happy because of the existence of God, Colgate toothpaste or the CNRS.'[1] With Lefebvre's agreement, Debord did not attend the session and the lecture was delivered 'cybernetically' on a tape recorder to heighten the alienating processes which was the central theme of the talk. Both Lefebvre and Debord declared the talk a great success. Similarly, the screening of *Critique of Separation* in Paris in February had attracted warm critical notice, which despite Debord's feigned indifference marked a further incursion of Situationist theory into the public domain.

The ranks of the Situationist International had also grown in number and now included representives from over nine countries. These new members included the Hungarian Attila Kotanyi, Jacqueline de Jong and, most significantly, a young Belgian schoolteacher of philosophy, Raoul Vaneigem, who, having been shown a copy of *L'Internationale situationniste* by Kotanyi and having already contacted Henri Lefebvre ('Guy, I know a young Belgian poet who is full of ideas,' is how Lefevbre had introduced Vaneigem), wrote excitedly to Debord to express his joy at the 'new possibilities' offered by the Situationists. Vaneigem, like many others, was invited to Paris, where he was vetted as to suitability as a Situationist comrade. Vaneigem was accepted and soon became a key member of the group.

During the same period Constant, aware that divisions between himself and Debord were soon to make a target for polemical attack (the word 'technocratic' was being ominously used of him in conversation), felt compelled to resign. 'I am still not sure if that is what happened. You couldn't understand everything in the Situationist International,' he commented some forty years later.[2] Pinot-Gallizio, much to his surprise, found himself excluded in the same month on the grounds of his love of art. Most importantly, in the wake of Constant's resignation in the spring of 1960, Vaneigem and Kotanyi (who also lived in Brussels) were responsible for the Situationist International's 'Bureau for Research into Unitary Urbanism', previously the fiefdom of Constant.

The first signs of Debord's increasing discontent with the organisation showed at the fifth conference of the Situationist International held at the end of August 1961 in Gothenburg. Having spent so much time with Jorn in Denmark and Sweden, Debord was perfectly at home in Scandinavian countries, despite not understanding a word of any of the languages he encountered and the slow and reluctant progress he made with his English. Gothenburg in August was a city of water and light, easy cafés and cosy bars. Over preliminary drinks, however, the Germans and Scandinavians sensed that Debord was not his usual charming self, although his alcohol quota was steadily maintained, and that something was about to happen.

Debord was indeed on the offensive even before the conference began. His main targets were the Germans of the SPUR group and Jörgen Nash, the younger brother of Asger Jorn. There had always been a fierce sibling rivalry between Jörgen and his elder brother, mainly centred around the fact that the younger man had never quite managed to get his own artistic career off the ground. The pair had nonetheless collaborated amicably enough on projects, even publishing a text together under the auspices of the SI in Copenhagen in 1960. Jorn had however decided to take his leave of the Situationist International a few months before the Gothenburg conference. The split was one of the most amicable in the annals of the group and Jorn agreed to continue funding the organisation with the proceeds of his painting. Debord had explained to Asger, during a marathon drinking session in Copenhagen, that he felt that the group needed to move into a harder, more political phase where theory could be matched by action. It was not enough to play pranks on professors and subvert research seminars and exhibitions. It was time to see if Situationist theory could keep its promises of revolution, and translate that theory into operations on the streets. Debord envisaged riots, revolutionary festivals, perpetual agitation. ('Our time no longer needs to draft poetic agendas; rather, it needs to execute them,'[3] Debord wrote, explaining this period). Jorn admired Debord's courage and they together planned a separate project, a journal called *Mutant* to protest against the proliferation of nuclear technology (no issue was ever written or published). But Jorn, aware that he was primarily an artist and not an urban guerrilla, tacitly withdrew from the fray, pledging cash, support and allegiance (indeed Debord and Jorn remained close friends until Jorn's death in 1973).

Nash was alone at the Gothenburg conference and quite unprepared for the broadside that Debord and his cronies, Vaneigem and Kotanyi, launched against him. The idea was to purge the group of all artists and artistic tendencies. Against Nash's wishes a resolution was passed declaring the production of any work of art as 'anti-Situationist'. The SPUR group, whose energies had hitherto been concentrated on subverting the art establishment from within, found the ground pulled away from beneath them. Alex Trocchi, now back from the United States, was in on the plot to purge the group and, from Paris, sent a message of support to Debord. The 'Nashist conspiracy', as they were called by the French and Belgian Situationists, found themselves completely isolated.[4]

The Hamburg Theses

Nash's first reaction was to retreat and lick his wounds. The atmosphere in Gothenburg had been nasty; the promise of physical violence had not been very far away.[5]

Debord, Vaneigem and Kotanyi travelled back to Paris via Hamburg, where they embarked on a three-day drinking spree in the most appealing quarters of the city. They drank mostly around the docks and in the red-light district, the Reeperbahn, not only the base for the Beatles, Rory Storm and the Hurricanes, Swinging Blue Jeans and other young English rockers, but also home to a thriving 'beatnik' or 'existentialist' youth culture which modelled itself on the Parisian scene. The Situationists produced from this alcoholic brainstorm a text for internal circulation, 'The Hamburg Theses', which, with later additions from Trocchi in Paris, according to Debord himself, were much more extreme than anything which they had produced before. 'The Hamburg Theses' stated that 'specialists of thought, logic, language and artistic language, of dialectics and philosophy, had generally abandoned or had not inherited the principal themes, results, historical ambitions, courage in critical judgement, methodological hopes, dreams and desires of their predecessors.'[6] The debate in the SI in the past year or so had been between culture and revolution. For Debord the two could not be separated, indeed culture did not exist if it was not revolutionary. It was intolerable, therefore, that Situationists should be involved in making art which, by definition, belonged to the dead cultural order. Situationists, argued Debord, should not seek to make art but rather build new forms of communication. It followed from this that all artists were now to be ruthlessly purged from the ranks of the SI. Only in this way could total freedom, that is to say absolute revolt and the negation of all social forces, 'the construction of situations', be achieved in action. This was 'the realisation of philosophy', an activity which Debord stated would now replace for Situationists the making of art as a central goal.

The storm to come was however some way off in 1961 and 1962. The first priority was to establish the Situationist International as a fighting force. It had already been decided in Gothenburg that the SPUR group, or 'Spuristes', were not only surplus to requirements but that they were an actual threat to an organisation which needed to be as tight and compact as possible in order to negotiate all future hazards. The situation had been confused by the fact that all six issues of the journal *Spur* had been seized and confiscated by the Munich police as 'possibly subversive and obscene material' and the 'Spuristes' threatened with jail. Before they could be called to trial, the group decamped to Drakabygett in Sweden, where Jörgen Nash had a farm and a safe refuge. In Paris Debord signed the petition in support of his German comrades, who did not suspect that another menace awaited them.

In February 1962, Debord, Vaneigem, Kotanyi and Uwe Lausen, a former member of SPUR, launched their attack. They presented the other members of the Situationist International with an ultimatum which demanded the expulsion of all members of SPUR on the grounds that they had 'systematically misunderstood Situationist theses'. Appalled by this backstabbing, Jacqueline de Jong, Jörgen Nash and another Scandinavian Situationist Ansgar Elde dashed off a tract, 'Danger! Do not lean out', which described Paris as 'a seething cauldron of sorcery, plots, OAS assassinations, strikes, police informers, torture',[7] where even in the Situationist International it was 'brother against brother'. Unsurprisingly, when SPUR were finally kicked out in March 1962, de Jong, Nash and Elde went with them. 'I was disgusted,' said Jacqueline de Jong, who at this point refused to cede way and went on to found her own influential journal *Situationist Times*. 'We were lied to and tricked and it was all in the service of one man, Guy Debord, and his sense of self-importance. It was a betrayal and although I no longer care about Guy Debord at all, I am still angry at that disgusting treachery.

When I saw Debord in the street later on in Paris, during the time of the riots, it was I who turned away.'[8]

Responsibility for the Scandinavian section was handed over to a certain J. V. Martin, who immediately set up a journal, *Situationisk Revolution*, with Jorn's money and Debord's guidance. In the meantime, from his farm in Drakabygett, surrounded by the wounded and like-minded 'Spuristes', Nash defiantly announced the formation of a Second Situationist International which would devote itself to problems of art, architecture and urbanism. 'He was definitely a mad hippie. Debord was not wrong there,' Jacqueline de Jong said.[9] The Parisian politicos were megalomaniacs, Nash declared, only the New Imaginist Bauhaus, which would be set up under collective conditions in Sweden, could rightfully claim the title 'Situationist'. From Paris, the 'real' Situationists snorted with contempt and continued with their plans to further 'politicise' the movement.

There would now be fewer purges in the coming year, although Kotanyi, co-author of 'The Hamburg Theses', soon found himself thrown out on the grounds of 'rotten ideology' whilst Pinot-Gallizio was quite shocked to find himself excluded as an 'art lover'. The shift in tactics was announced by the pamphlet 'No Dialogue with Suspects, No Dialogue with Cunts', which, although published at the beginning of 1963, was in fact a résumé of the plans announced at Anvers in the summer of 1962. This shift towards action also meant pushing the editorial line of *L'Internationale situationniste* in a more explicitly political direction, eschewing theoretical or critical pieces on art or aesthetics in favour of statements upon present conditions. At least to begin with most of these statements were not too far away from the positions being held by Socialisme ou Barbarie, although Debord had not acknowledged his membership of the group nor admitted any kinship in thought to his Situationist comrades. In the pages of *L'Internationale situationniste*, the Situationists declared themselves against the Soviet Union, China and any other bureaucratic system which refused to concede the supreme power of the proletariat. They declared the Hungarian insurrection of 1956 to be one of the few authentic political events of the post-war period and had only contempt for the 'Stalinist' French Communist Party, whose craven complicity with Khrushchev's brutal suppression of the putsch with Red Army troops and tanks was shameful and morally disgusting. Eastern Europe was an empire built on an illusion, a fact which everybody knew but few had the guts to point out. Meanwhile, the ongoing bitter relationship between France and Algeria was not so much a post-colonial struggle, a war between a decaying capitalist power and its slaves, but a conflict between competing ideologies, one based on tyranny and the other on freedom. The political situation within France was a mirror image of this conflict. A total collapse of all social meaning, it followed from this, could not be far away and the Situationists exulted in this. Above all, what drew these strands of political analysis together was that they were all defined by the key term 'spectacle', which did not simply mean mass media representation of events but rather an agglomeration of forces, capital, state, media, which conspired to create a distance between ordinary people and the political events of their period.

This distance, the Situationists argued, could only be breached by people taking control of their own lives and situations. In part, like the members of Socialisme ou Barbarie, the Situationists owed much to György Lukács and Karl Korsch, who in the 1920s had done a great deal to disentangle the Hegelian-Marxist tradition from the Soviet model by emphasising the role of the subject and subjectivity in determining class consciousness. This was diametrically opposed, both Lukács and Korsch asserted, to 'the scientific rationalism' of the Soviets, which they and the Situationists excoriated as deterministic dogma.

There was a distinctly millenarian aspect to Situationist thought, which was at least in part the result of Debord's reading of the historian Norman Cohn's classic book *The Pursuit of the Millennium*, an account of how 'the subterranean revolts' of dissident religious groups, the Anabaptists, the Brethren of the Free Spirit and other heretics, at the end of the first millennium had sent shock waves through the structure of medieval society which were still being felt today. Their story exemplified the purifying and liberating forces of absolute negation as the motors of history; Debord was also impressed by its French title, 'Les Fanatiques de l'Apocalypse', 'The Fanatics of the Apocalypse', which struck him as a useful metaphor for the Situationist International.

Arguments

Debord also wanted to position *L'Internationale situationniste* as the most important purveyor of ideas in Paris. The first step towards this was to set up the journal as the replacement for *Arguments*, the most influential and prestigious forum for French ideas which had stopped publishing midway through 1962. *Arguments* had been founded by the soon to be distinguished figures of Edgar Morin, a sociologist (and part-time cinema critic), and the philosophers Roland Barthes and Jean Duvignaud. Its aim was to conduct research and discussion in the Marxist tradition, but away from 'the shipwreck of Stalinism'. Other figures included Kostas Axelos, who was interested in the influence of Martin Heidegger on currents in Western Marxism, and a floating group of radical intellectuals, many of them from Eastern Europe, who sought alternative strategies to the Soviet model.

Debord knew that Henri Lefebvre, who was also a contributor to *Arguments*, was a good friend of Axelos and, as soon as news of the journal's death was imminent, he began to pressurise Lefebvre to bring his influence to bear on a replacement. 'The idea had come up to stop editing *Arguments* because several of the collaborators in the journal, such as my friend Kostas Axelos, thought that its role was over, they thought they had nothing more to say. In fact I have the text by Axelos where he talks about the dissolution of the group and of the journal. They thought that it was finished and that it would be better to end it quickly rather than let it drag along. I was kept informed of these discussions. During discussions with Guy Debord, we talked about this and Debord said to me, "Our journal has to replace *Arguments*." And so *Arguments'* editor, and all the people there had to agree. Everything depended on a certain man [Herval] who was very powerful at that time in publishing: he did a literary chronicle for *L'Express*, he was also in with the *Nouvelle revue française* and the *Éditions de minuit*. He was extremely powerful and everything depended on him. Well, at that moment I had broken up with a woman very bitterly. She left me and she took my address book with her. This meant I no longer had Herval's address. I telephoned Debord and told him I was perfectly willing to continue negotiations with Herval, but that I no longer had his address, his phone number, nothing. Debord began insulting me over the phone. He was furious and said, "I'm used to people like you who become traitors at the decisive moment." That's how the rupture between us began, and it continued in a curious way.'

There was also, inevitably, a personal dimension to this fractious break-up. Lefebvre continued: 'This woman Eveline, who, I forgot to mention, was a long-time friend of Michèle Bernstein, had left me, and Nicole took her place, and Nicole was pregnant. She wanted the child and so did I: it's Armelle. But Guy Debord and our little Situationist friends sent a young woman to Navarrenx [Lefebvre's country house] over the Easter vacation to try to persuade Nicole to get an abortion. [. . .] Can you believe that this woman, whose name was Denise and who was particularly unbearable, had been sent to persuade Nicole to have an abortion and leave me in order to be with them? Then I understood. Nicole told me about it right away. She told me, "You know this woman is on a mission from Guy Debord; they want me to leave you and get rid of the kid." So, since I didn't already much like Denise, I threw her out. Denise was the girlfriend of that Situationist who had learned Chinese, I forget his name [René Viénet]. I'm telling you this because it's all very complex, everything gets mixed up; political history, ideology, women . . .' Despite this acrimonious situation, to assuage Debord, Lefebvre invited him and Bernstein down to Navarrenx to work on an article entitled 'You will all be Situationists'. 'We worked together day and night at Navarrenx, we went to sleep at nine in the morning (that was how they lived going to sleep in the morning and sleeping all day). We ate nothing. It was appalling. I suffered throughout the week, not eating just drinking. We must have drunk a hundred bottles. In a few days . . . and we were working while drinking. The text was almost a doctrinal résumé of everything we were thinking about situations, about transformations of life; it wasn't very long, just a few pages, handwritten. They took it away and typed it up, and afterwards thought they had a right to the ideas. These were the ideas we tossed around on a little country walk I took them on. With a nice touch of perversity, I took them down a path that led nowhere, that got lost in the woods, fields and so on. Michèle Bernstein had a complete nervous breakdown, she didn't enjoy it at all. It's true it wasn't urban, it was very deep in the country.'[10]

Michèle's 'nervous breakdown' had however less to do with the rural environment than with the fact that her period had just started, a particularly heavy one, and she had run out of sanitary protection. Despite the Marxist professor's enlightened views and Guy's revolutionary opinions, women's monthly cycles were both taboo and a mystery. Michèle laughed uproariously and then pronounced, 'It took a woman's menstrual cycle to show the limits of Situationist theory!'

CHAPTER 16

Gangland and Philosophy

1962–3

The purges of 1961 and 1962 left the Situationist group as a tight unit which operated in a more flexible manner and was more closely focused upon the political implications of Situationist theory. This did not mean a diminution of Situationist activity, but rather a shift towards more provocative and confrontational forms of action. One of the pranks which had particularly irritated Debord of late was the 'commando raid' launched by the Scandinavian section of the SI upon the famous statue of the 'Little Mermaid' overlooking the harbour of Copenhagen (the stunt was finally blamed on Nash or 'Nashist gangsters'). The exhibition of Situationist art organised by J. V. Martin at Odense in Denmark, 'Destruktion af RSG-6: En Kollectiv Manifestation af Situationisk International' in June 1963, was to be the last Situationist intervention in the artistic and presaged a new seriousness of intent. The final proof that the group had become sufficiently hardcore to sustain itself through the coming period of political struggle was that the Central Council which had summarily dealt with 'Nashist gangsters' and their artistic friends had no role any more and was duly dissolved. Debord himself had provided the Odense exhibition with five pieces, a series of 'Directives', which heralded the future direction mapped out in the 'Hamburg Theses': they included the messages 'Abolition of Alienated Work', 'Realisation of Philosophy', 'The Overcoming of Art'. These 'Directives', Debord had decided, would play a guiding role in the SI's development of a new series of positions in which debates about art had been definitively abandoned in favour of strategic political manoeuvres.

Spies for Peace

The exhibition in Denmark was, unlikely as it may sound, a work of homage by the Situationists. The inspiration was the activities of a direct action group in England called Spies for Peace. This group included the English anarchist Nicholas Walter (later of the *TLS*) and seven others who are to this day anonymous. Spies for Peace, having decided that marches and protests were not enough, set out to expose the British government's secret plans in the event of nuclear war. Their most daring act was to break into a secret government headquarters, called the Regional Seat of Government Number 6, or RSG-6, and, this in the days before photocopiers or internet, photograph or copy as many documents as they could, and finally distribute 3,000 of them. These, in an act of provocation well worthy of the Situationists, were posted to newspaper offices and the houses of celebrities. There were soon demonstrations at RSG-6 and news headlines in England and elsewhere. The police made several arrests, whilst newspaper columns fulminated against foreign agents, moles and traitors. The Spies for Peace had, however, covered their tracks well, throwing the typewriter they had used into the Thames and, wearing gloves, posting the documents from postboxes all over London.[1]

In Odense the Situationists distributed a tract, *Destruktion af RSG*-6 with the cover of the Spies for Peace text *Danger! Official Secret – R.S.G. 6*. Debord's principal contribution to the exhibition was however a theoretical piece, 'The Situationists and the new forms of action in politics and art'. The main thrust of this piece, faithful to the 'Directives' of the Odense exhibition, was that it was the first task of any contemporary revolutionary project to define itself against its own period. This meant the development of a critical theory which actively engaged with its era ('the overcoming of the thought of Hegel and Nietzsche, or the realisation of philosophy,' as Debord put it); the 'abolition of art', by which Debord meant the destruction of outmoded forms of representation or expression which did not contradict the 'technology of separation' which was the dominant characteristic of modern capitalism; and the strategic positioning of an avant-garde group against enemy forces, against what was already being referred to as the 'society of the spectacle'.[2] Debord also gave wholehearted approval to a group of 'revolutionary students' in Caracas, Venezuela, who had earlier that year launched an armed attack upon an exhibition of French art organised by the French embassy, stealing five paintings with which they set out to bargain for the release of imprisoned comrades. This form of operation, argued Debord, was the only way to make art of the past seem important.

The end of the Situationist International's 'artistic phase' did not mean, however, that Situationist propaganda and agitation came to a halt. If anything, Situationist activity veered even more towards the direct engagement with the enemy, which Debord now claimed to have always advocated as the guiding principle of the group. One of the first targets was Henri Lefebvre who, having disappointed Debord by failing to secure the substantial financial support of the publisher of *Arguments* for *L'Internationale situationniste*, found himself reviled in a tract as a vile plagiarist of the Situationist International.[3] The basis of this accusation was that Lefebvre had used notes on the Paris Commune, drawn up by himself, Debord and Bernstein during the ill-fated stay in Navarrenx, to illustrate the main points of an article he was writing for *Arguments*. The violence of the rhetoric took even Lefebvre, who was well used to the partisan politics of the Situationists and their set, by surprise (he was insulted as, amongst other terms, 'a hare-lipped Stalinist'). Most unpleasantly, he was accused of deliberately tricking the Situationists in order to dilute their work, although all he had done was to offer hospitality and as much moral and intellectual support as he could. From the Situationist point of view, with their only link with academe broken, all university intellectuals were now fair game.

Zeng! Zeng! Zengakuren!

In the spring of 1963, Debord and Bernstein met with T. Kurowaka and Toru Tagaki, who had been sent to Europe from Japan by the Tokyo-based student group Zengakuren to make contact with like-minded organisations in the West for propaganda purposes. Since the end of the Second World War, the Japanese Left had admired European, indeed mainly French, models of revolutionary action (French intellectuals had always been accorded great distinction in Japan and, indeed, Japan's leading writer of the period, Yukio Mishima, although politically on the right, was a sensitive reader of Bataille, Pierre Klossowski and others in the French Marxist tradition, even penning an admiring article on Bataille for the *Nouvelle revue française*). The model of the Chinese Cultural Revolution was, however, much nearer to home for Japanese radical groups than it was for disaffected French youth. The combination of French theory and Maoist practice was an incendiary one and when student riots did occur in Japan, as they did in the mid-1960s, they were bloody and more ferocious than anything which had been seen hitherto in the West.

Zengakuren represented the All-Japan Federation of Student Self-Government Associations. It had been founded in 1948 under the influence of the small but resolute Japanese Communist Party which, disgusted by Nagasaki and Hiroshima, was fiercely anti-American and pro-Soviet, and later, with the same verve and violent passion, pro-Chinese. By the end of the 1950s the group had split itself into several competing factions who all agreed on only one thing; they opposed Western capitalism and the Vietnamese war with the same venom. The leading faction, called Minsei (Democratic Youth League), which had the support of 65 per cent of the membership, was implacably pro-Communist. The pair who met with Debord and his supporters in a café in the Latin Quarter were members of the groupuscule called Sampa Rengo (Three-Faction Alliance), which was sceptical of Moscow, were supporters of the 1956 Hungarian uprising and who advocated violent resistance to all forms of state control.

As he admitted, Debord could obviously no more claim to be an expert on the nuances of the Japanese radical movement than he could confidently order a beer in Chinese. He was however flattered by the attentions of the Japanese delegation who had been sent copies of *L'Internationale situationniste* by René Viénet, a recent recruit to the ranks of the Situationists who was fascinated by political extremism in Asia (he was the 'Situationist who learned Chinese' whose name had slipped from Henri Lefebvre's memory) and who brought to the SI, as it left its 'artistic phase' behind, a hardline political nous and uncompromising guerrilla mentality.

As had been the case at the ICA in London, there were language difficulties (the Japanese apparently spoke appalling French) but Debord was willing to overlook these details in favour of wholehearted approval of Zengakuren's most extreme and dangerous actions, sanctioning the publication of a short piece describing Zengakuren 'commando raids' on American marine bases.[4] At the beginning of the 1960s Japan was undergoing profound social change. The impact of Western consumer goods and the lifestyle which accompanied them had led to a schizo-phrenic attitude amongst Japanese youth, who appreciated pop music, cinema, scooters and mini-skirts but were also violently anti-Western or anti-American, aware that a form of cultural colonisation was taking place which was every bit as damaging to traditional Japanese civilisation as the wars in Korea or Vietnam. The Sempa Rengo youth admired the Situationists for their use of the term 'spectacle' to describe the alienating effects of mass industrialisation. They were also impressed by Situationist insurrectionary tactics, ranging from the cultural terrorism practised in the pages of *L'Internationale situationniste* to the SI's more public attacks on art and popular culture, which were being developed to combat 'the spectacle'. In their turn, the Situationists congratulated themselves on providing a revolutionary theory which was truly international.

In the pages of *L'Internationale situationniste*, Debord often slyly mocked the notion that he was a megalomaniac by illustrating his most grandiose statements with apposite scenes from American science-fiction comic strips in which small élite groups either threatened to take over the world or were defending it from chaos. He was genuinely delighted that his theories seemed to be taking hold in the most far-flung and unlikely parts of the world (the Situationists during this period often cited the troubles in the Congo as further proof of their theories that the 'spectacle' of Western civilisation could not withstand a genuinely alienated and therefore revolutionary class of post-colonial, post-industrial 'workers').[5] The death of Marilyn Monroe, the Cuban Missile Crisis and the Profumo Affair were all cited in *L'Internationale situationniste* as proof of this thesis. Debord was particularly pleased with a 'detourned' poster made by the Scandinavian section of the famous shot by Tony Armstrong-Jones of Christine Keeler naked astride a chair in which she is given the words 'As the Situationist International has said, I'd rather be a whore than marry that fascist Constantin', a reference to a forthcoming royal marriage in Denmark.[6]

The shift in the Situationist International from its 'artistic phase' to its 'political phase', as defined in 'The Hamburg Theses' and implemented in the purge of members who had 'artistic tendencies', also saw Situationist rhetoric characterised by a new aggression which did not shy away from a threat of violence. They jokingly referred to the way in which the police saw them as potential gangsters. In the same vein, the expulsion of SPUR and the 'Nashist conspirators' had been treated in the pages of *L'Internationale situationniste* partly as a joke, but at meetings and during informal discussions there had been a palpable physical menace introduced by Debord. Debord had always been attracted to marginal, possibly dangerous groups on the edges of society and now often appeared flanked by toughs, some of whom were revolutionary comrades and others who were just drinking companions. One of the first things which had attracted Debord to Raoul Vaneigem was the philosophy teacher's stated ambition to bring together revolutionary theory with the nonchalant violence of *Les blousons noirs* ('the black jackets'), the bored suburban youth who like Britain's 'rockers' enjoyed motorcycles, leather and violence, displaying at all times a contemptuous disregard for the rest of society. Vaneigem was honoured to find himself pictured in *L'Internationale situationniste* in an aggressive pose alongside J. V. Martin with the caption 'Les épurateurs de l'Internationale Situationniste' ('the purifiers of the Situationist International'). The term 'épurateur' was a loaded one, with connotations of the 'épuration' which took place in Paris after the Liberation in 1944, when suspected collaborators were frequently shot without trial and women who had slept with the Nazi enemy tarred, feathered and spat at. Younger, newer and 'more political' Situationists, such as René Riesel, Rudi Renson and René Viénet, wore their hair long and greasy, sported dark glasses and leather jackets and feigned a thuggish demeanour. Debord too had changed physically. The constant drinking and erratic lifestyle had thickened his waistline and features, whilst the duffel coat and carefully tapered 'Roman crop' of the beatnik dandy had been discarded in favour of a tougher, more streetwise appearance. The revolutionary Situationists now deliberately courted trouble and it was not long in coming: Rudi Renson, sporting a long black beard and scruffy clothes, was arrested and refused entry to Denmark on the falsified grounds that he had no money or passport and 'a dirty look'.

'Mostly, I just walk around'

Debord's personal life was also undergoing great changes during this period.

The upheavals of recent years had meant that many friends had now left the scene, either excluded or sick of Debord's behaviour. The new 'political' comrades who now clustered around Debord were philosophically rigid, stand-offish and difficult to know. They could also be extremely boring. Michèle Bernstein, who had been complicit with the manoeuvres that had led to this new formation in the Situationist International, complained to Debord that although they had founded what seemed to be an effective fighting force, she was bored with the intransigent style and rhetoric of the new comrades. 'The new members after 1962 were extremely dry and dogmatic,' she explained. 'They had no sense of the wit or fun with which we had done things previously. They believed in revolution, which we all did, but in a way that made you sometimes hope that they were not going to have too much say in it. Guy was still himself at this stage, witty and arrogant, but he was flattered by these new people who looked upon him as a true leader. He had always been a leader before, but a leader amongst other extremely clever people. Only Vaneigem was clever amongst these new people. But now it was different, and I began to drift away, even though I knew interesting things were about to happen.'

Debord and Bernstein had been drifting apart for a long time. In part, this was due to the strain of living together as a couple who experimented with an open relationship but whose financial relationship was one of dependency. Michèle had moved on from writing horoscopes and was now earning good money as an advertising copywriter, with a growing reputation across Paris as a quick and skilful worker. The irony of the subversive activities of Guy Debord, sworn enemy of the mass media spectacle of the new consumer lifestyle, could hardly have been lost on the revolutionary couple, who justified Michèle's earnings to others as a form of *détournement*.

Debord was not in the least jealous of Michèle's burgeoning career. The sexual politics of the Situationist International were sometimes primitive ('I had to do all so-called women's work, from typing to cooking,' Michèle explained) but there was never any tension or doubt that the pair were intellectual equals. Debord was indeed immensely proud of the fact that Michèle had also published two novels, *Tous les chevaux du roi* ('All the King's Horses') and *La Nuit* ('The Night'), with the prestigious publishing house Buchet-Chastel. Although the works had made little impact on publication in 1960 and 1961, they have since acquired cult status on the Left Bank. When I asked her about the sexual ambiguity which is the central theme of the books she was vague: 'I don't know if I was bisexual then, even though I looked like a boy and was thought to be a dyke. Later I became more one way, and now,' she dismissed the subject with a flick of her cigarette, 'it seems an irrelevant matter to me.'

The two novels provide sharp insights into the inner life of the Situationist couple at this period. In *Tous les chevaux du roi*, Guy appears as Gilles, the revolutionary poet with 'something medieval about him'. The name Gilles for the Situationists evoked not only Ivan Chtcheglov, who signed himself Gilles Ivain, but also Gilles de Rais, who fought with Joan of Arc against the English before turning to necromancy and murderous paedophilia.

In Bernstein's novel Gilles reads the writings of members of Socialisme ou Barbarie and formulates his own theories on social space and the political meanings of poetry, the city, the passage of time. When he is asked what he is so busy with all the time, he replies 'reification'. 'It must be a lot of work,' his naïve young lover says, 'with lots of books and papers on a big table.' 'No,' replies Gilles, describing his activities in a phrase that would famously appear on the wall posters in Strasbourg in 1966: 'Mostly, I just walk around.'[7]

The characters of Gilles and Geneviève, the narrator, are quite clearly based on Guy and Michèle. They spend their time wandering around Paris, visiting galleries, talking and planning. Gilles, we are told, must shortly leave for Amsterdam to create a 'scandal'. At a dinner party given by older friends, probably with Surrealist sympathies, they meet a young girl, Carole, clearly based on Debord's real lover of the period Michèle Mochot, who enchants them by singing traditional French songs and playing the guitar.

Guy seduces Carole, whom he takes on night-time 'psychogeographical' wanderings through Paris ('Gilles knew how to reinvent Paris,' says Geneviève); Geneviève takes a male lover, then a female lover, and also seduces Carole.

Bernstein had borrowed the plot from Marcel Carné's film *Les Visiteurs du soir*, made in 1942. In this film, set in 1485, two young troubadors, Gilles and Dominique, are sent as emissaries of the Devil to wreak destruction upon the peaceful castle of the Baron Hugues. They do this by practising diabolical arts, singing enchanted songs and seducing and abandoning the innocent or the weak. The plot is a perfect allegory for the way in which the Situationist couple saw themselves putting the negative aesthetic of Situationist theory, which sought to subvert the language of the controlling social order, into practice in their own lives.

The second novel, *La Nuit*, written, Michèle claims, to make even more money (or to pay off the advance from Buchet-Chastel), revisits the familiar themes of adultery and polymorphous sexuality. The form of the novel is based on the strictures of the *Nouveau Roman*, then the prevailing fashion in France, which as practised by Michel Butor, Alain Robbe-Grillet or Nathalie Sarraute sought to replace conventional 'linear' narrative with a multiplicity of perspectives. The narrative is accordingly a disjointed series of inconsequential scenarios, mostly centred on Gilles and Carole's nocturnal adventures in Paris.

The real differences between Debord and Bernstein were not sexual. Within the closed society of the Situationist International affairs could be controlled and justifed in the name of experimental behaviour (there was even a slang term, 'marsupial', invented by Ivan Chtcheglov and used amongst the Situationists to denote an 'anti-woman', a sexually ambiguous individual).[8] Both of them were, however, growing restless with their domestic arrangements and feeling the need to move on.

Alice

In 1963 Debord, who had always assumed a 'droit de seigneur' within the Situationist group, deepened his relationship with Alice Becker-Ho, a strikingly beautiful young lesbian of mixed-race background, whose fiery character and intransigence reminded Debord of Éliane.

Alice was born in Shanghai on 6 August 1941 to a Chinese mother and a father from Alsace-Lorraine (annexed by Germany in 1871) who had joined the German Navy as a young man and ended up in the international city of Shanghai. At the outbreak of the First World War he had decided that he was French and, deserting the German Navy, found himself on the run. After the war he became a succesful financier in Shanghai, but when the Chinese Communists took over the city in 1947 he returned to France with his family.

When she first met Guy, Alice was twenty-one, an admirer of the militants of Socialisme ou Barbarie and delighted to be taken to dinner with Guy and Michèle by a mutual friend, Christian, whom Guy was advising how to avoid military service. Like the very real Michèle Mochot and the fictional Carole, Alice was seduced by the free-thinking and sexually playful Situationists. Within a matter of weeks Guy was sexually intoxicated with his young and beautiful lover, and soon after decided to move into Alice's tiny flat on the rue Saint-Jacques. Michèle was unperturbed, like her fictional self Geneviève, promising to withdraw somewhat from Situationist activity but still finance Guy's activities.

In the summer of 1999, the *Times Literary Supplement* had published an article I had written about the poetry of Alice Becker-Ho, a volume I had chanced upon quite randomly in the window of a shop in the rue Dauphine, devoured in a bar that afternoon, and written about straight away. I described the poems as an intimate communication with the dead lover, Guy Debord, and was struck by their stark, simple, hard brilliance.[9] Alice, in turn, had been startled by the article which had appeared about her in English, a language she does not read (she had been given the *TLS* by a friend from London). Suddenly I found myself invited to meet her at her apartment in the Marais.

The first thing that struck me about Alice was her shy and gentle manner. The apartment itself, in an eighteenth-century building in a quiet stretch of the northern part of the Marais, was elegant and spare. I was greeted by Jean-Louis Rançon and Patrick Mosconi, who had lived occasionally with Alice and Guy during his last years. It was early afternoon and Alice opened a bottle of burgundy. She proposed that we watch a recent video of Philippe Sollers defending Debord as one of the greatest thinkers of the century. Glasses were poured and we settled down to watch the film.

'Guy was a man who respected friendship,' she said later in our conversation. 'Friendship is a gift which can't be given back, although it can be taken away. That was what Guy said was its force, it was a kind of love which has its own power.' 'Was Guy a good friend to those who knew him?' I asked. 'Yes, he was,' she said, 'because he was always ambiguous, always aware of what the friendship meant and what it could mean. Ambiguity, in sex and politics, is a force also.'

'Who are the Situationists?'

The war against the spectacular society had to be continued, despite the shift in domestic arrangements in 1963, and indeed it was about to move into a new phase. In the *Times Literary Supplement* of 2 September 1964, there appeared an article penned by Michèle Bernstein which described the activities of the Situationist International who 'recruited only geniuses for the avant-garde task'. 'Among the first intellectual groups which have had a chance to get to know them,' she wrote, 'the usual reaction is to ask if the Situationists are serious or if they are utterly mistaken and destined for unparalleled depths of stupidity. The Situationists can guarantee that none of these doubts will be tenable in a hundred years' time.'

Michèle had been asked to write this article by Debord because she had the best English and because she was considered the best writer in the group. The political philosophy she announced in the *TLS* was pure Debord (she predicted a future in which art had been abandoned and work abolished). The tone was pugilistic and confrontational, entirely in keeping with the deliberate creation of a 'Situationist mythology'.

This set the perfect tone for the books which Debord, Vaneigem and Renson were currently writing, and which Bernstein described to the readership of the *TLS* as 'the only basis for a new definition of the revolutionary ideal in our time'. An article by Jörgen Nash, 'Who are the Situationists?', which was printed in the *TLS* alongside Michèle's piece was of course studiously ignored by the Parisians.

CHAPTER 17

The Situationist International
Anti-Public Relations Service

1964–5

I do not have the space here to explain what situationism is. It suffices, for the moment, to know that it is a way of contemporary thinking, like surrealism, dadaism, existentialism etc.

> Pierre Puttemans, *La Gauche*, 20 December 1962

This Situationist movement, called to revolutionise our era, was born in 1959 in a cellar in Schwabing. . . .Their 'ideas' have created adepts across frontiers and situationist groups will soon be founded in Paris, in Zurich, in Brussels and in Tel-Aviv.

> *Germinal*, 6 March 1962

Their principal activity is a soaring mental derangement . . . In the maximum of possible languages, the Situationist International spreads from abroad letters stuffed with the filthiest of insults. In our opinion the Munich judiciary has been too kind to them in handing out prison sentences and fines.

> *Vernissage*, no.9–10, May–June 1962

It was with unrestrained delight that Debord published in *L'Internationale situationniste* the above selection of texts from a variety of countries describing the Situationists. 'These selected quotations,' he wrote acidly, 'are in pursuit of an Oscar of Fantastic Confusionism, that the SI will one day award.'[1] The fact that the Situationists had established themselves as a troubling and mysterious presence across Europe was one source of satisfaction for Debord. Another was the way in which the forces of media, capital and state, which the Situationists had decided to take on, were so deeply ignorant and confused about the nature of this movement which might or might not be called 'Situationism'. Now two years into their political phase it was of crucial significance that the SI made an impact on the outside world.

For those with the patience or intellect to read the SI journal, the message was quite clear. In the article 'Technique du coup du monde' ('How to take the world'), Alexander Trocchi made it clear that they wanted nothing short of total war on contemporary culture, a war which would change the world. 'Revolt is unpopular,' he wrote. 'It is easy to see why. As soon as it is defined one provokes measures to contain it. An intelligent man will avoid defining himself as a rebel, which could be his death sentence. Moreover it is so limiting. We have no desire to seize the State, like Trotsky or Lenin, but to take over the world, a necessarily more difficult passage, as well as being more general and more gradual, less spectacular. Our methods will vary according to the empirical facts we meet here and now, there and later . . . taking over the world must be in the largest sense cultural.'[2]

It was this combination of megalomania, irony and intransigence which so confused the outside world. 'Confusionism' was by now a favoured term of contempt amongst the Situationists about the so-called 'Situationist Revolution'. What was overlooked or misunderstood was that they were also deadly serious in their belief that a tiny group of revolutionaries could bring the state, even the world, to the brink of being dissolved by making the right strategic moves as in a game.

This belief was their most effective weapon. As he was working out this theory and its implications, Debord developed his interest in war games, an interest he had held since childhood, found confirmed in Huizinga and which now provided a mirror for his theory of revolution as a game. In 1964, he was already working out the rules of his own invented war game, which he would publish as a text some thirty years later. In *L'Internationale situationniste* a small announcement appeared, under the rubric of the 'Situationist International Anti-Public Relations Service', which asked readers 'to verify objectively (in your own interests as well as ours) how near you come to our problems, and your ability to play a full role in our undertaking'. Readers were then invited to develop and destroy a chosen Situationist position. 'This is not a meaningless game,' the announcement warned.

The exclusion of Trocchi

The new, harder edge also effected Situationist propaganda. *L'Internationale situationniste* 9 of August 1964 reported on worldwide insurrectionary activity, from Prague and Czechoslovakia to Japan and Nigeria. Approval was given to all forms of apparently random violence, including that of the so-called *blousons noirs* in the Congo with their phantasmagorical guerrilla tactics (they were profoundly superstitious and believed that their leaders travelled at night in tiny aeroplanes and that they could be instantly transported from place to place), and three young French students who had been given stiff prison sentences in Barcelona for planting bombs.

Amongst the Situationists' most successful international efforts that year was a tract, 'Spain in the heart', which was distributed clandestinely in Madrid, Barcelona and the northwest of the country. It contained 'detourned' images of erotic pictures, illegal, subversive, popular and widely distributed in Franco's Spain, of naked young women, reclining and spouting revolutionary slogans such as 'There's nothing better than fucking with an Asturian miner. That's what I call a man!'

Debord was however less enthusiastic about avant-garde activities which escaped the remit of the SI. In September 1964 Alexander Trocchi was about to leave the Situationist fold for good. Although Debord had approved 'Technique du coup du monde', he had published it with the mitigating comment that Trocchi was no longer speaking for the SI or acting as a Situationist. By the second half of 1964, Trocchi had friendly relations and planned collaborations with such leading figures of the Anglo-American 'underground' as Colin Wilson, Timothy Leary, R. D. Laing and Allen Ginsberg, to whom he explained his 'Project Sigma', the 'invisible insurrection of a million minds' which he claimed would lead to a total transformation of human life. The curious, the fanatical and the drugged were fascinated by this charismatic poet who had something of a junkie Calvinist minister about him.

It was Trocchi's friendships which made his position even as a fellow-traveller of the SI untenable. Debord had nothing but contempt for the beat generation and 'beatniks': the burgeoning 'underground' scene and its leaders who preached love, peace and understanding were 'mystical cretins', unworthy of even serious scorn. Trocchi, however, was different. He had understood the Situationist project, but misunderstood its methods. 'Guy thought that the world was going to collapse on its own, and we were going to take over,' Trocchi said, remembering the point of his exclusion. 'I wanted to do that, to take over the world. But you can't take over the world by excluding people from it! Guy wouldn't even mention the names of the people I was involved with, Timothy Leary, Ronnie Laing. I remember the last letter he sent me: "Your name sticks in the minds of decent men." He was like Lenin; he was an absolutist, constantly kicking people out, until he was the only one left. Ultimately it leads to shooting people, that's where it would have led, if Guy had ever "taken over". And I couldn't shoot anyone.'[3]

Trocchi was permanently excluded in the autumn of 1964. His subsequent career saw him follow a zigzag trajectory through abortive projects, heroin addiction and a precarious living selling rare and antiquarian books in West London. 'Project Sigma', the plan which would transform the world, was left in dusty cardboard boxes in Trocchi's Kensington flat.

Theoretical man

Both Debord and Vaneigem had been hard at work on two key theoretical texts since late 1963. In her *TLS* article of 1964, Michèle Bernstein had indicated as much by referring to forthcoming Situationist texts which would mark a major shift in worldwide consciousness. Vaneigem, it was well known in Situationist circles, saw himself as less of a theoretician and as more of an agent of revolution, a provocateur in the old nineteenth-century Anarchist sense. Debord, it was equally well known, was at work on a project which would clarify the relation between the SI and the outside world in terms which would both resist the 'confusionist' propaganda of the internationl press and, more than this, offer a new analytical vocabulary which would redefine the way we thought about the world.

Debord began to use the word 'spectacle' with increasing frequency around the middle part of 1963. The term had been first used in print in *L'Internationale situationniste* 3 in 1959, in an article probably penned by Guy Debord, which gave rare approval to Alain Resnais' film *Hiroshima mon amour*. This film, scripted by Marguerite Duras, had caused a stir on its release when its unconventional treatment of a Franco-Japanese love story had led to its being dropped as France's official entry at that year's Cannes Festival, apparently on the grounds that it was too uncommercial, too literary and too political for American tastes. The film's visual content was uncompromising. The famous opening shots of the film present a montage of images of Hiroshima and the wounded, fragmented bodies of its inhabitants, intercut with images of a couple making love. These are accompanied by Emannuelle Riva's elliptical, stilted commentary. There is an essential separation between voice and image which marks out the film's theme of memory and dislocation.

It was precisely this aspect of the film which pleased Debord, who saw this deliberate disassociation of text and image as being in line with the various Situationist strategies that sought to 'reduce the cinema to nothing'. This technique, he wrote, marked a leap forward in the development of the 'cinematographic spectacle of the world' towards 'free cinema', a cinema which, like the 'free jazz' currently espoused by Ornette Coleman and John Coltrane, sought to extend the limits of the art to breaking point. 'It is likely that then', Debord wrote, 'the freedom of the cinema will be superseded, forgotten, in the development of a world where the spectacle will no longer be dominant. The fundamental feature of the modern spectacle is the representation of its own ruin.'[4]

The term 'spectacle' was here used for the first time not only to denote visual representations of the world which denied or distorted its reality, but also an ideology which shaped that representation. The phrase, as it was now being used by Debord, came from Nietzsche. In his first book, *The Birth of Tragedy in the Spirit of Music*, Nietszche had argued that the origins of all modern forms of thought lay in the realisation that life could not be truly represented in art.

This separation between art and life, for Nietzsche, had a political dimension. More specifically, it was traditionally argued by contemporary commentators that the 'chorus' in Greek tragedy represented the mood and will of the people. This, argued Nietzsche, was patently untrue, indeed an impossibility in a community which had not yet begun to conceive of political relations in terms of democracy or equality. The chorus were then passive spectators of a process in which they could neither participate nor act upon. 'What kind of artistic genre,' wrote Nietzsche, prefiguring Situationist positions on art, 'could possibly be extracted from the concept of the "spectator", and find its true form in the "spectator as such"? The spectator without the spectacle is an absurd notion. We fear that the birth of tragedy is to be explained neither by any high esteem for the moral authenticity of the masses nor by any concept of the spectator without a spectacle: and we consider the problem too deep to be even troubled by such superficial considerations.'[5]

The realisation of this separation, according to Nietzsche, was the moment which heralded the arrival of 'the second spectator' who was no longer passive or controlled by events. This 'second spectator' was also in this sense what Nietzsche called 'the theoretical man', the artist who was able to announce a break with the past and imagine the future. Towards the end of his life Nietzsche also began to use the term 'spectacle' to denote the lack of real meaning in the passing events of modern life. 'A riot or a newspaper in a big city are both deep down no more than "spectacle", an absence of authenticity,' Nietzsche wrote in a fragment from 1880, prefiguring early definitions of what the Situationists termed the 'modern spectacle'.[6]

Debord had come to Nietzsche partly on his own initiative and partly because Nietzsche was one of the more unorthodox sources often quoted by Henri Lefebvre. Like Martin Heidegger, his great contemporary interpreter, Nietzsche occupied an uneasy position in France and his followers were open to accusations of proto-Fascism. Such was the case with Georges Bataille, France's most important disciple of Nietzsche in the twentieth century, whose attempted anti-Nazi collaboration in the 1930s with André Breton, *Contre-attaque*, broke up in acrimonious circumstances with Breton accusing Bataille of 'sur-fascisme'. Nietzsche was however quoted frequently and with approval in *L'Internationale situationiste* from its earliest days.

Fanatics of the Apocalypse

The publication of *L'Internationale situationniste* 9 in August 1964 also marked a new sense of ambition in the Situationist group. The editorial, 'Now, the SI', written by Debord, made it clear that the Situationist International saw itself as a world-historical force whose critique had an importance beyond present conditions. This mood prevailed precisely because the Situationists, uniquely as Debord thought, had managed to develop a critique which stood in clear and total opposition to all other forms of cultural or political debate and activity. It was from this starting point that the total war against modern society could be launched: 'The path of total police control over all human activities and the path of infinite creation of all human activities are one: it is the same path of modern discoveries. We are necessarily on the same path as our enemies, most often preceding them, but we must be there, without confusion, *as enemies*. The best will win.'

In his reading of Norman Cohn's *Pursuit of the Millennium* Debord had been fascinated by Cohn's descriptions of how, at the end of the first millennium, myriad cults had developed around the doctrine of 'chiliasm' in Europe. Most of these cults, Cohn argued, were at the forefront of a series of revolts which 'sent tremors through the massive structure of medieval society'. This was because they believed not in the inexorability of Christ's coming but rather that his presence had to be earned.

This much also applied to the Situationist revolution. 'Now that the Situationists already have a history and their activity has carved out a very particular but undeniable central role for itself in the cultural debates of the last few years,' wrote Debord, 'some people reproach the SI for having succeeded and others reproach it for having failed. In order to understand the real significance of these terms, as well as almost all the intellectual establishment's judgements concerning the SI, it is first necessary to reverse them. The SI's element of failure is what is commonly considered success, that artistic value that is beginning to be appreciated in us; the fact that certain of our theses have come to be sociologically or urbanistically fashionable; or simply the personal success that is virtually guaranteed any situationist as soon as he is excluded. Our element of success, which is more profound, is the fact that we have not clung to our original pilot programme but have proved that its main avant-garde character, in spite of some more apparent ones, lay in the fact that it had to lead further; and that fact that we have thus far been refused any recognition within the established order.'[7] It was this position as a phantom presence on the contemporary scene which permitted the Situationists to define their aims in the following terms: 'While contemporary impotence blathers on about the belated project of "getting into the twentieth century" we think it is high time to put an end to the dead time that has dominated this century and to finish the Christian Era with the same stroke. Here as elsewhere the road of excess leads to the place of wisdom. Ours is the best effort so far towards getting out of the twentieth century.'[8]

Situationist influence, despite this intransigence and visionary quality, was also seeping over into the mainstream. In 1964 Debord had published the scripts of his first three films as a book, *Contre le cinéma*, published by the Institute for Public Vandalism (an invented soubriquet for Jorn's activities) with a preface by Asger Jorn which argued that Debord was, in the tradition of Godwin or Shelley, a poetic disturber of the peace. Much to his annnoyance, however, Debord also discovered that *Contre le cinéma* was being read by young *cinéastes* such as Jean-Luc Godard as a programme for filmic innovation rather than a call to arms against the 'spectacular society'.

The first months of 1965 also saw the publication of two Situationist-inspired experimental novels, *L'Illusion tragique illustrée* by Jean-Pierre George and *Autopsie de Dieu* by his brother François George, by the respectable publishing house Juillard. The George brothers were both extremely young (François was only twenty) and had been in friendly contact with Debord and Bernstein since 1962, assuming the status of disciples but not Situationists.

Despite Debord's initial approval of both of these works, the pair were frozen out of all contact and even attacked in the SI journal as 'annoying disciples', 'incoherent' fools who were liable to a French form of the 'Nashist' virus. What seems to have offended Debord the most was the way in which Situationist theories had been discussed and written about in the press without any reference to their origins and context. 'Quite simply,' he wrote, addressing himself to the George brothers and also the world, 'we have nothing left to say to these people.'[9]

Letters from afar

Other events through the course of 1964 and 1965 touched Debord in a more personal way. The first and most unsettling of these was the sudden death of Giuseppe Pinot-Gallizio in February 1964 at the age of sixty. Pinot-Gallizio had not only been instrumental in the first years of the Situationist International in establishing and deepening links with the Italian artists who had gathered round Jorn at Alba and Albisola, but had also been an inspiring influence during the first period of 'artistic activity'. His texts on industrial paintings were now an indispensable part of the Situationist canon. The break with Debord, which Debord had initiated in 1960 on the grounds that both Pinot-Gallizio and his son Giors Melanotte were still too close to the commercial art world when Debord was preparing for the shift from artistic to political activity, had hit Giuseppe Pinot-Gallizio hard. Maurice Wyckaert remembered that a dinner with Michèle and Guy at their flat on the rue Saint-Martin a few days after the exclusion was interrupted by someone outside throwing stones at the window and shouting. Debord, who was well aware that it was the drunk, hurt and aggrieved Pinot-Gallizio, continued his meal as if nothing was amiss. 'I don't understand everything he does,' said Wyckaert, the besotted disciple, 'but I knew that he was right.'[10]

Pinot-Gallizio's death was reported in *L'Internationale situationniste* 9 with none of the customary vitriol which Debord poured on his former comrades. 'Certain aspects of his tastes, and above all the influence of those around him, made his participation in the SI difficult,' Debord wrote in what was almost a forgiving tone. 'Being personally very inventive he was the very opposite of the falsified publicity campaign of the Nashists. The origins of the Situationist movement owe him a lot.'

Both Debord and Bernstein had also been recently saddened by the deteriorating condition of Chtcheglov. They had visited him several times since his incarceration but had found it increasingly difficult to bear the depressing circumstances in which he found himself. Despite his illness, diagnosed as a variant of schizophrenia, Chtcheglov could be disarmingly lucid and engaging. 'I am making Situationist propaganda with the staff,' he wrote. 'Why not?'

The situation was grim, however. 'What else can I tell you, my dear Guy?' wrote Chtcheglov in letters which were published in the SI journal as 'Letters from afar'. 'I am sick. I am full of woes, four hundred wishes, hatred, delirium, imprecations, morbid and jealous desire, threats, the blows of childhood, prophesies of unhappiness, listen to your mother.' Debord compared Chtcheglov's incarceration to a political exile or banishment, but there was nothing more, other than printing these letters in *L'Internationale situationniste*, which could be done.

The year 1965 began with another, more violent shock. Since 1963 Jeppesen Victor (or more usually 'J.V.') Martin had been a singularly devoted supporter of the Situationist cause in Scandinavia, working hard at serious agitation which included deliberate provocations such as distributing 'detourned' erotic comic strips attacking the likes of well-known politicians or the Danish Royal Family as whores or fascists. Martin was therefore already well known to the police, who had received specific complaints about him from a Right-wing pressure group called Moral Rearmament, although the term 'Situationists' was by now known well enough in Scandinavia for the police to be already keeping a watchful eye on the likes of Martin and his dubious international pals. The baleful gaze of the watchful eye was intensified in March 1965 when, in the name of international co-operation, NATO decided that the German Army, for the first time since the Second World War, should practise manoeuvres on Danish soil. The area designated was Randers, a small town in Jutland which also happened to be the current residence of J. V. Martin, Denmark's most unpopular Situationist agitator.

When the German Army tried to enter Randers on the night of 16 March there were serious and violent confrontations between the police and demonstrators. Cars and lorries were stoned, tyres punctured and a military jeep stripped down. Martin was marked down by press and police as the ringleader. On 18 March, as he was leaving his house on Slogsgade, a bomb exploded, wrecking the house and its contents, which included paintings by Martin and Michèle Bernstein. Despite Situationist protestations that this was obviously a murder attempt by the far Right, the police arrested Martin himself, accusing him of staging a provocation. The plot thickened with the arrest of a mysterious figure known as Kanstrup, a mercurial figure who claimed to have infiltrated neo-Nazi groups under the aegis of the East German security forces. Kanstrup had clearly been working for the Danish police in the same way by attempting to infiltrate the Situationist-coordinated peace groups assembled in Randers. The fact that he had left a second bomb behind in a taxi only served to underline the amateurish performance of the Danish police.

Back in Paris, the riots, the bombs and general disorder were greeted with approving pleasure. Debord criticised the police and was angry and shocked about the apparent assassination attempt. He was, however, not surprised at police tactics, but welcomed the fact that the Situationists were now able to cause serious disruption on an international scale.

CHAPTER 18

Exit Far Left, The Mysterious Mr K

1965–6

Towards the end of 1965, Debord devoted himself to the manuscript of *The Society of the Spectacle*, which he worked on in Paris and in Cannes. Satisfied that the Situationists now had an international presence, he also pondered how the group's next move might up the stakes a little further.

He was at this point obsessed with the notion of the 'mass secret', a piece of falsified information whose patent falsity was no bar to its effectiveness. In July 1965, on holiday and drinking wine in Cagnes-sur-mer in the company of Michèle Mochot and a motley crew of transient friends – who, according to Michèle, included Frédérique Donnet, the waitress at a bar called Le Club, an Irish would-be writer called Brian O'Toole, Yvette Dieudonné, the owner of Le Club, a painter called Maguy Favrot and Michèle's sister Claire – Debord came up with the idea of conducting a small social experiment. 'We were bored,' said Claire Mochot. 'We were sitting on the *terrasse* of Jimmy's, on the place du Château de Cagnes, feeling gloomy, drinking wine. We had to come up with something.'[1] To general approval and applause from the dissolute and restless troupe, Claire came up with the idea of circulating a false rumour around the 'stupid village'. They gave each other secret names (Debord was 'Tungsten': others on the same theme of chemical hygiene were called Chloride and Fluoride) and under the guise of meetings they boozed long and hard into the Mediterranean night. A plot was hatched: Michèle and Claire were to make a hundred or so posters which warned the public to 'Beware of the Milk!' One early morning the conspirators fanned out across Cagnes-sur-mer with the posters and stuck them in prominent places (the painter Maguy desisted at this point, claiming it was 'too dangerous'). No milk was sold in Cagnes-sur-mer that day. Better still, the following day the conspirators were able to read in *Nice-Matin* that an entirely unconnected strike had broken out in the region's dairies. Thinking that the posters were put there as a public service the inhabitants of Cagnes were grateful that they had had early warning. Guy was not only amused, returning gleefully to Jimmy's Bar where he convened the succesful conspirators, but saw the incident as proof of his theory that an avant-garde group guided by a sense of adventure and intuition, with the weapon of the 'mass secret', could intuitively connect with disruptive currents in the wider world.

Theoretical positions

On the grounds that the Situationist group was in transition at this point, no issue of the journal appeared in the course of that year. Instead, Debord confined his activities to the collaborative publication of a series of anonymous pamphlets, the most incendiary of which was an analysis of the current situation in Algeria, *Address to Algerian Revolutionaries*, which encouraged revolutionaries to 'burn the Koran in public places'. To Debord's satisfaction, this tract was secretly circulated in Algiers and Oran by Mustapha Khayati, who had been introduced to Debord by a mutual friend, Béchir, in 1964 and who was in contact with pro-Palestinian underground movements in Paris and the Mahgreb.

In Paris, however, Debord was considering his own options. Seventy people had now passed through the Situationist International, but only Debord and Michèle Bernstein remained from the original eight who had gathered at Cosio d'Arroscia. Throughout the course of 1965, Debord assured himself and other members of the group that he had kept the promises of revolutionary Surrealism intact. A critical stage, however, had now been reached.

For Debord, the most important problem was to assert himself as the chief strategist of the group. He had long since been considered the group's leading theoretician, but he now wished to assume a leadership role which would allow him to steer the group from theory to practice. Although Debord had initiated most of the purges which had taken place since 1960, he was still a long way from being in a position of complete control.

In part this was due to the non-hierarchical structure of the group, a key principle of its organisation which made such a position an impossibility. It was also due, however, to opposed forces within the Situationist camp. Although, for example, his relationship with Bernstein was as close as it had ever been, she not only held considerable sway over the newer members of the group, but also had a personal charisma which made her a natural leader.

Similarly, Mustapha Khayati, who had only been in the group for a relatively short period of time, was a potential rival who commanded respect for his intellectual rigour, as well as his daring and imaginative nature. Raoul Vaneigem, having left Brussels to base himself in Paris, was another obvious contender for a leadership position.

It was an axiom of Situationist thinking that the conflicting personal and political positions of the group were to be reconciled in the realisation of theory. If the movement from theory to practice was to be successful, Debord thought, it had to be done in a way which would not compromise the group's theoretical position. This meant, in the first instance, that they had to rethink the organisational structures of the revolutionary movement.

Interventions

In *L'Internationale situationniste* of March 1966, the Situationists launched scathing attacks on all their old adversaries: the elders of the French Communist Party, Louis Aragon, Roger Garaudy and Louis Althusser, were predictably excoriated as 'cunts', 'priests' and 'faggots'. They also invented new enemies by denouncing friends and allies. A key target was Jean-Luc Godard, then the most famous and influential avatar of stylish Left Bank radicalism. Godard had privately praised Debord to 'situphile' friends and had even expressed the wish to make overtures towards the Situationist group. This had been reported to Debord who, not for the last time, insulted Godard in print as 'a cretinous Swiss cunt'. Graffiti which bore the legend 'Godard is the biggest Swiss cunt of all' appeared outside cinemas on rue de l'Odéon and rue de l'École de Médecine.

Having poured scorn on his enemies and opened fire on those closest to him, Debord then justified his scorched-earth tactics by declaring that the Situationist International was now ready to launch the next phase of their war against the spectacle on their own terms.

It was an irony, however, that, as Debord sought to distance himself from the cultural mainstream of the Left, his ideas were becoming fashionable currency in the Parisian radical imagination. More particularly, 'situationism', the term Debord despised as a simplification of his theories by the intellectual *petites têtes*, seemed to have become a catch-all term for a freewheeling bohemianism which allegedly allied the rigours of the French tradition of Marxism with the sexual philosophy of American-style Beatniks. Towards the end of 1965 the journal *Arts* published a piece about 'situationism' which managed to be mildy approving and patronising in equal measure. To their mutual disgust, Michèle Bernstein and Debord were singled out as a sexy 'intello' Left Bank couple, on the model of Jean-Paul Sartre and Simone de Beauvoir, who advocated revolution ('a hundred years too late') from their headquarters on the rue de Buci.

The corollary of this unwanted attention was that, despite its non-appearance in 1965, back copies of *L'Internationale situationniste* were eagerly sought after. The first issue of 1966, with the journal's rackety finances (it was still largely funded by Michèle Bernstein's professional activities) bolstered by its unexpectedly fashionable status, therefore had a print run of thousands rather than hundreds. This meant that, although it was sold in a handful of shops around the Latin Quarter and Saint-Germain-des-Prés, the circulation of *L'Internationale situationniste* was now far greater than any other equivalent publication. The journal's influence, moreover, could be measured by the fact that copies regularly reached London, Milan, Berlin and New York, where 'pro-situationist' groups were being set up. In the first issue of 1966, the Situationists proudly announced their affiliation to the Japanese radical 'autonomist' student movement, the 'heroic' Zengakuren, whose two leaders T. Kurowaka and Toru Tagaki had been impressed by Debord at their meeting in 1963. Debord insisted on publishing a photograph of *L'Internationale situationniste* translated into Japanese and available in Tokyo.

Debord's approval did not extend, however, to those bookshops in the immediate vicinity of his favourite drinking haunts which sold *L'Internationale situationniste* without the consent of the leadership. When Debord fell out with Pierre Guillaume, the owner of the bookshop La Vieille Taupe, and his former comrade in Socialisme ou Barbarie, a Situationist delegation was dispatched to the premises on rue des Fossés-Saint-Jacques to create 'a direct intervention' and seize any remaining copies of the journal.

Similar treatment was meted out to Francis Maspéro, whose bookshop on the rue Saint-Séverin was frequented by Louis Althusser, as well as his disciples from the École normale supérieure. Maspéro, who was also editor of the journal *Partisans* ('a horrible compromise between Stalinism and Trotskyism', according to Debord) which provided a first platform for soon-to-be luminaries Régis Debray and Jacques Rancière, had the misfortune to be denounced in person and in print as 'a Stalinist arsehole'. The term 'Maspérisation' also entered the Situationist lexicon and became, in future copies of *L'Internationale situationniste*, a favoured weapon in the Situationists' extensive armoury of abusive epithets.

Things

On a more serious note, Debord had been greatly offended by the young novelist Georges Perec. Until the mid-1960s, Perec was still an unknown who, aside from an occasional article for Maspéro's *Partisans*, had written little and continued to work as a humble archivist at the CNRS, the scientific funding council which, as a particularly austere outpost of the French Civil Service, could not have been further removed from the clamour of Left Bank politicking and avant-garde in-fights.

In 1965, however, Perec was taken by surprise when his novel *Things*, subtitled *A Story of the Sixties*, was awarded the Prix Renaudot, the second most important literary prize in France. Perec, who had failed his university degree and who was not yet thirty, found himself with a best-seller on his hands and, briefly, the talk of literary Paris. Perec was even more surprised when his book was almost immediately translated into Russian, Polish, Czech and Serbo-Croat and became a hit on the other side of the Iron Curtain, where it was popularised as an anti-capitalist parable.

Debord's anger, however, had been provoked by the feeling that Perec had plagiarised key Situationist ideas and stripped them of their political meaning. *Things* tells the story of Sylvie and Jérôme, two young market researchers, who are dazzled by the new consumer society of 1960s France. Although they are characters who have no political ideas they 'drift' through Paris, in imitation of the Situationist *dérive*, in a way which parodies and subverts the Situationists' own subversive techniques. Debord particularly resented the way in which these characters represented a generation whose existence was defined by 'the decor of the commodity-spectacle' but whose politics conformed to the Leftist shibboleths that the Situationists had sought to overturn.[2] More stinging still, Debord felt that he had been satirised.

In the pages of *L'Internationale situationniste* the group had presented a critique of advanced capitalist society which exposed the reality of the 'society of the spectacle' as total alienation. To see this critique turned into the object of satire demanded a response which not only demonstrated Debord's contempt for the 'commodity culture' of Georges Perec, Alain Robbe-Grillet, Claude Lelouch or Jean-Luc Godard, but which also laid down the Situationist rules of engagement.

Returning the gift

The seventh congress of the Situationist International was acrimonious even by the high standards of acrimony which the group had set from its inception. In a fractious atmosphere, which was not helped by the intense heat in the Paris streets of early July 1966, it began, predictably enough, in a café on the rue Brisemiche near the rue Saint-Martin and Les Halles, and with two expulsions.

Firstly, the Dutch Situationist Jan Strijbosch, who had aroused suspicion through his friendships with various members of Amsterdam communes linked with the Dutch Provos, was expelled for calling for the return of Rudi Renson. Renson, a Dane, had resigned a year earlier and could now only be considered – as Debord explained – as 'totally inactive' and, more obscurely, 'a case of a pure and simple disappearance'. Similarly, the Romanian Anton Hartstein, an earnest student of Hegelian theory who had come from Bucharest to study at the Sorbonne, had been unfortunate enough to ask Debord for clarification during a debate and was therefore excluded for 'theoretical insufficiency' and 'probable stupidity'.

The overall theme of the Congress was, ironically enough, unity. More specifically, the group had come together to discuss how they should organise themselves internally and what links should be established between the several international groups which were now appearing. The reason for this was that, although the group had now settled into a committed hardcore of twenty members who were mainly French and were based in Paris, it was necessary to ensure that the group maintained its pre-eminent role at the vanguard of international revolutionary activity. This was especially important as the group stood poised to enter its phase of 'practical agitation'.

Debord had been particularly inspired, in the summer of 1965, by the riots in the black ghetto of Watts in Los Angeles. The pictures of burning shops and wrecked cars were full of revolutionary potential. These were not simply race riots, he wrote in *Decline and Fall of the Spectacular Economy*, a tract which was quickly translated into English and distributed in New York in late 1965, but an insurrection provoked by disgust for the consumer society.[3] For Debord, the riots were a pure form of *potlatch*. Debord wrote that the blacks had taken the gift offered by the spectacular society and thrown it back in its face. In a festival of arson and looting, Debord told the Congress, they had created a pure situation which disrupted the controlling narrative of the spectacle.

The organisation of the Situationist group, unanimously agreed by the Congress at the final meeting of July, was predicated on two key principles informed by Debord's reading of the events in Los Angeles. Firstly, aside from the editorial committee of *L'Internationale situationniste*, whose work was necessarily dependent on the confidential handling of financial and administrative constraints, there was to be no secrecy or hierarchical structure. The group was henceforth to be considered a fighting unit which was dedicated to 'a unitary critique of the world' and the 'decolonisation of everyday life'.

Secondly, and most importantly, the revolutionary organisation, like the blacks who rejected the prizes of victory over the society of the spectacle by burning its gifts, the group vowed itself to 'a dialectic of negation'. In concrete terms, this meant that the group had to 'explicitly aim to dissolve itself as a separate organisation at the moment of its victory'. This was a key defining principle of Situationist strategy which, sooner than Debord had anticipated, guided the group's first direct hit on the French media.

Abolish everything!

In the spring of 1966, five pro-Situationist students at the University of Strasbourg ran for election for the presidency of the Student Union with a promise to wreck the institution by spending all its money. To their own astonishment, as well as that of the majority of the bored and apathetic student body who could scarcely be bothered to vote, the group of five, led by a pair of perenially squabbling would-be Situationists, André Schneider and Bruno Vayr-Piova, found themselves in power.

Although the five were more than ready to stay faithful to their election promises, and indeed, in their short spell in office, had proved remarkably adept at wrecking lectures, they found themselves unable to agree with each other on the best way of implementing their promises to destroy the university. They decided, therefore, to contact the Situationists who had originally inspired them, by writing to the box number which appeared in issue 10 of *L'Internationale situationniste*. A friendly reply was sent from Paris and, in due course, a delegation arrived from Strasbourg to meet with Debord and Mustapha Khayati in Paris in the summer of 1966, shortly after the seventh Congress.

Debord was not particularly impressed by the students, whom he considered naïve and hotheaded, nor did he care for Édith and Théo Frey, Situationist sympathisers based in Strasbourg, whom he was shortly to expel from the group for plotting against him. (Along with Herbert Holl, Jean Garnault, René Gailer and others, these were the so-called 'Garnaultins', named after Jean Garnault because he was apparently 'the most irrelevant member of the group', who like the 'Nashist gangsters' before them were accused of subverting the SI.) But he did see the potential of the situation. Immediately he set Khayati to the task of writing a pamphlet which would provoke an extreme response, possibly even violence, from the university authorities.

It was Khayati's idea to print ten thousand copies of the pamphlet in an elegant green jacket, which not only disposed of the entire funds of the local Student Union, but which would be credited to the Association fédérative générale des étudiants de Strasbourg (AFGES) and the Union nationale des étudiants de France (UNEF), the most important national organisations for students in France.

The autumn term in Strasbourg began with a series of carefully choreographed incidents which, although dependent on genuine student ire, were nonetheless carefully stage-managed by Debord from Paris. The university authorities, already suspicious of the *voyous* ('hooligans') in charge of the Student Union, had their fears confirmed by the charged atmosphere of tension and defiance which, although provoked by a floating hard core of only twelve or so pro-Situationist students, had now spread across the campus. Posters appeared, some of them inspired by the American anarchist group 'Black Mask', celebrating the rioting blacks of Los Angeles as revolutionary heroes. More disturbing still, students were not merely complaining to their teachers about the effects of the 'Loi Fouchet' (the recent reforms which had been introduced by the Gaullist minister Christian Fouchet to alleviate overcrowding in the universities), or the scarcity of books in the library, but challenging the intellectual and social authority of the university.

The opening shots were fired on 23 October at Abraham Moles, a Professor of Sociology, who was about to give his first lecture of the academic year, and found himself being verbally assaulted by the leaders of the Student Union, before being chased from the lecture hall by a posse of students throwing tomatoes.

It was not, however, the first time that the unfortunate Moles had been the target of Situationist scorn. As a researcher into the psychology of urbanism, he had been curious about Situationist ideas on the subject and, in 1963, through the intermediary of his friend and colleague Henri Lefebvre, had innocently written to Debord. Debord had immediately rebuffed him as a 'cretin' and 'pornographic daydreamer'. His humiliation in Strasbourg was, in Situationist terms, a well-executed and well-deserved act of cultural terrorism.

Events took a more serious and disturbing turn, at least from the point of view of the university, with the widespread distribution of tracts and pamphlets calling for the dissolution of all forms of authority. On 16 November, the journal of the AFGES, *Nouvelles*, devoted its front page to a communiqué from 'Black Mask'. The markedly pro-Situationist tone of the journal was even more evident in a critique of the Dutch provos, and support for Zengaruken.

Still more provocative was *The Return of the Durutti Column*, a series of comic strips depicting the student union takeover, designed by a pro-Situationist student, André Bertrand, which were plastered over the walls of the corridors of the university. The now famous pictures had a direct and powerful impact. They demonstrated the polemical force of the Situationist technique of 'detourning' advertising images: they included two cowboys discussing reification over a Marlboro cigarette; Lenin crying 'Fuck the Revolutionary Young Communists' and two toothbrushes discussing Anarchism. Most significantly, the comic strip paid overt homage to what Raoul Vaneigem called the Situationists' 'guiding light': the image of a ragged column of Anarchist troops in the Spanish Civil War, led by Catalan revolutionary and bandit Buenaventura Durruti (Durruti's name was misspelt in Bertrand's strip), 'going from village to village, destroying the entire social structure, leaving the survivors to rebuild everything from scratch'.

There was more to come. Bertrand promised in *The Return of the Durutti Column* that students would soon be able to procure 'the most scandalous publication of the century'. This was *On the Poverty of Student Life, considered in its economic, political, psychological, sexual and especially intellectual aspects, with a modest proposal for its remedy*, mostly written by Khayati, with amendments made by Debord in Paris. Although the main argument of this text was directed against the university and its humiliation of the student ('after the policeman or the priest, the student is the most universally despised being'⁴) it went far beyond its remit into Situationist theory and practice. There were predictable attacks on Godard, Perec, Althusser; there was praise for the insurrectionists of Berlin, Kiel, Shanghai and Barcelona; solidarity was expressed with Zengakuren and London-based radicals who produced the pro-Situationist newsletter *Heatwave*. Above all, there was the identification of the alienating force in student life as the spectacle of everyday existence. The student was therefore part of the 'new proletariat' which the spectacle had created and was constituted by 'all those who have no power over their lives and know it'. 'The student is a product of modern society, like Godard or Coca-Cola,' Khayati wrote, 'his alienation can only be contested by contesting the whole society.'⁵ The duty of the avant-garde, having made this critique, was 'to create a situation which made all forms of retreat impossible'. However, the 'new proletariat' would only give themselves to 'the game of revolution' if, like the Watts riots, it was 'a festival' in which transforming the world was an expression of poetry as well as politics. The pamphlet concluded with two principles of 'the revolutionary game' which, eighteen months later, would be daubed on the walls of the Sorbonne and flashed in news reports across the world: 'Vivre sans temps mort' ('Live without dead time') and 'Jouir sans entraves' ('Come without limits').⁶

'A little social experiment'

As promised by the students, this tract was published in a potlatch which consumed all the Student Union funds. On 22 November, the day of the official opening ceremony of the university, the representatives of Strasbourg's *haute bourgeoisie*, which included the Bishop of Strasbourg, the chief of police and the mayor, filed into the Salle Aula, the grandest lecture theatre in the Palais Universitaire, to be handed by smartly dressed members of the AFGES the elegantly bound copy of *On the Poverty of Student Life*. . . . When Maurice Bayen, Rector of the university, stood up to begin the inaugural ceremonies, there was mounting horror on the faces of the assembled dignitaries as it became clear that they had been duped by the very 'hooligans' they had sought to keep away. Worse still, in anticipation of the scandal they had planned, Schneider, Vayr-Piova and Khayati, wearing leather jacket and dark glasses, styling himself as 'K' and playing the role of 'adviser', had organised a press conference with three local journalists on 23 November, ostensibly to discuss the rising tension on campus.

It was Debord, however, who had a guiding hand in the events. Having ordered Khayati to stress that the SI played no active role in it, he nonetheless ordered that Situationist theory control events. Thus, in a dramatic *coup de théâtre*, Schneider read out the 'final communiqué' of the

AFGES which announced its auto-dissolution. The group had achieved its revolutionary goal and the game was over.

Students were now encouraged by their elected representatives to occupy the university and steal books and food, whilst the campus psychiatric clinic was declared a centre for mind control. Mayhem and chaos were unleashed in a 'revolutionary festival' which, in six short weeks of disobedience, brought the university to its knees. Such events were bound to attract media attention beyond Alsace-Lorraine.

The 'scandale de Strasbourg' began at a local level. *Le Nouvel alsacien* was outraged by 'Situationist beatniks' who had affronted 'the dignity of the city'. But very quickly it became a media firestorm which raged for several weeks in the pages of the national press. The betrayal of public trust and, most especially, the misappropriation of public funds outraged opinion. Above all, the consensus was that although it was evident that something was rotten in the French universities, there were darker forces at work which threatened – said Communist Party officials, politicians of the Left and Right, businessmen, professors, union leaders and priests – the very substance of Western civilisation. In *France-Soir* the students were described as 'ultra-revolutionaries' who led a shadowy conspiracy. *L'Aurore* of 25 November spoke of 'utopian anarchists taking control of the UNEF'. *Le Monde* on the same day referred to a mysterious political movement called 'international situationism'. 'How many are there?' asked *Le Républicain lorrain*. 'Where do they come from?'

Other news reports, much to the astonishment of Debord in Paris, compared the events to the 'happenings' organised by the Amsterdam Provos and San Franciscan hippies of Haight-Ashbury. *Le Figaro*, appropriately enough as the mouthpiece of the fiercely patriarchal Gaullist government, adopted a sterner tone and warned of the legal repercussions against the students, who threatened to waste all the annual turnover of the AFGES, which, as accumulated income from coffee bars, student canteens and travel offices, represented some two million francs.

The university, still reeling from the shock of the scandal, moved quickly against the students. On 27 November Maurice Bayen denounced them in the pages of *Paris-Presse* as 'psychiatric cases' and accused them of electoral fraud. There would be severe implications, he suggested, if this proved to be the case. The academic staff of the university were, in the main, behind him. A Professor Lhuillier declared to a packed lecture theatre, 'I am for freedom of expression. But if there are any Situationists amongst you, you can leave now.'[7]

However, despite Bayen's threats, and concerted efforts made by other student organisations as well as the *anciens* of the AFGES who had been unseated in the original election, it proved impossible, by legal means, to dislodge the pro-situ students from the non-occupation of the official positions. The chaos continued until late December, when, on the advice of deputy-mayor Paul Wach, Bayen placed the student union under the control of the courts and the five students were disbarred on the orders of a judge. In court, Judge Llabrador described the students as 'scarcely more than adolescents, lacking all experience of real life. Their minds confused by ill-digested philosophical, social, political and economic theories, and bored by the drab monotony of everyday life, they make the empty, arrogant and pathetic claim to pass definitive judgements on their fellow students, their teachers, God, religion, the clergy and the governments and political systems of the entire world. Rejecting all morality and constraint these students do not hesitate to commend theft.'[8]

'A little social experiment'

Guy Debord could scarcely have put it better himself. Indeed, despite Debord's earlier reservations about SI involvement with the Strasbourg affair, the court process itself, and the judge's comments, proved to be a spectacular propaganda *coup* for the Situationist group. Llabrador's comments were described by the Situationists as 'disarmingly lucid' and reprinted in various pamphlets. The British section of the SI translated Llabrador's text and published it in the tract *Ten Days Which Shook the University*, which was read as a radical manifesto as far away as the LSE and Berkeley.

In December 1966, the *Sunday Telegraph* in London published a piece which described events at Strasbourg in ironic terms and painted a lurid picture of international subversives, led by the leather-jacketed 'mysterious Mr K', travelling around Europe, fomenting rebellion in campuses and, more importantly from the point of the *Telegraph*, exciting the libidos of a generation of winsome revolutionary anarchist teenage-girl students. This was not at all how Debord had imagined the SI might make its first impact upon the world, but it did confirm his theses on the hall of mirrors which was the modern media spectacle. And it was Debord who, during a visit to Strasbourg in the company of Donald Nicholson-Smith, ordered Khayati to describe the Strasbourg affair to a perplexed *Telegraph* staffer as 'a little social experiment'.

The events at Strasbourg proved to Debord that the game of subversion, when taken to an extreme point, had the potential to overwhelm the controlling forces of the 'spectacularised economy' in 'a festival of unreason'. Strasbourg was more than just a student prank and this had been proved by the extreme reaction the students had provoked by literally throwing money away. The blacks at Watts were right: only by throwing the gifts of the consumer society back in its face can a revolutionary situation emerge.

There were however immediate and more pressing problems within the

Situationists' ranks which had no connection with the ambitious aims of Strasbourg events. Debord had been under attack from the far Left for some time. In January 1967 these same enemies had jokily distributed a fake Mass card signalling 'the death of Guy Debord, dead in the Situationist International, Strasbourg, 3 January 1967'. The expulsion of the 'Garnaultins' in the same month was a further mini-crisis which seemed to divert energy and resources away from the revolutionary momentum which Strasbourg had served to anticipate. It was clear to Debord therefore that the coming months were perhaps the most crucial in the shift from theory to practice which he had been actively animating since the Situationists had begun their political phase in 1962.

CHAPTER 19

Heatwave

1967

Although the events of the Strasbourg scandal were largely misunderstood by most people in France, who had until then never heard of the 'International Situationists' and their revolutionary strategies, it was apparent nonetheless to even the most casual observer that something serious was happening in the French universities. Most clearly, disaffected youth were now a force to be reckoned with. The mass media were not slow to react to this and the Situationists found themselves either cult heroes or the objects of public opprobrium.

One unexpected consequence of this new fame was that despite Debord's strident antipathy to the cinema, Situationist issues and arguments were now material for the big screen. In his feature film, *Brigitte et Brigitte*, for example, the young film-maker Luc Moullet took *On the Poverty of Student Life* as the source text for his story of two young provincial students who come to Paris and find themselves in a variety of difficult, potentially humiliating situations. Moullet had formerly been a fan of Jean-Luc Godard. He had however been fascinated to find in Situationist texts a preoccupation with daily life which mirrored his own preoccupations with the deadening effects of work and routine. These themes were also present in the most recent work of the great Jacques Tati, who although no reader or follower of ultra-Left theory was a sensitive and perceptive critic of the currents flowing through French society. His 1967 comic masterpiece *Playtime*, in which modern society and the mechanised city of Paris is mercilessly lampooned to the point of destruction, is in many ways a model of ludic Situationist subversion.

Closer still to the Situationist critique was Jean-Luc Godard, whose 1967 film *Weekend* painted a nightmarish picture of suburban *anomie* and the destructive power of the consumer spectacle. The Situationists were still vehemently against Godard at this point and Debord was particularly annoyed by the closing sequences of *Weekend* which portray a revolutionary organisation as a cannibalistic gang of terrorists quoting Maldoror and devouring each other. 'It was inevitable', said Debord when he heard that

Godard was off to London to film the Rolling Stones, 'that he should work with other cretins.'

In the pages of *Le Monde*, the Strasbourg students were publicly applauded in a petition signed by such notables as Henri Lefebvre, Alain Touraine and Jean Baudrillard. Olivier Todd, the future biographer of Albert Camus, then a hard-working young journalist, also wrote sympathetically of the events in Strasbourg for *Le Nouvel observateur*, a mainstream Left-wing publication. According to Todd, although the 'dada-marxist' arguments of the Situationists had something 'Lutheran' about them, they also represented the genuine sense of despair prevailing amongst young French people within or without the universities. Praising the pamphlet *On the Poverty of Student Life* . . . and the extremist tactics which brought the university to a halt, Todd declared 'there is definitely method in their madness.'[1] Even *Le Figaro littéraire*, a journal diametrically opposed to the politics of *Le Nouvel observateur*, thought that the Situationists might have a point. In a piece which reproduced key sections of the *Durutti Column* posters, Dominique Jamet quoted a young girl at Strasbourg: 'Oh, of course the revolution won't be made by the people at Strasbourg or youth alone. But there are periods when every person can take control of his life, when man goes beyond himself, when there is an abundance of ideas, of courage, of activity superior to what men seem capable of in other moments. The Commune, the Spanish revolution, Ukrainian anarchism, the Hungarian revolution are such moments. The meaning of an organisation like the Situationist International is to make the future possible.' In a prophetic coda Jamet added, 'And the young girl says softly: "We are vowed to great actions." She seems to believe it's true.'[2]

Internationalists

The events at Strasbourg had brought the Situationist International a notoriety which extended far beyond the borders of France and a momentum as a revolutionary movement which Debord rightly calculated would be difficult to stop or control. In Italy, England, Germany, Sweden and Belgium, all sorts of disaffected youths seized on the nomenclature 'Situationist', which in the wake of Strasbourg had acquired a glamorous, even dangerous, cachet.

In France, the years 1966 and 1967 were also dominated by British and American cultural influences which clearly had an ambiguous relationship with the 'spectacle'. In pop music, *Pet Sounds*, *Blonde on Blonde*, *Revolver* and *Sergeant Pepper* announced a new literacy and sophistication in a medium otherwise derided by so-called serious listeners for its cretinous style and content. In the cinema also, the recent films of Joseph Losey (*Accident*) and John Schlesinger (*Far from the Madding Crowd*) were acclaimed as artistic masterpieces.

Even more intriguing were the rumours filtering through to Europe of the New York avant-garde and its demonic guru Andy Warhol, whose icy aristocratic contempt and deliberately nihilistic attacks on the emptiness of the consumerist society and its 'spectacular' effects in cinema and art seemed exactly to match the Situationists' critique. In 1966, Warhol had just finished making *The Chelsea Girls*, his six-hour masterpiece of anti-cinema in which dykes, drug addicts, neurotics talked endlessly, pointlessly into and away from the camera. Although no one in Paris or Rome had yet seen *The Chelsea Girls*, it became an immediate legend across the continent and Warhol a hero of the revolutionary avant-garde. In Italy, Warhol was declared the inheritor of the mantle of Pasolini or Fellini; in France Warhol's work was seen as a savage indictment of the hollowness of contemporary life and his work an attack on all forms of its representation or 'spectacle', a term which had by now gained currency in avant-garde circles in New York and Europe, and which was about to enter everyday language.

The esteem was not reciprocated, however: Warhol apparently disdained Europe and few of the genuinely politicised members of European avant-garde movements were able to make headway in New York. The reason for this was a mixture of snobbery and genuine indifference to shifting trends in Europe. According to Brigid Berlin, heiress, best friend, confidante to Warhol and star of *The Chelsea Girls*, the European scene, and in particular the Situationists, were an irrelevance: 'We really didn't give a fuck, I didn't give a fuck,' she recalled. 'Our politics were certainly not those of the Left, and they never were at any point what you might call Democratic. We had nothing to do with any radicals, and certainly never had anything to do with the French. We were interested in, or at least Andy and I were interested in, fame, glamour, art and emptiness, not politics. We never mentioned it.'[3]

Pop art and pop music did however have a real social and political impact in France. In July 1966 the first edition of the rock journal *Rock & Folk*, the future bible of a generation of French rock fans, had hit the news-stands and given French youth their version of the much-admired British or American 'underground' scene. The films of Luis Buñuel (*Belle de jour*) and Roger Vadim (*Barbarella*), the 'pop art' collaborations of Serge Gainsbourg and Brigitte Bardot, similarly all contributed to the notion that sexual and political 'liberation' was truly in the air. This was, it seemed, not merely French but a truly global phenomenon. The two most important catch-phrases of the mid-1960s were 'the global village' and 'the medium is the message', both coined by the Canadian theorist Marshall McLuhan whose pamphlets *The Gutenberg Galaxy* (1962) and *Understanding Media* (1964) cheerfully predicted the end of text- or print-based culture. McLuhan's misplaced faith in the global village led him, despite his lack of understanding of the forces he was describing, to predict accurately the rise of a bland, homogenous culture which knew no national boundaries.

For many, the second half of the 1960s was also characterised by the slowly dawning nightmare of Vietnam, the launch of the Chinese Cultural Revolution, the Arab–Israeli Six Day War and, closer to home, growing discontent on campuses across Europe and the United States. In Amsterdam, the 'provos', with the former Situationist Constant in their number and taking Huizinga's *Homo Ludens* as the guiding theory of their revolution, set about disrupting the ordinary life of Amsterdammers through the course of 1966 and 1967. Their targets were the 'Provotariat', the bored youth of Amsterdam's grim suburbs who were numbed into passivity by television, work and a stultifying urban environment. In true Situationist fashion, no one could tell if the 'Provos' were serious or joking when they proposed 'the white chicken plan' to turn policemen into social workers or to abolish the 'asphalt terror of the motorised bourgeoisie' by giving away free white bicycles. They organised 'love-ins' and 'happenings' in a marijuana fug in Amsterdam's Vondelpark and ran candidates for the Amsterdam city council. Demonstrations, sometimes violent but mostly stoned and benign, were a weekly festival and a tourist attraction for would-be hippie students all over Europe.

For the Situationist International it was important to measure these seismic shifts in public consciousness against what they perceived to be, for good or ill, real political activity. They therefore took positions against both China and Israel on the grounds that they both represented a form of spectacular politics which excluded debate or dissent. 'The point of the explosion of ideology in China', penned by Debord, attacked the bureaucratic dictatorship and its French supporters – the fashion for wearing Mao collars amongst pop stars and Leftist intellectuals was then at its height – as dupes. Israel, or rather the Six Day War, was more complex and led to a row in Donald Nicholson-Smith's home near the Porte Saint-Denis in late 1967 when, annoyed by Mustapha Khayati's rigidly pro-Palestinian stance, Michèle Bernstein closed the evening by singing the Israeli national anthem.

Around this time Debord asked her to consider becoming 'clandestine' like Asger Jorn before. Her role was never again under discussion, although her presence was thereafter keenly felt: when he was asked about her role in the group's activities after 1967 Debord would reply enigmatically that 'Michèle has good advice'.[4]

'The Seeds of Social Destruction'

For Debord it was also important for the Situationist International to capitalise on its burgeoning international notoriety and extend its theatre of operations into the English-speaking world. Most importantly he wanted to penetrate America, home of Marshall McLuhan and the site of the Watts riots. Given, however, that Debord's English was at this stage somewhat primitive and largely incomprehensible to native English-speakers ('I don't think Guy thought that English suited his philosophy of the world,' commented Ralph Rumney. 'I think he thought it rather beneath him.'[5]) and that the rest of the group was not much better, it was important to recruit Situationists who could speak the language and negotiate the nuances of the Anglo-Saxon pop culture which looked set to take over the world.

Americans would have been useful. There were however few likely candidates amongst the dope-smoking draft-dodgers who had fixed on London as their cultural capital. In England the 'underground' went overground in July 1967 with a conference at the rock venue The Roundhouse under the title 'Congress for the Dialectics of Liberation' which would last two weeks and bring together representatives of the revolutionary Left and the emerging counter-culture. The Congress had been called by psychiatrists at Kingsley Hall, led by R. D. Laing whose reputation as a radical anti-psychiatrist was at its zenith, and delegates included veteran political theorist Herbert Marcuse, a hero of the German radical Left, and Black Power leader and convict Stokeley Carmichael. Allen Ginsberg, in a speech entitled 'Consciousness and Political Action', chanted a mantra insisting that the work of his friend and love object William Burroughs was 'one of the best analyses of the present consciousness existing in the West'.

The Situationists in Paris were deeply suspicious of the revolutionary claims made by what Debord called 'drug addicts and idiots'. He had long since given up on Trocchi, who was now spiralling into a crippling heroin addiction, as his emissary in the English-speaking world and he now set two young English militants, Chris Gray and Charles Radcliffe, who had been impressed by the copies of *L'Internationale situationniste* they had come across on trips to Paris, the task of spreading Situationist theory via their journal *Heatwave* which Debord had already seen and approved.

The title *Heatwave* was inspired in roughly equal parts by the Utopian notion of 'an explosion of revolutionary energy which would transform the face of the world', and demonstrating a nuanced pop sensibility which was entirely lacking from the Parisian Situationists. The cover of the first edition of *Heatwave* was a shot of riots on Brighton beach above the headline 'Seeds of Social Destruction'. Inside arguments were made in favour of *stilyagi* ('hooligans') in the USSR, the *blousons noirs* in France and Mods and Rockers in England as catalysts for change who, like Isou's 'youth front' almost a generation earlier, owed no allegiance to the existing social order. A review of Dave Wallis's novel, *Only Lovers Left Alive*, once mooted by Andrew Loog Oldham as a film vehicle for the Rolling Stones, described a future where adults have committed suicide by taking 'easyway' pills and youth has taken over.

Radcliffe had been associated with various libertarian or anarchist groups for some time, having already published several articles in the London-based journal *Anarchy*. With the tacit approval of Debord himself, Radcliffe and Gray declared in *Heatwave* that their aim was to 'transform in its totality the nature of human experience'. In conversation and in print, the pair impressed the Parisians to the extent that Chris Gray was given the daunting task of translating Vaneigem's key theoretical text, *Banalités de base*, into English (a rushed and rather approximate translation was extensively circulated on British campuses as *Totality for Kids*).

Two other young British Situationists, Donald Nicholson-Smith and Timothy Clark, who had arrived in Paris with parallel interests in Marxist philosophy and art history, had been inspired by meetings and a burgeoning friendship with Guy, Michèle and others, to set about the task of spreading the Situationist message to the English-speaking world. To this end they composed a pamphlet in collaboration with Gray and Radcliffe which they called 'The Revolution of Modern Art and the Modern Art of Revolution'. With a sophisticated wit and demonstrating a uniquely Anglo-Saxon pop vocabulary (The Who were quoted as exemplars of 'spectacularised revolt') they attacked all contemporary cultural phenomena, from William Burroughs to Pop Art, as con-tricks and rackets. Revolution, they argued, will come. This time, however, it would not be consumerism, fashion, pop or art which led the way but the 'juvenile delinquents' who refused to believe that modern life offered anything at all of value.[6]

'The Revolution of Modern Art' was circulated only amongst those who were already committed Situationists. In contrast, the English translation of *De la misère en milieu étudiant*, translated as 'Ten Days Which Shook the University', was beginning to make an important impact in America and particularly in Britain, where the Situationist-inspired outfits such as the Hornsey-based grouping King Mob were starting to make their voices heard. The hippie underground in London, who had heard the good news from Strasbourg, immediately seized on the term 'Situationist' as a catch-all term for aggressive and provocative actions. Dick Pountain and Alan Marcuson, occasional contributors to *Friends* and other more peripheral underground magazines, joined in angry King Mob demonstrations at the Indica Gallery, the fashionable haunt of Paul McCartney, Marianne Faithfull and other leading lights of the West London scene, in the name of Situationist revolt. They had been introduced to the term 'Situationist' by Chris Gray, who had disseminated texts and ideas from Paris via a sympathetic Notting Hill commune.[7]

For South-African-born Alan Marcuson, who was shortly to become the first editor of UK *Rolling Stone*, the attraction of Situationist ideas was their apparent emphasis on unfettered subjectivity as the catalyst for revolution. 'The Situationists were the first people ever to provide me with a rational explanation of our irresponsible behaviour and urges and to see everything,

Chez Moineau,
22, Rue du Four:
(*standing*) Fred, Mel and a
friend of Vali; (*sitting, from
left to right*) Serge Berna,
Vali, Michèle Bernstein,
Joel Berlé and Paulette
Vielhomme

Pierre Feuillette and Guy
Debord on the boulevard
Saint-Michel

Michèle Bernstein and
Guy Debord on the
balcony of the Hôtel de
la rue Racine

(*Main picture*) Guy Debord, April 1952
(*Clockwise, from below right*)
Éliane; 'The Romanian messiah':
Isidore Isou, 1951; Gil Wolman

(*Above*) Cosio D'Arroscia, 1957. 'The wreckers of civilisation': (*from left to right*) Pinot-Gallizio, Piero Simondo, Elena Verrone, Michèle Bernstein, Guy Debord, Asger Jorn and Walter Olmo.
(*Left*) Pegeen Guggenheim, Walter Olmo and Guy Debord at Cosio D'Arroscia
(*Below left*) Guy Debord, Michèle Bernstein and Asger Jorn in Paris
(*Below right*) Ralph Rumney at Cosio D'Arroscia

Poster for the publication of *L'Internationale situationniste*, no. 11, October 1967

(*Facing page*) Rue Gay Lussac, May 1968

Suicide de Guy Debord

Son œuvre ultime

L'auteur de « la Société du spectacle » a mis fin à ses jours. Cet homme secret a-t-il été rattrapé par la société qu'il n'a cessé de dénoncer ?

GUY DEBORD, penseur de fond, imprévisible aventurier révolutionnaire, moraliste de grand style, s'est donné la mort mercredi soir. L'annonce-éclair en a été faite hier, en fin d'après-midi. Du spectaculaire sans images. Le défunt les avait en horreur. Il a vécu jusqu'au bout dans une obscurité assumée, donnant ainsi à sa critique de la société du spectacle l'éclat de sa propre pratique. La plupart de ses admirateurs découvriront son lieu de vie, en Haute-Loire, en même temps que son suicide.

Voici néanmoins deux ou trois choses que l'on sait de cet écrivain délibérément discret. Il

Guy Debord.

Supercapitaliste et révolté, assassiné cette semaine dans le parking Foch, Gérard Lebovici, l'agent des stars, était devenu un homme sous influence

Le Journal du Dimanche

Dans l'ombre de Lebo, un mauvais ange nommé Debord

PAR
PIERRE FRIEZ

les Inrocku+i

hebdo musique, cinéma, livres, etc. Du 24 au 30 sept.

Guy Debord

l'avant-garde meurt mais ne se rend pas

N'ECRIVEZ JAMAIS

(*Main picture*) 'The avant-garde dies but never surrenders'

(*Left*) Rue Mazarine, Paris, 1998

absolutely everything, in terms of political activity,' explained Marcuson. 'They were much more fun, their writings were more fun, they were a more interesting group of people, they were doing more interesting things, their pamphlets were more interesting than the boring fucking Trots, who really were the most tiresome bunch of people I have ever come across.'[8]

Dick Pountain also saw straight away that the Situationist project was at a considerable remove from the West London alternative scene. 'They wouldn't tolerate any kind of tendencies or whatever and also our take was different from theirs: they were high-powered French intellectuals, we were rapidly becoming street hippies. They didn't like the street culture, they saw it even then as part of the "Spectacle"; they didn't like drugs although they did drink vast quantities of Calvados and red wine. They were undoubtedly correct – they predicted perfectly that it would all be co-opted and turned into a huge commodity, which it was. The "Spectacle" is a very Hegelian notion. It was their idea of what the modern state uses instead of physical coercion to keep people in their place. The state still has coercion as a last resort, but by and large they don't need it. The "Spectacle" is the mass media, very much bread and circuses brought up to date with the modern media, TV, film, stardom, the control of everyday life by work disciplines and all this kind of stuff. The Situationist revolution was to be the revolution of everyday life which involved breaking with all of those things. This naturally fitted together with the hippie thing – except that they couldn't stand hippies.'[9]

The young Malcolm McLaren, future scandal-monger and manager of the Sex Pistols, and Jamie Reid, future Sex Pistols designer, were amongst those who first heard the clarion call. Pountain recalled first seeing McLaren at a noisy King Mob event at the London School of Economics at an unspecified date in the mid-1960s: 'Only a minority supported us; the majority wanted to be quiet and respectable, but these two guys came out of the crowd and joined in with us and said "We're with you". They were a couple of art students from Goldsmith's and one was called Fred Vermorel and the other was called Malcolm Edwards. They both had long, dirty khaki macs, a couple of impoverished art students. And of course Malcolm went on to finer things and became Malcolm McLaren, and in a lot of ways the whole Sex Pistols scam was the putting into practice of a lot of Situationist theories. It was a betrayal of it in the sense that it became part of the "Spectacle", but he did really shock the bourgeoisie of the whole country, which is something that King Mob never did.'[10]

'I'd heard about the Situationists from the radical milieu of the time,' recalled McLaren in an interview much later, describing his experiences while a student at a variety of London art schools and polytechnics. 'You had to go up to Compendium Books. When you asked for the literature, you had to pass an eyeball test. Then you got these beautiful magazines with reflecting covers in various colours: gold, green, mauve. The text was in French: you tried to read it, but it was so difficult. Just when you were getting bored, there were always these wonderful pictures and they broke the whole thing up. They were what I bought them for: not the theory.'[11] Above all, McLaren was fascinated by the idea of *détournement*, destroying art and turning the weapons of the spectacular society upon itself. 'I learnt all my politics and understanding of the world through the history of art,' he said. 'Plagiarism is what the world's about.'

'The Situationists were a buzz-word,' recalled Jamie Reid, who was then briefly a student at Wimbledon Art School. 'There was definitely something going on in France that we thought we had to know about. The problem was that no one knew what it was. We just knew it was better than everything else.'[12] Other like-minded individuals such as Antony H. Wilson, who would go on to manage Joy Division, New Order, Happy Mondays and name his Manchester nightclub The Haçienda after a phrase in Ivan Chtcheglov's 'Formulary for a New Urbanism', also sensed that Situationist politics was something apart from other Leftist movements: 'I was at Cambridge with other would-be Situationists like Paul Sieveking [future writer for the *Sunday Telegraph*] and I was a member of a group called the Kim Philby Dining Club which I think had some people from the Angry Brigade involved. We all wanted to destroy the system but didn't know how. We knew about Strasbourg and the Situationist tactics of creative plagiarism and basing change on desire. The Situationists offered, I thought then and I still think now, the only future revolution I could imagine or want.'[13]

Back in Paris the Situationists professed both contempt and indifference to the pop culture which was exploding all around them and upon which they had such an accidental impact. Tim Clark recalled Debord working in his room: 'Writing was one social activity amongst others . . . [the room was] an austere cell, with nothing on the shelves but a few crucial texts (Hegel, Pascal, Marx, Lukács, Lautréamont's *Poésies*) laid open at the relevant page, and the entryway to Debord's minuscule apartment through which friends and comrades continually passed. The process was meant to be seen, and interrupted. One moment the deep ventriloqual dialogue with *History and Class Consciousness*; the next the latest bubble for a comics *détourné*, or the best insult yet to Althusser and Godard.'[14] This was clearly a world apart from the marijuana fug of a West London crash pad.

Terrorist bibles

The key event of 1967 for the Situationists was neither in the realm of art, film or pop music but rather the publication of Guy Debord's *The Society of the Spectacle* in November 1967 and, several weeks later, Raoul Vaneigem's *Traité de savoir-vivre à l'usage des jeunes générations* ('Treatise on how to live for young generations', usually translated into English as *The Revolution of Everyday Life*). These were the two great works of Situationist theory which had been promised since Michèle Bernstein's article in the *Times Literary Supplement* and which aimed to make explicit what the Situationists meant when they had promised, in 1957, 'to wreck this world'.

The two works were, however, radically different both in content and tone. Vaneigem had been a teacher and a promising literary artist. His book was dense with allusion, intimate, sinuous and emotional. He veered into digression, anecdote and allegory with the deft ease of the practised writer. Vaneigem's reference points were Lautréamont, Céline, Antonin Artaud, Jacques Vaché, Norman O. Brown, Gérard de Nerval, as well as the nineteenth-century anarchist bomber François-Claude Ravachol and the anarchist thinker Max Stirner. Vaneigem argued for the unleashing of radical subjectivity as the agent of transformation in the modern world: this meant total sexual freedom (including breaking of the incest taboo), life as the endless pursuit of play and a new 'science of pleasure'. Above all he imagined the coming revolution as the inevitable result of revolutionary practices applied to everyday life. It was in the 'micro-society' of the Situationist International that these revolutionary techniques had been most effectively developed and it was the Situationists who therefore led the way: 'Guerrilla war is total war. This is the path on which the Situationist International is set: calculated harassment on every front – cultural, political, economic and social. Concentrating on everyday life will ensure the unity of the combat.'[15] Vaneigem quoted Guy Debord and Asger Jorn as authorities on subversion and prophets of the coming 'new world' in one of the clearest and most accessible definitions of Situationist subversive practice: 'In 1960, Jorn wrote: "Subversion is a game made possible by the fact that things can be devalorised. Every element of past culture must be either re-invented or scrapped." Debord in *Internationale Situationniste* no. 3 developed the concept further: "The two basic principles of subversion are the loss of importance of each originally independent element (which may even lose its first sense completely), and the organisation of a new significant whole which confer a fresh meaning on each element." [. . .] The art of subversion,' concluded Vaneigem, 'is an integral part of all forms of resistance to the organisation of everyday life.'[16]

This language of Vaneigem's book, poetic, fiery, imperious, had an immediate appeal for members of the European and American underground movements for whom 'Situationism' had so far been no more than a buzz-word with the same currency as hippie, beatnik, provo, mod or rocker. However, this was not the case with Debord's book. This was the text which Debord had been working on since 1963, had been thinking about for even longer, and which was intended as the next, crucial stage in the Situationist project – the dissemination of a theory which, if properly understood by its readers, would change the way in which they looked at the world absolutely and for ever.

The publishing house of Buchet-Chastel offered Debord a contract in 1966. Edmund Buchet himself knew Michèle Bernstein well (he had of course published her first two novels as well as *Young Adam* by Alex Trocchi on her recommendation). He had an inkling that life with Debord as an author would not be easy. 'He told me in advance that he didn't want to have his photograph published, that he would give no interviews and that he would not appear on television,' wrote Edmund Buchet in his autobiography.[17] Buchet was evidently somewhat perplexed by Debord: 'I think advertising and marketing may be rather delicate,' he wrote, hugely underestimating the severity of Debord's position and the challenges to come.

The book was published in an elegant, plain white jacket, with a small photograph of Debord and the rubric: 'Guy Debord, born in Paris in 1931, is the director of the revue *L'Internationale situationniste*. He has also made several films which are out of circulation.'

The text itself was divided into 221 theses, rigorously numbered and ordered, each one developing or building upon the previous argument or assertion so that, in the true Hegelian fashion which Debord admired, the theory as a whole contained the sum of its parts. If the first influence was Hegel, there were also elements from Karl Marx and from twentieth-century thinkers such as Karl Korsch, Gyorgy Lukács and Anton Pannekoek, who were considered to be the inheritors of the 'young' or 'true' Marx, the revolutionary theorist of alienation whom Henri Lefebvre had set in contrast to the official Marxism of the French Communist Party. To this extent, it seemed, *The Society of the Spectacle* could be read as part of the general debate on the French Left outside the French Communist Party, a debate which included Edgar Morin, Henri Lefebvre, the Socialisme ou Barbarie group, about the primacy of everyday life in revolutionary theory and practice.

The essential arguments from the book were all developed from the famous opening thesis: 'The whole life of those societies in which modern conditions of production prevail presents itself as an immense accumulation of spectacles. All that was once truly lived has become mere representation.'[18] Debord prefaces *The Society of the Spectacle* with a quotation from Ludwig Feuerbach's *The Essence of Christianity* which attacks the worship of sacred images, which are in themselves representations of an illusion.

From this starting point Debord develops the concept of the 'Spectacle' in 221 numbered paragraphs, which in classically Hegelian fashion build upon the succeeding arguments. Debord begins by reconsidering nineteenth-century Marxist definitions of alienation before concluding that in the modern world alienation is the result of living in a society which is characterised by its fragmentary, dispersed nature. Human beings in the modern world have no sense of purpose or any tangible feeling of authenticity and are 'separated' from themselves and their products. This is because everywhere and in all spheres of human activity reality is consistently being replaced by images. These images then become reality.

Debord does not simply attack the obvious visual manifestations of modern society – advertising, television and the mass print media. He analyses in a rather more nuanced fashion the way in which the fragmented aspects of modern life are brought together in the images which the spectacular society makes to represent itself. This process is most clearly seen, he says, in the development of the modern cult of celebrity which serves to represent all the qualities – happiness, tragedy, freedom – which are missing in the anonymous lives of spectators.

Media stars are spectacular representations of living human beings, distilling the essence of the spectacle's banality into images of possible roles. Stardom is a diversification in the semblance of life – the object of an identification with mere appearance which is intended to compensate for the crumbling of directly experienced diversifications of productive activity. Celebrities figure various styles of life and various views of society which anyone is supposedly free to embrace and pursue in a *global* manner. Themselves incarnations of the inaccessible results of social labour, they mimic by-products of that labour, and project these above labour so that they appear as its goal. The by-products in question are *power* and *leisure* – the power to decide and the leisure to consume which are the alpha and omega of a process that is never questioned. In the former case, the government power assumes the personified form of the pseudo-star; in the second, stars of consumption canvas for votes as pseudo-power over life lived. But, just as these celestial activities are truly *global*, neither do they offer any real choices.[19]

In recent years, the term 'society of the spectacle' has itself become a cliché, entering the post-modern lexicon to describe any contemporary process, from the playful pursuit of designer consumerism, economic and cultural globalisation, the internet, celebrity worship or the way in which Western democratic political parties occupy interchangeable positions having abandoned the anachronistic distinctions of Left and Right. Having entered the language of contemporary life, the term 'society of the spectacle' is also somehow understood to imply a complicity with its illusory nature.

The defining mood of the book *The Society of the Spectacle* is however one of disgust. In the first instance, and in the first part of the book, this is reserved for the interplay of opposing forces which are united in the revolting falsity of the 'Spectacle'. In the later chapters, the disgust hardens into contempt, as Debord chillingly and brilliantly dissects two key ideas which have become shibboleths of the age: 'incessant technological progress' and the 'integration of state and economy'.

It follows from these notions, he writes, that the 'Spectacle' cannot simply refer to the mass media, whose products are but a 'limited' manifestation of the spectacular society, but relates instead to a rather more complete form of social organisation which gives the spectator the feeling of participating in society, providing him with the illusion of consumer choice, political democracy and so on, whilst at the same time remaining at an untouchable distance from him. From this premise Debord develops a series of perspectives, ranging over the city, mass production, art, travel, the passage of time, the alienated individual in an automated age, which showed how the living, thinking subject is made into an object by the 'spectacular society' which has robbed him or her of the possibility of choice or participation.

The originality of *The Society of the Spectacle* lay in the way in which Debord was able to draw together other strands of thought, Machiavelli, Charles Fourier, the Spanish renaissance poet and courtier Baltasar Graciàn, even Shakespeare, which were either entirely outside the Marxist canon or who, like Fourier, were so marginal as to be outside current debate. Even more surprising was the inclusion of the likes of Lewis Mumford, the distinguished American professor of history who held a chair at the Massachusetts Institute of Technology and who styled himself 'a radical conservative'. Mumford's works on the historical development of cities contained plenty of learned insight and shrewd historical analysis but precious little Marxism. Debord quoted Mumford in the section of *The Society of the Spectacle* entitled 'Environmental planning', a section which described how cities, instead of fulfilling their original role as free spaces of human activity, had become subservient to the demands of capital and consumerism. Resistance to this process, Debord explained, was precisely the real meaning the Situationists sought in the city.

The overall intention of *The Society of the Spectacle* was, however, firmly in the Marxist tradition in the sense that it was conceived as a work of theory which aimed at a direct impact and intervention in the world. In 1992, Debord restated with acerbic clarity how he had meant the book to be received: 'This book should be read bearing in mind that it was written with the deliberate intention of doing harm to the spectacular society. There was never anything outrageous, however, about what it had to say.'[20]

Inevitably the *Traité* and *The Society of the Spectacle* were read together in the French press and little regard given to the nuances which separated Debord and Vaneigem. What was surprising however was the large amount of space which the two books were given in the mainstream press and the famous names of those who had been invited to review the books. This was principally because in the wake of Strasbourg 'Situationism' and

'Situationists' had come to be perceived as a major social problem which, unlike the mods and rockers in England or the provos in Amsterdam, seemed to have a dangerous political content.

In the pages of *Le Monde*, Pierre-Henri Simon, a distinguished *belle-lettriste* of the Académie Française, noted that both Debord and Vaneigem were well into their thirties, a fact which did not stop them giving bad advice to their juniors. With barely contained rage Simon launched an attack on Vaneigem and Debord, 'our future Saint-Justs in black leather jackets', which not only scorned their erudition but attacked the premises of 'Situationism' as badly conceived symptoms of a deeper malaise, one which arose from a post-war culture which had lost all sense of purpose and dignity.[21] Robert Kanters (who had been mocked in *L'Internationale situationniste* 6 for an article on Colin Wilson and the 'Angry Young Men of England') was hardly any more sympathetic in *Le Figaro littéraire*, describing the ideology of the two books as a failure: 'Because it underestimates in a cavalier fashion the philosophy of the day, because in the detail it confuses the true, the false and the doubtful without blushing, the anti-modernism of Messrs Debord and Vaneigem will probably never manage to constitute in the world which it hates a powerful form of thought, action, or both together, like surrealism or existentialism. Rather I would see them more like the ideological sects of the ancient world or the heretical groups in the Middle Ages, to whom the author of the *Traité de savoir-vivre* refers often.'[22] Most vehement of all, however, was François Châtelet, a contributor to *Arguments* who had been criticised in earlier editions of *L'Internationale situationniste*, and who, in the Left-leaning *Le Nouvel Observateur*, devoted two pages to the books and to a general consideration of the mayhem in France and across the world which they seemed to be causing. 'These books, the very existence of Situationism, as a glimmer of light flickering between Copenhagen and New York,' wrote Chatelet, 'are at least symptoms. Certainly, Situationism is not the spectre which has been haunting industrial civilisation, any more than communism was truly the spectre haunting Europe since 1848. But it is an idelogical sign. Here are two writers – in the most literal and banal sense of the word – who have read, who have a polemical sensibility, who legitimately hate the world in which they are forced to live! They form a group, they publish a journal, they pronounce their theoretical perspectives, which are results, without doubt, of many discussions of a philosphically demanding nature. What is all this then? Quaint analyses where everything is all mixed up, from Sade to Bataille, from Marx to Freud, from Fourier to Lautréamont and where all these things are brought together in the name of revolutionary spiritualism.' Most damning of all was the opening comment: 'We were waiting for a Situationist manifesto. What we got was two terrorist "bibles" which are beyond analysis.'[23]

Chatelet, 'a Marxist and a piece of shit', was later honoured with a comprehensive and offensive riposte in *L'Internationale situationniste*, as was Claude Lefort of *La Quinzaine littéraire* (who had evidently patronised Debord as presenting almost a doctoral thesis on Machiavelli). Other reviews of the Situationist books were also engaged upon and summarily dealt with in the journal. It was perhaps hardest of all for the venerable and esteemed Pierre-Henri Simon to defend himself against the Situationist charge that he was 'a panicky old cunt'.[24]

CHAPTER 20

Days of Rage

1968

The year 1968 marked a key date in the cultural history of the twentieth century. It was a year that had many precedents: the Popular Front of 1936, the Paris Commune of 1871, the revolutionary insurrections of 1848, 1831 and even the Revolution of 1789 were all cited as models for the drama of the revolutionary year of 1968. However what was most extraordinary amongst many extraordinary events that year was the way in which, in May, a local dispute between staff and students at an obscure university on the outskirts of Paris became the catalyst for an insurrectionary revolt which brought France to its knees and which shook the rest of the world.

When, during the 'événements' of May, they saw their slogans daubed on walls and their arguments the focus for national and international debate, this was also clearly the finest hour of the Situationist International. It was the moment when avant-garde theory had made the crucial shift to the practice of the revolution of everyday life.

For Debord himself, it was to be the moment when the revolution he had predicted for so long was at hand. It was to be the nearest he ever came to such a triumph, a prize which he described in Clausewitz's terms as ultimate victory, the moment when the enemy, no matter how powerful his forces, is overthrown by a single direct blow which hits upon 'the centre of gravity of the whole war'. In the immediate aftermath of 1968 the Situationists and their admirers often described the events of May in these terms and compared the insurrection to the Paris Commune of 1871. However, the closest historical precedent to 1968 was 1848, a year when a revolutionary fever had swept across Europe like wildfire and Paris itself was convulsed by a series of bloody conflicts which brought the state to its knees. Although the insurrections were failures, they had consequences and outcomes, from the Paris Commune to the October Revolution of 1917, which could not possibly have been foreseen by the participants in the riots that tore apart the poorest quarters of Paris in June 1848.

In 1968, across the United States, South America, Western Europe, the Eastern bloc and in the developed capitalist nations of the Far East, governments were openly and often violently confronted in a chain of rebellious uprisings, spearheaded by disaffected youths, which challenged the very basis of the post-war world order. In the Western industrialised countries the common factors were disgust with the war in Vietnam, a disgust which was heightened by the militant disaffection of the American Blacks within the United States itself. In the Eastern European countries, revolt was directed against a hierarchical system, controlled from Moscow, which brooked no individual or collective dissent. In the Far East, particularly in Korea and Japan, anti-capitalism and anti-Americanism presented a united front. Everywhere, the rallying cry of the youths who made the revolts was against the bourgeois social-democratic compromises made in the post-war world and the 'alienation' engendered by dominant cultures where material comfort was the highest social value. As in 1848, it was most crucial for the reigning powers that nowhere did rebellion become a revolution. The inevitable focal point for this feverish activity, which so vividly recalled 1848, was however again Paris, the world capital of revolutionary movements, which for insurrectionists as far apart as Mexico and Tokyo was the defining point of reference.

Spectacular times

There was little to suggest in the first few days of 1968 that within five months the French government would find itself paralysed by the most serious and bloody insurrection in the streets of Paris since the Commune in 1871, and that in the wake of this revolt French society would be torn open and separated into two opposing, bitterly divided camps.

Despite the aggravated colonial conflict in Algeria and the political dangers and tensions which had come in its wake, there was none of the sense of fury and anger in Paris in the mid-1960s which, for example, characterised political movements amongst the young in Germany where dissatisfaction with the state was already hardening into political violence. Although Ulrike Meinhof, the future leader of the notorious Baader-Meinhof gang, was at this stage still a journalist for the Leftist magazine *Konkret*, there had been since the early 1960s an increasingly harder edge creeping into student rhetoric and actions in Germany. The student leader Rudi Dutschke, whose charisma was enhanced by his long, straggly hair, leather jacket and jeans, caught the mood by declaring, 'We must hate certain elements in society but we must also feel guilty about doing so. I have advocated the use of violence in practical circumstances, yes, but only against objects and property, not people.'[1]

Even more radical elements within West Germany were the members of Kommune I, a Surrealist-inspired group of anarchists based in Berlin, whose prime motivations were a love of hallucinogenic drugs and a thirst for outrage. In the wake of a fire in a department store in Brussels in 1967, Kommune I had distributed pamphlets claiming the fire was the work of anti-Vietnam activists and suggested moving the Vietnamese front to Western Europe: 'Three hundred satiated citizens and their exciting lives came to an end, and Brussels became Hanoi,' the pamphlet callously and sarcastically stated. 'Now no one needs to shed tears for the poor Vietnamese people over his breakfast paper. As from today he can simply walk into the made-to-measure department store of KaDeWe, Hertie, Woolworth, Bilka or Neckermann and discreetly light a cigarette in the dressing room.' During the subsequent trial on the charge of incitement to arson, the two most influential members of Kommune I, Fritz Teufel and Rainer Langhans (previously an officer in the West German Army), did their best to disrupt the solemnity of the court with their flippant and defiant responses which aimed at complete disregard for state apparatus.[2]

The activities of marginal groups such as Kommune I took place against a background in which it seemed that the whole of German society was being forced into opposing camps. The case for extra-parliamentary opposition, at least in the eyes of Dutschke and his followers, was strengthened in 1966 with the announcement of a coalition government in Bonn, organised between the Christian Democrats and the Social Democratic Party. The government, which had already agreed military and foreign policy, now apparently served only the interests of international policy-makers. 'The youth of our country will turn its back upon the state and will move either to the Left or Right,' growled the novelist Günter Grass in response to the coalition. Tension was heightened in 1967 when, during the controversial visit of the Shah of Persia to Berlin, Benno Ohnesorg, a student at the Free University of Berlin who had never taken part in a demonstration and whose wife was pregnant, was shot dead by plain-clothes police. Twelve thousand people marched through Berlin behind his coffin. A year later, on 11 April 1968, when Rudi Dutschke was almost killed by a gunman (he was shot twice in the head and once in the chest when riding his bicycle), West Germany was divided between those who were appalled at such a naked assault upon the forces of true opposition and others who suspected that Dutschke had thoroughly earned his assassination attempt. Either way it seemed that the fledgeling democracy of the West German State was in a precarious position.

In other European countries during the same period, particularly in Italy and Holland, the proliferation of Maoist or Trotskyist literature was matched only by an increased belligerence amongst the young. Over half of all Italian universities in the period 1967–8 had been occupied after conflicts led by groups such as the Maoist Guardie Rossie and the Situationist-inspired Uccelli group ('The birds'). In Holland and Denmark, the street demonstrations led by the Provos were all too frequently spinning beyond police control.

In France, in contrast, aside from the incidents in Strasbourg and a copycat strike at the University of Nantes in May 1967, which had a markedly less explosive impact, there were few signs that a storm was brewing. The year began indeed with de Gaulle firmly at the head of a government whose authority, despite the setbacks of the Algerian crisis, was largely unchallenged in the mainstream political arena. Student disturbances such as those at Strasbourg or Nantes were largely explained, even by sympathetic Leftist commentators, as aberrations, the fruits of too much material comfort and boredom rather than any serious political confrontation. French youth culture, typified by the phony sneer of would-be Elvis Johnny Halliday and a gormless vogue for inane dance crazes, was a long way from the genuinely radical musical shifts and turns of the Beatles, Stones and The Who in Britain and the dissident, sophisticated dissonance of Frank Zappa and the Velvet Underground in the United States. All these circumstances supported the eye-witness view of the British Marxist historian Eric Hobsbawm that what happened in France in May was 'totally unexpected and totally unprecedented'.[3]

According to the Situationists, however, the signs were all there for those who could read. The cracks in French society had already started to show, they argued, as far back as 1958 or 1959, the years when the Algerian war had placed the greatest strain on government, intellectuals and ordinary people. Since the Second World War it had been taken for granted by most of the European Left that revolution was an anachronism or an impossibility. This was of course the exact opposite of what the Situationists believed in and had been arguing for since 1957.

In the pages of the *L'Internationale situationniste* Debord had icily pointed out that it was not Vietnam or 'black consciousness' or dissatisfaction with reforms which had led to the ferocious Watts riots of 1965, but purely and simply a rejection of everything that modern life stood for in material terms. It was this complete negation of the spectacular society, he further argued, which was not only the catalyst but also the actual form of the revolution to come. He compared this form of uprising to the POUM insurrection in Barcelona in 1936, the conflict which George Orwell witnessed and described in *Homage to Catalonia*, and pronounced this was how the 'total transformation' would come about: 'A rebellion against the spectacle is situated on the level of totality, because even if it were only to appear in the single district of Watts, it is a protest of people against inhuman life; because it begins at the level of the real single individual and because community, from which the rebelling individual is separated, is the true social nature of man, human nature: the positive supersession of the spectacle.'[4]

Preludes

The revolt began at the University of Nanterre, a monstrous edifice of glass, steel and concrete which had opened in 1964 as a 'model university' for a future generation of technocrats. Nanterre was just outside the city limits of Paris and only accessible from central Paris by *métro* or a long and complicated bus route. Set amidst makeshift buildings and rotting slums which housed mainly North African workers in genuinely Third-World conditions, it was hard to imagine a university campus further removed from the light, buzz and action of the Latin Quarter. By 1967, the campus was also wildly overcrowded, with some 12,000 students housed in cheap residences which, to make matters worse, were subject to draconian house rules. For most of the students who were not able to escape into central Paris on weekdays or weekends, life was reduced to twice-weekly ciné-clubs, the occasional severely controlled 'dance party', table tennis and television. Through the course of 1967 there was a series of student strikes, largely provoked by the so-called 'dormitory laws' which forbade any intermingling between the sexes without the written permission of parents. The Situationist theses on the poverty of student life, distributed by the pro-Situationist students René Riesel, Jean-Pierre Duteil and Gérard Bigorgne, were eagerly devoured as potent truths. By the beginning of 1968 the campus was ready to explode.

A great deal of the disruption throughout 1967 had been the work of the TSRF (Tendance syndicale révolutionnaire féderaliste, or Syndical Federalist Revolutionary Tendency) who were a libertarian socialist group with about forty members, most of whom had joined the group in the wake of the Strasbourg scandal. Along with their comrades and occasional rivals in the LEA (Liaison étudiante anarchiste, or Anarchist Student Liaison Group), who had been established in Nanterre since 1964, the TSRF were admirers of the Situationist International, whom they were constantly trying to impress. Shortly after the Strasbourg scandal, members of the TSRF had distributed copies of *The Return of the Durutti Column* and *On the Poverty of Student Life* in Nanterre. In June 1967 the TSRF and LEA finally made real contact with their heroes Debord and Vaneigem, who were both just about to publish their first books, and were advised by the Situationist duo that a good start to the revolution would be made by throwing tomatoes at Henri Lefebvre as he gave a lecture in the ground floor of the building. Like the earlier attack on the 'cybernetic tortoise' Abraham Moles in Strasbourg this would almost certainly ignite fires in important parts elsewhere in the University of Paris, explained the Situationists. Jean-Pierre Duteuil, then a leading figure in the LEA, remembered the encounter as one between leaders and the led: 'It was during a meeting in a bistro near Jussieu between representatives from the LEA and the SI, led by Guy Debord, that the Situationists, acting like great masters of the game, consented to provide the anarchists with pamphlets; but they also suggested that they should be thrown first during Lefebvre's lecture. It was really quite clear that they were using the LEA to settle old scores. The anarchists, who had nothing against Lefebvre, refused to throw the things but accepted the gift.'[5] On the day of the planned attack on Lefebvre, the anarchists limited themselves to handing out copies of *On the Poverty of Student Life* before engaging the nonplussed Lefebvre in lively but orderly debate.

The catalyst for the really serious trouble which spread through the campus in the early part of 1968 was the visit on 8 January of the French Minister for Youth, the well-meaning but hopelessly out-of-touch François Missoffe, who had himself not so long ago published a massive tome on the problems of youth. Missoffe had come to the university to open the new swimming pool in the Cité Universitaire but was baffled to find himself booed and jeered by the students. One of them, a self-assured, freckle-faced character named Daniel Cohn-Bendit, complained loudly to Missoffe that his book had avoided the issue of young people's sexual problems. Missoffe dismissed the complaints, telling Cohn-Bendit that a quick dip in an icy pool was the most effective remedy for sexual frustation. Cohn-Bendit accused the minister of sounding like a member of the Hitler Youth. The minister said nothing but soon afterwards Cohn-Bendit was singled out by a zealous minor official for deportation (he had dual nationality, having been born in France of German Jews who had fled the Nazis). In retaliation the students began sticking up posters of plain-clothes policemen known to frequent the campus and denouncing the dean and his administration as 'tools of the prefecture'.

This was the work of the self-styled *Enragés*, a minuscule group of students led by René Riesel, who had avowed themselves to total war against the university a month previously. Riesel, along with Cohn-Bendit and Gérard Bigorgne, had already been threatened with expulsion by the dean, the well-meaning and Left-leaning Pierre Grappin, if they continued with their concerted campaign of agitation. Incensed by this, they had named themselves after the *Enragés* of 1789, a popular movement who were amongst the most vehement and extremist critics of the revolutionary government. Many of the slogans of the *Enragés*, calling for government by the masses and an end to hierarchical government, were taken up by the Hébertistes, violent atheists and revolutionaries who frightened even Robespierre. 'We were paying homage to the most radical revolutionary groups,' explained Riesel in 1998 in a rare interview with *Libération*, placing his small cohort in a direct lineage with the French Revolution. Their ranks included the soon to be notorious names of Patrick Cheval, Pierre Carrère, Patrick Negroni, Pierre Lotrous, Bernard Ager and Angeline Neveu.[6] Their headquarters was the café Zimmer at place du Châtelet, on the edge of the Right Bank, and they were distinguished by a uniform of leather, jeans, beards, long hair and dark glasses. Most importantly however the *Enragés* were accountable to no one, especially not their comrades in less enraged and determined groups.

Appropriately, in the wake of the poster campaign and rumours of 'black lists' of students, there were a number of scuffles with riot police called in by the university, which quickly escalated into a situation beyond the university's control when more than a thousand students gathered on 26 January to demonstrate and repel the police in the main hall. A month later students of social psychology voted to boycott examinations and a pamphlet, 'Why do we need sociologists?', was handed out in the corridors by the hard-core elements who had been at the centre of the skirmishes with the law and who would soon name themselves the 22 March Movement, after the earlier occupation by students of the administrative building of the University of Nanterre. The occupation had been launched in defence of an anarchist anti-Vietnam demonstrator known only as Xavier who had been arrested some days before, but it took on international significance when the students discovered that 22 March was also the day of the closure of the University of Warsaw after weeks of parallel disturbances.

The role of the *Enragés* in the events of 22 March was limited but dramatic. Over a hundred and fifty students launched the occupation of the building. Having gained entry, there was a general air of confusion and no small measure of hesitation amongst the crowd who had breached the entrance. The *Enragés*, in contrast, were cool, aloof and bent on total destruction; they stayed only twenty minutes or so in the main hall before setting out for the key offices, which they ransacked, swigging from newly found bottles of whisky and brandy, urging the other students to set fire to all university documents. Other more moderate students resisted this and Daniel Cohn-Bendit, who sensed the hidden hand of Guy Debord behind all this loutish mayhem, said that this could not be supported. The *Enragés* left disgusted at the lack of revolutionary will, spending the rest of the evening getting drunk on stolen booze in a café near gare Saint-Lazare. They refused to affiliate themselves with the newly born Movement of 22 March and scarcely reappeared in Nanterre. Much to Cohn-Bendit's surprise and even chagrin (he had already openly expressed disdain for Guy Debord as divisive, cunning, sectarian and an all-round 'nasty bastard'), Situationist slogans appeared mysteriously around the campus on a frequent basis, including 'Never Work!', 'Take your desires for reality', 'Boredom is counter-revolutionary'. Students, police and University authorities were equally baffled at their provenance.

Events and Situations

By the end of December 1967 all the English members of the SI had either resigned or been kicked out. The attempts to build 'an English section' or 'an American Section' had so far been a fiasco, characterised by a visit Debord had made earlier in the year to London where Chris Gray had assured him that he had a cadre of twenty or so hard-core revolutionaries already assembled. Debord was furious to find, at the address he had been given in Notting Hill, a pair of Gray's associates – who were the entire cadre – drinking cans of McEwans export beer and watching *Match of the Day*. Debord took it out on the bookshelves, a ragbag of hippie and anarchist literature, which he emptied on the floor. There was no more talk of 'an English section' from this point on.

In Paris, however, the SI began 1968 on Debord's terms and in its tightest and most organised form. Most crucially, it seemed that the theses and predictions of the Situationist International were taking on a concrete form in the larger stage beyond Paris. The year began with the anti-Moscow politician Alexander Dubcek elected as First Secretary of the Czechoslovak Communist Party. In the same month, to coincide with Tet, the Vietnamese New Year, Vietcong guerrillas and conventional forces from North Vietman attacked thirty-four provincial towns across the country, even penetrating and managing to hold part of the US Embassy in Saigon for more than six hours. The American response was to declare the Communist offensive a failure and to counter with an overwhelming series of air and infantry attacks upon civilian as well as military targets. The unfolding news of the slaughter was truly appalling. The images of the unburied bodies of Vietnamese civilians unleashed a great wave of anti-American feeling across the globe.

Anti-US riots in Tokyo, led by Zengakuren, the Vietnam Solidarity March in London and the arrests of Bobby Seale and other Black Panthers in the United States confirmed that the 'old world' was on the defensive. The assassination in April of Martin Luther King and then, an event which had an even greater impact on the Situationist milieu, the attempted assassination of Rudi Dutschke in Germany proved also that the 'old world' was an enemy to be taken seriously. The rioting in West Berlin and other German cities was directed principally against the Right-wing millionaire Axel Springer, whose media empire had whipped up anti-Dutschke and anti-student feeling amongst the conservative citizens of Germany. The result was a divided society where, as the journalist and historian Neal Ascherson reported, 'even nicely dressed middle-class schoolboys and young girls talked about "unmasking the state apparatus" and "institutionalised violence under late capitalism"'.[7]

In April 1968, an internal document written by Debord was circulated amongst members of the Situationist International to prepare them for a new period in the history of the SI. In this text, 'The Question of the Organisation of the Situationist International', Debord divided the history of the group into three phases. The first had been devoted to the foundation and establishment of the SI and the 'overcoming of art'. The second phase had been the development of a critical theory of the 'spectacular society'. The third, which was yet to come, was the formation of a genuine revolutionary movement which would be capable of overthrowing this society. The 'situationist vogue' which, in the wake of Strasbourg and Nantes, was embraced by students and journalists alike was something, Debord argued, which the Situationists could use to carry their message to an even greater audience. This was indeed the strategic opening which Debord had calculated would lead to the revolutionary moment. On the eve of the explosion of May 68, the Situationists were still a tiny group. However, as press, television and radio coverage in France and elsewhere was already proving, much to Debord's satisfaction, their name was legion.

The point of explosion

The evening of Friday 3 May 1968 was warm and humid. For most French people the most surprising fact so far had been the unusual warmth of the day which promised a fine weekend and possibly an even finer summer. By the early evening, however, first radio reports announced to an astonished public that across the Left Bank of Paris there was a riot going on.

Michèle Bernstein, who was then living not far from the Sorbonne, had spent the early part of the evening preparing dinner and listening to music, completely unaware of the dramatic events that were unfolding less than half a mile away. Around eight o'clock in the evening she was visited by an agitated Guy Debord in the company of Alice Becker-Ho. 'They were both very excited,' she recalled. 'Both of them were saying, do you know there's fighting in the streets of Paris and we are winning, this is it, we cannot turn back now. I didn't know what to say or do. It was very exciting and I wanted the students and the SI to beat the police, but I had not expected it to come like this and so quickly, and nor did Guy and Alice. But they were ready to do anything necessary, even though they had no plans or tactics worked out.'

The events of the day had taken everyone by surprise. At midday, there had been a meeting at the Sorbonne between activists from Nanterre and the Sorbonne to talk over the disciplinary charges brought against members of the 22 March movement, including Daniel Cohn-Bendit and René Riesel, and which were due to be heard on Monday 6 May. The meeting was fractious, a feeling which was exacerbated by the police presence around the Sorbonne and the activities of Occident, an extreme Right-wing student movement whose members were handing out pamphlets in the Sorbonne courtyard and the place de la Sorbonne threatening to frogmarch Cohn-Bendit to the German border and 'to have done with all Bolshevik agitation in the universities by all means'. By 4 o'clock, as the atmosphere grew increasingly tense, the Sorbonne had been surrounded by the CRS, the Compagnies Républicaines de Sécurité, notorious for their heavy-handed and violent methods which had been developed and refined in breaking up miners' strikes in northern France. Shortly afterwards, on the grounds that students were apparently wearing helmets and smashing up tables to use as clubs (this was exactly what the *Enragés* in the building were doing), the CRS began arresting anybody who looked as if they might be an activist or a militant, giving them a hiding in the process. Students began pouring out of cafés, libraries, bars, with the cry 'Libérez nos camarades' and throwing stones at the police wagons carrying away the arrested students. As the street-fighting grew ever more intense, the decision was taken to close the Sorbonne, something which had only occurred once in the Sorbonne's seven-hundred-year history, when the Nazis had shut the university in 1940.

Events then began to move with a fierce momentum and, for the government at least, the logic of a nightmare. That night, as battles raged across the Latin Quarter, the National Union of Students (UNEF) and the lecturers' union called a strike. The following morning *Le Figaro* railed against 'guttersnipes, fit for the remand home rather than for the university'. The judiciary worked overtime through the weekend, handing out suspended sentences and then, enraging the students in revolt even further, prison sentences. Three demands were put to the university authorities by the unions: to re-open the Sorbonne, to withdraw the police and to release all those arrested. The authorities, unaware of the forces they were about to unleash, refused. The battle lines were now clearly drawn and the stage set for the firestorm which was soon to engulf all of France.

CHAPTER 21

Paris Awakes!

1968

Monday 6 May began with the Sorbonne surrounded by police, CRS riot control squads and *gendarmes mobiles*, a battle-hardened military organisation. The atmosphere across the Left Bank that morning was one of muted violence, with no sense that the streets would be any quieter that evening than they had been over the weekend.

It was apparent that President de Gaulle himself did not really appreciate the strength of the threat posed to civil order by the disturbances, whilst Prime Minister Pompidou, the only one amongst his ministers who might have understood the seriousness of the disorder, was still away on a diplomatic trip to Aghanistan and Iran. This left Louis Joxe, a journeyman politician lacking Pompidou's charisma and insight, in charge alongside the Minister of the Interior, Christian Fouchet (whose reforms as the former Minister of Education were being blamed for this trouble), and Alain Peyrefitte, then Minister for Education. Not one of these politicians could agree to a solution, leaving power effectively and disastrously in the hands of the police.

Enraged from the outset by the taunt 'CRS-SS', the police behaved with consistent and brutal disregard for individuals and their safety. Young males unfortunate enough to fall into police hands were viciously beaten in public view. Girl students were punched, kicked and sexually abused. A nurse recalled her arrest and detainment at the detention centre at Beaujon over the weekend: 'We got out of the bus and were beaten up; then going between two ranks of CRS, I reached a stadium surrounded by barbed wire. . . . A CRS man said to me, "Come along, I'll shave you, curly locks." He hit me. An officer intervened but the girl ahead of me had all her hair cut off. I was taken to a cell, three metres by six. After five hours it contained 80 of us. We had to stand up. I could see the courtyard; a young man went by half naked, legs lacerated with baton blows, bleeding, holding his stomach, urinating everywhere. A young woman who'd been with him told me the CRS beat him till he fainted, then undressed him and hit his sexual organs until his flesh was in ribbons.'[1] The Café de la Mairie on the place Saint-Sulpice, a student hangout and popular with the writer Georges Perec amongst others, had been flushed out by police raining blows on its student clientèle. Protesting that he was an innocent foreigner, a young man was smashed in the face by a CRS man and told, 'Yes, and you've come to shit on us in France.'[2] Similar scenes were repeated through the day across the Left Bank.

The key flashpoint however was the appearance of eight students, the so-called 'Nanterre Eight', at a special disciplinary hearing of the University of Paris to be held at the Sorbonne in the morning. The world's press, alongside hundreds of student supporters, was there to meet them as they marched across the courtyard and into the building singing the 'Internationale'. They were the members of the 22 March movement, Olivier Castro, Michel Pourny, Daniel Schumann, Yves Fleischl, Ploix, Jean-Pierre Duteuil and, inevitably, Daniel Cohn-Bendit, who had now been renamed 'Dany Le Rouge' by the press. Alongside the Nanterre comrades, walking ahead with a genuinely rock'n'roll swagger which matched his long hair, jeans, beard and dark glasses, was René Riesel, intimate of Guy Debord, and the unmarked representative of the Situationist International.

Crime and punishment

The hearing was of course a farce. The meeting was set up as a trial, with the students accompanied by 'lawyers', members of the Faculty of Letters including Henri Lefebvre and Alain Touraine, who were to plead the case. René Riesel set the tone by deliberately mocking the seriousness of the set-up, annoying even 'Dany Le Rouge' with his demeanour. Duteuil recalls him 'taking off his leather jacket, which he rolled into a ball and used as a pillow, after lying down on the noble wooden floor which had seen so many noble shoes. Touraine and Lefebvre looked at him hard but kept their mouths tight shut.'[3]

Outside the *Enragés* and Situationists, with Guy Debord in their number, were handing out leaflets entitled 'La rage au ventre' ('Fire in the belly'), attacking Trotskyist lies, pro-Chinese propaganda and the 'anarchist Daniel Cohn-Bendit'. 'Let's sort this out ourselves!' it proclaimed. The leaflet was not intended as an act of support or solidarity with the 'accused' but as a call to further provocation. 'Already violence has caused the little chiefs of tiny groups to keep their gobs shut; the mere contestation of the bourgeois university is insignificant when it is all of society which must be destroyed. Long live Zengakuren! Long live the Committee of Public Health of the Vandalists (Bordeaux)! Long live the Enragés! Long live the Situationist International! Long live the social revolution!'[4] The trial of the 'Nanterre Eight' was abruptly halted when the first sound of tear-gas canisters exploding in the courtyard outside could be heard and dozens of students began hurling missiles at the police.

More clashes were to follow. The morning had seen a peaceful demonstration by students on the Right Bank, marching through the centre of Paris in the name of peace and solidarity. Shoppers, business people, office workers were mildly sympathetic to the students' cause, these were after all their own sons and daughters marching for rights and freedoms. As the marchers made their way across the river to the rue Saint-Jacques and the Latin Quarter, the police, from nowhere and completely unprovoked, charged the lines with an unprecedented ferocity. The enraged students fought back: paving stones were ripped up and hurled at the police; parked cars were turned into barricades.

The evening which followed was the bloodiest yet. More than 600 protesters were wounded and 422 arrests were made. Many students had made for place Denfert-Rocherau to the south of the Latin Quarter, whose many junction roads allowed easier escape from the police. Further north, place Saint Germain-des-Prés, the boulevard Saint-Germain, the rue du Four, rue Mouffetard and place de la Sorbonne became war zones.

Fighting intensified throughout the week. On Tuesday a student demonstration had reached the Arc de Triomphe, the arch-symbol of Gaullist France, where red and black flags now flew unchallenged. By Wednesday, surprised and impressed by the courage of the students, workers in Marseilles, Toulouse, Strasbourg and Rennes gave their support to the students. There were efforts by the Communist Party to calm the situation. The veteran Communist poet Louis Aragon, in the eyes of the SI the betrayer of Surrealism and a 'Stalinist cunt', was wheeled out to speak to the people. At first the Communists had condemned the disturbances. Georges Marchais the future Secretary-General had railed against what he called 'false revolutionaries' in the Communist newspaper *L'Humanité*. It was inevitable therefore that when Aragon began to patronise the 'false revolutionaries' at a street meeting opposite the Odéon, claiming that they reminded him of his own youth, he was met with cries of 'Long Live Stalin!' and the order to 'Go home and watch TV!'

By Friday evening there were more than 30,000 students and workers on the streets of Paris, thirsting for quick and radical change. The police were now just watching. In homes across France, as over sixty barricades were built in the streets of the capital between place de la Contrescarpe and rue des Feuillantines, transistor radios reported all night, with an increasing sense of expectation, as the rebellion seemed about to become a revolution.

Shortly after midnight an order was given in the Ministry of the Interior to clear the barricades. Guy Debord was mainly on the rue Gay-Lussac, a short step away from the flat he then occupied with Alice Becker-Ho on the rue Saint-Jacques. He visited other sections of the besieged Latin Quarter along with Christian Sébastiani, Alain Chevalier and other students who seemed 'advanced' and, according to Alice, understooood that 'never had the passion to destroy seemed so creative'.

The fighting was more frightening and more vicious than anyone had anticipated. Amazingly, no one was killed (although the Situationists did later advance the view that any dead or missing persons might easily have been passed off as road accident victims). Although the CRS had managed to clear the square facing the Luxembourg Gardens, the rue Gay-Lussac, which lay slightly to the south, was proving more difficult. CS grenades, previously only ever used in Vietnam, were hurled at the insurrectionists, whilst buckets of water were thrown from apartment windows to help the rioters. The rioters also fought back hard, setting fire to cars and hurling Molotov cocktails at the police lines. Girls, foreigners, workers all joined in the struggle. When dawn broke, the streets were an empty, scarred battleground where Situationist and Anarchist slogans painted by Debord's friends provided the clearest description yet of what had motivated the fighting. These included 'TAKE YOUR DESIRES FOR REALITY', 'THE IMAGINATION TAKES POWER' and 'EVERY-THING IS POSSIBLE'.

The Occupation of the Sorbonne

There was more to come. On the Saturday morning the police vans and troop-carriers which sped relentlessly across the Left Bank were spat at, booed and hissed. Pompidou, returning as quickly as he could from the Middle East, immediately reversed government policy, emptying not only the Sorbonne but the whole Latin Quarter of the police. Raymond Aron, the distinguished Gaullist intellectual, expressed the mood of even the most conservative elements in France by stating that 'for a regime which for more than ten years has governed France with more authority than any other French Government has ever possessed, the discovery that there was such a fund of violence must have been both staggering and bitter'.[5]

On Monday 13 May, the trade unions joined the students and declared a one-day general strike. Two hundred thousand demonstrators from all over France gathered in central Paris to challenge de Gaulle and his government. Pompidou had by now given the order for the police to leave the Latin Quarter. Believing that the worst was over de Gaulle had followed Pompidou's advice and gone ahead with an official trip to Romania. However, as the marchers dispersed again at Denfert-Rochereau, the slogan first whispered then shouted was 'Occupy the Sorbonne!' Small groups of *Enragés* and Situationists had already entered the building and by nightfall the venerable seat of learning was in the hands of determined revolutionaries who, with the world watching, would now take the game one step further.

Guy Debord was amongst those who first entered the Sorbonne. The Salle Cavaillès, named after the distinguished philosopher of mathematics who had been shot by the Germans in 1943, was renamed Salle Jules Bonnot, after the Anarchist leader notorious for his murderous bank robberies and who was shot by police while being arrested in Choisy-le-Roi. A flag, painted the night before by Michèle Bernstein, claimed the building in the name of the Comité Enragés-Internationale Situationnistes.

The Situationists were not in sole control of the building. Paint-bombs and graffiti also announced the presence of Maoist, Trotskyist and Anarchist factions. But the propaganda campaign launched by Debord made it seem that it was the Situationists who held the real power. 'Although I had never met him before, I knew by his way of speaking and holding himself that this was the great Guy Debord,' commented Jean-Marie Bienvenu, a hardworking student of mathematics and an avid reader of Situationist texts. 'He spoke beautiful impeccable French, and was composed and serene, in the way you would be if you were just about to launch your finally deadly moves in a game of chess.'[6]

Compared to the dull or turgid prose of the other groups, the Situationists' graffiti were provocative, witty and determinedly poetic. The slogans, 'And what if we burned the Sorbonne?', 'How can we think freely in the shadow of a chapel?', 'Let us be cruel!', 'Down with the toad of Nazareth!', were traced on paintings and walls by René Viénet and Christian Sébastiani on the orders of Guy Debord. Erotic images accompanied by other detourned Situationist texts – 'Never Work', Live without Dead Time, Come without Limits' – were festooned through the corridors. A text from Raoul Vaneigem was scrawled upon a wall: 'Those who speak of revolution and class struggle, with explicit reference to daily life, without understanding what is subversive in love and positive in the refusal of constraints, have a corpse in their mouths!'[7]

The following day saw a long chaotic meeting in the main assembly hall in which Debord played a central role. The debate was centred on the question of whether to demand reforms in the university or whether to press for an end to Gaullism, even capitalism. A third element, distinctly a minority of Situationists and sympathisers organised by Debord, argued for the 'abolition of classes, salaries, spectacle and survival'. In the name of the *Enragés*, René Riesel declared that 'Examinations have been abolished by the barricades.' To barracking from moderate elements, he called on the assembly to demand the release of all rioters, including looters (the example of the Watts riots had not been forgotten by the Situationists), attacked the professors of the university and, again to a generally hostile reception, denounced all Leftist leaders as 'Stalinists'. Despite the booing and catcalls, he was elected to the first 'Committee of Occupation', an executive group of fifteen delegates with a twenty-four-hour mandate.

In reality the 'Committee of Occupation' had no actual power over the sub-groups which were mushrooming in the building, mostly organised by the Students' Union, nor did it have any control of events which were taking place outside the Sorbonne. Inspired by the students' example there was a wave of occupations across France organised by workers and intellectuals – writers, doctors and architects announced the dissolution of their professional associations; workers occupied factories and shops; even footballers demanded 'football for the footballers' and the immediate sacking of those who made 'a profit from football and insulted footballers'.[8]

As they were being undermined by the Students' Union and they saw their power base withering away in front of their eyes, Debord, Riesel and the other Situationists in the 'Salle Jules Bonnot' decided upon a last throw of the dice and, in support of the workers at the Sud Aviation factory at Bourguenais (who had actually been on strike before the student riots) published a document calling for 'immediate occupation of all the factories in France and the formation of workers' councils'. The Students' Union had deliberately made sure that the Situationists were short of paper, radio equipment (the students who controlled the technical side of things tended, for some reason, to be 'Right-wing') and other material needed to spread this message. Riesel went to the windows of the 'Salle Jules Bonnot' and, using his rock-star charisma as best as he could, asked for volunteers to form a 'gang' who could help overcome the conservative elements. The Situationists and their sympathisers then fanned out through the building, grabbing hold of any free telephones or radio equipment, often using force and intimidation, and contacting Agence France Presse and other agencies to pass the message on to the outside world.

Non-Situationists of all hues claimed that they were being betrayed and manipulated by an élitist gang whose agenda was not that of the students. The situation was changing from hour to hour. On 15 May 300 people occupied the Théâtre de l'Odéon. The following day a strike was declared at the Renault works at Boulogne-Billancourt. A spontaneous march was organised from place de la Sorbonne to Billancourt in support of the strike in which most of the *Enragés* and Situationists participated. Returning to the Sorbonne on 17 May they found that the 'Committee of Occupation' had been taken over by extremist Left-wing groups, allied to hardline Trotskyist or Maoist factions. In disgust, Debord ordered his troops to leave the Sorbonne. Two photographs show Debord on the platform of the General Assembly. In the midst of the crowd, he is serious, calm and determined. The fact that the students had not understood the Situationists' tactics was a mistake on their part and a mark of their stupidity. But it did not mean that the revolutionary game was finished.

Wildcats

The Situationists claimed that they had effectively been in charge of the Sorbonne, and therefore symbolically at the head of the revolutionary movement in France, for three days. During that time the hand of Guy Debord could be clearly discerned in each of their statements and actions. These included the propaganda posters which called for 'The occupation of factories. Power to the workers' councils. Abolition of the society of classes. Down with the society of mercantile spectacle. Abolition of alienation. End of the university.' Characteristic of Debord's mocking sense of grandeur was a telegram to the Politburos of Peking and Moscow which read: 'Tremble Bureaucrats Stop The international power of workers councils will soon sweep you away Stop Humanity will not be happy until the day when the last bureaucrat will be hung with the entrails of the last capitalist Stop.'[9]

The abandonment of the Sorbonne was not, however, in Debord's eyes a defeat but a tactical withdrawal which enabled the Situationists truly to engage with activity in the streets. Their first action, decided in a meeting led by Debord in a flat on Île de la Cité, half a mile from the occupied Sorbonne, was to found a new movement, 'The Council for the Maintenance of Occupations' (CMDO), which would continue to spread the revolutionary message which the students, because of their unconscious affiliation to the bourgeoisie, were unable to understand. The notion of workers' councils was not new: the idea of such councils, 'soviets' in Leninist terminology, as a product of revolutionary crisis was well established on the extreme Left. What was original, however, was the theory, postulated by Debord, that the spontaneity which the Situationists embraced as a general principle would undermine any potential 'Leninist-Stalinist' threats to the autonomous power of the councils.

After handing out a tract, 'Report on the Occupation of the Sorbonne', attacking cretinised students, the second action of the group was to slip past police lines to take over the Institut pédagogique nationale on the rue d'Ulm, the prestigious headquarters of teacher education in France, adjacent to the even more prestigious École normale supérieure, then occupied by intransigent Maoists who could be extremely violent if crossed. The new group included Guy Debord, Raoul Vaneigem, Alice Becker-Ho, Mustapha Khayati, René Riesel, Gérard Bigorgne, Christian Sébastiani, François de Beaulieu and Jean-Louis Rançon, constituting a loose alliance of Situationists, ex-students, ex-workers and, most importantly for Raoul Vaneigem, 'young hooligans'. Debord himself made his headquarters on the rue d'Ulm, where he ran across two former comrades, Marc O, whom he was pleased to see, and Jacqeline de Jong, whom he ignored completely as an 'excluded and excommunicated' personage.[10] (Isidore Isou was also seen at this stage, apparently climbing onto the tops of cars and shouting that the revolution was 'a Letterist invention'. He was led away by friends and supporters before any serious conflict with diehard Maoist thugs.)[11]

The slogans of the Situationist-controlled 'Committee of Occupation' of the Sorbonne were now reworked and made into stylish and eye-catching posters by friendly striking printers in the southern suburb of Malakoff. These were distributed in the Paris area by the CMDO in a fleet of twelve or so mostly stolen cars, and in Nantes by activists in frequent faithful contact with the SI. Food, petrol, tobacco and of course alcohol were in short supply. The CMDO, in the spirit of Jules Bonnot, took happily to smashing shop windows and taking what they wanted and siphoning petrol from parked cars (the nearer the police station the better, as there tended to be less surveillance). Although not a member of the CMDO, Michèle Bernstein was happy to provide what she could, rustling up an impromptu banquet for the hungry and exhausted revolutionaries Debord and Becker-Ho whenever they called unannounced.

The atmosphere during these weeks of May was joyous. The group moved to the cellars of a building opposite the Institute, where a red and black flag and slogans dreamed up by the CMDO announced their territory. In the spirit of the Paris Commune of 1871, whose rebels had composed seditious songs which were 'a danger to the state', they took to 'detourning' traditional French songs into rebellious anthems or writing their own songs. Alice Becker-Ho composed a hymn to the destruction wreaked on the rue Gay-Lussac, 'The Song of the CMDO', which was immediately taken up as a battle cry. Vaneigem composed a song, 'La vie s'écoule, la vie s'enfuit' ('Life drifts away'), whilst Jacques Le Glou was more contemporary, transforming the banal hit 'Il est cinq heures' ('It's five o'clock') by Jacques Dutronc into a revolutionary call with the rallying cry 'Paris s'éveille' ('Paris Awakes').

The occupation of the Institute on the rue d'Ulm and the communal life there in the centre of Paris seemed idyllic, but it could not last for ever. Events were spinning far faster and far more wildly than the Situationists could have predicted or understood properly. For one thing the police repression, which swung properly into gear from the mid part of May onwards, was far more brutal than anyone could have expected, even given the low standards set in the first part of the month. The wave of strikes which started at Cléon, Flins, Le Mans and then, on 14 May, at Billancourt looked set to bring the government down. This position could not be tolerated by anyone in power. As postal workers, teachers, shopworkers, civil servants all joined in the strikes, it seemed that France was about to descend to a level of anarchy and lawlessness which it had not seen since 1871. 24 May marked the turning point when de Gaulle spoke to the French nation on television, stressing the need for 'a mutation in our society . . . a more extensive participation of everyone in the conduct and result of the activities which directly concern them'.

This was however no capitulation on de Gaulle's part. The night of 24 May was the most frightening and violent yet. Barricades went up in Bordeaux, Nantes and Lyons, where a police officer was killed. In Paris, some 30,000 demonstrators marching towards the place de la Bastille found their path blocked by police. They began tearing up paving stones, café chairs and tables, and anything else they found in their path, hurling them at the police who were now in trouble as they tried to defend the Town Hall, the Élysée Palace and other main buildings of state. The Stock Exchange was unguarded. In a pack of heavily armed and violent hooligans, chanting 'Temple of Gold', Debord, Becker-Ho and other Situationists made their way towards the building which was duly set ablaze.

This, though, was the beginning of the end. The economic life of the country had been paralysed and appeared to be on the brink of being destroyed. A deal had to be made with the unions to avoid the nightmare scenario of students and workers in alliance against the government. In the Hôtel du Chatelet on the rue de Grenelle, at 3 o'clock in the afternoon, union bosses and government representatives hammered out a deal which they thought would signal the end of the conflict. The deal was almost unanimously rejected. The parties of the parliamentary Left, with François Mitterrand and Pierre Mendès France, opportunistically seized on this rejection and proposed a coalition of the Left, with themselves at the helm. In the meantime de Gaulle had left the country to meet with his generals stationed on the Rhine to reassure himself of their support if the true crisis ever really came.

But the crisis never did come. At 4.30 on 30 May, de Gaulle spoke again to the French nation. This time he announced elections within forty days and 'civic action against subversion' and the threat of 'totalitarian communism'. The patriotic France, de Gaulle's natural constituency, rose as one: there was a triumphant parade of thousands up the Champs-Élysées, waving *tricolores* and chanting 'France back to work', 'Clean out the Sorbonne' and, more notoriously, 'Algérie Française' and 'Cohn-Bendit to Dachau'.

On 30 May the CMDO and the Situationists published a tract called 'To all Workers'. 'Comrades,' it read, 'what we have already done in France haunts Europe and is soon going to threaten all the dominant classes in the world, from the bureaucrats of Moscow and Peking to the millionaires of Washington and Tokyo. In the same way that we have made Paris dance, the international proletariat is going to come back and assault the capitals of all states, all the citadels of alienation.' Within twenty-four hours in Paris, the supporters of de Gaulle, of traditional France and traditional values, were dancing to a different rhythm and singing words which were in stark contradiction to those of the libertarian Left who had brought Paris closer than it had been for over a hundred years to revolution.

An incident at the end of May demonstrated a new harder edge to Debord which the events seemed to have awakened. At the École des Beaux Arts Debord had been corrected by someone who thought that the CRS should not be fought but won over to the cause of revolution. After all, argued the interloper, would it not be necessary to have a police force to put down the counter-revolution? Debord stood still, took off his glasses and, before anyone could say a word, had smashed his interlocutor in the face with all his force. Debord was not a big man. But he had never been afraid of physical violence, especially when it took his opponent by surprise. For Debord and his Situationist comrades this was the most important lesson of the events of May 1968.

CHAPTER 22

In Time of War

1968–9

The crackdown, which began with de Gaulle's return to Paris on 30 May and the street demonstrations which followed his televised address to the nation, was swift and effective. By the first week of June, strikes were crumbling across France, except in the most solid working-class areas where the desire for change was at its most militant. Two workers were killed in clashes with police at the Peugeot plant in Sochaux; at other factories throughout the country the paramilitary tactics of the CRS were met with fierce and determined resistance.

In Paris, the government outlawed all street demonstrations and banned eleven student groups, using an old law made by the Popular Front of the 1930s which, ironically enough, had originally been aimed at Right-wing groups. A notable exception to these measures was the extreme Right-wing group Occident: other leading and notorious Right-wingers were rumoured to be flooding back into France from North Africa and other flashpoints. Daniel Cohn-Bendit had already left the country, smuggled out by comrades. The death of a young schoolboy photographer, Gilles Tautin, killed in a skirmish with heavily armed CRS men, gave the movement a martyr and at his funeral workers and students of all denominations vowed to avenge him. But the movement was also exhausted, lacking direction and leadership and, most crucially, now at the mercy of a familiar parade of Left politicians, Guy Mollet, François Mitterrand, Pierre Mendès France, whose rhetoric was little altered by the convulsions of May. De Gaulle effectively had a free hand.

In the Sorbonne, the situation had degenerated to the point where capitulation was only a matter of time. The cellars and corridors were now running with rats, the students themselves were now filthy and lice-ridden. The free-wheeling and lawless atmosphere had become a magnet for every dope-dealer, whore, minor criminal and apolitical, gormless hippie in Paris. A group of mercenaries called the Katangais, made up of army deserters and petty thugs from the suburbs, had tried to impose some order on the 'revolutionary festival' which was rapidly becoming a nightmare which to some acid-tripping students resembled scenes painted by Hieronymus Bosch rather than the imagined Utopia. The thuggish bullying of the Katangais irritated everybody and they were finally expelled, leaving the 'commune' to be taken by the police without a struggle on 16 June. 'The joke was over,' declared the Situationist International, who held no grudge against the Katangais, even according them respect as genuine underclass toughs.

The Situationists instead reserved their contempt for the weak-minded and divided students whose vacillation and lack of rigour had meant that they had missed the revolutionary moment.

Going underground

On 15 July 1968, Debord led a final meeting of the CMDO at the Faculté de médecine in the 7th *arrondissement*. It was decided to dissolve the CMDO and offer membership of the SI to comrades who had proved themselves worthy of the nomenclature 'Situationist' during the heady days of May. Given the increasingly severe nature of the police counter-attack against the May revoutionaries, it was also agreed that now would be a good time to get out of France.

Debord did not leave Paris straight away but went into hiding in a flat in the rue Niger in the 12th *arrondissement* owned by Monique, another one of Michèle Bernstein's friends. After a few days spent collecting and sorting papers and dodging the few police patrols which ventured into the placid backwaters to the south of place de la Nation, he made for the Vosges and then for Brussels. On familiar ground, and in the company of Raoul Vaneigem, Alice Becker-Ho, Mustapha Khayati, René Riesel and other refugees from Paris, Debord started planning the next stage of Situationist activity.

It worried Debord that the Situationists were in danger of becoming legends. Their name now had an international currency as a byword for anarchy and subversion and Debord was very aware of how this might dilute the meaning and impact of theses and actions which had been worked out in rigorous fashion. In Paris, Nantes, Lyons and Strasbourg all kinds of groups were claiming allegiance to the Situationist International or declaring themselves 'pro-Situ' (this also had financial implications as Debord was to realise later when the eleven issues of *L'Internationale situationniste* were reprinted as pirate editions by a group in Nantes who made a handsome profit from their 'détournement' of SI texts). Abroad, although their texts were poorly distributed and little understood, the Situationists had, in Jamie Reid's words, 'captured headlines around the world and the imagination of a generation'.[1]

In America, libertarian groups such as Black Mask and Up Against the Wall Motherfucker declared themselves inspired by 'Situationism'. In England, the occupation of Hornsey Art School during May 1968 had brought together like minds who would briefly become the journal and organisation King Mob. In the universities of Cambridge, Essex and Sussex, Situationist texts in poor translations were devoured by figures as diverse as Anthony H. Wilson and Paul Sieveking, as well as the students who would later become the Angry Brigade, the proto-terrorist organisation which launched a series of bomb attacks on 'spectacular targets' in the later 1960s and early 1970s and whose name was taken from the *Enragés* of Nanterre.

This kind of fallout had been predicted by Guy Debord prior to the events of May and had to be avoided at all costs. His first actions in Brussels were therefore to plan a propaganada campaign which would counter the calumnies of the press and official media on the one hand, and, on the other hand, distinguish the Situationists, their ideas and their activities, from their so-called comrades and self-styled allies on the international Left.

The first part of this counter-attack was to publish a true account of what had actually happened in May. It was not difficult to find a publisher since in the immediate aftermath of May publishing houses fell over one another in pursuit of the 'revolutionaries' and their stories. A deal was quickly brokered with Gallimard, whose managing director Claude Gallimard had been impressed by the important reviewers who had lined up to take potshots at Raoul Vaneigem's book, which Gallimard had himself published, and Debord's *The Society of the Spectacle*. The prestige of these authors, whose predictions appeared to have come true and who had dirtied their hands in street-fighting, was now incalculable. For Debord the deal with Gallimard was also something of a victory since it had long rankled with him that Vaneigem, whom he considered as his intellectual inferior, had been published by the more important publishing house.

'Forget us!'

The book *Enragés et situationnistes dans le mouvement des occupations* was written in Brussels by the exiled Situationists Debord, Vaneigem, Khayati and Riesel, typed up by Alice Becker-Ho and published by Gallimard in the summer of 1968 with René Viénet as the designated author (this was something of an in-joke amongst the Situationists as Viénet had been slyly nicknamed 'Obélix' by Debord on account of his oafish manner). The text itself was a dry and rigorous account of the barricades, the occupation of the Sorbonne and the dissolution of the CMDO, not without shards of humour and typically Situationist invective ('Whoever has got a smelly arse makes ideology!' was a characteristic epithet which had annoyed Daniel Cohn-Bendit). Most striking of all however was the collection of photos scattered throughout the text of the riots and the Situationist graffiti around the Sorbonne. These had been collected by Viénet and Christian Sebastiani, the two Situationists who had been mainly responsible for these actions. The overall impact of this was to leave the reader believing that the revolutionary events of May had been guided and shaped by the poetic aphorisms of the Situationists rather than the accidents, mistakes and contradictions of history. The overall argument was clear: the responsibility for the failure of 1968 was the inability of the students to respond to and live out the desires which had been expressed on the walls of the Sorbonne. The final statement was combative: 'A fire has been lit which will never go out . . . the spectacular society will never sleep again.'[2]

Amongst the books which were published through the course of 1968, the most notable was Philippe Labro's *Ce n'est qu'un début* ('It is only a beginning') which quoted Situationist slogans but made scant reference to Debord and the Situationists' *Les Enragés* . . . , and stood out as a stylish and still defiant text. Pierre Viansson-Ponté in *Le Monde* was less than convinced, accusing the Situationists of being pretentious self-publicists and ludicrous fantasists whose most ridiculous claim was not that May 1968 had been their invention but that world revolution would ensue from their theoretical arguments.[3]

This kind of response was now expected in the Situationist camp. Less predictable was the way in which Situationist writings were becoming bestsellers. By the end of October 1968 the text of *On the Poverty of Student Life* had sold over sixty thousand copies whilst stock of both Debord and Vaneigem's books had all been sold out by June (Debord was again annoyed by the way in which Gallimard was quickly able to publish a second edition of Vaneigem's text, whilst his own book, published by the gentlemanly Buchet-Chastel, stayed off the shelves until 1969). Former Letterist sympathisers Jean-Louis Brau and Éliane Brau (formerly Éliane Papaï, Debord's lover in the early days of the Letterists) also brought out books to critical disdain and public approval.[4] Most remarkable of all was the fact that in December 1968, much to his own amazement, Debord's currently unavailable book *The Society of the Spectacle* was shortlisted for the prestigious Prix Sainte-Beuve, named after the nineteenth-century literary journalist most famous for his philosophical and critical writings and often termed the father of modern French criticism.

Debord and the other Situationists-in-hiding had now been back in Paris for some months and were even frequently to be seen at their old haunts. Debord was not however the first Situationist to be courted by the literary world. In June 1968 Vaneigem had been invited by Jean-Pierre Faye, on payment of the nominal fee of thirty francs, to become a member of the Writers' Union, a powerful force in the world of French literature and politics. Vaneigem's response was suitably contemptuous: 'Pieces of shit, musty crusts of intellectual shithouses, thick cunts, the smell of your own decomposition must have gone to your head and made you mad if you think that a Situationist would join your crappy little gang. . . . You'll soon understand that the time for this kind of joke is over for you. Times are changing. Next time, we'll fucking kill you, you arseholes.'[5]

In this letter Vaneigem captured the true mood of the times. The Situationists, now battle-hardened street-fighters, were also not above moving from verbal violence to real violence, smacking people hard for slights against the group, all in the name of 'direct justice'. A spate of attacks, not linked to Debord but apparently in the name of the SI, had been reported around Left-wing Paris. One unfortunate victim was Jean Maitron, who in his book *La Sorbonne par elle-même*, dashed off in the summer of 1968, had apparently committed the error of playing with or distorting Situationist slogans and arguments. The case for Maitron's defence was not helped by the fact that his publisher and associates were directly linked to the hated Communist Party. On Debord's orders the SI sent Maitron a letter demanding a public apology. When, a few weeks later, it was clear that none was forthcoming, a delegation, again presumably on Debord's orders, visited Maitron's apartment, where they insulted him and started smashing up the place, destroying family heirlooms and other items. The attack was written up in *Le Monde*, where the Situationists were described as louts, and Maitron gave an emotional account of the attack on the radio. The syndicalist newspaper, *La Révolution prolétarienne*, not previously noted for its promotion of family values in the name of revolutionary change, railed against 'terrorists in the grass' and continued, 'The militant worker knows how to use raw language, but uses it with circumspection. As for breaking furniture, he also knows how to break faces.'[6]

Debord's reply to the judging committee for the Prix Sainte-Beuve was no less robust, although somewhat more courtly in style. Disgusted by the effrontery of the literary establishment who wanted to give him a prize, he wrote to the avuncular figure of Edmond Buchet, the editor who had originally commissioned *The Society of the Spectacle* believing it was a history of the theatre, thus: 'As you know, I am radically hostile to all literary prizes. So please let this be known to all persons concerned so that they might avoid a blunder. I must even confess to you that if such a regrettable eventuality were to come about, I would no doubt be unable to prevent the consequences: the young Situationists would certainly be angry with the jury who awarded this distinction, indeed they would take it as an outrageous insult.'[7]

Buchet, not a little shaken by this response, informed the press that his new and daring young author might be rather difficult with literary honours, circulating Debord's letter amongst literary journalists. In the literary gossip pages of *Le Figaro Littéraire*, Bernard Pivot, who some twenty years later would go on to host France's most popular and influential television book programme *Apostrophes*, wrote about the 'ferocious Situationist' who could not 'accept being fêted by bourgeois society at a cocktail party hosted by the consumer society'. 'It is true that we weren't at Nanterre or the Sorbonne,' ironised Pivot, 'but a lovely little restaurant near the Élysée palace, but all the same we may well have had some heckling and even violence if the jury of the Prix Sainte-Beuve had given it to Guy Debord.' One of the rare photos of Debord, described as 'the occult pope of Situationism', appeared alongside the piece.[8] The Prix Sainte-Beuve went elsewhere that year.

The war against the literary establishment carried over into the New Year of 1969. The catalyst for this fresh outbreak of hostilities was the fact that Antoine Gallimard, the father of Claude Gallimard, had apparently been boasting at a dinner party that, having published Vaneigem's book and *Enragés . . .* , the Situationists were practically employees of the Gallimard publishing house. When this came to the ears of Debord and the Situationists they fired off a splenetic letter to Claude Gallimard making their position plain: Antoine Gallimard was 'a shit, a cunt' and a 'scraping from a bidet'. The letter continued: 'Two Situationists have published books with you. You will have no further contact with Situationists and from the two in question you will have no more books. You are so thick and wretched that it is useless to add any more insults. For the IS: Guy Debord, Mustapha Khayati, René Riesel, René Viénet.' Claude Gallimard, with a dry wit, decided to respond in kind: 'I was amused to find that you have found out that I was my father's son. Since you enjoy a good time, don't you think that we could have a drink together with the aforementioned Antoine Gallimard who, thick as he is, has a certain sense of humour . . . there is nothing of substance in your letter which might change our relationship.' This incensed the Situationists even more: 'You've no reason to find anything amusing in our letter of 16 January . . . Stick it up your arse. Forget us.'[9]

After May

Such minor spats were mere diversions and far from being the real substance of 1968, which had been the most important year ever in Situationist history, the year in which they had taken on a world role in the game of global revolution. There were inevitably tough consequences and even harder real challenges to come. The first of these was to construct some sort of analysis of the events which might contribute to a future strategy that would move the game to another level. The second was to find the way forward out of a conflict which had left the Situationists at the end of 1968 both inspired and exhausted.

It was clear that May 1968 had provided the best testing ground so far for

Debord's theories. In conversations around the end of the year and in early 1969, however, he questioned whether more could have been done, whether errors had been made (leaving the Sorbonne in the hands of Cohn-Bendit and the Students' Union had been a crucial calculation), and whether the Situationists had truly been able to connect, to fuse theory with practice in the revolutionary moment. Initial analyses of events however proved that it was the cowardice and compromise on the part of the non-Situationist students which had cost them the game. This left Debord at the end of December even more glacial and hardline than he had ever been before.

The actual role which the Situationists had played in the events of May was more difficult to define, even for those who had been in the thick of things. More than twenty years after the events, Debord assigned the Situationists and himself the central roles in the drama of the streets, claiming at the same time that these roles had been badly interpreted by commentators and historians of the period. 'All my life I have seen only troubled times, extreme divisions in society, and immense destruction; I have joined in these troubles,' he wrote in the opening pages of *Panegyric*. 'Such circumstances would no doubt suffice to prevent the most transparent of my acts or thoughts from ever being universally approved. But I do believe several of them could have been misunderstood.'[10] Debord saw the Situationists' role in the development of events as less to do with the students' generalised aims, which were really only reforms rather than revolution, and more directly linked to the creation of a situation, a moment in time in which absolute change could occur. This was, as he saw it, the culminating point of over a century of dissident activity in aesthetic and political theory which was at the heart of the avant-garde programme: 'It was modern poetry, for the last hundred years, that led us to there. We were a handful who thought that it was necessary to carry out its programme in reality, and in any case to do nothing else.' It was carrying out this programme, moving from theory to practice, Debord insisted, which had been the central important and, to non-Situationists, most shocking aspect of May 1968. 'It is sometimes surprising – to tell the truth, only since a recent date – to discover the atmosphere of hate and malediction that has constantly surrounded me and, as much as possible, kept me hidden. Some think that it is because of the grave responsibility that has often been attributed to me for the origins, or even for the command, of the May 1968 revolt . . . An angry queen of France once called to order the most seditious of her subjects: "There is rebellion in imagining that one could rebel."'[11]

Twenty years on, Debord had hardly modified the position he had developed as 1968 drew to a close. If the movement and the events had been a failure it had been the failure of so-called intellectuals and students to grasp the real nature of the enemy, which was not the nineteenth-century version of capitalism, the still cherished enemy of the French Communist

Party as well as Maoist or Trotskyist groupuscules, but the 'spectacle', the advanced form of capitalist organisation which had colonised the very texture and substance of everyday life and thought. The real questions which should have been asked in 1968, according to Debord, were not questions of how to abolish capitalism and restructure economic systems, or questions of womens' and minority rights, or reform of the *lycées* and universities, but how quickly and most effectively could modern society be dissolved and destroyed? This meant, more precisely, engaging with the 'spectacle' as a 'totality' – a term used by Hegel approaching and defining the process of revolutionary, absolute change, a change in which the passage of time could be felt as the ground trembled beneath your feet and the world turned. Debord believed that the SI, alone amongst the revolutionary groupuscules which had swarmed over the Sorbonne and Latin Quarter, had remained faithful to the most important promise of the early avant-gardes, which were to connect with and transform their time.

'Abolish alienation!' was a cry which had a more powerful and absolute resonance therefore than any committee decision taken in the Sorbonne to reform examination structures or the academic hierarchy. 'The Situationists have already abolished everything,' was the keenest rallying cry in the streets.

However, despite these reflections twenty years after the events, the reality was that amongst the many complex and contradictory factors which had contributed to the explosion of May 68, it was the simple but deadly threat of coalition between workers and students which, for most commentators, had looked most likely to bring down the state. The fact that this had not happened was, for most historians of the aftermath of 1968, also the real cause of the failure of the movement. It was certainly this coalition which the government had initially identified as the real threat. For the police the threat was also likely to come from the militant (and perhaps armed) wings of Maoist and Trotskysist groups which seemed to be organising on paramilitary lines, evoking in their rhetoric dangerous memories of the Resistance and the Commune. For the powers at the centre of French political life, in the immediate aftermath of 1968 the Situationists were apparently irrelevant, a marginal group of 'cultural terrorists' who were notorious for insulting editors and publishers, but who were of even less significance to mainstream political currents than the films of Jean-Luc Godard or the novels of Alain Robbe-Grillet.

But it seemed to nearly everyone who was there at the time that it was the presence of the Situationists which had made the events unique. Although a 'small band' they had worked hard, with graffiti and provocations and street-fighting, to ensure that their presence was felt everywhere. In the slipstream of events which succeeded May, Situationist slogans indeed became the defining memory of the insurrection in the popular imagination as well as in the more rarefied atmosphere of Saint-Germain-des-Prés. In the Sorbonne, on the streets, in cafés and bars, in the media, Situationist slogans and theses had entered the language and taken on a new and powerful currency.

The inescapable conclusion, drawn by media commentators, academics, historians, was that the revolution which had not happened still marked an important ineradicable change in the philosophical language of political engagement. The demands which the Situationists made, for desire instead of commodity, for real life instead of 'spectacle', were 'impossible', according to all mainstream politicians of Right and Left, but also on everyone's lips. The hardest question which Debord had to ask himself was whether the avant-garde had missed its time.

This was not the case, at least according to General de Gaulle. In his televised speech of 30 May, the speech which had rallied the comfortable classes to their counter-revolt, he isolated the real enemy of bourgeois France. They were not Communists, or Maoists or students or workers, but 'dangerous classes' consisting of the disaffected, the rootless, the bored, those who lacked any stake in society and sought its overthrow by any means necessary. 'This explosion,' thundered the General, 'has been provoked by groups who are revolting against modern society, against the society of consumerism, against the mechanised society, whether it is Communist in the East, or capitalist in the West. These are groups who have no idea what they will replace modern society with, but they take delight in negation, destruction, violence, anarchy.' Guy Debord could not have put it better himself. As de Gaulle's speech made clear, the real revolutionary forces, those which brought France closest to the brink, were composed of those elements in society who did not believe in the value of the cheap gifts which consumerist economics offered them. They were bored, negative, entirely destructive.

CHAPTER 23

Is the Reichstag Burning?

1969–70

When, in the first few months of 1969, Paris appeared to return to something like normality, the Situationists turned their attentions to Italy. Events in France the previous year had made an enormous impact on the Italian political landscape. Throughout the first part of 1968 the country had been in turmoil, with universities occupied by students and violent street disturbances in Rome, Turin, Milan and other major cities. Most crucially, Pietro Nenni, the longtime champion of the Socialist cause in Italy, had increased division on the Left when he had forced his party into coalition with the Right-wing Social Democrats and became part of Aldo Moro's Centre-Left grouping in the Italian parliament. Nenni's 'historic compromise' provoked disgust and anger among younger groups on the Left who had also turned their faces away from the monolith of the Italian Communist Party and replaced its chief theoretician Antonio Gramsci with Mao, Castro or Trotsky. The year 1968 had seen demonstrations against de Gaulle in Florence, where militants had marched carrying the banners of the Vietcong and Mao, street-fighting in Rome and Genoa in the name of 'self-management' and 'the abolition of alienated work', and the red-and-black flag of international Anarchism raised over the Palazzo Campana, the distinguished heart of the University of Turin.

For a long time Debord had cultivated a visceral attachment to Italy. He was very conscious of his own Italian origins, and even before he could speak Italian in any form that would be understood by a native of the country, he liked to affect Italian manners and sayings, addressing Italian comrades and friends with as much of the language as he could muster. It was not by chance that the Situationist International had been founded in the Ligurian Alps and that during its 'first artistic period' some of its most important and influential members were Italian. The break-up with the Italians such as Pinot-Gallizio had been genuinely difficult, since Debord had a lingering affection for who they were and what they represented, and was not characterised by the rancour and spite which marked the exclusion of the German or Scandinavian 'artistic gangsters'.

In 1969 the Situationist International looked very different from what it had been in 1957 in Cosio; its newer members had been in battle, were coarser and determinedly anti-artistic. The likes of Viénet and Riesel enjoyed pushing people about, using tough language and with their leather jackets and straggly beards could not have been further removed from the spry rakish elegance of earlier members such as Ralph Rumney or Asger Jorn. Debord, alone amongst his comrades, preserved a taste for refinement and exquisite language and this was partly expressed in an intellectual attachment to Italian ideas and writing. It was not only political turbulence which attracted Debord to Italy but also a fascination with the ideas of Machiavelli and Castiglione.

Death to the state

An Italian section of the Situationist International was founded in Milan in January 1969. It had three members, Claudio Pavan, Paolo Salvadori and Gianfranco Sanguinetti, each of whom had come into close contact with Guy Debord in Paris and who could be entrusted with the responsibility of carrying Situationist agitation in Europe to new heights. They were soon joined by Eduardo Rothe, a Venezuelan who had sought political asylum in Italy.

They quickly distinguished themselves as an energetic and fearless group of activists. The first edition of *Internazionale Situazionista* was drawn up, edited and published in the first few months of 1969. The positive reaction of the Italian underground and Leftist community, who bought over four thousand copies within a few weeks of its publication in Milan, proved to Debord's delight that he had been right to see Italy as the new theatre of operations. The Italian Situationists did not lack physical courage either, taking part in the fierce riots in Reggio di Calabria that summer. Nobody in Italy was quite sure who had organised the protests – students or workers – which had taken the Rome government quite by surprise, as so far very little of the tension of the big cities had seeped over into the south of Italy. The protests lasted over three months with the protesters taking effective control of the town, displacing Communist and Socialist officials. The Situationists declared this a victory for 'self-management' and began describing events in Reggio as the beginning of 'a new superior level' in the crisis afflicting Italy. It was 'the first insurrection of the Italian revolution' and therefore on a par with previous historic insurrections dear to the Situationists such as Kronstadt in 1917, Barcelona in 1936, Budapest in 1956. It was, most importantly, 'a popular revolt against the state'.[1]

According to the Italian Situationists, however, it was also clear that such a revolt would mobilise the murky forces, Fascist, neo-Fascist, Mafia or simply merely corrupt, which lay at the heart of the Italian nation. It was important, therefore, they stated clearly and quite unequivocally, that Reggio was also, unlike the revolts at Battipaglia and Caserte which had also been praised by the Situationists, a revolt which had been led by no one and seemed the autonomous work of the masses. The workers' councils, advocated as the way forward from the Sorbonne in 1968, found their living corollary here in the sleepy *mezzogiorno* of Italy.

Debord approved of all the actions of this new group. In the mercurial and flamboyant figure of Gianfranco Sanguinetti he had also found a comrade in arms. Sanguinetti shared Debord's taste for excessive drinking, sexual intrigue and reckless, daredevil brinkmanship. Sanguinetti was then only twenty, scion of a wealthy family in the north who had embraced Communism with fervour. Above all Sanguinetti had a rare talent for stylish literary and political provocation. Debord and Alice were very quickly seduced and entranced by the handsome and flamboyant figure who had turned away from Gramsci and the Italian Communist Party in favour of life as unlimited subjectivity. Sanguinetti was very quickly entrusted by Debord with what would soon be the crucial role of strategist in Italy.

In homage

As Situationist activity intensified in Italy, the mood in Paris in contrast was characterised by exhaustion and drift. Having been intially exhilarated by May 68 and its aftermath, the group was lacking focus and direction. Debord now sensed that the Situationist International would soon come to a crossroads. Michèle Bernstein remembers Debord in the early spring of 1969 as uncharacteristically gloomy. 'You could tell that he was exhausted,' she said. It seemed that even the self-styled master strategist did not now know which way the group should turn.

The year began with a stunt which recalled the activities of the earlier, more ludic Situationist International. During the Second World War a statue of the libertarian hero Charles Fourier had been unseated from its plinth on boulevard de Clichy, opposite the well-to-do school Lycée Jules-Ferry, and dismantled. As a mark of homage and defiance, Pierre Lepetit, a Situationist sympathiser and teacher at the École des Beaux Arts, had made an exact copy of the original which, although it weighed over a hundred kilos, was seated on the plinth by a group of *Enragés* and Situationists in less than fifteen minutes with the rubric 'In homage to Charles Fourier from those who manned the barricades on the rue Gay-Lussac'. It was a fine day in early March and there was a festive atmosphere in the group which included Viénet, Riesel, Sébastiani, Alice Becker-Ho (but not Debord) at the *terrasse* of a neighbouring café. Although the statue was removed by police and municipal workers with a crane a few days later, Debord heartily approved of the action which he considered a great success, particularly the way in which the restoration of the statue of the great poetic anarchist had provoked a round-the-clock police guard which had to be maintained until the offending object was removed. 'Never before', wrote Debord, 'had *détournement* been at work in such a domain.'[2]

The festive atmosphere was however short-lived. Of late the group had been marked by acrimony, personal rivalry and sexual jealousy. The high profile and prestige which the Situationists had attracted in the wake of May 68 was now distorting behaviour. The group had attracted fellow-travellers, sympathisers and fans, loosely and sometimes contemptuously termed the 'pro-Situs'. This made the inner circle, those who were proper members of the Situationist International, even more élitist and exclusive. Most meetings now took place in the apartment of René Viénet, not far from Les Halles. When discussions were concluded the group would go down to the nearest café to drink and continue debate in the presence of their 'pro-Situ' fans who were rigorously excluded from all debate. Sexual rivalry was as high on the agenda as political debate (one unfortunate 'pro-Situ', Angeline Neveu, who had the temerity to switch her sexual allegiances from Patrick Negroni to someone else, was barred from the group on the grounds that she was 'a manipulator. She wants to destroy the SI').[3]

Debord himself, at the centre of the inner circle of the SI, viewed such behaviour and petty machinations with haughty disdain. He also kept himself at a great distance from his admirers, even to the extent that many who had been attracted to the SI because of the prestige of *The Society of the Spectacle* and the group's leading role in May 68, became rather unsure about what precise role Debord played in the group. 'Debord was not someone who was central at the level of human relations,' said Patrick Negroni, who was himself at some remove from the inner circle. 'The behaviour was on a collective level, almost generational. Vaneigem had as much influence, it seemed even more on the younger people.'[4]

Debord's distance at this stage was not merely a ploy. He confided to Michèle Bernstein that he really had little faith in the present generation of Situationist 'partisans' and that he was unsure which way to take the group now that the revolutionary moment seemed to be passing into history. He had already decided to leave the Latin Quarter, scene of so many recent conflicts, and which now, newly paved and with a strengthened police presence, seemed to him like an occupied country. He moved camp in the late spring of 1969 from the cramped quarters on the rue Saint-Jacques to a well-appointed apartment, with a balcony and a telephone, on the rue Saint-Martin across the river. It seemed the first point of retreat.

Venice has conquered Guy Debord

Debord was also exhausted by the responsibility and physical hard work that he was putting into the twelfth and, as it turned out, final edition of *L'Internationale situationniste*. This was the edition which would aim to make some kind of sense out of the confused events of May 68, which would interpret the storms which were breaking out across the world from Berkeley to Warsaw University, and show that the SI still led the way in terms of strategic and tactical approaches to the practice of revolution. The debates amongst fans, pro-Situs and the lesser Situationists who swaggered at café tables in the Marais and around Les Halles now seemed to Debord to be so much hot air. With an uncharacteristic haste, at the end of July, when he had written and prepared for publication almost all the texts for the twelfth edition of the journal, Debord announced that he had had enough, that he was resigning as editor and that the journal was the responsibility of René Viénet. Given Viénet's preference for impressing women and thuggish posturing rather than writing it was unsurprising that the thirteenth edition of the journal never saw the light of day.

The mood of acrimony was carried over into the eighth conference of the Situationist International which was scheduled to take place in Venice on 25 September 1969, shortly before the publication of *L'Internationale situationniste* number 12. Venice was chosen partly because, impressed by the voracious activity of the new Italian section, Debord wished to place himself at the forefront of their activity. A second reason was that since the summer of 1968 the SI, like all of the other groupuscules who had participated in the 'revolutionary festival of May', was now coming under intense scrutiny from the French intelligence services – the fear of 'infiltration' by these groups was another reason to keep fans and 'pro-Situs' at bay – and it was thought Venice was a suitable distance from Paris.

The group who assembled in late September in the Giudecca district of Venice were however completely different both physically and intellectually from the sharp intellectuals who had founded the group at Cosio. Since this was Venice, they cut an even deeper contrast and seemed even further removed from the early 'psychogeographical' dreams of the first Situationists, dreams which had been recorded by Ralph Rumney who had stalked the beat poet Alan Ansen in 1957 across these same streets, alleys and canals.

This was also one of the largest conferences which the Situationists had organised, with eighteen members of the SI from Scandinavia, Holland, Italy and France and their attendant girlfriends, pals and fellow-travellers. Most of the debates centred on the crucial question of which way the SI should turn now. Should it return to artistic and political agitation? Or was it possible to take the revolutionary game which had been started in May in Paris one step further towards total transformation?

Debord was depressed at the way things were turning out and moment-
arily lost his concentration and grip on SI affairs. The conference, and
therefore the group, now seemed to be slipping into the hands of those
who favoured 'direct action', even though no one knew precisely what
this meant, over the development of a new theory which might match
the shifting conditions of the time. The CMDO was taken as the model
form of organisation – although what had characterised the CMDO was
precisely its disorganisation – and the Central Council of the SI dissolved.
The consequences of these two decisions were the beginning of the end of
the SI. Crucially, as the editorial control of *L'Internationale situationniste* was
now in the hands of Riesel, de Beaulieu, Sébastiani and Viénet, each of them
loudly anti-intellectual, Debord realised that it would now be impossible
to maintain anything like the torrential flow of ideas which had driven
Situationism towards its realisation in May 1968. What had looked like
a historic moment was beginning to seem more like a fiasco.

There was worse to come. As the conference was breaking up, Mustapha
Khayati, still one of Debord's sharpest and most trusted lieutenants,
announced to a stunned group of Situationists that he had decided to leave
the group and commit himself to the Palestinian cause. Khayati's support
for his Arab comrades had long been a sore point amongst the Situationists,
most of whom denounced all forms of nationalism, and some of whom, such
as Michèle Bernstein, were resolutely opposed to the cause of Palestine. All
Situationists opposed political terrorism, which was seen as playing into the
hands of the enemy, and the 'Holy War' which was being launched against
the West from the Middle East was considered by Debord as anathema,
less a revolutionary struggle than medieval nostalgia. Khayati had been
in touch with Israeli Leftists and representatives from various Palestinian
groups in Venice throughout the summer of 1969 (an infiltrator known as
Mustapha Saha, a student from Nanterre and associate of the 22 March
Movement, had further confused these manoeuvres by passing himself
off as Khayati and quizzing known Situationist sympathisers on their
activities that summer). Khayati finally decided to throw in his lot with
the Popular Democratic Front for the Liberation of Palestine, a group led
by Nayef Hawatmeh who espoused an unholy marriage between Islam and
Marxist-Leninism and who was supported and funded from East Germany.
When Khayati left, the SI, much to Debord's disappointment, lost its only
bridge to the Arab world and, no less important, a strategic thinker of great
literary talent and political acumen.

'We prophesied nothing'

The twelfth and final issue of *L'Internationale situationniste*, written almost
entirely by Guy Debord, was published in Paris and Venice in September

during the final acrimonious conference. The tone was rancorous, sombre, defensive and gleefully ironic in equal measure. This tone was most evident in a long essay, 'The Beginning of an Era', which analysed the events of May and their consequences for the international revolutionary classes. At his most lucid and penetrating, Debord considered the language which had been used by commentators to describe May 1968. The vocabulary, even the very term 'events', was, he argued, a way of masking what had really happened, which was that a tiny band of dedicated revolutionaries on the rue Gay-Lussac had brought France to the brink of the most complete transformation in its history. It was no accident, Debord began, that *The Society of the Spectacle* had been published six months before the disturbances began. The Situationist impact on developments was further confirmed by the fact that it was the *Enragés* . . . book which had been the most stolen book in Parisian bookshops after the barricades had been taken down. Anyone who doubted that the real issues of 1968 had been defined by the Situationists had only 'to read the walls', where Situationist slogans (scrupulously collected and reprinted in Walter Lewino's book *L'Imagination au pouvoir*, published some months later) had guided and shaped events. The conflict had therefore not been about workers and students but about the commodification of life and its rejection by a generation who had, for an essential moment, glimpsed the possibilities which lay beyond 'the spectacle of non-life'. That this had occurred was not the result of political theory in action, but because the Situationists, alone amongst the movements of their time, had grasped the essential forms of alienation which made modern life so horrible and pointed them out. 'We prophesied nothing,' wrote Debord. 'We had simply pointed out what was already present. . . . If many people did what we wrote, it was because we essentially wrote the negative that had been lived by us and by so many others before us. What thus came to the light of consciousness in the spring of 1968 was nothing other than what had been sleeping in the night of the "spectactular society", whose spectacles showed nothing but an eternal positive façade.'[5]

It was conceded that tactical errors had been made. It was regretted that the Sorbonne had been at the centre of the movement of occupations. If the centre had moved instead to a single, large factory where workers' councils could have taken practical control of events and materials then the outbreak of a revolutionary civil war would only have been hours away. All of this was hypothesis, but Debord was deadly serious about the reality of armed conflict, even if this provoked foreign intervention, an eventuality which he would have welcomed as raising the stakes: 'Everything would once again have hinged on the European proletariat: double or nothing.' The same intransigent and fearless tone was caught in the concluding remarks, which also seemed to hint ambiguously at the expediency of political violence in the struggles to come: 'Now this critique is arming itself. The "sunburst that in one flash reveals the features of the new world" was seen in France that month of May with intermingled red and black flags of workers' democracy. The follow-up will come everywhere.'[6]

Other articles in the final *L'Internationale situationniste* mocked international press accounts of the Situationists and their activities, refuted the critical reviews of Situationist books in the mainstream press, and attacked the wretched Jean Maitron who had been so effectively 'terrorised' by the Situationists' hoodlum wing. It was noted that the term 'Situationists' had now officially entered the language and the Situationist International maliciously reproduced the hopelessly askew entry from the prestigious Larousse dictionary which described the Situationists as 'a group of students advocating an effective action against the social situation which favours the present generation'.[7] There were pieces from Vaneigem and Riesel, speculating and theorising about the future shape of revolutionary organisations. A short piece on the expulsion of the English Situationists in 1967 shed further light on what had been a typically mysterious execution of policy by revealing that one of the things that had irritated Situationists (more precisely Debord) was the proximity of the group to the American anarchists of the journal *Black Mask*. Vaneigem had been dispatched to New York, the piece revealed, to develop contacts but had refused to have any connection with Ben Morea, the publisher of *Black Mask*, on the grounds that he was intellectually dishonest. It was also perceived that an alliance between the Americans and the English, who were friendly and sympathetic towards Morea and who visited him in New York, would be a very bad thing and a potentially destabilising force in Paris. Thus it was that the first attempts at creating an American section of the Situationist International had been stillborn.

Although the tone was sombre, with little of the playful and acidic wit typical of earlier issues, all of the articles in this *L'Internationale situationniste* were combative. Its enemies were now being engaged with everywhere: 'It is easy to recognise throughout the world,' wrote Debord, 'the new tone with which a radical critique is pronouncing its declaration of war on the old society, from the graffiti on the walls of England and Italy to the extremist Mexican group Caos, which during the summer of 1968 called for the sabotage of the Olympics and of "the society of spectacular consumption"; from the acts and publications of the Acratas in Madrid to the shout at a Wall Street demonstration (AFP, 12 April), "Stop the Show".' The war was quite definitely not over.

The strategy of tension

It was in Italy that the most effective forms of combat were being put to the test. The French May was already moving into history, as were the students' protest in the Italian universities. France enjoyed a relatively tranquil transition back to Gaullist normality and small groups, such as La Gauche prolétarienne, who advocated armed conflict, were quickly suppressed by legal sanction, police and intelligence service infiltration and public distaste for violence. In Italy however the soured revolution had only further poisoned an already ailing political system. The move towards violence was immediate and widespread. Debord wrote approvingly of the 1969 revolts in Battipaglia, which left two dead, and the prison mutinies in Turin, Milan and Genoa, which 'pushed the crisis to a higher level and reduced even more the bureaucrats' margin of manoeuvre'.[8] He wrote admiringly, as if describing a vignette from the Spanish Civil War, of how 'in Battipaglia the workers kept control of the town for twenty-four hours after the police opened fire, seizing arms, laying siege to the police holed up in their barracks and demanding their surrender, and obstructing roads and trains'. This was clearly the kind of activity which, Debord claimed, if implemented in France at the crucial moment in May 1968, would have taken France to within an hour of civil war.

In Milan, where anti-capitalist and anti-Fiat demonstrations had predictably taken ugly turns, he also approved of the demonstrators' urge to vandalise and to wreck the elegant quarters of this most mercantile and spectacular of cities. 'On this occasion,' he wrote, 'the Italian situationists took up the French methods in the most appropriate manner.' This remark also turned out to be a premonition. On 12 December 1969, the centre of Rome and the Piazza Fontana in the elegant centre of Milan were rocked by twelve bombs in succession. There were few casualties in Rome, but in Milan sixteen people were killed and ninety injured.

The immediate police reaction was to pursue and intimidate all those they suspected of 'red extremism'. Members of radical groups of all hues were rounded up and subjected to fierce interrogation. Leading anarchists who had died in police custody were alleged by the police to have 'committed suicide'. Across Italy a wave of revulsion spread through all social classes and even liberal commentators in the Milanese and Roman press approved of the measures taken. The editors of the Leftist journals *Potere operaio* and *Lotta continua* were tried and sentenced. The leading Milanese publisher Giangiacomo Feltrinelli, a wealthy and notable Left-wing propagandist and an intimate of Fidel Castro, had his passport taken away and was indicted for incitement to subversion and being the leader of an international terrorist organisation called 'Tricontinental'. Copies of books by Mao, Marx, Castro and even Hegel and Sartre were seized from bookshops around the country. The Italian nation was in deep panic.[9]

The Situationist International did not approve of bombs, but it did not approve of hysteria either, especially when emotions swung away from the promise of revolution. On the morning of 19 December a pamphlet entitled

'Il Reichstag bruccia?' ('Is the Reichstag burning?') could be found scattered around the Piazza Fontana and factories throughout Milan. It was signed by 'Friends of the Internationale' and published in the names of Sacco and Vanzetti, two Italian anarchists who were condemned to death in Massachusetts in 1921 for alleged armed robberies and whose innocence became a *cause célèbre* throughout the world. The text had in fact been composed by the Situationist International and it accused the Italian state of having a hand in the Rome and Milan bombs. Terrorism was denounced as most commonly a 'primitive and infantile demonstration of revolutionary violence' and the fruit of 'failed revolution'. These particular massacres, it was argued, were, however, a new, more spectacular form of violence, sanctioned by the state in order to frighten and coerce the populace. This form of terrorism was the brutal exposed reality of the society of the spectacle.

When the Situationists wrote this text, which caused an outcry on the Left as well as the Right, few even on the extreme Left dared to think that this was possible let alone already happening. It would be several years before the role and the activities of the Italian intelligence services known as 'Gladio' and their hand in the bombings would be fully known and revealed in the international press. It was the Situationists who had been the first to unveil the new tactics mounted by the spectacular society in its self-defence, the deliberate provocation and even murder of its citizens which would ward off threats from the insurrectionist Left with the so-called 'strategy of tension'. Debord was proud but not pleased that the Situationists had been the first to decipher the meaning of these events. But in late 1969, as Italy stood on the edge, aware that their position in Italy was now unsafe and that they would be under attack from all quarters once it was realised who had written the pamphlet, the Italian Situationists were called to France by Debord, who now sought their theoretical input in future developments.

CHAPTER 24

Without Dead Time

1970–1

The return to Paris was not without its complications. The conference in Venice had left Debord exhausted and disillusioned. His leadership of the SI had been unquestioned since the group's inception in 1957 and every action taken by the group was ultimately Debord's responsibility. The events of 1968 had signalled a turning point in the Situationist micro-society as well as in the world outside: younger, newer and brasher recruits, like Viénet and Riesel, who had made their mark on the barricades on the rue Gay-Lussac, were no longer content to play second string in an organisation which claimed to challenge the very notion of leaders and leadership. Debord was certain that, with the exception of Vaneigem, these latter recruits lacked the intellectual sophistication to carry on the revolutionary game. His problem therefore was how to cut himself away from these later Situationists whilst preserving the integrity of the group's tactics and remaining faithful to the strategic aims which he had been developing so effectively since 1957. It seemed at first that it was a problem of organisation – a collective internal document on this theme had been produced in October 1969 – and so Situationists were asked to gather their thoughts on this matter for a series of meetings which would take place in May.

In the meantime, Debord gave himself more resolutely than ever to the pleasures of alcohol. He had become noticeably heavier and more jowly than he had ever been before. He still drank mainly wine, and profited from his frequent excursions to Italy in the company of Sanguinetti to make himself an expert on the wines of the country and the best ways to drink them. He particularly loved the small bars of the Oltrarno district of Florence, mixing in marginal and semi-criminal environments as well as the most elegant cafés. Harder spirits had rarely made an appearance but grappa and cognac were now staples of his drinking life. Above all, as his drinking intensified and sessions extended themselves over days, he savoured the poetic possibilities which drink uncovered by steering him inexorably and irrevocably from any connection with the routine organisation of daily life. More than ever, drinking became a way of overcoming not only the mediocre demands made on the individual by the spectacular society, but also a way of overcoming space and time through a futile but essentially beautiful activity. 'First, like everyone,' Debord wrote, 'I appreciated the effect of slight drunkenness: then very soon I grew to like what lies beyond violent drunkenness, when one has passed that stage: a magnificent and terrible peace, the true taste of the passage of time. Although in the first decades I may have allowed slight indications to appear once or twice a week, it is a fact that I have been continuously drunk for periods of several months; and the rest of the time I still drank a lot.'[1]

When in Paris at this stage, Debord frequented not only the Left Bank bars and cafés where he had been known for nearly twenty years, but also, from his new base in the rue Saint-Martin, began to seek out a drinking life which lay beyond the confines of the area between the rue de Seine and the place de la Contrescarpe. He enjoyed the anonymity and the random encounters with people who had little time for or indeed scorned the intellectual hothouse of the Left Bank. 'Guy was extremely normal,' said Alice Becker-Ho. 'He did not want people to think that he was interested always in politics, philosophy, and that he could not speak normally. He liked ordinary people, and they liked him.' One such friendship, well away from 'politics and philosophy', was established with a certain Suzon Marzin and her daughter Christine, a resolutely eccentric pair who owned a second-hand furniture shop in the Marais not far from the flat on the rue Saint-Martin. Alice Becker-Ho had visited the shop in search of a frame for a bed and had been immediately enchanted by Suzon's witty and disordered manner. Dinners followed and the shopkeeper, who loudly professed her disdain for books and other intellectual nonsense, found herself at the heart of the Situationist community, dining with Michèle Bernstein, Sanguinetti, René Viénet and others. She remembers long conversations with Debord about her life, her father's life and above all that Debord was a good listener, even if his manner could offputtingly be that of schoolteacher. 'Guy Debord knew how to listen to me,' she said. 'When I made a mistake in French he made me start my sentence again. He was a very intelligent man.'[2]

Debates to save the SI

Less gentle was the sort of intimidation which certain Situationists practised and which, in the wake of the well-publicised attack on Jean Maitron, looked dangerously like becoming as much a hallmark of Situationist activity as it was of rival Maoist or Trotskyist groups. Another incident occurred when a Situationist delegation drove to Lyons. Their aim was to 'punish' the editor of the journal *L'Archinoir* who had had the temerity to write a tract called 'To the SI'. The unfortunate editor was smacked around his apartment until blood began to flow. The Situationists stopped the punishment beating at this stage, aware that they might have gone too far.

Debord was not afraid of violence but he was, despite his regard for Sanguinetti and Viénet, disgusted and angered by this sort of behaviour. The question of organisation and the publication of the 13th issue of the *L'Internationale situationniste* under the guidance of Vaneigem now weighed even more heavily upon him. It was clear to Debord by the spring of 1970, which he spent mainly in Paris with Alice and other intimates, shunning any semi-public appearance in his familiar cafés, that the Situationist International was facing a crisis which might have terminal consequences. Debord had relinquished his editorship of the journal and therefore effective control over the direction of the SI, but it was clear that those who were taking over or were about to take over had little understanding of what steps should be taken to move the group forward, or, more urgently, save it from a steep decline. It was essential to Debord that the SI did not simply become known as one of the many disparate elements who had contributed to the failed revolution and thereby entered the museum of dead avant-gardes. Above all, therefore, the Situationist International had to be saved from itself.

Endless documents were produced for debate and discussion. The key themes were 'theoretical orientation' and 'organisational methods'. It was tacitly agreed that, although it was the theses and arguments of the Situationists which had most effectively provoked the events of May 68, and that it was their subsequent actions which had been the most inflammatory (the SI conceded nothing to Cohn-Bendit and others), there had been errors and these were largely to do with their lack of planning and foresight about what form of organisation might proceed from the revolutionary moment. The 'workers' councils', inspired by the Leninist Soviet model were both unoriginal and effectively unworkable, even a direct contradiction of what the Situationists had originally promised as a revolutionary festival or, as Viénet described it, 'a banquet'. The real problem, as Debord expressed it, was that councils tended to be organisations moulded out of pre-existing conditions and ideology and therefore contrary to the demands of Situationist practice. The key to the desired fusion between theory and practice was to bring the Situationist theses to the working class, whose boredom, defined by the dominating nexus of work, leisure and commodity fetishism, preserved their separation from theory. Debord proposed literature as a possible solution, suggesting a theoretical text which 'would be the opposite of the Communist manifesto' called 'Problems of the Classless Society'. Other suggested publications were a book of selected Situationist aphorisms and maxims, which would in the Nietzschean manner provide a guide to the philosophical language of the group and so illuminate its practice. Debord also suggested, most controversially, the composition of a *History of the Situationist International* and a film of *The Society of the Spectacle*. The latter was potentially difficult and certainly walking a tightrope, apparently contradicting a theory which set out to destroy the civilisation of the image. Debord justified this practice however in the name of *détournement* and promised a film which would ruin all other films.

The history, and the historification of the SI, was more difficult to justify to other Situationists, who were so surprised by this that the flow of documents circulating between Amsterdam, New York and Paris suddenly concentrated on this one issue which seemed to signal the end of the group and its activity. For Debord however it was a master stroke, silencing debate and leaving him space to think and manoeuvre. Most urgently, it seemed to signal for the Situationists that maybe their historic moment had passed.

The resignation of Vaneigem

The internal debates looked set to destroy the Situationist International. The last great act of the group had been the tract in Milan published by the Italian Situationists, whilst in Paris acrimony and simmering violence were now never too far from the surface at any given meeting. Relations between Debord and Vaneigem were particularly bad, with Debord suspecting Vaneigem of organising a 'putsch'. Paranoia on both sides was exacerbated by the rumour, constantly and consistently murmured by Debord's supporters, that Vaneigem had only made a fleeting appearance during the events of May 68.

At the same time further efforts were made to develop the Situationist International's influence abroad. In the United States, the first edition of a journal in English called *Situationist International* had already been published in June 1969, modelled on the French edition and written by Robert Chasse, Bruce Elwell, Jon Horelick and Tony Verlaan. The group was in regular contact with Paris and under the close control of Debord himself, who was particularly keen on Horelick and Verlaan extending operations out into the wider world of mainstream publishing. Throughout the course of 1970, with Debord's encouragement, they pursued without success a variety of publishing houses, including Doubleday and Random House, seeking to sell the translation rights to *La Société du spectacle* and the *Traité de savoir-vivre*. The reactions ranged from the lacklustre to the openly hostile, with the Situationists treated as something halfway between a terrorist group and a student radical groupuscule.[3]

Between 17 and 19 January 1970 delegates from the international sections of the SI met in Wolsfeld in West Germany and finally, poignantly, in Trier, a gloomy provincial town which was also the birthplace of Karl Marx. The mood in the SI was, however, dreary and desultory rather than apocalyptic.

There was, most noticeably, a sense in the international sections that the SI had run its course. J. V. Martin, still a robust and committed Situationist, complained that Situationist actions and provocations were now actually making very little impact in Scandinavia. Other sections remarked on the inability of the SI to mark out new territory or adopt new critical positions. Certainly in France, it was clear that the swaggering leather-jacketed Situationists who had occupied the Sorbonne with such style and bravura did not have the intellectual qualities to maintain the strategic momentum which 1968 had given them. The SI seemed doomed to drift and impotence. The conference broke up gloomily.

The most crucial point in the slow break-up of the SI was the rupture with Vaneigem. He was accused of cowardice, of not fully participating in the events of May with the courage and authority which a Situationist ought to possess in such a moment. Vaneigem was also a threat to Debord and one of the few remaining Situationists who could intellectually match Debord step for step. The campaign against Vaneigem became a full-blown war in the November of 1970, when Riesel, Viénet and Debord established a tendency which explicitly attacked everything which Vaneigem stood for.

Vaneigem was mortally wounded and, his position untenable, resigned on 14 November. He took it personally and considered himself to have been betrayed by Debord for reasons which even now he cannot fathom out. The two had been leaders of a movement which for a moment looked as if it might truly change the world but which seemed now to be degenerating into a spiteful contest of egos and wills. 'The tendency that established itself in the French section on 11 November 1970 has the merit of being the last abstraction to be able to achieve expression within, on behalf and in the name of the SI,' wrote Vaneigem in his letter of resignation. 'If it is true that the group has never been anything other than the very unevenly distributed abilities and weaknesses of its members, there is no longer at the critical moment we are now facing any discernible community, or even tendency to make us forget that each and every one of us is alone in answering for himself. How did what was exciting in the consciousness of a collective project manage to become a sense of unease at being in one another's company? This will be for historians to establish. I feel no vocation, be it that of historian or intellectual, retired or not, to become a war veteran . . .'[4] When, as a kind of historian, I asked Vaneigem how this split could be explained if not as a personal dispute, he answered that he had not changed his position for a minute since he wrote his letter of resignation. 'I confess that neither the memory of the past nor the passion of a history which is unfinished is worthy of any kind of judgement. As for the rest, if I was at the age when one limps from memory to the tomb what could I tell you that you don't know already? . . . There is too much to do to worry about answering for the past.'[5] Faithful to his word Vaneigem, now resident in the Belgian countryside, continues to write brilliant, poetic and imperious works of social theory and criticism.

Vaneigem was henceforth dubbed 'Ratgeb' in a derisory gesture by Debord and his followers. By the end of 1970 there were only five Situationists left (Christian Sébastiani had been thrown out for chatting to Mustapha Khayati who, as an 'exclu', was now *infréquentable*). Of these only Sanguinetti seemed to rise above the general level of intellectual mediocrity, demonstrating a daring and a flair for provocation which recalled the heroic days of the SI before May 68. Even his skills however were not enough to stop him, in early 1971, from being arrested and thrown out of France as a suspect terrorist who was alleged to have been involved in the December bombings in Milan. Guy Debord too, like many of his milieu, was now receiving more attention from the police and the French intelligence services than was comfortable.

Letters to an editor

No less serious and engaging for Debord was the dispute which flared up between the Situationists and Giangiacomo Feltrinelli over the publication in Italian of the twelve issues of *L'Internationale situationniste*. Feltrinelli had long been attracted to the Situationists, as he had been to other radical groups in Italy and beyond. He was alleged, for example, to have close links with Ulrike Meinhof and Andreas Baader, who had not yet started their terror campaign in West Germany but were already moving outside the law. Feltrinelli had put them up at his country house outside Milan when they were on the run.

Feltrinelli was something of a paradox: he was a romantic, a millionaire publisher, known in Milan and Rome for his stylish and elegant manner, with connections in high places on both sides of the political divide in Italy. The Feltrinelli publishing empire continues as a major political and literary force in Italy today: the shops in Rome and elsewhere are roughly the equivalent of Waterstone's in London and Barnes and Noble in New York. He was also a radical dreamer, who since 1949 had dedicated himself to collecting archive material and publishing radical texts ranging from Lord Russell of Liverpool to Marx, Castro, Mao, Gramsci and Lenin. In 1964 he had travelled to Cuba to meet Castro, whom he now flaunted as a personal friend. As, in the wake of 1968, events in Italy had taken a serious and potentially violent turn, Feltrinelli had founded his own underground guerrilla organisation, the Gruppi di Azione Partigiana (the Partisan Action Group, or GAP). Feltrinelli dreamt of a revolution on the Cuban model, led by a ragged partisan army of workers, and was rumoured to be storing guns and bombing equipment in the hills above his country residence. There were also actions: bomb attacks on political parties, on factories, on the US Consulate were all claimed by GAP. Then there was Radio GAP, the result of Feltrinelli's wide experience of the media, which broadcast mainly around Milan. It began its broadcasts, 'Attention, this is Radio GAP, the Group of Partisan Action!'[6]

To the Situationists Feltrinelli was an opportunist menace. They knew of GAP and his terrorist dreams and refused to have anything to do with him. However, Feltrinelli had already published *De la misère en milieu étudiant*, which had no copyright, in an Italian translation that had been widely read and applauded on Italian campuses. When they were approached by Gian Piero Brega on behalf of Feltrinelli, who wrote to the Situationists asking for foreign language rights, Debord wrote back a stinging reply, calling Feltrinelli 'a Stalinist reptile' and the 'subaltern policeman of democracy'. Brega, himself no slouch with polemical insults, replied in kind, describing Debord to his face as a 'sick nutcase' and advising him to seek medical help, whilst wishing him a quick recovery. A yet more sinister letter was sent from the SI to Brega, this time signed by Sanguinetti. The tone was far from jocular, as Sanguinetti insinuated that Brega was not 'far from reach' and that he was 'personally responsible' for Feltrinelli's duplicity. 'It is your hide,' wrote Sanguinetti, 'that we will take it out on.'[7] These letters were reproduced by Sanguinetti, who plastered them around the elegant and prestigious Brera district of Milan, a stone's throw from La Scala and Feltrinelli's main bookshop, as a further provocative gesture.

These threats and actions, which certainly signalled violence to the uninitiated reader of Situationist texts, were to have repercussions which neither Debord nor Sanguinetti could have predicted. Most notably, when Feltrinelli was killed in mysterious circumstances, allegedly preparing a bomb, the attentions of media and police were concentrated on the SI and their texts. In the pages of *L'Espresso*, below a photograph of the grieving Feltrinelli family and their legal and medical advisers, a half page was given over to describing the threats of the SI against Feltrinelli and 'a certain Guy Debord' who ran operations 'from Paris, where else?'[8]

Debord and Sanguinetti were not surprised by this turn of events – had not the Italian Situationists pointed out at the time of the Piazza Fontana bombing that modern terrorism and mysterious assassinations were all creations of 'spectacular society'? – but they were stunned and unnerved by the way in which the SI had become identified in the public imagination with precisely the terrorist organisations which the SI denounced as playing into the hands of the enemy. There were claims, in the *Corriere d'Informazione*, that the SI had been demanding an initial payment of a billion lire from Feltrinelli: 'From that to murder,' wrote the journalist, 'there is only one step.'[9] If the polemic with Feltrinelli demonstrated anything it was the fact that, in the falsified conditions created by the 'spectacle' in defence of itself after 1968, words could quite literally kill.

The spectacular times of the SI

In the meantime, in spite of their silence on external affairs and their internal wranglings, the Situationist International was also becoming a legend. In October 1971, under the terms of a deal brokered by the Dutch Situationist Tony Verlaan, the Amsterdam publisher Van Gennep undertook to reprint the twelve volumes of *L'Internationale situationniste* in its unabridged form. Debord was clearly delighted with this, firstly because he had always loved Amsterdam and considered it a natural home of Situationist activity and, secondly, because this move displaced the mooted thirteenth volume of *L'Internationale situationniste* from the original Situationist canon. Debord was also content that the resignation of Vaneigem made it less likely that such a volume would appear. The deal with Van Gennep made this almost definite and restored Debord to his central position as strategist and prime mover. Debord also appreciated the publicity handout, which in Situationist style Van Gennep produced in the form of a comic strip in which the Situationists, including a stubbled, jowly Debord, were depicted boozing in a dive near the Amsterdam docks in the company of Marx and Hegel.

For the first time the Situationists were also receiving warm reviews in the mainstream. In Paris, Denis Lahaye in *Le Monde*, reviewing the Van Gennep reprint, wrote approvingly of the SI, 'who have always refused, in the name of the revolution, any form of association or assimilation with Leftism, [and] set the totality of its history as an absolute, which must now produce its own supersession.'[10] In England, in a review of the same edition, an anonymous *TLS* commentator noted that, as well as costing only £3, less than the price of the individual copies, 'the volume provides a fascinating record of the groupuscule which began in the French tradition of political-cultural sectarianism and ended by playing a prominent part first in the disturbances at Strasbourg University in 1966 and then in the more dramatic 'events' of May 1968.'[11] This much, both accurate and true enough in Situationist terms, satisfied Debord that the Van Gennep deal had been worthwhile. There was in the brief note however also a troubling point to do with the 'commercial' aspect of such a publication, which, as the reviewer pointed out, placed crucial arguments out of context or above their historical time in a 'highly marketable commodity in a clearly spectacular way'.

This was also a pattern which was beginning to emerge in a disturbing manner in the plethora of articles which were appearing in the French underground press to occupy the space left by the SI's self-imposed silence. In *Actuel*, the self-proclaimed *Rolling Stone* of France and the bible of French hippiedom, an article entitled 'The Big Shots in the Situationist International' confusedly described the SI as being like a 'delirious village fête' which aimed at destroying language, authority and urbanism.[12]

Alongside the headline a 'détourned' pornographic poster in the 'pro-Situ' style depicted a half-naked woman quoting revolutionary sentiments as she pulls the underpants of a man to whom she is clearly about to deliver a blow job. Debord was depicted as a 'secret figure, without the charm of André Breton, who brings with him several carefully ordered myths'. Less severe was the description of Raoul Vaneigem, a more 'generous person, to whom women flocked impetuously'. All in all, the article gave the impression that despite its revolutionary rhetoric and almost comical seriousness, the Situationist International was not really to be distinguished from any group which had sprouted out of the detritus of 1968, other than the fact that the Situationists were obviously good at inventing slogans.

As the 1960s stuttered to a close, the SI, who despised 'cretinous' rock music, ignored fashion (through the course of the 1960s the formerly dandified Debord famously dressed like a down-at-heel provincial schoolteacher), and deplored drugs (but not wine), were in danger of being seen as an integral part of the French experience of 1960s radicalism which included Jean-Luc Godard, the Rolling Stones, Pink Floyd, LSD and Mao-style collarless suits. This form of 'recuperation' by the 'spectacle' was as inevitable as it was distasteful to the members of the SI. It was this fact that, after the arguments, break-ups and debates over internal organisation and terrorism, in Debord's mind finally signalled the end of the Situationist International.

CHAPTER 25

Fall-Out

1971–2

The decision to end the activities of the Situationist International had been taken by Debord shortly after the Venice conference. The reasons were various but also straightforward: Debord found it impossible to work with a group who were not only his intellectual inferiors but had also strayed away from the discipline which he alone was able to impose on the group. There were also other human factors involved. Debord was now forty years old and a good fifteen or twenty years older than most of those left in the group. His taste for luxury, fine wines, good living and the art and literature of Renaissance Europe was distinctly at odds with his younger leather-jacketed comrades who, like most of their generation, were inspired as much by Jimi Hendrix, The Who, dope and speed as by Marx, Hegel and Machiavelli. Whatever alliance may have earlier been possible or even necessary (after all Debord himself could not have done the things they did) between the young shock troops of the Situationist International and the generation of Debord, it was now clearly at an end.

The recent actions of Riesel, Viénet and in particular Vaneigem, each of whom seemed to completely misunderstand the problem now facing the group, only served to confirm these points. It was better that the group pass away into history than to allow the true impact of its actions and theses to be blunted by a false historical perspective. The revolutionary project was now, albeit temporarily, at an end.

Despite Debord's reluctance to endorse any activity outside his ever more tightly closed circle of intimates, there were a number of publications and public manifestations of the Situationist ethos in the years of transition, 1971–2, which he judged to be worthwhile. The first of these was, in September 1971, unusually enough a book from the mainstream publisher Éditions du Seuil called *Les Origines du gauchisme* ('The Origins of Leftism') by Richard Gombin. 'Gauchisme' was now a term which had passed into common usage in France to denote dissident varieties of Marxist thought which functioned outside the parameters (and the pervasive controlling structures) of the French Communist Party which since the decisive events of 1968 for many young people, despite its huge working-class support, seemed more than ever to be a clumsy, anachronistic monolith. Debord was both surprised and pleased to find that Gombin, who was by training an academic sociologist, had traced the development and impact of Situationist ideas with great clarity, emphasising that what made the Situationists so different from their revolutionary peers in the movement of 1968 was their ability to constantly and consistently draw theory back to real, lived experience. This, said Gombin, was closer to the revolutionary practices of nineteenth-century theoreticians of anarchy such as Max Stirner, whose central argument was that the individual ego is the sole creator of moral order, and therefore separate from the official or unofficial Marxism preached by either Maoists, Trotskyists, Leninists and others. In the spirit of Stirner, argued Gombin, the SI had pursued their revolutionary aims not simply by developing theoretical positions but, in the white heat of the events of 1968, proving that revolution could only come from those who had already set about the task of turning revolutionary theory into the practice of everyday life. Debord judged this appraisal to be at least 'honest'.[1]

Another publication, which this time came not only with Debord's approval but also a semi-official Situationist imprimatur, was published in January 1972 under the title *L'Internationale situationniste, Protagonistes/Chronologie/Bibliographie, avec un index des noms insultés*.[2]

For those who had been reading and following the activities of the Situationists for the past ten years or so, this text provided an invaluable and accurate record of the floating membership of the organisation, the various splits and changes of direction taken by the group and, in the tradition of the Surrealists and the Dadaists, a gleefully spiteful and detailed record of every insult which the Situationist International had heaped upon its enemies. These ranged from calling Jean-Paul Sartre 'a money-grubbing commodity and mangy dead dog' to describing John Cage as a 'Buddhist mental retard'. Others, less famous but no less despised in the Situationist canon, were faithfully described as 'cretinous cunts', 'defrocked Stalinists', 'salaried bastards and imbeciles', 'liars, tricksters, cretins' and so on.

The book had been compiled by Jean-Jacques Raspaud and Jean-Pierre Voyer, both briefly intimates of Debord's inner circle, who declared themselves members of the self-styled Institut de préhistoire contemporain ('Institute of Contemporary Prehistory'), a Hegelian joke at the expense of more earnest Leftist groups who were still waiting for 'History' to begin. The publisher was Champ Libre, an enterprise run, maintained and controlled by the mercurial figure of Gérard Lebovici, a succesful enterpreneur and highly respected figure in cinema circles in France who had also dedicated himself to publishing and distributing radical texts inspired by the currents swirling around 1968. Both Champ Libre and

Lebovici would shortly come to play a pivotal role in Debord's life and activities. For the time being, however, the singular importance of this text was that it also clearly announced, to the few members left as well as its readers, that the Situationist International was over.

Less satisfactory in Debord's view were the activities of those, such as René Viénet, who no longer accepted Debord's authority or discipline and who were functioning almost as renegades. Viénet had lately turned his attention to film-making, taking pieces of contemporary or near contemporary Chinese cinema (as a former student of Chinese at the Sorbonne he continued to pursue his fascination with the Orient) and 'détourning' them into Situationist works. The first of these, *Wang Ping: du sang chez les Taoistes* (Wang Ping: Blood and the Taoists), appeared on Left Bank cinema screens in 1971 and was a Chinese Kung Fu B movie which had been subtitled with texts from the twelfth issue of *L'Internationale situationniste*. Debord was amused by this adventure, as he was with Viénet's later projects which included another 'detourned' Kung Fu film, *La Dialectique peut-elle casser des briques* ('Can dialectics break bricks'), and a 'détourned' piece of Chinese soft porn film, *Une petite culotte pour l'été* ('A little pair of panties for the summer'), but he was unsure about what Viénet was really up to. Viénet's translation of *De la misère en milieu étudiant* into Chinese did not really seem to Debord to be a particularly useful action: most importantly, Viénet made no reference to the organisational structure within the SI which Debord had been at such pains to clarify at the Venice conference a year earlier.

'Outlaw aristocrats'

René Viénet resigned from the Situationist International in February 1971, citing 'personal reasons'. These were evidently less to do with a distaste for revolution than an inability to understand that, however occluded his power base may have been, it was ultimately Guy Debord who was in sole command of the Situationist International. Having been personally excluded from the social life of the small circle around Debord, Viénet, who was personally every bit as arrogant and vain as Debord himself, had no option but to resign. In his subsequent actions, which were both erratic and charming at least to Debord who approved from a suitable distance, he nonetheless remained faithful to the ideas and techniques he had encountered in the SI.

The break-up with René Riesel was far nastier. Debord was annoyed that Riesel had not had the presence of mind to resign earlier, when more intelligent minds than his own, Vaneigem, Beaulieu, Sébastiani and others, had seen the writing on the wall and ceded their hand. Debord put this stupidity down to stubbornness and began describing Riesel, who by his own admission was no intellectual and preferred sex and rock'n'roll to Hegelian philosophy, as 'a Shakespearean fool'. It had been Riesel's physical courage which had played such an important catalytic role in the events of May 68. Now that he was deemed irrelevant he was forced to leave in the September of 1971, pursued by a lengthy and vitriolic character assassination which Debord had also circulated to the few Situationists left standing. 'Riesel had watched with glee', Debord began, 'as several rivals of his decided to call it a day, since he imagined that this would enable his own career to move forward. The new situation obliged him however to undertake various tasks for which nobody could have had less aptitude. A revolutionary at seventeen, in 1968, Riesel had the rare misfortune of growing old before his nineteenth birthday had come round. Never had such a loser given himself over in so desperate a manner to such extremes of ruthless ambition, whose every means is denied him. He attempted to hide this ambitious streak, and the bitter envy that its continual frustration leads to, beneath that dodgy veneer of confidence proper to the weakling who you know lives in constant fear of a harsh word or a boot making contact with some part of his anatomy.'[3] Debord went on to accuse Riesel of sexual jealousy and even fraud and theft. Clearly, it was not enough to throw him out but he also had to be smeared as he went.

These final exclusions meant that the Situationist group was now reduced to Sanguinetti – who had dissolved the Italian section on Debord's orders and moved to Paris – and Debord himself. Debord particularly admired Sanguinetti, who had proved himself a reckless and daring comrade in Milan, where he had narrowly avoided an assassination attempt by 'Stalinists', and Paris, where he lived clandestinely until he was deported in July 1971. Such adventures only enhanced Debord's view of Sanguinetti. Despite his apparent distaste for press coverage, Debord also took a secret pride in the way in which the Situationists, now effectively reduced to two people, could cause journalists to describe them as 'Elusive and covert plotters [. . .] They reject all legal restraints and conformist principles, even socialist ones. The practice of fellowship is not one these outlaw aristocrats of the revolution go in for.'[4]

The collapse of a world

The end of the SI was formally announced in April 1972. This took the form of a small book, signed by Debord and Sanguinetti, but apparently written solely by Debord (Sanguinetti's name appeared in tribute to him as he was expelled from France), published by Champ Libre, and called *The Real Split in the Internationale, public circular of the Situationist International*.[5]

The text consisted of a long, theoretical section, 'Theses on the Situationist International and its time', and a number of appendices, including Vaneigem's letter of resignation and the SI's response to Vaneigem which accused him, amongst other crimes, of being away on holiday in the South of France during the most tumultous events of May 68 which, worse still, he only found out about 'through the mass media'. The main focus of the text was however the relationship between the ideas of the Situationist International and their historical impact on a precise moment in history. This relationship, Debord indicated, was based on the indubitable fact that Situationist theory functioned equally well as premonition and as prophesy. 'The Situationist International', the opening thesis announced, 'emerged in a moment of world history as the thought of the collapse of a world, a collapse which has now begun before our eyes.' Situationist ideas, the following thesis elaborated, were now everywhere, 'from California to Coimbra, Scotland to Spain, Belfast to Leningrad, [they] work their way in secret or are proclaimed in open struggles . . . this is because the SI itself is merely the concentrated expression of a historical subversion which is everywhere at the present time.' The reason for this phenomenon, which could still turn into a revolutionary process, was because, 'At the bottom, people are no longer prepared simply to put up with what is in the offing. Moreover, it is the demand to live that has at present become a revolutionary agenda. The resolve to make one's own history oneself is the secret underpinning of all the "wild" and "incomprehensible" acts of negation that are currently holding the old order up to ridicule.'

The Situationist International, which had been the first to diagnose the degradation of daily life which was now everywhere accepted as the most fundamental of modern revolutionary principles, was however in danger of succumbing to the modern-day disease of placing style over substance. The danger came from the Situationists themselves who did not see that the game had moved on, and 'pro-Situ' fellow-travellers who had been seduced, most heinous crime of all, by the SI's *image*: 'An inevitable part of the SI's historical success led it in turn to be contemplated, and in the course of this contemplation, the uncompromising critique of everything that exists had come to be positively acknowledged by an ever expanding constituency of losers who had themselves begun to evince revolutionary sympathies.' All Situationist sympathisers, Debord concluded unerringly, would now henceforth be declared enemies.

The Real Split was not however a mere settling of scores. It also advanced and moved on many of the arguments of *The Society of the Spectacle* and, in particular, presented a withering analysis of modern conditions of production and consumption in which 'the executive is the epitome of the consumer-spectator'. This is because, unlike the genuine proletariat in the factories, the managerial or executive classes do not fully acknowledge their status as cogs in the machine of production, emphasising their distance from the proletariat by consuming higher value consumer goods. This is, argued Debord, 'man as a thoroughly dependent creature who feels duty bound to lay claim to freedom itself, idealised in the semi-affluent nature of his activity as a consumer'. It was this man, 'the former student', Debord warned, who was also shaping the physical conditions of the modern world: 'The work and leisure requirements of the executive are what now dictate the transformations currently laying hold of our urban fabric, from office blocks down to the tasteless fare dished up in restaurants where his strident tones leave other diners in no doubt about how much training his voice has received from exposure to airport Tannoys.' The executive, the man who thought he owned the world, was, said Debord, no more or less than 'le plouc', an old French slang word still in use, which denoted a gormless rural oaf, completely at odds with his environment. The same term, he went on, should be applied to women in modern society whose idea of liberation was to harbour the same needs and ambitions as the 'executive oaf'. The result of this process, in which 'executives always pretend to have wanted what they have got, and the distress occasioned by their secret dissatisfaction' was described by Debord as a new form of alienation, a 'gilded destitution'.

It was also important that these sections of *The Real Split*, beautifully lucid and penetrating as they are, marked a turning point in the evolution of Debord's style as a writer. Echoing Bossuet, Graciàn and Machiavelli, the writers and thinkers he now took as masters, Debord placed the Situationist International against its time in an admirably clear and aphoristic manner which, quite deliberately, struck an icy tone of detachment from the author's era. 'Never once have we been involved in anything either politicians of the most extreme left-wing variety or the most progressive-minded intellectuals get up to in the way of business, rivalries, and the company they keep. Now that we can moreover pride ourselves on having achieved the most revolting fame among this rabble, we fully intend to become even more inaccessible, even more clandestine. The more famous our theses become, the more shadowy our own presence will be.'

It was the dissolution of the SI which completed this process. This was moreover entirely in keeping with the principles advocated by Hegel, whose dialectical method Debord used in order to justify the split. More precisely, the 'scission' was an active demonstration of the Hegelian principle of *Aufhebung*, the term used by Hegel to describe the dialectical transition in which a lower stage is both annulled and preserved in a higher one and which is commonly translated as 'sublation'.[6] Debord quoted Hegel on the dialectic as the *envoi* to the book: 'One party proves itself to be victorious by breaking up into two parties; for in doing so it shows that it contains within itself the principle it is attacking, and thus had rid itself of the one-sidedness in which it previously appeared. . . . So that the schism that arises in one of the parties and seems to be a misfortune, demonstrates rather that party's good fortune.'

The game of absolute negation played by the Situationist International under Debord's direction, he was asserting here, had always been entirely faithful to this principle, which meant not that to destroy was to create but that destruction was in itself an absolute value. It followed from this that Debord could finally assert that 'Whoever cares to study the course of the SI's life will find therein the history of the revolution. At no time has anything ever managed to traduce it.'

Le roi Lebo

The end of the Situationist International did not mean however that the revolutionary game had come to an end. The end of one phase of activity was simply the beginning of another. The end of the Situationist International had therefore been decided by Debord shortly after his first meeting with Gérard Lebovici, the man whose life would be most closely interlinked with Debord's own over the next fourteen years.

Lebovici was also approaching forty when he met Debord. His life and career had however taken him in a completely opposite direction. He was born in Paris, on 25 August 1932, into a family of Romanian Jews. As it was for Isidore Isou and many others of that generation it was the war and Lebovici's Jewishness which were the defining features of his childhood and adolescence. The family fled to the southwest of France as the war approached Paris, but this did not prevent Lebovici's mother Marie being arrested and deported to Auschwitz where she died.

Lebovici's father, Jacob, never recovered from this shock and died shortly after the Liberation of Paris, leaving Gérard, who was dreaming of becoming an actor, in sole charge of the family import-export business. Gérard was determined, however, to pursue his acting ambitions and briefly managed to work for the small theatrical troupe Compagnie Marie. In 1960, abandoning both the family business, which by then had provided him a lucrative income, and his acting career in one bold move, he founded his own agency for budding actors and theatrical artistes.

Lebovici now came into his element, engineering the careers of known and unknown actors. Buoyed by early success and ever-confident, Lebovici, still only in his early thirties, rapidly bought up rival agencies including the prestigious Société André Bernheim which included in its roster none other than Jean Gabin, the idolised master of the French gangster movie. Other friends, acquaintances and clients included Yves Montand, Catherine Deneuve, Simone Signoret, Brigitte Bardot and Alain Delon. In late 1966, Lebovici, now a powerful and glamorous prime mover on the film scene, met an equally glamorous and enigmatic young woman, Floriana Chiampo, who had recently divorced and come to Paris from the small town of Ivrea with her small son Lorenzo to work as an editorial assistant on *Lui*, the French equivalent of *Playboy*. Lebovici fell immediately in love, not only with Floriana but with the radical ideas she brought with her from an Italian political scene already about to boil over. Through Floriana Lebovici came into close contact with a milieu of Communists, Anarchists and others who not only despised his world but actively sought to destroy it. Like the Italian publisher Giangiacomo Feltrinelli, Lebovici was unable to resist the lure of danger.

At the historic moment of May 1968, Gérard Lebovici, the mercurial power-broker of the French film scene who was respected by financiers and bankers as an entrepreneur of creativity, energy and flair, was both intoxicated and incited to action by the real fighting which was taking place in the streets of Paris and the libertarian philosophies behind the slogans. In the immediate aftermath, he dreamt of putting his money and influence at the service of the revolution by founding a publishing house which would keep the fires lit by the events of May still burning. At the end of May 68, in a plush apartment on the Île Saint-Louis, a few hundred metres away from the tear gas, coshes and barricades, he outlined to his friends, including the young Communist militant and future novelist Gérard Guégan, his plans for an editorial policy which would function as a consistent form of provocation and subversion.

'Gérard really did want to change the world,' Guégan told me thirty-two years later in a small Japanese restaurant behind the rue du Louvre. 'I can remember the conversation as if it were yesterday. His only real problem was that he lacked actors for his dramatic ideas.'[7] Guégan was a spry and fit man of sixty-odd years with obvious charisma and a witty turn of speech. Later, outside on the boulevard, he demonstrated his physical agility by high-kicking his way through traffic. 'I'm getting older,' he said, 'but I've still enough energy for women and drink and politics.' I liked him a lot but, given his reputation amongst former Situationists as 'a proven liar', it wasn't necessarily the case that he would tell the truth.

According to Guégan, it was he who provided Lebovici with the concrete means to set up the publishing house. 'You have to understand that Lebovici did not understand the world of working-class politics or the ultra-Left. How could he? He was a bourgeois from the trading classes who knew only how money works. So he asked me, a working-class militant, for advice on how to make the revolution. And I told him that the best way was to be daring and publish what he knew to be the most subversive texts possible. And then we agreed the title of the publishing house would be Champ Libre (Free Field).'

By 1971, Champ Libre had established itself as the major literary focus for the diverse elements which had contributed to the events of May. Publications included an anarchist polemic, *À bas les chefs!* ('Down with bosses!') by Joseph Déjacque, a homage to the Amercian Black Power movement, *Free Jazz Black Power* by Philippe Carles, and a primary school teacher's account of the revolutionary moment of 68, *Journal d'un éducastrateur*, or 'Journal of an educastrator'. Rights had also been recently acquired for the notorious *Anarchist's Cookbook* and the collected works of Timothy Leary.

All of these texts, challenging as they were for the older generation, were also conventional enough to be found on radical bookshelves in Paris, or indeed Amsterdam, Milan or London. It was the meeting with Guy Debord at the bar La Palette on the rue de Seine, then as now a fashionable haunt of art dealers and their clients, which took Gérard Lebovici a step beyond the limits of radical chic and into the truly unstable world of underground subversion. 'It was no secret that it was only after he had met Debord for the first time, and remember that I was there, that Lebovici really thought he stepped beyond the law,' said Guégan. 'He said to me straight after that meeting: that man is brilliant and dangerous and the really fascinating thing is that I don't know why.'

PART FOUR

Silence, Exile

1972–84

Peoples who have been driven out by sheer necessity are very formidable and, unless confronted by good armies, can never be held back.

Machiavelli, *Migrations*

I have no need to travel very far, but I have considered things with a certain seriousness, according them each time the full measure of the months or years that they seemed to merit. Most of the time I lived in Paris, exactly in the triangle defined by the intersections of the rue Saint-Jacques and the rue Royer-Collard, rue Saint Martin and rue Greneta, and the rue du Bac and rue de Commailles. And I have in fact spent my days and nights in this restricted space and the narrow frontier-margin that is its immediate extension; most often on its eastern side and more rarely on its northwestern side.

I never, or hardly ever, would have left this area, which suited me perfectly, if a few historical necessities had not obliged me to depart several times. Always briefly in my youth, when I had to risk some forays abroad in order to further extend disruption; but later for much longer, when the city had been sacked and the kind of life that had been led there had been completely destroyed – which is what happened from 1970 onwards.

Guy Debord, *Panegyric*

CHAPTER 26

Prince and Bandit

1972–3

The meeting with Lebovici was also of crucial significance to Guy Debord. Initially Debord had thought of Champ Libre as the potential backer of his planned film of *The Society of the Spectacle*. To this end, Jean-Pierre Voyer had been tidied up, abandoning his leather jacket and jeans for an ill-fitting suit, and dispatched to Champ Libre's headquarters, a modest two-room flat on the rue des Beaux-Arts, as 'Guy Debord's business representative'. The plan was to seduce Lebovici into financially backing the film *The Society of the Spectacle* on the grounds that Champ Libre had not as yet made a direct intervention in the spectacular world of the cinema, Lebovici's natural habitat. Lebovici, who had been a declared fan of the Situationists for some time, was intrigued but also, as a shrewd investor, cautious about the commercial potential of such a film. Voyer was sent away with a non-committal answer, whilst Lebovici did some research, telephoning friends and colleagues to see whether they thought such a project worthwhile. A brief meeting was convened at a café, La Charette des Beaux-Arts, between Jean-François Bizot, editor of the underground bible *Actuel*, two of his colleagues and Guégan and Lebovici. Although the project was worthwhile, the group concluded over drinks, there was clearly no financial mileage in backing the film, which indeed might well have spelt commercial disaster for the fledgeling publishing house. A message was sent back to Voyer, however, that a literary collaboration, far less expensive and risky, was not out of the question.

It was Lebovici's good fortune that this signal coincided with the fact that Debord had been unhappy with his original publisher, Buchet-Chastel, for some time and was looking for a way out of this commitment. Debord complained loudly about the fact that Buchet-Chastel had cashed in on the Situationists' notoriety in the wake of 1968 by adding the subtitle 'The Situationists' Theory' to a reissue of *The Society of the Spectacle*. Debord was also impressed by the way in which Champ Libre, without making any apparent concession whatsoever to the demands of capitalism, was able, through the agencies of the lawyer Georges Kiejman, a close friend of Lebovici, to avail themselves of the distribution facilities and network of the Gallimard publishing empire.

The only real question under discussion at the meeting at La Palette, which finally took place in 1971, was whether Lebovici would dare to defy the law and publish Guy Debord by breaking copyright with Buchet-Chastel. Debord, ordering beer for himself and coffee for Lebovici and Guégan, explained that as far as he was concerned the relationship with Buchet-Chastel was over: he had sent a registered letter informing the company that they were no longer to consider themselves as his publisher and that was the end of the affair. Guégan claimed to be less than impressed by Debord; he described him as physically a tiny man, 'with the tiny babyish hands which he flapped about to make a point, but Lebovici could not resist the challenge which Debord had thrown down and agreed on the spot to become his publisher'.[1]

There were of course other details to be considered and Lebovici suggested a meeting with Georges Kiejman to discuss these. It was Kiejman's idea not simply to break with Buchet-Chastel, but to denounce the original contract as invalid. It was now Debord's turn to be impressed and he declared himself ready to press ahead with any appropiate court action. Gérard Guégan, who was also at this meeting, could not work out whether Debord was being sarcastic or not when he addressed Kiejman, whom he apparently held in great respect, as 'Maître', the French appellation for members of the legal profession.

'O per fortuna o per virtù'

It was no accident that the meeting with Lebovici preceded a period in which Debord sought to dissolve nearly all the ties and alliances of the previous decade. The first and most obvious of these was the Situationist International, which was dissolved with the publication of the *The Real Split in the International* by Lebovici in the spring of 1972. Other more intimate alliances were also ineradicably changed at this time. The first of these was Debord's marriage to Michèle Bernstein; they were divorced on 5 January 1972. There was little emotion involved. The complexities of Debord and Bernstein's life together had been formed out of a shared passion for games, both sexual and political, and the end of the marriage was simply the end of this alliance. Bernstein, Debord and Alice Becker-Ho had all enjoyed the ambiguous and thoroughly un-bourgeois set-up their relationship involved, so that the divorce announced no more than a change in the financial relationship between Bernstein and Debord. More specifically, Bernstein was no longer duty-bound to support Guy's activities as the reins of financing the continuing project of Situationist subversion was handed over to Gérard Lebovici. The marriage between Alice and Guy, which was formally made on 5 August that year at the Town Hall of the Marais, was similarly a financial arrangement. 'Guy married me so that I could have the benefit of his work if he ever died or went to jail,' said Alice, 'that was the only reason for it. We loved each other and sometimes we loved other people, but we had no respect for the institution of marriage. It was simply a way of preserving what Guy, we, had if times were tough.'

Debord had also decided to leave Paris, the city he loved but which seemed to be changing before his eyes into a monstrous version of the spectacular society which he had so recently predicted. Debord explained his need for exile as both cause and consequence of his changing relationship to the city, which since the failure of 1968 seemed to be accelerating towards its own extinction. He described this process eloquently in *Panegyric*, written in 1989 supposedly as Debord's autobiography:

> I believe that this city was ravaged a little before all the others because its ever renewed revolutions had so worried and shocked the world, and because they unfortunately always failed. So we have been punished with a destruction as complete as that which had been threatened earlier by the Manifesto of Brunswick or the speech of the Girondist Isnard: in order to bury so many fearsome memories and the great name of Paris. (The infamous Isnard, presiding over the Convention in May 1793, had already had the impudence to announce prematurely: 'I say that if through these incessant insurrections the national representatives should happen to be attacked – I declare to you, in the name of all of France, Paris will be annihilated; you would soon have to search the banks of the Seine to determine whether this city ever existed.')
>
> Whoever sees the banks of the Seine sees our grief: nothing is found there now save the bustling columns of anthill of motorised slaves [. . .]. It could almost be believed, despite the earlier testimonies of history and the arts, that I was the only person to have loved Paris; because, first of all, I saw no one else react to this question in the repugnant 'seventies'. But subsequently I learned that Louis Chevalier, its old historian, had published then, without too much being said about it, *L'Assassinat de Paris* ('The Assassination of Paris'). So we could count on at least two righteous people in the city at the time. I did not want to see any more of the debasement of Paris. [2]

It is striking that in this text Debord, faithful to his own premise as articulated in *The Society of the Spectacle* that modern travel or tourism is a chimera, describes his own movements across Europe as inextricably linked to historical moments and imperatives (Debord never took an aeroplane or indeed travelled outside of Western Europe). This is partly swagger, but also a formulation of the notion, dear to Debord, that history and subjective experience are one and the same. The references made here are however deliberately contradictory and confusing: little, for example, in the Situationists' recent behaviour seemed to suggest an affiliation or sympathy with the Manifesto of Brunswick or the Girondins, one of the more moderate groupings during the French Revolution. Similarly, the book on Paris by the venerable historian Louis Chevalier was essentially a conservative work, bemoaning the modernisation of the city from the point of view of a historian who saw the city as a monument to the past.

It was however precisely Debord's ideas on the city which explained his current movements and, above all, his present decision to move his headquarters to Florence, a city which incarnated for Debord the ideal city-state of the Renaissance. Florence was in this sense, more than Paris, the ideal city he described in *The Society of the Spectacle*: 'The city is the locus of history,' he wrote, 'because it embodies at once a concentration of social power, which is what makes the historical enterprise possible, and a consciousness of the past.'[3]

On the advice of Gianfranco Sanguinetti, Debord and Alice first rented a house (from the Catholic Church, no less) in Pieve in the idyllic hills of the Chianti region to which they periodically retreated from Paris for long periods. They then acquired, with Lebovici's money, a fourteenth-century *palazzo* in some state of disrepair at 28 via Delle Caldaie, a narrow street in the old part of Florence. He actively sought out the bars of the semi-criminal underworld and revelled in the fact that, like the poet Li Po, he had 'hidden his fame in taverns'.[4]

It was from here that Guy would make sorties to the bars of the Oltrarno district, to the south of the river Arno, extending drinking sessions over days in the bars and in a favourite *vinaio* (a traditional Florentine wine cellar) in this artisanal medieval quarter. He also fell in love, briefly and under the watchful eye of Alice, with a young Florentine, 'perhaps because of her beautiful, bitter smile'.[5] All of this activity, financed by the patron Lebovici, seemed to Debord to be entirely consistent with his belief, developed from the writings of that other great Florentine Machiavelli, that the city and the citizen are linked together in the practice of what Machiavelli calls *virtù*. This word is used by Machiavelli at the end of the first chapter of *The Prince* to describe how a prince can govern a new state, 'o per fortuna or per virtù' ('either by fortune or by prowess'). This latter word has been variously translated into English as 'prowess', 'ability', 'skill', 'strength and wisdom'. Its real meaning for Machiavelli is closer to its Latin cognates, *vir* (man) and *virtus* (what is proper to a man). This has less to do with 'virtue' as a moral quality but rather 'virtuosity', a model and technique of artistic and political behaviour. Opposed to *virtù* in Machiavelli's vocabulary is the quality of *ozio* (indolence or corruption), and it is this latter quality which destroys the civic qualities in citizens and ultimately the city itself.

In Renaissance Florence, Debord found a philosophical justification for Situationist practice, which was a form of *virtù*, of relentlessly daring, bold, even reckless activity.

'A historical film'

Sightings of Debord in Paris were now becoming less and less frequent, and even the stuff of legend. His relationship with Lebovici had only further enhanced his mysterious image, as more and more of Lebovici's friends and associates began to complain about the influence which Debord seemed to wield over Lebovici, previously known as a hard negotiator and nobody's fool under any circumstances. Indeed, in the business world, Lebovici was going from strength to strength: in 1972 he had founded Artmedia, a new agency which quickly became the dominant force on the French media scene, including Yves Montand, Gérard Depardieu, Catherine Deneuve, Jean-Paul Belmondo and others on its roster. The headquarters was on the avenue Georges-V, the most exclusive and expensive part of Paris, a stone's throw from the Champs-Élysées and a world away from the radical politics and poetic games played out by Debord in the drinking dens of backstreet Florence or Left Bank dives. It was Artmedia, however, which continued to generously fund Debord's lifestyle, much to the disgust and consternation of those who thought they knew Lebovici well enough to comment on his new-found friends. A new office for Champ Libre had been set up on the rue de la Montagne-Sainte-Geneviève, almost next door to the former Letterist headquarters at the Tonneau d'Or. It was here, if at all, Debord could be found, drinking with Lebovici, who would let it be known via his secretary that he was not to be contacted during these meetings. Debord was disparagingly described as Lebovici's 'guru' and respected associates such as François Truffaut openly commented to friends about his state of mind.[6]

The one thing which Lebovici did not have to worry about was money which, due to the success of Artmedia and other projects, was more easily available than it had ever been. It was this financial security which prompted Lebovici to resuscitate the idea of filming *The Society of the Spectacle*. On 8 January a contract was signed between Debord and the newly formed Simar Films, which strangely enough had the same address as Champ Libre. Debord himself received 300,000 francs against royalties of 20 per cent, an advance which was generous enough by any estimation, let alone for an untried, underground subversive who had loudly and consistently declared himself against the cinema.

The making of the film seemed at first an improbable, even impossible task. How could the severe Hegelian theses of the text possibly be transformed into cinematic material? And who would want to see such a film?

Worse still, was this not merely a form of collaboration with the dreaded enemy, 'the spectacle'?

The simple answer to this was that the film was conceived as yet another act of *détournement*, which this time involved 'kidnapping' scenes from pre-existing films. The fact that some of these films were Hollywood productions, and therefore guarded by battalions of highly paid and highly skilled lawyers, made the theft of copyright all the more dangerous and enticing. In the pre-video era, however, it was not easy to get hold of film copies, let alone to steal scenes from them. To this end, Debord, Alice and Lebovici set out to charm André Mrugalski, an acquaintance of Lebovici's who was a senior technician at ORTF (Office de radiotélévision française, then the main French broadcasting organisation), inviting him to dinner and making a fuss over his children. Mrugalski did not wish to jeopardise his career by getting caught up in such an adventure, and so a certain Martine Barraqué, another acquaintance of Lebovici and a skilled film editor, was duly courted. Barraqué, in contrast, was intrigued by the air of conspiracy around the project and Lebovici's laconic replies to her questions about theft and piracy, to which he replied he was making a revolutionary film and not entertainment. Barraqué had been invited to participate in the making of the film by Suzanne Schiffmann, then working for François Truffaut. After a brief and mysterious meeting with Lebovici at the offices of Artmedia, she found herself invited into the inner circle of Alice and Guy, in attendance at long, festive dinner parties and seduced by the clever and witty conversation.[7]

Through her connections in the film world, Barraqué was able to get hold of most of the films Guy asked for and arranged for private screenings in the sole company of Alice and Guy during which scenes would be chosen and duly (and expensively) copied by Martine. Recording the soundtrack, which consisted of Debord reading extracts from the book, was easier, although the tape had to be carefully edited to get rid of Debord's smoker's cough and the phlegmy noises he made, the result of heavy drinking. The atmosphere was lighthearted and after recording the team, which now comprised about five people, would often finish a session at a *guingette*, an old-fashioned open-air cabaret, not far from the Marne (the sessions were recorded in Jonville-le-Pont, an hour or so out of Paris).

The final film, which was in black and white, was a sombre product, apparently a long way removed from either the delicate wit which had informed much earlier Situationist versions of *détournement*, or the bold devil-may-care attitude which had characterised more recent revolutionary practice during May 68. The opening scenes of the film were engaging enough, featuring nude shots of Alice and stills from *Lui* and *Playboy*, each evoking the cool cynical eroticism of many of the illustrations in *L'Internationale situationniste*. Thereafter, as image accumulated upon image

– the Kennedy assassination, the Beatles getting off a plane, appearances from Mao, Nixon, Mitterrand, scenes from *Battleship Potemkin* and *The Charge of the Light Brigade* – and Debord's monotone delivery continued, the dreariness of the film itself seemed at odds with the lucidity of Debord's text. There was also something already anachronistic about Debord's choice of images (the Beatles were portrayed in 1964, for example) which seemed to indicate that, perhaps for the first time, Guy Debord the master strategist whose idea of the avant-garde was that it always made contact with its time was losing his grip and falling out of touch.

The film was released on 1 May 1974, on the eve of Valéry Giscard d'Estaing's victory over François Mitterrand. Despite a select few screenings for the press in cinemas on the Champs-Élsyées and elsewhere, its distribution was confined to a small art house cinema on the rue Gît-le-coeur. It met a muted response: 'pro-Situ' militants disturbed a few screenings of the film on the grounds that it was a betrayal of everything the Situationists had stood for, but otherwise the public ignored the film. *Le Monde* ironised about 'Debord's theoretical western' and drolly dismissed the film as yet another by-product of 1968.[8] Even the big Hollywood companies, whose work had been so openly pinched, including films by John Ford, Orson Welles and Sam Wood, it seemed could not be bothered making a fuss. As a provocative work of *détournement* it seemed to miss its target entirely.

This was not the opinion of some of those who have seen the film recently. The Yale academic Thomas Y. Levin, for example, has described the film as 'a turning point in the history of the cinema', citing Walter Benjamin to support his thesis. Levin writes that the film, 'in its practice of citation without quotation marks, [. . .] insolently throws back at spectacular society the images with which it depicts itself. Indeed one could say that Debord's critique consists in an incriminating, analytical quotation of the spectacle. This marks a turning point in the history of the cinema that, according to Debord's Hegelian logic, is nothing less than the *Aufhebung* (sublation [i.e. obliteration]) of the medium. In a way, in this film, the cinema, at the end of its pseudo-autonomous history, gathers up its memories. Debord's film is simultaneously a historical film, a western, a love story, a war film – and none of the above.'[9]

This is indeed how Debord conceived of the work and it was on these grounds that he refused to consider the film a failure. It was not, he insisted, intended as a celebration of the revolutionary moment but rather a commentary on its passing away. The quotations from Machiavelli, Marx and Clausewitz on the illusory value of the image could not have therefore been more apt. Most crucially, if the filmed version of *The Society of the Spectacle* did not or could not connect with its time, this was only proof that the age itself was in the process of moving further and further away from the possibility of revolution. For Debord and Lebovici, this only confirmed their belief that the art of subversion lay also in the subversion of art. There was however a melancholy tone in the film *The Society of the Spectacle*, not only in the mournful baroque soundtrack music by Michel Correte, but noticeable also in the way that defiance was portrayed as a hopeless, even suicidal form of activity when placed against the passage of time: 'Are we really living proletarians?' was the text inserted alongside a close-up of the Anarchist Durruti. 'Are we really living? This age that we count on, and where everything we count on is no longer ours, can it be called a life? And can't we recognise how much we keep losing as the years pass by?'

The death of Jorn

On 1 May 1973, in the hospital of Aarhus in Jutland, Asger Jorn died. He had been suffering from lung cancer for some months, but had informed few people how near to death he was. He had last seen Debord and Alice in the December of 1972, when Debord had presented him with an essay in homage to him, 'De l'architecture sauvage' ('Wild architecture'), dedicated to Jorn's house in Albisola, the site of the many drinking parties, conversations and theoretical artistic activities of the 1950s which had ultimately led to the formation of the Situationist International. For Debord the house was both a work of art and a place of real, lived experience, a place of totemic importance which he compared to the fantastic creations of Le Facteur Cheval, the postman in an obscure town in Provence who constructed out of stones, shells, cement and broken glass an 'Ideal Palace, part Gaudí cathedral, part Temple of Angkor, part grotto' which became, when discovered by Breton in the early 1930s, 'one of the meccas of Surrealism'.[10]

Remembering Jorn also reminded Debord too that 'good humour was never in short supply in Situationist scandal, and was at the centre of ruptures and violent arguments, incredible justifications and unplayable strategies. Those who ask themselves vainly what history might or might not have been, in "the manner of" it would have been better for humanity if those people had never existed, will spend a long time trying to work out if the Situationists, towards 1960, might not have been calmed down, by a lucid and recuperating reformism, by giving them a few towns to build, instead of pushing them to the limit and forcing them to unleash on the world the most dangerous subversion which it has ever known.'[11]

Debord also made it clear for the first time in this text what Jorn's role had been and how important his contribution was. He wrote that Jorn, who had supported the group financially and morally, even after his exclusion, had been 'a Situationist more than anybody else [. . .]. No one had contributed like Jorn to the origins of this adventure: he found people across Europe, and so many ideas, and even in the most delightful wretchedness, frequently supplied what was needed to pay off the most pressing debt which we accumulated with printing presses.'[12]

Guy and Alice were in Florence, living without a telephone (on Debord's strict orders) in the old house on via Delle Caldaie when Asger died. Debord learned of his friend's death when he read his obituary in *Le Monde* in a bar in the Oltrarno district. The shock was all the more powerful because neither Guy nor Alice had any idea of how ill Asger had been. At the end of March, Jorn had sent them a letter, almost a farewell letter, to their address on rue Saint-Martin to tell them that his illness had moved into its final, fatal phase. Debord had never seen the letter.

Like the final split with Michèle Bernstein and his exile from the Paris he loved, for Debord Jorn's death marked a decisive break with a past which he had yet to come to terms with. Debord did not as yet have a great sense of his own mortality, although he was now in his early forties, paunchy, out of condition and resignedly addicted to an excessive daily consumption of mostly wine and spirits (whisky had lately featured as a favourite late-night drink). But Jorn's death did remind him both of the fragility of existence (he talked more often about death with Alice than he had done before) and that time was passing. He was not yet ready to surrender to melancholy or pessimism with regard to the continuing project of subversion. But the world had changed, and Debord was not certain whether he was ready or able or willing to change with it.

CHAPTER 27

The Courtier

1974–5

There was an elegiac tone in the essay for Asger Jorn which was finally published in December 1974, a year or so after its composition. Although it was mostly concerned with the art of Jorn and its application in the 'concrete appropriation of space' as represented in his garden at Albisola, Debord began the piece by recalling the early ambitions of the Situationist International and considering the extent to which the group had remained faithful or not to those original dreams. 'We know that the Situationists, to begin with, wanted to at least build cities,' Debord wrote, 'the environment which would suit the unlimited diffusion of new passions. But obviously it was not easy: consequently we have been obliged to do much more. And along this way several partial projects have had to be abandoned, a good number of our excellent capacities have not been used: it is even more absolute and sad that these capacities have not been put to good use for hundreds of millions of our contemporaries [. . .]. The fifteen years which have passed since the meeting at Cosio d'Arroscia have started to change the world, but not our intentions.'[1] Although the mood was melancholy, almost wistful, it was also defiant. It was clear that although the Situationist International was dead, Situationist promises still had to be kept. However, 1974 was a turning point in the history of the generation which had tried to make the revolution of 1968: it was, more notably, the year that the radical Left became the new establishment.

The first and most important events of the year were the death of Georges Pompidou in March and the election in May of Valéry Giscard d'Estaing. This narrowest of victories for the Right seemed to mark the end of the revolutionary adventures of the 1960s, as former radicals now turned their attentions to political struggles in mainstream arenas. The newspaper *Libération*, for example, founded in 1972 by a group of intellectuals including Jean-Paul Sartre and Michel Foucault, in Debord's eyes was an important step away from violent contestation towards a Leftism which would be made up of professional dissenters whose aim was not to change society but to reform it. Similarly, the journal *Tel Quel*, still under the control of Philippe Sollers, was now casting off its vestigial Maoism and turning its attention towards technical problems of post-Marxist theory as they applied to literature and psychoanalysis.

It was no coincidence that it was at this point that Julia Kristeva, who had become Sollers's lover, now emerged as the most important voice in the *Tel Quel* group, championing a new form of criticism which centred on the singularity of subjective experience, laying the emphasis on women's experience. Sexual freedom and gender roles had pushed themselves to the top of the cultural agenda, whether in the form of the increasingly powerful women's movement in France (whose leading voices were Kristeva and the young Luce Irigaray) or the soft-focus erotica of the first *Emmanuelle* movie. The other big cinema hit of the year was *Les Valseuses*, starring a young Gérard Depardieu and Patrick Dewaere as suburban hooligan losers. The sexual crudity and violence of the film also seemed to mark an end to 1960s idealism: its appeal to audiences at both ends of the political spectrum seemed to mark the end of an era of potential revolution.

The art of politics

What had changed most definitively for Debord was not the possibility, or the need, for revolution but the fact that the idea of a collective enterprise had collapsed. Other forms of organising and promulgating subversive activity had therefore to be found. It seemed, in the first instance, that the best way to channel this impulse was through Champ Libre itself, to which Lebovici seemingly offered a free hand to Debord as 'literary director'.

Although he assumed this role, Debord also preferred to keep himself at some distance both from the day-to-day running of the group and the authors themselves. Debord had long since believed in the importance of invisibility and invisible agitation as a key Situationist technique and principle (the terrifying events in Italy, in the wake of the Piazza Fontana bombing, had convincingly borne this theory out) and he saw his position as a way of furthering what Alexander Trocchi, now long disappeared from view, had called 'the invisible insurrection'.

Amongst the books which Debord was reading in Florence and in Paris were Baltasar Graciàn and Baldassare Castiglione as well as, inevitably, Machiavelli. The importance of these books was that they offered social, philosophical and political theories which not only sought to provide a model of cultivated behaviour but also, no less importantly, an ideal of action and interaction which formed the basis of the model Renaissance society. Debord found here parallels with his own previous experimental notion of the Situationist International as a micro-society; in these texts he discovered a way of preserving the notion of a micro-society which was defined less by its collective decision-making process but rather by forms of individual behaviour. Friendship, honour, and the practical uses of the classical ideals of reason and self-knowledge were now becoming central to Debord's thought, behaviour and ultimately his writings.

In Castiglione, Debord found justification for his emphasis on activity and writing which engaged directly with its time, but also looked beyond, to future readers who had not been born yet but who might find in his texts a constitution of philosophical ideas closely linked to the comple demands of real life. Castiglione's most important work was his book *Il libro del Cortigiano* ('The Book of the Courtier'), written in 1528. This was translated into French in 1580 by Gabriel Chappuis and republished by Champ Libre in 1987 (it was also translated into English by Sir Thomas Holby, and apparently read by Shakespeare, as *The Courtier*). This book was not only a treatise on how to be a perfect courtier ('known for all men as someone who is excellent,' writes Castiglione) but also a historically accurate and detailed account of life at the court of Urbino, the representation of a perfect city-state. The perfect courtier, according to Castiglione, is one who is able to bring together military and literary skills and use them with equal facility. Most importantly for Debord, Castiglione is concerned with the individual and his action, rather than with society as a collective whole. In this sense Debord's reading of Castiglione marks a decisive shift in his thinking away from social analysis and towards an individualistic theory of behaviour. It was also important for Debord that Castiglione argues against the false idealism of the Christian doctrine, stating that all moral judgements are both subjective and reversible ('Truth it is, many things seeme at the first sight good, which are ill: and many ill, that notwithstanding are good').[2] Most crucially, the book celebrates a perfect age based on a political philosophy which gives equal importance to the full measured enjoyment of the material aspects of life as well as theory or speculative thought.

Baltasar Graciàn, writing a hundred years or so after Castiglione, offers a vision of the world which is slightly darker than that of his predecessor, probably the result of his education at the hands of Castilian Jesuit priests and his early career as a writer of the chronicles in Zaragoza and Madrid. For this reason he is often quoted as an influence on Schopenhauer. For Debord, Graciàn's most important work was *El oráculo manual y arte de prudencia*, which was translated into French by Amelot de Houssaie in 1684 (and reissued by Champ Libre in 1972) as *L'Homme de Cour*, or *The Courtier*. In this book Graciàn presents 300 maxims which aim to instruct in the proper ways of conduct those who live alongside princes and men of power. Graciàn emphasises above all the specifically Spanish qualities of *desengaño* and *agudeza*. The first of these is to be translated as 'disillusion', but to be understood as a refusal to be fooled by the world and its appearance. The second, *agudeza*, is a term most often used in relation to the *conceptista* poetry of Góngora and Graciàn himself. The term *conceptista* is generally understood in Spanish as meaning 'witty, allusive or involved' and *conceptista* poetry is distinguished by an extreme form of concision, lack of similes and an essentially medieval approach in which the poet establishes an occult relationship with the universe.

What mattered most for Debord in the writings of Castiglione and Graciàn was that they defined rules of moral and political action in a society which had not yet lost the sense of itself as a unified entity and in which the individual could therefore still influence great events. So, although the turn to an individualistic philosophy seemed a retreat, and to this extent was symptomatic of the introspective mood of the post-68 Left in the 1970s, it was also however, at least on Debord's own terms, a way of seeking to clarify present and future strategy in 'the society of the spectacle' in which the individual had been reduced to a mere spectator.

Cannibal economy

Debord had very quickly made himself the confidante and hero of Lebovici and was immediately in a position of influence over Champ Libre. The pivotal figure was still at this stage Gérard Guégan who, with his Marseilles accent and impeccable working-class credentials, effectively ran the literary and political side of the business whilst Lebovici picked up the bills. For a short while Debord was happy to let this situation continue, limiting himself to suggestions that certain books, such as those by Castiglione, Graciàn or Clausewitz (a bestseller, much to the surprise of the Champ Libre staff), be published, and not insisting too hard in case Guégan, who already had a reputation as a pugnacious and arrogant colleague, felt he had to prove that it was he who was really in charge. The situation suited Debord, who was evidently pleased to be applying in practice the arts of invisible power which he learned from his study of Renaissance political theory. More effectively, these texts confirmed for Debord the Hegelian notion that negative action always leads to a culminating point which consumes both abstract and practical desires in a movement forward towards the positivity of a new situation, a new world. It was Debord's interpretation of this notion, which was obviously closely related to the Marxist dialectic, which François Bott, the former enemy of the Situationists, described as 'the cannibal economy of the Situationist International'.[3]

The point of conflict was the increasingly business-like drift of Champ Libre, which under the energetic control of Guégan was turning into a success and becoming something of a name to be reckoned with in Parisian publishing circles. In early 1974, with a highly talented young team which included Raphaël Sorin, Jean-Yves Guiomar and Alain Le Saux, Guégan set up 'Chute Libre' ('Free-Fall'), which under the Champ Libre imprint published detective novels. A journal, *Les Cahiers du futur* ('Future notes'), was set up by Guégan at the same time.

Debord was clearly jealous of the younger man's success. According to Guégan this was in part because Debord had drifted away from any direct contact with radicals and radicalism and, from his new aristocratic position, could not understand the current debates and issues around women's rights, gay rights, Black Power and the liberating forces of sex, drugs and rock'n'roll. 'Debord seemed to belong to another generation, another age,' Guégan said to me, revisiting an old conflict which still visibly angered him, 'he could not understand or control the forces that were in Champ Libre, and which were about to make it such a success and make it so important. He talked about war, Clausewitz, strategy, Machiavelli, but none of this could mean anything to the new proletariat who he had nothing in common with. I'm from Marseilles, you are from Liverpool, we know what working-class people are. Guy Debord, for all his talk of "the dangerous classes", could not bear to be with ordinary working people – you could not imagine him on the terraces at Marseilles or Anfield. He used to surround himself with bullies and thugs, but he was always physically scared. He tried to control you instead in the most sinister ways.'[4]

Given the long-simmering personal animosity between Debord, the aloof and aristocratic master-strategist, and Guégan, the hard-headed working-class militant, it was no longer possible for Champ Libre to remain under the control of a team which, as Debord and Lebovici saw it, seemed bent on turning the enterprise into a professional organisation such as *Libération* or the underground magazine *Actuel*. The flashpoint was an initial meeting between Lebovici and the young team around Guégan who demanded complete control over Champ Libre, reducing Lebovici's role to that of a mere financier. This was obviously unacceptable to Lebovici, who had founded Champ Libre not as a plaything, and certainly not as an ordinary capitalist business, but as the direct antithesis of his day-to-day role as a mercurial and gifted prime mover in Parisian media circles.

In September 1974, after long and alcoholic conversations with Debord, Lebovici decided to sack Guégan and his supporters. The excuse was that Guégan had been seeking to publish his novel *Les Irréguliers* with Champ Libre, an act of self-publication that was clearly repugnant to any publishing house worth its salt (the fact that Guy Debord also published his works with Champ Libre, to which he had an intimate affiliation, was overlooked). The row rattled on through October, with an acrimonious exchange of letters between Guégan and Lebovici, each accusing the other of duplicity and mendacity. A meeting was finally called on 4 November in La Coupole, the distinguished literary brasserie on boulevard Montparnasse, formerly the haunt of Hemingway, Lenin and Cocteau amongst others, between Lebovici, Gérard Guégan, Raphaël Sorin, Jean-Yves Guiomar and Alain Le Saux. Lebovici, wearing a venerable trench coat and an inscrutable expression, was adamant that Guégan had to go and asked for his resignation. Guégan refused and his team stood behind him. In that case, said Lebovici, the only possible solution was to separate Champ Libre from Guégan and his supporters. The meeting lasted thirty minutes.

Several hours later Lebovici was hospitalised suffering from severe stomach cramps. Evidently what he saw as a betrayal had cut him to the quick. No less distraught were Guégan and his supporters, convinced that the whole situation had been stage-managed by Guy Debord, who, skilfully using the arts of manipulation he had learnt from his Renaissance masters, had outplayed them and outflanked them, and now stood as the central driving force behind Champ Libre. 'Guy Debord took control,' said Guégan. 'It's what he wanted all along, and we were tossed aside because he could not share power. From then on we knew that he was a fantasist but also a dangerous megalomaniac.'

Refutations/Reputations

Debord was from now on rarely seen in the offices at Champ Libre, which was now run on a day-to-day basis by Lebovici's wife Floriana. Catherine Nicole, who worked as a copy-editor for Champ Libre and edited all of Debord's texts, claimed never to have seen him in seven years. Lebovici would hand her handwritten manuscripts with great care and confidentiality, emphasising in conspiratorial tones that not a word was to be changed.

The editorial team at Champ Libre was now greatly reduced, yet for the time being no less effective than it had been under Guégan. The office administration was managed by Hortensia Biscarreti di Ruffia, recruited by Floriana from her Italian connections, whilst Roger Grégoire and Jean-Pierre Voyer took on the roles of 'representatives' of the company, a job which for most of the time meant no more than writing letters to authors turning down their books because of their insufficient revolutionary qualities. Voyer still considered himself a militant as well as a publisher. Grégoire had been involved with the American anarchist organisation Black and Red, which had its home in Detroit, then one of the most politicised and violent cities in the United States, and maintained his contacts with American revolutionaries (this was of great importance for Debord, who was still seeking an American publisher for *The Society of the Spectacle*).

Despite his strictly observed absence, very quickly the company began to take a form and a direction which could only have been shaped by the imagination of Guy Debord. This meant, in the first instance, that the publishing list of Champ Libre was, from Clausewitz to Jean-Pierre Voyer, entirely dictated by Debord's tastes and interpretations. Equally significant was the fact that the publishing house, almost alone amongst its peers, refused all forms of publicity, never sought literary prizes and turned down all requests for interviews with journalists who were intrigued by the still-burning radicalism of Champ Libre, as well as by the Janus-faced Lebovici, who was, by day, now at the height of his fame as a movie mogul but who also embraced the most dangerous underground politics and associates.

Perhaps the most significant fact of all was the way in which Champ Libre accelerated towards a series of political and philosphical positions which put it on an almost unassailable distance from even its most radical rivals and peers. The mood of the Left in mid-1970s France was one of retrenchment and taking stock of what exactly had been the failure and implications of 1968. The fact that the Right had edged into power in 1974 had provoked further soul-searching amongst those on the Left who now conceded that 1968 was a defeat, and who examined their own actions and consciences for the causes of this failure. The women's movement, anti-racist lobbies and gay liberation now dominated the agenda in pursuit of 'rights', which if they could be achieved were taken as victories and advances and markers of how much society had moved forward since the dark days of Gaullism. Champ Libre stood apart from these currents, publishing books which talked of a degraded era, advocated war as a nobler form of action than politics and, under Debord's direction, scorned the pursuit of 'rights' as the pursuit of the most mediocre gifts of the society of the spectacle. For the rest of the decade, as the French Left swung towards a social-democratic majority and consensus, Champ Libre maintained, in its public actions and its publications, an icy distance from the mood of the times.

Debord, whose cult of secrecy was now becoming the stuff of legend in Leftist circles and elsewhere, also became the object of rumours concerning his alleged new-found wealth acquired from Lebovici. According to these rumours, Alice Becker-Ho was now putting on great airs and would not move around Paris unless taken to her destination in a chauffeur-driven car. Debord himself had a great taste for luxury, a villa in Italy and a fine eye for antiques. He paid his staff, on his films or in his houses, with cash, like a gangster or an aristocrat.

These rumours occasionally irritated or bored Debord and Alice, but mostly left them indifferent. More serious was the way in which the film of *The Society of the Spectacle* had been received by a generation of critics whose obvious aim was to reduce Debord's ideas to rubble in order to preserve their own contemptible status in 'the spectacle'. He decided that it was not enough to ignore the critics but to refute them utterly and entirely. To this end, he asked Martine Barraqué to work with him again on a short black-and-white film, *Réfutation de tous les jugements, tant élogieux qu'hostiles, qui ont été jusqu'ici portés sur le film 'La société du spectacle'*

('Refutation of all judgements, whether in praise or hostile, which have been made up until now on the film *The Society of the Spectacle*'). As in the original film, Debord cut shots of examples of degraded spectacular society (polluted cities, alienating processes of production, alienated workers) with Hollywood representations of war or combat. These were placed alongside newer material, such as newsreel film of the recent revolution in Portugal in 1974 which had been led by a pro-Left military (it was not only the military metaphor which appealed to Debord but also the reports that revolutionary workers were drinking up to five litres of wine per day). Debord did not attack individual critics as he would have done during the days when the Situationist International was at its height, but rather caught the tone in an icy phrase from Chateaubriand which appeared at the beginning of the film: 'There are times when one must expend scorn with economy, because of the great number of those who deserve it.'

The final break with Michèle Bernstein and Ralph Rumney

The film did little or nothing to kill off the rumours about Debord in Paris (Guégan was currently spreading the idea that Debord had gone mad) or to enhance the reputation of the dead Situationist International, which was already in the eyes of many former radicals no more than an embarrassing museum piece. By now Debord himself had either lost or severed contact with the leading figures in the group.

A final, more touching last meeting occurred in late 1974 when Michèle Bernstein turned up for dinner at Alice and Guy's flat in the company of Ralph Rumney, whom she had recently married. Through the course of the 1960s Ralph's career had veered from brilliant excess to catastrophe. After being thrown out of the Situationist International, an idea into which he had put his heart and soul, Rumney had turned his full attention to painting, with no little success, acquiring a reputation as a daring and intellectually gifted young man. He divided his time between London, Venice, Brussels and Paris, where he scintillated at dinner parties around the Guggenheim circle and developed a formidable reputation as a wit and a dandy, as well as a painter.

The world had collapsed around Rumney on 8 March 1967 when his wife Pegeen Guggenheim killed herself with an overdose of sleeping pills. The marriage had never been stable, not because of Pegeen's depressive tendencies, but rather because Peggy Guggenheim, who had been suspicious of Ralph from the start, was determined that her daughter should not marry this impertinent and feckless Englishman. The night that Pegeen died was only the beginning of the nightmare for Ralph, who found himself accused by the Guggenheims of aiding and abetting her suicide. Their prestige, reputation, money and lawyers made it impossible for Rumney to overcome the slurs. The reality was that Pegeen had suffered from depression for years and used threats of suicide frequently to gain control over Ralph and a marriage that often seemed to be falling apart at the seams.

Pegeen's death had quite simply been a response to Ralph's absence in Venice, where in a dispute over his papers he had found himself handcuffed and deported. He had returned to Paris to a distraught Pegeen who now thought that Venice, where her mother still lived, was finally closed to her. Angry at Ralph for his carelessness, and fearing that this marked a final break with her mother, she started drinking whisky, weeping and remonstrating with the exhausted Rumney. She finally wished him good night and went to sleep in the maid's room, leaving Rumney to sort out the children, the cat and other domestic arrangements in the morning. It was after having delivered the children to school that Rumney found her dead.[5]

The press were alerted straight away and Rumney, to avoid journalists clustering at the door of the flat, was obliged to flee across the rooftops, pausing only to give his version of events to Eleonari Marmora, a trusted journalist on the Italian newspaper *Il Giorno*. The children were seized by the Guggenheims and Rumney forced to live undercover in Paris, where he was nonetheless trailed constantly by Guggenheim's private detectives. Sensing that the police and possibly a jail sentence were coming ever closer, on the advice of a friend he asked to be interned at La Borde clinic, the psychiatric centre where Ivan Chtcheglov had ended up and where Félix Guattari was presently in charge. After several months in La Borde, Rumney made for London, where he was out of reach of Guggenheim's lawyers but, penniless and desperate, was obliged to take a job as a telephone operator, a far cry from the art world of Paris and Venice and even further from the revolutionary impulses of the Situationists who were poised for the events of May 1968.

Rumney returned to Paris in 1970, drinking heavily in the Rosebud on boulevard Montparnasse and making a kind of living working as a translator and editor for ORTF. The art world was not very far away, however, and it was not long before he was again in the company of former comrades and friends such as Gil Wolman and François Dufrêne. The world seemed even smaller when, one evening at a drinks party held in the gallery of Lara Vincy on the rue de Seine, he ran into Michèle Bernstein. The pair almost fell upon each other, reliving adventures and entertaining each other with accounts of time past. The friendship turned to love and within months the pair were married, living in the rue Saint-Martin, near the construction site of the Beaubourg and practically neighbours of Guy Debord.

The dinner party at Debord's flat had been Ralph's idea; he had been asking Michèle to arrange it in the hope that old wounds might have been healed. The evening got off to a bad start, with Debord treating Michèle as his exclusive property, with Ralph, who was reminded of the sexual jealousy which had predominated at Cosio, frozen out of the conversation. Michèle was also clearly uneasy about all this tension.

The breaking point came when, after dinner and made amiable by the wine, Rumney began to talk of his difficulties in getting papers from the police which would enable him to get a resident's permit in France. Jokingly, he asked Guy, with all his connections, whether he could help him out with his problem. At this suggestion that he had dealings, crooked or otherwise, Debord flared up, shouting at Bernstein and Rumney that he was not a cop and that they should now leave and never see him again. Alice escorted them to the door. Neither Bernstein or Rumney ever did see Debord again.

According to Rumney, the argument had only been a pretext for throwing him out, and it was clear that the old rivalry still remained. Alice gives a different version, stating that the argument had shattered Guy and that he had really loved Ralph and felt betrayed. 'When they left,' she said, 'Guy was violently sick, which he never was, throwing up, pale and ill. And also I can say honestly that it was the only time I have ever seen him cry.'

CHAPTER 28

The Last Chance to Save Capitalism
1975–6

'I would have had very few illnesses,' wrote Debord, 'if alcohol had not in the end brought me some: from insomnia to vertigo, by way of gout. "Beautiful as the trembling of the hands in alcoholism," said Lautréamont. There are mornings that are stirring but difficult.'[1] At the age of forty-four Debord was overweight and suffering from gout, an affliction usually associated with a much older age group and which was extremely painful. This was living proof, if any were needed, that not all the rumours circulating around Paris concerning Debord's refined tastes were untrue. In recent years, with Lebovici's financial help, he had developed a taste for luxury which mostly centred on a love of fine wine and food. Michèle Bernstein had noted, at their last meeting, that Debord had lost the sharp angular features of his youth and was puffy and pale. 'He loved excess, and for a time this was sex, and another time it was food and drink. He was never drunk, or you never saw him drunk, but it was impossible for him not to drink,' Michèle explained. 'Guy loved intensity, intense moments,' explained Alice, 'and at this time it was intensity in the ordinary good things of life, food, drink, sex. There were no restraints, that was the only rule.'

The elegant aphorism from Lautréamont quoted by Debord to justify his alcoholism was a typically defiant philosophical justification of a way of life which was already bringing him down: he found sleep difficult, and brooded and worried long into the night. Along with the gout came digestive difficulties, not helped by a wheezy smoker's cough. Exercise was of course out of the question and the burgeoning 1970s cult of fitness and the body, only now being imported into France from America, was dismissed with the same sneer that had been levelled by the adolescent Debord at bathers in Cannes.

However, his failing health worried his friends and intimates, including Alice and the eternally indulgent Lebovici. As Debord naturally refused to limit his intake of alcohol (he now habitually began the day with either beer, wine or, in cases of extreme need, Russian vodka) or moderate his diet, it was decided that at least a healthy environment might improve matters. This was not the most important reason why Debord and Alice had started looking for a country residence in the Auvergne. More pressing was the need to escape Paris which, for Debord, had been brutalised by the changing shape of development in the 1970s, but it was nonetheless, at least for Alice, an important factor. The house had been found towards the end of the previous year in a place called Champot, a tiny hamlet near the equally obscure village of Bellevue-la-Montagne in the furthest reaches of the Auvergne, then as now one of the wildest and most inaccessible parts of France, a good six hours at least on the straightest road from Paris.

The early part of 1975 was spent settling in and enjoying the new house, which was rarely empty and most often filled with guests from Paris and elsewhere. Martine Barraqué, whose work on the film of *The Society of the Spectacle* had been so cherished by Debord, was amongst the first to visit the couple in the Auvergne. She found that in the countryside Guy was relaxed, witty, charming, something again of the legendary drinker and raconteur who had led the Situationist International. He, in turn, nicknamed Martine 'La voyelle', a play on the masculine term *voyou*, meaning hooligan or outlaw, by which the ex-Situationists now referred to themselves. Guy held forth every evening at the head of a long wooden table which dominated the main room, smoking a pipe, drinking slowly but steadily, tapping ash onto the table and telling stories, jokes, or theorising on the political condition of Europe. Martine also noted that drinking was not exclusively an evening activity but that the couple now seriously devoted their lives to a permanent state of intoxication. There was also, to say the least, a quite marked sexual tension in the air, as if Guy was both provoking and enticing his guests with the possibility of fulfilling sexual desires they might not have suspected they had. Both Guy and Alice proclaimed themselves to be free to follow their own desires and they pointed this out to guests, whose choice it was to follow their instincts.

Despite his various complaints and illnesses, Debord felt confident and optimistic in the new house at Champot and, in conversation with frequent visitors such as Gianfranco Sanguinetti, began to draw up new plans and projects. The first of these was to oversee the reissue of the twelve volumes of *L'Internationale situationniste* which Lebovici had agreed to publish under the imprint of Champ Libre that summer.

The second plan, which involved the re-activation of former Italian Situationist comrades, was far more complex. But it was also to be one of Debord's most daring, skilful and accomplished political actions and entirely consistent with the first promises of the Situationist International to turn the world on its head by exposing its reality as a construct. As Debord put it, 'understood in its totality, the spectacle is both the outcome and the goal of the dominant mode of production. It is not something added to the real world – not a decorative element so to speak. On the contrary, it is the very heart of society's real unreality.'[2] This analysis, an early thesis in *The Society of the Spectacle*, was the starting point of Debord's notion that power is always and everywhere hidden from view, even though modern democracies pride themselves on the apparent visibility of the mechanisms of power. It was still possible, Debord argued, that this state of affairs could be subverted by the simple act of pointing out the occluded nature of real political power and the unreality of democratic procedure.

Twentieth-century baroque

'At that time,' wrote Debord, describing his periodic bouts of exile from Paris in the mid-1970s, 'Italy was once again losing its way: it was necessary to regain sufficient distance from its prisons, where those who stayed too long at the revels of Florence ended up.'[3] The disorder which apparently prevailed in Italy was evidently much to Debord's taste: 'the distance' he needed to keep from its prisons was a mark of how involved he would become in one of the country's main political scandals of the period.

In 1975 it was clear to most Italians of all political complexions that the country's political situation had never really recovered from the series of crises which had marked its history through the 1960s, and in particular the movements of 1968 and 1969, and that if anything, accelerated by the oil crisis of 1973, the situation had worsened, become serious, and that democracy itself was in a fragile state. The principal reasons for this political quagmire were, in no particular order, a fragmented party system, a politicised legal system, illegal, anti-democratic and subversive activities from the security and intelligence services, and clientelism – the acquisition of political power through the time-honoured exercise of patronage rather than popularity. Added to these factors were the specific tensions heightened by conspiracy theories and mysterious acts of terrorism. The occult world of Italian politics, where few verifiable facts were ever made public, was therefore almost impossible to penetrate or understand, even by informed insiders. The confusion was heightened by the activities and agitation of semi-clandestine organisations naming themselves National Vanguard, Mussolini Action Squad, New Order and Black Order. In early 1974, at an anti-Fascist rally in Brescia, eight people had been killed by a bomb thrown by an unknown hand. Later that year twelve people were killed in Bologna by a bomb on the Italicus express train between Rome and Munich, again no one knew by whom or why the bomb had been planted (the Fascist group the Black Order later left a note in Bologna claiming responsibility and declaring that government members who 'are engendering Marxism in Italy by dissolving neo-Fascist Organisations' had to bear responsibility for the deaths).

There was however a growing feeling, even amongst moderates of the

Right and Left, that since the Piazza Fontana bombings of 1969, it was unthinkable that the state did not have links or influence on these so-called 'Black terrorists'. These suspicions had deepened in the wake of the attempted *coup d'état* of 1970, organised by a former submarine commander, Prince Junio Valerio Borghese, otherwise known as 'the Black Prince', who assembled some 200 members of his 'National Front' outside Rome, urging them to take power by force. This comic-opera failure was made less hilarious for many Italians by the revelations that some of Borghese's men had actually got inside the Ministry of the Interior building, an act which could not have been accomplished without the active collaboration of senior officials in the Andreotti coalition government, including most notably General Miceli, a senior figure in the intelligence services.

In 1972 two neo-Fascists, Franco Freda and Giovanni Ventura, were arrested and tried for the Piazza Fontana bombings. Tension was heightened across the political boundaries when it emerged that a certain Guido Giannettini, an agent of the Italian security services, was exposed as a conspirator and that well-known figures on the anarchist or libertarian Left had been pushed to 'suicide' by the police.

Parallel to the frightening proliferation of 'black terrorism' was the emergence of the Red Brigades, originally conceived as a response to Fascist violence and the increasingly mysterious powers of the state. The origins of the Red Brigades lay in an alliance forged between Communists and left-leaning Catholics who, in the 'hot autumn' of 1969, when tension in Milan was reaching fever-pitch, formed a 'metropolitan political collective'. In July 1970, at a meeting in the Ligurian town of Chiavari, this movement named itself the Proletarian Left and espoused an agenda which would combat all forms of state violence, whatever shapes they took. By 1972, the loose alliance of Proletarian Left and workers' groups, styling themselves the Red Brigades, began to perfect the art of political kidnapping, holding 'proletarian trials' of bankers and industrialists. In the early stages these activities, alongside the firebombing of car plants and factories, were largely of a symbolic nature and attracted a good deal of tacit support from otherwise moderately Leftist voters and supporters. This support even extended itself to the first kidnapping of a state official, the magistrate Mario Sossi who was known for his anti-Left views and hard line on radical prisoners. The symbolic form of resistance continued until the shooting by police of an unarmed activist, Margherita Cagol, the beautiful, intellectual militant who had dedicated her life to the struggle and who died in 1975 at the age of thirty; thereafter the rallying cry of the Red Brigades was 'Never again without a rifle!'[4]

It was to combat the rising tensions in Italy that the parliamentary Left in Italy, represented in the main by the Italian Communist Party under the leadership of Enrico Berlinguer, sought the *compromesso storico*, 'historic compromise', with the Christian Democrats, who had been the main party in power controlling all of the coalition governments through the 1970s, even those of a centre-Left direction. Berlinguer had been persuaded by prominent Catholic Communists, led by the Catholic intellectuals Franco Rodato and Antonio Tàto, that the proletariat, in the form of white, working-class, urban manual labourers could never constitute a majority in a country which was also dominated by rural, Catholic values. The 'Italian way' of Communism, Berlinguer had announced to a party Congress as far back as 1972, was to seek to reconcile these contradictions. At the back of his mind, however, was the chastening example of Chile, where a narrowly elected Left-wing government had been destroyed in a *coup* led by General Augusto Pinochet, but which had been organised, paid for and tacitly supported by the CIA and the United States government. In order to avoid this scenario Berlinguer was to persuade his intransigently Marxist intimates that a compromise with the Christian Democrats offered a route to Socialist power.

It was against this background that a mysterious tract appeared under the imprint of the publisher Ugo Mursia in August 1975. The slim volume was entitled *Rapporto veridico sulle ultime opportunita di salvare il capitalismo in Italia*, 'The True Report on the Last Chance to Save Capitalism in Italy', and signed by the equally mysterious 'Censor' whose name evoked the original function of the Roman office of supervising public morals. 'Censor' quoted Shakespeare, Machiavelli, Hegel and Thucydides and wrote with brilliant classical lucidity. The book, which accurately described the structures of power and the uses of state-controlled terrorism, caused a political storm in Italy.

The central thesis of the book, written from the standpoint of a believer both in Christian Democracy and high bourgeois values, was that only by allowing the Italian Communists into an alliance with the Christian Democrats could capitalism and the bourgeois order in Italy be saved from the subversive classes who were threatening revolutionary violence. This did not mean that the Communists would be given any power, and even less tolerable was the possibility that they might have any say in modes of production and consumption, but that the illusion of power would be enough to defuse any future threat of subversion. This was a classically executed argument, every bit as precise and cynical as Machiavelli, aiming at the exercise of statecraft with all the guile and feint deception of the Florentine master.

The argument that the illusion of power masks access to real power was of course ecstatically received by Christian Democrats who were reluctant to take Enrico Berlinguer's advances and promises without reassuring themselves that they would still be in charge. It was assumed, partly as a result of the classical tone of the text and partly because of the erudition on display, that these were the thoughts of an insider within the political process; its cynicism thus gave the text even higher prestige.

A commentator in *Il Giorno* asked, 'So what does this mysterious "Censor" have to say of interest? . . . "This society suits us because it is there, and we want to maintain it in order to maintain our power over it." What society is "Censor" talking about? It is capitalist society from San Francisco to Vladivostok, the society in which those who control the movement of capital manage to make the masses work by strength or by "an incomparable power of illusion". . . . The final part of this pamphlet is written with an absolute aristocratic cynicism.'[5] It was this latter aspect of the text which compelled the journalist in *Europeo* to describe admiringly 'the real and authentic manifesto of political and economic power in Italy'.[6] In *Il Resto del Carlino*, a conservative publication, a reviewer was astonished, fascinated and convinced by the interpretation of recent events in Italy: 'And having come to this point, you ask yourself: "who is this 'Censor' who is so intimate with the secrets behind events" . . . what you read about the "hot autumn", of the strategy of tension and the massacre at the Piazza Fontana, means that the author must remain anonymous, given what he knows and what he has to say about these serious affairs . . . until now the thesis of a "massacre by the State" has only been put forward by far Left groups, even the Italian Communist Party is officially lukewarm on the matter. But it is stupefying that it should be publicly revealed by a convinced conservative, whose only concern is to preserve capitalism.'[7]

The pamphlet was of course a hoax. 'Censor' was in reality Gianfranco Sanguinetti, who had drawn up the text with considerable help from Debord (the references and classical allusions were key markers for those such as the academic sociologist Mario Perniola, who were keen Italian readers of *L'Internationale situationniste*). Both Debord and Sanguinetti were delighted that the pamphlet had managed to nail its target so effectively and they boasted gleefully of how they had almost brought down another government, embarrassing not only those on the Right who had so cheerfully approved of 'Censor's' most diabolical and Machiavellian theses, but also those on the Left who had been working hard to convince their supporters that the forthcoming compromise was not a betrayal. Most importantly, the fact that readers of both Right and Left had left unchallenged the main argument that power was an occult force in Italy and Western Europe was proof that this notion was true. The interpretation of the violent terrorism and confused rhetoric which characterised the political scene in Italy, although shocking to many Italians, was soon proved by revelations about the government and security services to be correct. There was therefore also a prophetic tone to Censor's remark in English, 'Frailty, thy name is Italy!'

For Sanguinetti the book was also an act of revenge. He had been on several police black lists since 1968 and was, in the wake of the Situationist denunciation of the Piazza Fontana bombing, variously suspected of involvement in bombings or other associated activities covered by the rubric 'red terrorism'. His case had not been helped by his deportation from France in 1971, which had left him extremely bitter, angry and deeply sceptical of the due process of the law. Since then he had lived a semi-clandestine life, moving between Italy and France as Debord's most steadfast drinking partner and chief conspirator. In March 1975, Sanguinetti had once again been quite arbitrarily arrested by the Italian authorities and spent some months in prison, whilst the police attempted fruitlessly to relate him to recent discoveries of arms caches or have the Situationist International proscribed as a terrorist organisation. *Rapporto veridico* was Sanguinetti's response: a measured, imperious and wholly succesful *détournement* of the political language at the time which mocked and destroyed those in power who were also destroying Italy.

It was also however Guy Debord's book, and would certainly not have existed without Debord's strenuous guiding hand over theoretical and editorial matters (Sanguinetti was an elegant writer, but he lacked discipline and was given to excessively florid touches in his prose). Debord was now dividing his time fairly equally between Florence and Champot. In the overheated political climate in Italy this was not without certain dangers to Debord, Sanguinetti and those around them. These were risks that Debord was more than willing to embrace: 'So what did I do during that time?' he wrote later in *Panegyric*. 'I did not try too hard to avoid dangerous encounters; and it is even possible that I cold-bloodedly sought them out.'[8]

Out of time

As the French translation of *Rapporto veridico* was being published and publicised by Champ Libre in the early months of 1976, Sanguinetti was still a fugitive sought by police in France and Italy. He was turned back again at the French border on 11 February on the strict orders of the Minister of the Interior, Raymond Marcellin, probably acting on false information given to him by the Italian and French intelligence services. On 24 February Champ Libre paid for a half-page advertisement in *Le Monde* for a text drawn up by Debord which mocked the petty repressions taking place on European borders and echoed the confidence gained from the recent Italian adventure in counter-propaganda: 'The effective existence of Gianfranco Sanguinetti himself is highly debatable,' the text read, 'either as a personality involved in a Western samizdat operation, or as the target of a liberal-advanced gulag.'[9]

Yet despite the relative success with this latest venture, it seemed that

Champ Libre, and Debord, were increasingly out of step and becoming isolated in Paris both intellectually and emotionally. The Situationists seemed to more and more people to be no more than a memory of images, ideas and emotions which constituted the 1960s. Outside of Italy, political life in Western Europe was characterised by a move towards centrist and consensus politics. The fact that it was Debord and the Situationists who pointed out that terrorism, as their experiences in Italy had demonstrated, created this state of affairs was less an irony than a sign that no one wanted to hear such a radical, apparently perverse critique. Vocabulary and manners were changing fast, and the language of Marxist Hegelianism used by lesser lights around Debord was rapidly becoming unfashionable, even embarrassing.

Champ Libre itself had now been reduced to a hard core of dedicated staff, comprising Floriana, Hortensia and Catherine Nicole. The business was able to survive, subsidised by Artmedia and Lebovici's other interests, but it had drifted a long way away from either commercial or intellectual success. 'There were whole days when I saw no one,' said Catherine Nicole, who was not really interested in politics or literature and found the job 'rather flat'.[10] Debord was still drawing up plans for publication and talking them through with Lebovici, but the enterprise seemed afflicted with a curious sense of isolation and stagnation.

In the late spring of 1976, Debord received news which shocked him to the core. It came in the form of a letter from his half-brother Patrick Labaste. The terrible news was that Michèle, the half-sister he had always felt close to and admired for her good looks and capricious wit, was dead.

Michèle had always idolised Guy and, unlike Patrick, who despite his physical resemblance to Debord in his voice and in his manner could not have been politically further away, she was excited and inspired by the heroic actions of the Situationist International. Her own life, however, had been far from glittering: she had never taken up a career and from an early age veered between alcoholism and recuperation. Her good looks – in her youth she was quite stunning – had blurred but never quite faded. She had never found happiness or fulfilment in her life and each of her three marriages had been marked by her attempts at suicide. Her third marriage, to a Lebanese businessman, had taken her to Cameroon, to the obscure town of Douala where, in the course of a boozy and depressed evening, she ingested a fatal combination of sleeping pills and alcohol. She died later that night. Nobody knew whether it was an accident or suicide.

The two brothers were reconciled in grief. Even a friendship briefly flourished, and visits were made to the Labaste residence where, on one famous occasion, in the spirit of the 'potlatch', Alice and Guy turned up on the thirty-fifth birthday of Patrick's partner Catherine with thirty-five presents. Such pleasant and ordinary domestic scenes were, however, a rarity in Debord's life. The death of Michèle had hit Debord hard, but this was not the reason why his own drinking was so relentless. Financed by Lebovici, Guy and Alice set out to live life as far as possible away from the constraints of the society of the spectacle: this principle justified the drinking for days on end, the journeys between Italy, France and other European cities (Barcelona and Seville were other favoured destinations) and their aristocratic disdain for work, leisure, the mediocrity of consumerism. But it could not stave off the creeping suspicion that a way of life that had once been heroic was turning into something darker, even tragic.

CHAPTER 29

Fortresses, Firebombs and Films

1977–8

The characteristic feature of the house at Champot was its extreme isolation. In the warmer months this made the place especially attractive to Parisian guests, who delighted in its distance from the city and the relatively tough and wild nature of the surrounding countryside. In the wintertime, however, the Auvergne is one of the most inhospitable areas in France, high winds and frequent storms making existence particularly difficult for those who seek to make a living from the land.

The architecture of the Auvergne reflects both the uncompromising landscape, of extinct volcanoes, inaccessible ravines and grassy upland hills, and its political instability. It was not until the eighteenth century that the Auvergne lost its reputation as a land of brigands, insurrectionists, and anti-monarchist agitation. Many houses were constructed as a defence against roaming bands and private armies as well as the elements. The weather changed constantly and almost instantaneously from calm to wild and savage storms. The house at Champot seemed at times under siege from the elements, a factor which made the house feel like a fortress. This provided the perfect metaphor for the way in which Debord, the retired revolutionary general, was now beginning to conceive of himself and his relation to the outside world.

It was with a a rare touch of the elegiac that Debord acknowledged this new status and the irony of his latest position, bringing together the poetic, the military and the political in his descriptions of the house in *Panegyric*:

I even stayed in an inaccessible house surrounded by woods, far from any village, in an extremely exhausted mountainous region deep in a deserted Auvergne. I spent several winters there. Snow fell for days on end. The wind piled it up in drifts. Barriers kept it off the road. Despite the exterior walls, snow accumulated in the courtyard. Logs burned in the fireplace.

The house seemed to open directly on to the Milky Way. At night, the nearby stars would shine brilliantly one moment, and the next would be extinguished by the passing mist. And so too our conversations and our celebrations, our meetings and tenacious passions.

It was a land of storms. They would approach noiselessly at first, announced by the brief passage of a wind that slithered through the grass or by a series of sudden flashes on the horizon; then thunder and lightning were unleashed, and we were bombarded for a long while and from every direction, as if in a fortress under siege. Just once at night, I saw lightning strike near me outside: you could not even see where it had struck; the whole landscape was equally illuminated for one startling instant. Nothing in art has seemed to give me this impression of an irrevocable brilliance, except for the prose that Lautréamont employed in the programmatic exposition that he called *Poésies*. But nothing else either: neither Mallarmé's blank page, nor Malevitch's white square on a white background, nor even Goya's last pictures, where black takes over everything, like Saturn devouring his children.

Violent winds, which at any moment could rise from one of three directions, shook the trees. Those on the moors to the north, more dispersed, bent and shook like ships surprised at anchor in an unprotected harbour. The compactly grouped trees that guarded the hill in front of the house supported one another in their resistance, the first rank breaking the west wind's relentless assault. Farther off, the line of the woods disposed in squares, over the whole half-circle of the hills, evoked the troops arranged in a chessboard pattern in certain eighteenth-century battle scenes. And those almost vain charges sometimes made a breach, knocking down a rank. Piled-up clouds traversed the sky at a run. A sudden change of wind could also quickly send them into retreat, with other clouds launched in their pursuit.

On calm mornings, there were all the birds of the dawn and the perfect chill of the air, and that dazzling shade of tender green that came over the trees, in the tremulous light of the sun rising before them.

The weeks passed imperceptibly. One day the morning air announced the arrival of autumn. Another time, a great sweetness in the air, like a quick promise always kept, 'the spring breeze'.

In regard to someone who has been, as essentially and continuously as I, a man of streets and cities – one will thus appreciate the degree to which my preferences will not overly falsify my judgements – it should be pointed out that the charm and harmony of these few seasons of grandiose isolation did not escape me. It was a pleasing and impressive solitude. But in truth I was not alone: I was with Alice.[1]

During the long winter days and nights in Le Minour, when there were no guests or they were exhausted from conversation and entertaining, Guy and Alice spent many hours drinking and playing war games. Games of strategy had always fascinated Debord; it was an interest which long preceded his discovery of Johan Huizinga and could indeed be traced back to childhood when, to escape Manou, his mother or his siblings, he would retreat to the back of the house in Cannes and obsessively plan campaigns with his lead soldiers. In 1975, in a second-hand shop in Paris, Debord had come across an old war game which he had renovated. A brass plate, made by René Viénet, was attached to the side of the game. It read: 'Kriegspiel Clausewitz Debord'.

The rules of the 'game of war' were entirely based on the theories of Clausewitz and on the basis of eighteenth-century warfare, that is to say wars which were fought across territories not yet fully defined by nationhood or empire. Each territory in the game was divided into arsenals, fortresses, a mountain pass and nine mountains, which were untraversable, blocking fire and communications. The aim was the complete destruction of the military potential of the adversary, to be achieved by destroying all combat units or taking all the enemy's arsenals.

In this the game was also faithful to Huizinga's notion, for so long a central part of Situationist strategy, that the essence of a war is also the essence of art. As in art, it is the lightning strike of bold gesture, unpredicted and unpredictable, which is most likely to destroy an enemy's positions and clear the field for new manoeuvres. The war game was also most poignant, as Debord was assuming a new status as a thinker rather than a revolutionary participant in his age, a poetic suspension of the passage of time as in the poetry of Mallarmé or the paintings of Malevitch. 'In the unfolding of this Kriegspiel,' Debord wrote, 'all time is equal: the solstice of war where the climate never varies and night never falls before the inevitable conclusion of the conflict.'[2]

It was also of great significance for Debord that Clausewitz had been a contemporary of Hegel and that his theories on the meaning and use of war were developed against the background of European revolutionary conflict. Clausewitz's ideas were therefore a perfect corollary of Debord's understanding of the Hegelian notion that history can only move forward when men in any given age are prepared to wage war against its most deeply held beliefs in the name of a higher culture. This was of course, as Huizinga put it, the 'aristocratic and agonistic' life of the warrior. It was also important for Debord that the house in Champot allowed him to think and act in this way: he was able again to justify his retreat from the city, the world, in the name of Clausewitz, citing a favourite aphorism from the chapter 'Fortresses', which stated that, 'The efficacy of a fortress is plainly composed of two different elements, the passive and the active. By the first it shelters the place, and all that it contains; by the other it possesses a certain influence over the adjacent country, even beyond its guns [. . .]. Fortresses in mountains are important in a similar manner. [. . .] they may be regarded as the true buttresses of the whole defensive system.'[3]

Children of the revolution

As Debord retreated to the Auvergne and further into himself, the ideas which he had developed for so long in isolation or with the Situationist International were taking on their own momentum and 'spectacular' meaning. 'Our ideas are in everyone's mind' had been a key axiom in the early 1960s. Now it seemed that the term 'Situationist' was becoming charged with a certain and explosive currency in the English-speaking world which went far beyond its first meaning as a form of cultural activity that would reshape the human imagination.

In the first instance the word began to be associated with a small group of 'adventurists' in the UK, the so-called Angry Brigade, who captured headlines in the early 1970s. The members of the Angry Brigade were allegedly either Sussex or Cambridge drop-outs or Stoke Newington and Notting Hill hippies. They had arrived at their political positions through their readings of Marcuse and Spanish Anarchists as well as the Situationists. Some of them had travelled to Paris during the events of May 1968 and returned to England even more confirmed in their belief that the state could only be destroyed by a small, disciplined organisation which attacked the most obvious manifestations of the consumer society. Their main targets were therefore property, shops and other representative agents of 'the repression of proletarian life' such as banks, the BBC, the Miss World Show or the embassies of Right-wing governments.

The bombings associated with the Angry Brigade had started as far back as 1968 with a series of attacks on the Spanish Embassy in Grosvenor Square, then the Bank of Spain, Iberia Airways, two Italian consulates and an Italian trade fair, all of which gave rise to the initial suspicion that a European terrorist network was at work. A second wave of attacks on specifically British targets did however identify the groups as home-grown. Shaken by events in Northern Ireland and the rise of the IRA, the government imposed a media blackout and made it a priority to 'smash the Angry Brigade'.

Even the name of the group, which first appeared in the groups' communiqués in 1969, was the cause of confusion. It was first of all associated, by cultural commentators on the Left and then the police, with the French *Enragés* and it was therefore presumed that the activities were the work of pro-68 students. Another view proposed links with the International Brigades of the Spanish Civil War, whilst others, more conspiratorially minded still, doubted that the name and the group itself was anything more than a phantom.

What was not in doubt was that in Britain in the late 1960s and early 1970s there was an orchestrated campaign to systematically wreck the apparatus of the state. The Angry Brigade formed a perfect secret army: 'The Angry Brigade is the man or woman sitting next to you,' read *Communiqué no. 9*. 'They have guns in their pockets and hatred in their minds. We are getting closer.' The campaign included 123 attacks on property between 1968 and 1972. Eventually Jim Greenfield, Anna Mendelson, Hilary Creek and John Barker, all apparently the guiding lights in the group, were sentenced to ten years' imprisonment for 'conspiracy to cause explosions'. The previous December another member, Jake Prescott, had been sentenced to fifteen years on the charge of 'conspiracy'.

The main debates on the Left in the wake of the Angry Brigade trials centred on the fact that the group were clearly guilty of the worst kind of élitist 'vanguardism' and that their actions, although 'technically brilliant', as the Trotskyist journal *Red Mole* put it, were also likely to make police and state repression more heavy-handed.

The Angry Brigade had no direct connection with any of the Situationists in Paris or elsewhere. One of the central leads in the police investigation was however the use of the word 'spectacle' in several of the Brigade's texts. The first communiqué announced that 'Fascism and oppression will be smashed. Embassies (Spanish Embasssy gunned Thursday), High Pigs, Spectacles, Judges, Property.' Later communiqués were also capable of their own form of violent poetry which echoed Situationist language:

> 'If you're not busy being born you're busy buying.'
> All the sales girls in the flash boutiques are made to dress the same and have the same make-up, representing the 1940s. In fashion as in everything else, capitalism can only go backwards – they've nowhere to go – they're dead.
> The future is ours.
> Life is so boring there is nothing to do except spend all wages on the latest skirt or shirt.
> Brothers and Sisters, what are your real desires?
> Sit in the drugstore, look distant, empty, bored, drinking some tasteless coffee? Or perhaps BLOW IT UP OR BURN IT DOWN. The only thing you can do with modern slave-houses – called boutiques – IS WRECK THEM. You can't reform profit capitalism and inhumanity. Just kick it till it breaks.
>
> Communiqué 8
> The Angry Brigade[4]

The above communiqué was dated 1 May 1971. The same day a bomb planted by the Angry Brigade exploded, with no casualties, in the fashionable Biba boutique in Kensington High Street.

It was not long before Special Branch officers were investigating students at Cambridge, Sussex and other 'centres of agitation' to see who in the university library had been reading *The Society of the Spectacle* and other Situationist texts labelled as 'seditious' by the police. Gordon Carr's book, *The Angry Brigade*, published in the wake of the trials, devoted a long opening chapter to describing the dangerous influence of Situationist ideas and the warped, terrorist philosophies of Guy Debord and Raoul Vaneigem.

The result of the police campaign and then Carr's book was to effectively blacken the Situationists' reputation in more respectable Left-wing circles in Britain, to the extent that even an astute commentator on the changing currents of the European scene such as Robin Blackburn, editor of the influential *New Left Review*, was able blithely to connect Debord's milieu with that of the Angry Brigade, stating categorically, 'I can't help thinking that there was a link between the Situationists and the Angry Brigade.'[5] In English underground circles the Situationists were now regarded as terrifying megalomaniacs and their contribution to the events of 1968 was consequently diminished or derided. In a 1977 edition of *International Times*, still the most radical magazine in London outside the burgeoning punk scene, Heathcote Williams identified the Situationists as the spoilers of the revolutionary party:

> Paris '68 was rich in nameless wildness, but it was marred by a small group of embittered scene-creamers, who called themselves Situationists, and who tried in typically French fashion to intellectualize the whole mood out of existence, and with their name tried to colonize it. Failed activists and mini-Mansonettes who boasted that all their books and pamphlets ('Leaving the 20th Century', 'The Veritable Split in the Fourth International' etc.) had been produced from the proceeds of a bank robbery when even the most lavish of them could have been produced for the price of a few tins of cat food from Safeways (one tiny exception being 'Ten Days that Shook the University' by Omar Khayati). Their heroes are a legion of mad bombers, Valerie Solanas, Nechayev, the IRA et al.[6]

Williams's thinking on this matter entirely matched the thoughts of Inspector Roy Habershon of the Special Branch. Habershon was the 'Situationist cop' who had been assigned to smash the Angry Brigade but found himself utterly baffled by the politics of the hippie communes his officers were trying to infiltrate. He was convinced throughout the investigation, however, that the Situationists had something to do with international terrorism and that they provided the key to understanding the Angry Brigade. The mere term 'Situationist' was more than enough to incriminate the stoned students and spaced-out hippie chicks who were constantly arrested and re-arrested during this period.

Flowers in the dustbin

The term 'Situationist' was to enter the English language properly with the arrival of the Sex Pistols, who crashed onto the stage in 1976 declaring war on all preceding forms of rock culture. The Pistols' manifesto was clearly laid out in the first single, *Anarchy in the UK*, a shattering slice of violent glam rock whose message was pure negation. A nation's traumas were brought swiftly to the surface on national television, as the group swore and drank on Thames Television's *Today* show. In Manchester, with Vivienne Westwood dressed as a Nazi slag dancing on the side of the stage, they childishly wrecked the studio of Granada Television's *So it Goes*, the local rock show presented by Anthony H. Wilson. In the wake of the *Today* incident, the newspapers fell over themselves to thunder against 'The Filth and the Fury' and denounce the punk rock followers of the band as 'foul-mouthed yobs'. Meanwhile a generation of teenagers in provincial Britain decided that youth and rock music were still powerful allies and began to form bands based on the premise that the rebel poses of an earlier generation could still have a currency in the stagnant cultural universe of the 1970s.

The iconic image of Johnny Rotten defacing posters of the Beatles and the Rolling Stones in a record shop in Soho was elegantly heretical, in the best Situationist manner, and sent out shock waves of alarm through a moribund music industry. The artwork for their record sleeves was similarly destructive and inspiring in equal measure, from the 'detourned' images of the Queen with a safety pin through her nose to the famous cover of *Holidays in the Sun* which, borrowing its images from a Belgian Tourist Board poster, showed the members of a happy family declaring 'I wanna go to the New Belsen' and 'I wanna see some history'. The Sex Pistols' lyrics were no less subversive and beautifully negative: 'We're the flowers in the dustbin, we're the poison in the human machine, we're the future, your future', ran the middle eight section of *God Save the Queen*, the record which when it reached the number one spot in the charts during the Queen's Silver Jubilee celebrations was effectively blacked out of existence by radio, television and newspapers. This was a perfect confirmation of the Situationist notion that the society of the spectacle cannot admit negative forces which it cannot control or contain.

The Sex Pistols had not been created by accident. Their manager Malcolm McLaren and designer Jamie Reid were both products of the libertarian scene based around West London (future Pistols photographer Joe Stevens had been picked up more than once as a suspected Situationist terrorist) and directly influenced by the London Situationist offshoot King Mob, an abbreviation of the slogan 'His Majesty King Mob' which had been painted on the walls of Newgate prison during the Gordon Riots of 1790. McLaren and Reid had based their ideas for the group and its actions on specific theoretical positions developed by King Mob.

King Mob's main enemies were the orthodox Left in all its manifestations and all forms of cultural spectacle. They made heroes of Jack the Ripper and the ten-year-old child killer Mary Bell and they decorated the house of the murderer John Reginald Christie with the slogan 'Christie Lives!' Other plans included blowing up a waterfall and Wordsworth's house in the Lake District and an idea for a totally disgusting rock band which would make 'cash from chaos'.[7]

As far back as 1969, Chris Gray, briefly a Situationist and active in King Mob and its American brother organisation, the Motherfuckers, had scrawled graffiti for a completely revolting pop group across Victoria Station. King Mob also reprinted a Motherfuckers flyer from 1968 which declared: 'There is no longer any distinction between theory and action. We are outlaws. We are the forces of CHAOS AND ANARCHY. We are everything they say we are and proud of it.' The statements were reproduced on the Jefferson Airplane album *Volunteers* and Charles Radcliffe, another former Situationist, was declared 'political adviser' for the group. Most crucially, a clutch of Situationist texts, translated by Chris Gray with graphics by Jamie Reid, had been published in 1974 as *Leaving the Twentieth Century: The Incomplete Work of the Situationist International*. Although the original edition sold only 4,000 copies, it became a much sought-after item when the connections between Reid and the Sex Pistols became known.

It was soon clear to those who had been following closely that the Sex Pistols had been constructed out of the collision between French theory and the iconoclastic energy that characterised British youth culture. This was first spotted in Paris, where the Sex Pistols made a brief foray in September 1976 and where their paint-spattered clothes, festooned with slogans in the style of the hooligans of the early Letterist International, made an immediate impression at the Café Deux Magots and led one press commentator to identify Malcolm McLaren as a 'couturier situationniste'. .

The reaction from Paris from Debord and the former Situationists themselves was however largely one of indifference. The same applied some twenty years later when I asked Philippe Sollers about his impression of the impact the Situationists had had in Britain and, in the manner of a High Court judge enquiring 'And who, pray, are the Beatles?', he claimed with exquisite mandarin charm never to have heard of the Sex Pistols. Debord himself remained faithful to his own musical tastes, largely consisting of traditional French folk songs and more latterly the jazz of John Coltrane or Art Blakey's Jazz Messengers.

Only Michèle Bernstein recognised, watching the Pistols on British television, that something was happening which was the result of theories and ideas she had been part of in the 1960s. 'I understood the Sex Pistols straight away,' she said, 'and I don't listen to rock music much but only to opera. But I saw in Johnny Rotten that he would have been like us at Chez Moineau, he was obviously a brother.'

Wisdom will never come

Debord viewed these various popular manifestations of 'Situationism' with some contempt. 'It was as if', said Bernstein, 'nobody else had the right to revolt or say no. Guy had always been a man who could make you laugh and be charming and witty with everyone. He was extremely seductive. Obviously I did not know him after a certain period. But I knew people who did, and they tell me that they saw this side of him less often than before.'

In January 1977, Debord began shooting the film *In girum imus nocte et consumimur igni* in Venice. The film's main theme was the large and widespread form of historical amnesia which he now saw as the defining point of the society of the spectacle. The shoot was scheduled for a week but took only three days, the rest of the time in Venice being spent in bars and restaurants where Debord spent much of Lebovici's money and astonished the film-crew workers with his apparently insatiable appetites for refined food and good wine. The making of the film had not been without its complications, the least of which had been the difficulty in getting the film equipment across the French border, where it was immediately seized for some time by Italian customs officials. On arrival in Venice, noting the emptiness of the streets and squares, Debord suspected that police infiltration had accounted for the apparent absence of Italian comrades.

Debord was not slow either to suspect that those working for him might also be against him. This was largely based on the not unreasonable assumption that the crew – which was made up of André Mrugalski (or 'Mru'), Bernard Largemains and Richard Copans – disapproved of the time spent drinking and eating. Debord considered this to be an insult to his chosen way of life and then began to suspect sabotage.

Shooting was ended abruptly on the evening of the second day when Debord suddenly called a halt to proceedings and walked away from the crew, followed by Alice Becker-Ho, with the enigmatic words, 'And there you are, the shortest jokes are the best.' When Mrugalski later telephoned Debord in his hotel for an explanation, Debord replied, 'Mru, don't take me for a cunt', and slammed down the phone.[8] The three crew members returned to Paris, not knowing now whether they would be paid at all. Meanwhile Lebovici was summoned to Venice, where he spent several days with Guy and Alice sampling the finest culinary and alcoholic delights that the city could offer.

Despite the chaotic circumstances of its production *In girum imus nocte et consumimur igni* turned out to be Debord's most beautiful and finished film. It took the form of a fragmented, deeply literary meditation on failed revolution which, as the palindromic title suggests, circles around the central motif of the passage of time. 'There was then on the Left Bank of the river,' intoned Debord, quoting Heraclitus and evoking the lost world of his youth in Paris in the 1950s, 'a quarter where the negative held sway.' 'It was in Paris,' he said elsewhere, 'a city then so beautiful that people preferred to be poor there than rich elsewhere.'

The film, as cinema and text, is also a model of *détournement*. Accordingly, Debord quotes from texts by François Villon, Bossuet, Pascal, and steals footage from films by Marcel Carné, John Ford and Orson Welles (now a particular hero of Debord, as demonstrated in his taste for Welles's lifestyle as well as his art) in support of the notion that 'real life' cannot be fully erased from history or memory by the 'spectacle'. Amongst the few films which Debord openly admired was Alain Resnais's *Hiroshima mon amour*, chiefly because it was a film which placed memory and subjectivity against historical time. Debord, in his own cinema, borrows from Resnais the technique of preserving an essential separation between images and an intimate commentary. In this way the text of *In girum imus nocte et consumimur igni*, like Marguerite Duras's original script for Resnais's film, takes on a singular importance of its own.

The tone of the film was in equal parts defiant and elegiac. There were images of Saint-Germain-des-Prés, Alice, Éliane Papaï, accompanied by a sound track of Couperin and Art Blakey. Above all, the film, with quotations from Heraclitus, Shelley and Omar Khayyam, centred on the image of water flowing, an image which, Debord pointed out in his notes to the text of the film, stood as a metaphor for the passage of time.[9] This theme seemed even more apposite with the publication, in the early part of 1978, by Champ Libre of the text of *In girum imus nocte et consumimur igni* as part of Debord's *Oeuvres Cinématographiques complètes 1952–78*. This publication indicated the passing of another period in Debord's life, that of film-maker and artist. Thereafter, all of Debord's activity was to be marked by defensive actions rather than offensive operations.

CHAPTER 30

Terrorism and the State

1978–80

For those who had not been Situationists or close followers of their debates and activities in the 1960s it was all too easy to make connections between the group and the various terrorist groups who dominated the political agenda in Europe in the 1970s. The reasons for this were obvious: Situationist terminology such as 'spectacle', 'separation' and 'spectacular domination' were now staples of myriad revolutionary groups, from the Angry Brigade in Britain to Azione Revoluzionaria and the Red Brigades in Italy. Debord himself was often deliberately ambiguous about the subject (few of his friends of the period will even now broach the subject without the greatest circumspection), and included in *In girum* a still of Andreas Baader and Ulrike Meinhof of the German Red Army Faction as the commentary quotes '*Bella Porta Romana*', a Milanese prison song which contains the line 'the best of youth die in prison'. It was little wonder that in the atmosphere of virtual civil war which prevailed in Italy in the late 1970s, as pirate editions of Debord's book proliferated, influential journals such as *L'Espresso* could desribe the Red Brigades as 'waging a war against the "society of the spectacle"'.

At the end of April 1979 a slim volume by Gianfranco Sanguinetti called *Terrorismo e il stato* ('Terrorism and the State') appeared in a few radical Italian bookshops, including the Rome and Milan branches of Feltrinelli's posthumous empire (Feltrinelli's was now, despite the demise of its founder, the leading booksellers in Italy) and the Communist Party flagship Renascità on Rome's via delle Botteghe Oscure. By the end of the summer the book, which purported to reveal for the first time 'state secrets', was completely sold out. Unlike Sanguinetti and Debord's earlier collaboration, this was no hoax but a genuine and apparently very well informed unmasking of the state apparatus which shaped and controlled the 'spectacular' impact of terrorism on Italian society. Its central thesis was that 'the terrorist infection is a colossal and viable enterprise which ensures the jobs of thousands of journalists, cops, secret agents, gentlemen of the robe, sociologists and specialists of all denominations'. The main argument of the book was that it was not however a question of 'disagreeing' with terrorism but understanding how it worked. Sanguinetti begins by making a distinction between *offensive* terrorist operations, such as those of the PLO or the IRA, which he says will always fail, and *defensive* operations, such as the bombing of the Piazza Fontana, which because they are controlled by the state are nearly always succesful. Sanguinetti makes a further distinction between 'direct' terrorism, which attacks the population (as was the case with the 'black terrorism' of Piazza Fontana), or 'indirect' terrorism, which frightens the population by apparently placing the state in danger (this was the role, he argued, of the Red Brigades). Once these principles of the 'spectacular' effects of terrorism have been understood, he argues, it becomes clear that the task of the true subversive is to turn the weapons of state-controlled terrorists, whether they are 'direct' or 'indirect', back against the state. Published in the wake of the grisly killing at the hands of the Red Brigades of the Christian Democrat leader and architect of the 'historic compromise' Aldo Moro, in May 1978, these were, to say the least, unpopular and incendiary opinions.[1]

They were also, however, strategic theories which came, at least in part, from Guy Debord, whose journal *L'Internationale situationniste* was now banned in Italy on the grounds of its subversive influence. From the early spring of 1978 onwards, and centring on the killing of Moro, Debord had conducted a long and serious correspondence with Sanguinetti on the value and meaning of terrorism in modern society. It was this correspondence which had been at the origins of *Terrorism and the State*. The dialogue centred on the fact that Debord was convinced that the Red Brigades, either as dupes or through infiltration, had to be classified as an armed weapon of the state, whose strategy was to preserve a social-democratic consensus by brandishing the spectacle of illusory terrorism as its negative corollary. Sanguinetti was less than convinced about this point of view, seeing the Red Brigades as heroic freedom fighters who were misguided but essentially noble. Sanguinetti's opinion changed sharply when, after a long period of police surveillance, he found himself arrested on 13 May 1978 by eighteen armed policemen, little more than a week after Moro's body had been found in the boot of a Renault car in Rome, on the charge of possession of arms. During the investigations Sanguinetti was to find that his membership of the Situationist International was what really counted against him, as the prosecuting counsel sought to draw parallels between certain Red Brigade documents and those of the Situationist International.

In their correspondence Debord had signed himself Cavalcanti after the fourteenth-century poet Guido Cavalcanti, a friend of Dante whose reputation was that of a studious, bizarre and violent character. Appropriately, Cavalcanti had been deeply involved in Florentine politics and a poet. His central theme was the destructive force of human suffering. The exchanges between Debord and Sanguinetti (who signed himself Niccolò, after Niccolò Machiavelli) were a dialogue whose central purpose was, in the manner of their Renaissance heroes, to define rules for future intervention in the occult practice of statecraft. More precisely, unlike the armed terrorism of the Red Brigades and other related groups, Sanguinetti and Debord understood that what was really at stake in the conflict between terrorist organisations and the Italian government was not so much the prize of power, but the unmasking of the true nature of power. Accused of possessing weapons by the police, Sanguinetti's response was this would be a useless thing to do because 'it seems to me that the civil war has not yet begun'.

Debord was however now beginning to suspect even Sanguinetti of misunderstanding his own theories and severely underestimating the real danger he was in. At the moment of Aldo Moro's murder, Sanguinetti was in Milan, where he immediately prevailed upon a former comrade, who he had come across by chance in the street, to be seen publicly with him to provide an alibi. Having decided that this strategy was short-lived in its usefulness, Sanguinetti ignored Debord's advice to go underground and retreated to his country house at I Fagionili, where he made a great point of being seen by the villagers and the *carabinieri*, and thus avoided keeping his face off the front pages as a suspect who had mysteriously 'disappeared' in the aftermath of Moro's killing.

Although Debord himself largely approved of *Terrorism and the State*, he had been irritated at the way in which Sanguinetti had missed his opportunity to intervene in Italian affairs at the moment of the death of Moro, which was for Debord the crucial instant when the unmasking of the 'spectacular' operations of the state might have provided the revolutionary opportunity. Instead by reworking their dialogue into the theory of *Terrorism and the State*, which was published too late after the event, Sanguinetti had proved himself ineffectual at the point of crisis. More particularly, Debord was unconvinced by what he saw as Sanguinetti's naïve argument that unmasking the mechanisms of power, such as pointing out that the Red Brigades were 'indirectly' controlled forms of state terrorism, was enough to provoke a revolutionary situation.

It was therefore Paolo Salvadori who was entrusted with the Italian translation of *The Society of the Spectacle*, which Debord planned to publish in Florence at the end of 1979. In his preface to this edition Debord expressed his opinion that the Red Brigades had a 'function of a general interest, which is to disconcert or discredit proletarians who really rise up against the state, and maybe one day to eliminate some of the most dangerous of them'.[2] This was clearly at odds with Sanguinetti's belief that even if the Red Brigades were under state control their manipulation could be met with with counter-manipulation.

Debord approved of Salvadori both for his literary skills and for his

unwavering and often explosive dedication to the cause; complaining of
the inadequacies of the first Italian translation of *The Society of the Spectacle*
by De Donato, Debord wrote with warm approval of how 'Paolo Salvadori
right away, having gone to find those responsible for such an excess in their
offices, had hit them and even literally spat in their face: for such is naturally
the way good translators act when they meet bad ones.'[3]

Letters from an editor

Despite these differences the friendship with Sanguinetti remained warm.
Sanguinetti wrote a letter to Debord, giving a long account of his political
persecution in the overheated climate of 1978 and his narrow escape from
a long prison sentence. Sanguinetti still thought enough of Debord and his
ways to remind him that he still had a hundred litres of a 1975 Chianti to
be drunk on Debord's arrival in Italy. In the same letter, in a rare insight
into the uninhibited sexual life of Guy and Alice in Florence, Sanguinetti
described the chaotic state of the Italian terrorist milieu with reference to a
well-known prostitute they had both used at Debord's house in Florence:

> You cannot imagine, from a distance, the real state of things in Italy in the
> escalation of madness, on the one hand, and the degradation of everything
> which exists in general. And even what I put forward as an argument about
> the terrorist phenomenon are not merely rantings which do not have any
> base in reality. You may remember the whore, from Naples or Rome, who
> was at Caldaie one day, and seemed so excited when you were stroking
> her cunt, with four hands; you maybe remember that she had a brother,
> who was as immoral as her, and they were as incestuous as each other
> and didn't care to hide it. Anyway, as it happened this brother met a
> well-known terrorist, whose name he didn't want to tell me, and I don't
> remember the name of the brother and his whoreish sister. He told me,
> this brother, that despite his doubtful morality, he was astonished by the
> insane slackness which prevailed amongst these people who were capable of
> many things (useless for us and too spectacular) that you would think you
> were back in the time of Nechaev and Dostoevsky. So I think it's better for
> those of us with certain principles not to get involved with whores, incest
> or terrorists![4]

Away from Italy and its potentially lethal complications, Debord and
Lebovici were more than happy to get involved with stirring up as much
trouble as they could in the French literary and political scene. Having, for
the time being, abandoned film and full-blown Situationist activity, Debord
turned his attention to the art of the *lettre d'injure* ('the letter of insult'), an
epistolary form of spiteful and vindictive assault which the Surrealists, and

even more importantly from Debord's point of view, Arthur Cravan, had developed into a fine art.

The targets were apparently random, ranging from former comrades such as Isidore Isou, Mustapha Khayati and Gérard Guégan to the rock singer Renaud, who having invited Lebovici to his daughter's christening, had the invitation sent back with a typically offensive letter:

> Dear Sir,
>   I have indeed noted the birth of your daughter and sincerely congratulate you despite the dubious taste of the advertising-style announcement which you sent me. I am not surprised that you no longer have any taste or your style; your recent songs have provided ample evidence of this absence . . . I would prefer it then that you forget me, announce the births of your future children to people who are concerned about them and accept the truth of the statement, which is happily not the exclusive prerogative of Stalinist liars, 'we are not on the same side.'

Amongst the crimes imputed in the letter to Renaud was that of refusing to write a song about Jacques Mesrine, the gangster whose recent escapades in and out of prison had made him a folk hero for many on the Left. This status had been confirmed by the publication in 1977 of Mesrine's memoirs, *L'Instinct de mort* ('Death Instinct'), by Éditions Jean-Claude Lattès. When Mesrine was shot dead by police on 2 November 1979, both Debord and Lebovici were appalled by the opportunistic republication of this book by Lattès, mainly because they had decided that Mesrine was exactly the prototype of outlaw poet who should be published by Champ Libre.

'Even his [Mesrine's] death could not shake your indifference,' Lebovici complained to Renaud.[5] The enraged Renaud, whose songs were explicitly political and who prided himself on his working-class roots and language, wrote furiously back:

> You'd better watch out, you cunt, instead of hiding in your office giving orders to your dumb blonde secretary to tell me you're not in. You've got no balls, Lebo, so you'd better forget me fast, and I warn you not to send me any of your shitty little letters or you will certainly get a taste of what a pair of pointed leather boots feels like in the chest.[6]

Lebovici and Debord (most of the letters signed by Lebovici were composed or engineered by Debord) also seemed to take a particularly malicious pleasure in upsetting even those who were their friends. Chief amongst these was the lawyer Georges Kiejman, who had done so much to extricate and defend Debord from his previous publisher Buchet-Chastel (even to the extent of privately condoning Champ Libre's acts of 'piratage' over *The Society of the Spectacle*). He was astonished to find himself attacked and insulted by Debord and Lebovici for the apparent crime of defending the sworn enemy of the maverick publishers Gallimard in a recent lawsuit, a crime which was compounded by his refusal to take on the case of a certain Elisabeth Gruet who, unknown to Kiejman, just happened to be enjoying a close friendship with Debord at the time. It was Debord who sent the final insulting letter informing Kiejman in the most elegant prose that he was to be relieved of his position as Champ Libre's lawyer. Kiejman's response was a short note to his former friend Lebovici: 'You poor stupid cunt!'

There were obvious contradictions at work here however. More precisely, Lebovici was now at the zenith of his power over the world of the French cinema, so why did he spend so much of his time insulting, irritating and alienating those around him for the most trivial of reasons? Those who had observed his climb to power, such as François Truffaut, thought he was literally going mad. Others, who knew the name and the reputation of Guy Debord as an arch-manipulator and sinister guru of far-Left violence, whispered of Red Brigade violence, citing Debord's frequent disappearances over the border and mysterious liaisons in Italy. By the same token, why did Guy Debord, whose reputation as a thinker and a strategist was now fast fading away, waste his undoubted talent on such childish squabbles?

According to Georges Kiejman at least part of the answer to this puzzle lay in the fact that both men quite literally brought out the worst in each other. 'Gérard found someone who gave a meaning to his life,' Kiejman commented, still puzzled by Lebovici's baffling adoration of Debord.[7] 'They were like two schoolboys,' commented Michèle Bernstein, quite acidly and with no shred of affection for these antics. 'I did not see Debord at this time, but I knew what was going on and the various games that he was playing with Lebovici. That's all it was, a series of games, and if people were upset or hurt then too bad. Even though we had no contact then, Guy knew that I thought it was pathetic and stupid and a waste of his mind. But I also think that is what he wanted to do, as with food, as with drink, as with sex, to just waste things in a pure potlatch. That was the secret of the game.'

The Spanish Cockpit

Throughout the 1970s Debord had been drawn almost as much to Spain as he was to Italy. In part this was a form of political nostalgia: the earliest days of the Letterist International had seen the group call for a restarting of the Spanish Civil War and make one of their headquarters in the suburb of Aubervilliers, which was populated with republican *émigrés* from the war. One of the fascinations of the Spanish Civil War for Debord was the prominent part that Anarchists, and in particular his chosen hero Bienaventura Durruti, had played in the struggle. He was also developing an interest in Orwell, whose *Homage to Catalonia* was now becoming a totemic text along with Franz Borkenau's account of Stalinist crimes in Spain, *The Spanish Cockpit*, which would later be reprinted by Champ Libre. The Portuguese revolution of 1974 seemed briefly to offer a parallel to the earlier conflict but as it soon became clear that its impact would be limited his enthusiasm was shortlived.

The first Spanish city which Debord grew to know well was Barcelona, which even during the greyest periods of the Franco era in the 1960s was still able to present a cosmopolitan and even daring face to the world. Franco had never quite managed to stamp out the bars and brothels of the Barri Xines, the red-light labyrinth of streets and alleys at the bottom end of the Ramblas whose nocturnal life was described with such scabrous accuracy by Jean Genet in *Le Journal du voleur* ('The Thief's Journal') and Georges Bataille in *Le Bleu du ciel* ('The Blue of Noon'). Debord delighted in the louche atmosphere of the place, as well as in the cheap and freely available alcohol (Debord's endless thirst was often slaked in the Bar Marsella on Carrer nou de la Rambla, a dim-lit bar which specialised in a form of absinthe which had long been illegal in France: it is still there, serving the most potent forms of alcohol in Western Europe). Several excursions were made in the company of Lebovici to Barcelona in the early 1970s, mainly as a way of paying homage to the country's revolutionary history. 'In Barcelona,' said Alice, 'Guy was always aware of what had happened there not long before. I remember one evening, during the Franco period, we were in a workers' café with Lebo, when a woman came in asking for money. None of the workers had any or much to give, but Lebo gave her a substantial sum. She was obviously a bit mad or crazy, but only in the way you would be if you had to live like her on the street. And then she stood in the middle of the café and sang the Internationale. Nobody dared move, because you could still be arrested or whatever. But everyone appreciated it silently. It was the only gift she could give us, Guy said, and it was a magnificent one.'

The death of Franco in 1975 unleashed forces and passions in Spain which the Spanish thought they had long repressed or forgotten. The term *desmadre* ('excess', 'chaos' or 'sudden leap') was used to describe the almost unanimous desire to turn life into a permanent festival. The atmosphere was perfectly captured by the journalist Francisco Umbral, who in his memoir of Madrid at the time of the 'transition', *Y Tierno Galván ascendió a los cielos* ('And Tierno Galván Went up to Heaven' – Tierno Galván was a popular Marxist mayor of Madrid), describes how he watched the funeral of Franco on TV, listening to Patti Smith's *Radio Ethiopia*, smoking a large joint and having anal sex with a friend.[8]

Although Debord visited the country less often than Italy, he nonetheless began to spend more and more time in Barcelona, Madrid, Cadiz and

Seville, particularly savouring the atmosphere in a country which was visibly changing from dictatorship towards a new and as yet undefined form of democracy and in which changes seemed to be taking place on a daily basis. The love affair with Spain also drove Debord and Alice to new heights of impulsiveness. One afternoon, whilst travelling across the *meseta*, the high tableland which is every bit as inaccessible and beautiful as the Auvergne, they fell in love with an old ruined house. The pair hurried into the neighbouring village and when told that it belonged to the local baker they immediately sought her and agreed a price there and then of fifteen thousand francs (fifteen hundred pounds). Only later, much further up the road, did they realise that they had forgotten the name of the village and that they had no maps to find a way back.

Debord also fell in with a beautiful young woman from the south of Spain called Toni Lopez Pintor. Her gypsy features fascinated him and, like Michèle Bernstein, nicknamed 'The Horse', and Alice, nicknamed 'The Asian One', she was affectionately inducted into the pantheon of Debord's lovers with the nickname 'The Andalusian'. 'I loved that Andalusian for a long time,' he wrote nostalgically in 1989. 'How long? "A period in proportion to our vain and meagre span," said Pascal.'[9]

Spain was a playground where Debord and Lebovici caroused and drank with abandon and, particularly in the Franco era, deliberately set out to provoke the bourgeois sensibilities of Catholic Spain with profanities and drunkenness. Alice recalled a night in one of Barcelona's best restaurants where the staff were evidently eager to get rid of their loutish French visitors. This only incited Debord and Lebovici further. They ordered coffee and brandy and, much to the chagrin of the waiters, insisted on drawing out the meal to its last dregs. Only when they were outside the restaurant did Alice reveal that the waiters had been so annoyed that they had not noticed that no one had paid the bill. 'A perfect example of post-capitalist economics,' laughed Debord.

Bank robbers

Debord had been moved by the plight of some fifty or so anarchists who had been held in Spanish jails since 1978 on charges of holding up banks and, in the spirit of Durruti, often giving the money away. In the November of 1980 Champ Libre published an anonymous pamphlet entitled *Appels de la prison de Ségovie* calling for their release. The tone and style of the opening text of the pamphlet, 'Aux Libertaires' ('To Libertarians') were clearly recognisable as Debord. In this essay he argued that the Spanish government preferred to make public examples of Basque or Maoist terrorists because they were no real threat to the power structures of the state. He felt sympathy therefore, he explained, with young anarchists whose radical form of critique took the form of rejecting all organised forms of syndicalism, favouring wildcat strikes. He did not denounce either the violence of these anarchists, who between 1976 and 1977 launched a series of firebomb attacks on German businesses in Spain in the wake of the mysterious deaths in prison of four members of the Baader-Meinhof gang and against French businesses after the controversial extradition of their lawyer Klaus Croissant from France. 'You should not be able to walk down a street in Spain without seeing their names. Songs should be heard everywhere which speak about them,' Debord wrote before concluding with the salutation, 'Long Live SOCIAL LIQUIDATION!'

With Lebovici, Debord set about planning a record of songs celebrating the imprisoned libertarians. The singer Mara Jerez, known to Debord from the old days at La Méthode, was approached with a view to interpreting the songs. Although the album was never recorded, Debord did get as far as writing a number of songs which were appended to the pamphlet.

It soon became inevitable that the Spanish would somehow have to relent. 1980 was the bloody year of Basque violence, with ETA claiming an unprecedented number of victims and practically paralysing the economic life of the region. In the face of this genuine threat, the Spanish government sought to re-establish its democratic credentials and in November 1980 six anarchist militants were acquitted in Madrid followed by further releases. In January 1981 Debord wrote to Michèle Mochot Brehat, one of his most long-standing allies and lovers, to express his pleasure at these verdicts, implying that he had been in part responsible for them, and in *Panegyric* he claimed, 'I played my part – and perhaps my greatest part – in the follies of Spain.'[10] Certainly this sort of victory was the best excuse there was, he told Michèle, for the longest and most extravagant sort of drinking party.[11]

CHAPTER 31

The World is Illusion

1981–3

The narrow victory of François Mitterrand's Socialist Party in the elections of 10 May 1981 was met by an outbreak of unparalleled delight across France. In Paris there were spontaneous celebrations all over the city, whilst place de la Bastille and the Champs-Élysées were turned into one long champagne-soaked street festival. This was the first real self-proclaimed Socialist government since the days of the Popular Front – or so it seemed for the generation which had fought the battles of 1968 and who now saw that those battles had not been in vain. The election campaign had been fought by Mitterrand on the issues of social justice and egalitarianism, from women's rights to reducing the working week and increasing the minimum wage. The leading theme was 'a clean break with capitalism', a slogan which claimed to fulfil the broken promises of May 68.

Debord greeted this new government with an indifference that slowly developed into contempt. He had now started spending his summers with Alice in Arles, a suitably sleepy and provincial town at the western tip of Provence whose reputation rested on the prestige of its bullfighters and its counter-revolutionary tradition, dating from 1792 and continuing until the 1980s when it was still a bastion of Right-wing activity. For Debord it was however of greater significance that Arles was almost equidistant between Spain and Paris, where he had now abandoned the apartment on the rue Saint-Martin in favour of Gérard Lebovici's stylish and plush apartment at 14 rue de l'Université in the tranquil and elegant surroundings of the 7th *arrondissement*. He saw Spain as potentially his most succesful theatre of operations yet and situated himself in Arles with a view to controlling and guiding the small forces in Barcelona where the Situationists, in the light of the Italian adventures, had developed a certain prestige.

Guy and Alice took over an apartment and then a house in the old quarter of the town at 33 rue de l'Hôtel de Ville. It was here that Debord held forth, delighting visiting comrades from Spain, Italy and other parts of France with his talk and always pouring himself another drink. There was no television in the house, but occasionally Guy and Alice would watch television in the house of a friendly old lady, who took the soberly dressed and exquisitely mannered Debord for a bank official.

Amongst those who visited Debord in Arles was Michel Prigent, a libertarian activist who, although never a Situationist, had maintained a friendly correspondence with Debord for over ten years. In the early spring of 1981 Prigent arrived at the house in the company of Lucy Forsyth, a young English student who been living off and on in southwest France in communal houses for some four years or so, following her involvement as a student in an occupation of the local university. Lucy was well acquainted with Marxism and radical ideas, having already translated and published some of Debord's texts in English under the aegis of Chronos Press, which she and Michel had established in London with their dole cheques in 1978.

As a forthright feminist Forsyth was however somewhat surprised by the domestic arrangements in an apparently radical household and felt it her duty to tell Guy what she thought of his drinking and the division of labour: 'When it was mentioned to him that an English situphile had slagged him off in print for starting to become an alcoholic, he replied with a big smile: "I've been one for a long time." I tackled him later about this very set and segregated division of labour between himself and Alice. (Don't get me wrong: she joined in the discussions as well, but in any disputes she always supported her husband.) His response about the household tasks was the completely unironic "Elle fait la vaisselle, je fais la révolution" ("She does the washing-up, I do the revolution") – which indicates a complete absence of any feminist politics, even at that late date in the Situationist circle. Gianfranco Sanguinetti [. . .] was reputed to boast that no feminist had ever darkened his threshold.'[1]

Rather than discussing the washing-up, Debord was still focusing most of his energy towards Spain. Over the kitchen table he would light his pipe and talk wistfully of the instability of the country and the potential resurgence of the revolutionary anarchist movement of 1936. Prigent and Forsyth were in Arles on their way to Barcelona, where they planned to smuggle into Spain copies of the *Appels de la prison de Ségovie* and help Spanish comrades make posters of Debord's 'detourned' revolutionary anthems. Debord was however intensely suspicious of the loyalties of his Spanish comrades, even sending Jean-François Martos, a young militant who would go on to write an orthodox and Debord-controlled history of the SI, down to Barcelona as his 'emissary' and to talk some sense to the 'Autonomist' groups.

When Debord finally saw the posters, according to Forsyth, 'he threw a wobbly'. This was because the Spanish had dared to alter some of his lyrics. 'He called them plagiarists and manipulators and a few traditional Spanish homophobic insults (at which we protested!),' continued Forysth. 'There was no libertarian sense of autonomous practice, when it came to altering

Debord's words. Our French friend, Arthur (who had so many surnames I never knew his real one, the favourite one was Cravan), was sent packing and friends were encouraged to break with him for his defence of these comrades. A couple of the Spanish friends involved in doing the posters then wrote to Debord explaining that they were autonomous libertarians, practising their autonomy, and that they judged it more apt to change the words. Debord quietly accepted this and was finally pacified. . . . This flight of paranoia of Debord's was definitely induced or enhanced by alcohol. He was already starting to suffer from alcohol-related gout quite badly at the time. I can recall an amusing episode when an old friend of Michel Prigent's from Arles, an Armenian tailor called César, was introduced to Debord – in fact they knew each other by sight as he, Debord and Alice had been the only people in Arles in the cinema when Buñuel's films had been playing. César was sixty and looked forty. He explained that he didn't drink alcohol and ate a lot of Bulgarian yoghurt. Debord commented "that's very good" and poured himself another large glass of whisky.'[2]

Another visitor to Arles was a former Situationist comrade, Maurice Wyckaert, who was passing through Arles with his wife Rob. Wyckaert noticed that Debord had grown very fat and, in obvious pain from gout, walked with great difficulty with the aid of a cane. He was still only fifty. Debord asked Rob to bring him back a walking stick from one of her frequent shopping expeditions to London.[3]

Arles was one of the great centres in France of authentic gypsy culture (it is no accident that the Gypsy Kings, the most famous if bowdlerised representatives of gypsy music in the world, hail from Arles) and Guy and Alice were fascinated by the underground gypsy world. The gypsies were authentic outsiders who took pride in rejecting all forms of social hierarchy and who defined themselves by their deliberate exclusion from stable social organisations. As Mitterrand swept to power and France seemed poised for the greatest radical changes since the Popular Front, Debord began to identify more and more with the gypsies of Arles, whose only loyalty was to an idea of freedom which they alone could articulate or define.

Debord was also at this point returning to the Middle Ages to explain present conditions. In April 1980, Debord had quietly published his translations of Jorge Manrique's famous *Coplas que fizo por la muerte de su padre* ('Verses on the death of his father'), some of the most famous poems in the Spanish language, the Castilian masterpiece of the late medieval period.

Jorge Manrique's themes stem entirely from medieval (and, in part, classical traditions): life as a journey, the great men of the past, the *'ubi sunt'* topic, the dead man's qualities as compared to those of famous men, personification of death, the temporary consolation of fame, the permanent consolation of salvation in Christ. In his postscript Debord writes that in five hundred years of translation of Manrique into French, there has been no one better qualified to do it than himself. Above all, Debord valorises in Manrique the objective relationship he has with his era. The passing of time, the ephemeral nature of all objects and the feeling of the world literally slipping away in front of your eyes are what, in Debord's view, make these poems important emblems of subjective revolt:

> It should be noted the literally pre-Machiavellian coldness with which the author of the *Coplas* speaks about the people whom the Manriques themselves slaughtered . . . and the fragility of all possessions. . . . The most beautiful feature is without doubt the lesson, so indirectly articulated, that one has to fight for 'one's own true king', that is to say the one which one makes oneself.[4]

Jorge Manrique opposes the world as a combatant in a spirit of resignation, which has been his enduring appeal for Spaniards through the centuries. What was important for Debord in *Coplas* was not only a refusal to concede defeat but also a mood of defiant melancholy. In his last works and statements to come, Debord would echo the themes of Manrique, and to a lesser extent François Villon whom he later quoted to support the melancholy notion that 'Le monde n'est qu'abusion' ('The world is illusion').[5]

Sophists and Cynics

The film *In girum imus nocte et consumimur igni* was finally released on 6 May 1981, at the height of Mitterrand's rollercoaster electoral campaign. The film was shown in three cinemas across Paris – Le Quintette Pathé, L'Olympic Entrepôt and Les Sept Parnassiens – finally settling down to a brief sojourn at Le Quintette Pathé in the heart of the Left Bank on rue de la Harpe and making a surprise appearance on two successive nights of the 3 and 4 June on Canal 68, a pirate Parisian television channel (both pirate radio and television were then undergoing something of a boom in France).

The critics were not kind. Although there were sympathetic or nostalgic echoes in some of the reviews (it was notable also that despite Debord's apparent insignificance and obscurity all the major French newspapers and magazines sent a reviewer) the overall tone was one of boredom, disappointment and melancholy. Pascal Bonitzer in the influential *Les Cahiers du cinéma* remarked on echoes of Georges Bataille in the film, recalling Bataille's mingled fear and delight when contemplating the portrait of the aged Hegel who knows the 'horror of being God'. Debord was not God but his system of thought, 'Situationism', which claimed to reveal the totality of the world was as terrifying as anything that Hegel's pursuit of the Absolute might reveal. 'The spectator and the critic, challenged and foreclosed by the film, might well smile in the face of what Debord himself asserts are his excessive claims,' wrote Bonitzer. 'Indeed they might well talk about a beautiful soul and paranoia.'[6]

In the pages of *Libération* Hélène Hazera described 'the conspiracy' in the cinema world against Debord, before writing a long and impassioned defence of the film, Debord and, above all, the theory of the 'spectacle'.[7] In *Les Nouvelles littéraires* the rancorous Guégan, dismissing Debord as a theorist of revolution, nonetheless conceded that this was a work to rank with Satie, Swift or Mallarmé.[8] Most other reviewers were however less generous: Louis Marcorelles in *Le Monde* described the film the work of a 'bourgeois lamenting the poor workers . . . strictly reserved for the tribe, the parishioners'.[9] The critic of *Télérama* (the French equivalent of the *Radio Times*) described the film as loaded 'with unbearable pretention: for dimwits in search of a guru'.[10]

Debord had anticipated this much, writing from Arles to Jean-François Martos in the early part of 1981 that he sensed that the film would not stay on general release for long. In the first instance this was because the film stood so self-evidently at odds with the mood of the times. As François Mitterrand's electoral campaign had picked up pace through the early part of 1981, there was a general sense throughout France that the world was changing and that many of the dreams of 1968 would now be realised, albeit via the democratic process which had been so fiercely rejected by most vehement *soixante-huitards*. The Mitterrand campaign, it was believed, was a vindication of those original dreams and not a betrayal, or so it was believed by many on the Left at the time.

What offended reviewers about *In girum . . .* was not that it merely struck a dissident note but that in this film Debord was relentlessly and tirelessly negative, conceding no space to those who saw the spectacle of democratic politics as offering the possibility of real change. This could not have been more out of touch with the Left-wing consensus in France at this point in history. It was this negativity, however, which Debord himself saw as the film's most salient virtue.

Most importantly, Debord in this film was deliberately comparing himself to the itinerant Sophists, described by Huizinga in *Homo Ludens* in a section which compares and analyses the potlatch as a critical instrument in war and politics with traditional Western forms of dissent. Debord had borrowed the title of the film from a quotation usually ascribed to the Roman orator Sidonius Apollinarius, who used it to describe 'the arabesques formed in the air by those notoriously blind insects, moths, circling around a lit candle at night'. The appeal of the Sophist philosophers for Debord lay in their emphasis on the use of the spoken word as the main instrument of debate and investigation. What had made the Sophists so hated was that they not only based their thoughts on entirely negative terms and definitions, but also that they were paid for teaching this method of acquiring *arete*, the Greek term for virtue or skill roughly equivalent to Machiavelli's definition of *virtù*, the word which describes the morality of a citizen's relation to his city-state. In the early 1980s Debord identified with all those, Sophists, Cynics, Manrique and Villon, who were obliged by force of circumstance to retreat from their original positions and place themselves at a distance from a world which had disappointed them. 'I am a remarkable example of what this era did not want,' was how he described himself.[11]

The Studio Cujas

While Debord in the first years of the new decade distanced himself further and further from public and political life, Gérard Lebovici seemed to be at the height of his powers. In 1982 he acquired AAA (Artistes Auteurs Associés), a film distribution company, which extended Artmedia's influence on the French cinema industry even wider. The first film distributed by AAA, the stylish if exploitative thriller *La Balance*, starring Nathalie Baye and Philippe Léotard, went on to attract a huge box office (4 million viewers) and won the four most prestigious César awards of 1982 (the French equivalent of the Oscars). Despite his success, however, Lebovici cultivated an air of mystery about his activities, avoiding all contact with the press, rarely using the telephone, even suspecting that his office was bugged. He talked more and more about abandoning the cinema in favour of his literary activities, imagining the acquisition of small and financially vulnerable publishing houses which would prop up the leading role of Champ Libre. For the time being however it was more than satisfactory that Lebovici's flourishing business activities should be 'detourned' in the favour of Guy Debord.

In October 1983, Gérard Lebovici bought a small cinema on the rue Cujas, a short step away from the Sorbonne. This was where the drunken nineteen-year-old Guy Debord had lain in the rain, declaring his love to the young Barbara Rosenthal some thirty years previously. It was a site charged with memory and meaning and this was why Debord had asked Lebovici to buy the place.

From October onwards the cinema on the rue Cujas had only one programme, the 'Programme Guy Debord', and played continually four films by Guy Debord, *La société du spectacle, Sur le passage de quelques personnes dans une assez courte unité de temps, In girum imus nocte et consumimur igni* and *Réfutation de tous les jugements tant élogieux qu'hostiles qui ont été jusqu'à ici portés sur le film 'La société du spectacle'*, announced to the public in a small advertisement as 'political films'. Lebovici explained his strategy to the previous owner of the Studio Cujas, Bernard Plégat, as akin to acquiring 'a museum which only exhibits one work. Or, if you like, a library which has only one book'.[12] The projectionist was under strict orders from Lebovici himself to stick rigidly to the programme, even if there were no spectators at all. The cinema was another form of potlatch, a gift given with no reciprocal obligation and therefore with an infinite capacity to provoke.

Cécile Guilbert, now one of the most important young novelists and essayists in France, was eighteen, bored and wandering around her native Paris on a sweltering day in June 1981, when on a whim she entered the dim, empty cinema, which resembled more a porno cinema than any of the glitzy corporate picture houses of the great boulevards. Inspired, moved and disturbed by what she had seen she hurried to look for a copy of the almost unfindable *Society of the Spectacle*, whose arguments struck her with the force of revelation. 'Debord for me was an adventure and a great discovery,' she says. 'Everywhere you read that France was changing and that democracy would solve all our problems, but in the film *In girum imus nocte et consumimur igni* Debord was telling us, in his grave and melancholy way, that the war was not yet finished, that it could not yet be finished whilst the spectacle was transforming life into non-life. I did not know then much about Hegel or (Marx's) *The German Ideology*, but I knew that what Debord was saying was true because I could see it all around: the spectacle of politics, the illusion of democratic power. I left the cinema feeling as if I had seen something transgressive, like a porno film or a novel by Georges Bataille, but most of all I knew what I had just seen was not cinema but something else.'[13]

The potlatch of the Studio Cujas continued until 7 March 1984, when the body of Gérard Lebovici was found in an underground car park on the avenue Foch, one of the most elegant avenues in Paris not far from the Champs-Élysées. He had died instantly, having received four bullets from a .22 calibre rifle in the back of his neck.

PART FIVE

Death of a Prince

1984–94

Since conspiracies are of such dangerous consequence alike to princes and to private persons, I cannot well omit to discuss their nature, for it is plain that many more princes have lost their lives and their states in this way than by open war, because it is given to but few to make open war on a prince, whereas anyone can conspire against him.

Machiavelli, *On Conspiracies*

I have been very interested in war, in the theoreticians of its strategy, but also in reminiscences of battles and in the countless other disruptions history mentions, surface eddies on the river of time. I am not unaware that war is the domain of danger and disappointment, perhaps even more so than the other sides of life. This consideration has not, however, diminished the attraction that I have felt for it.

And so I have studied the logic of war. Moreover, I succeeded, a long time ago, in presenting the basics of its movements on a rather simple board game: the forces in contention and the contradictory necessities imposed on the operations of each of the two parties. I have played this game and, in the often difficult conduct of my life, I have utilised lessons from it – I have also set myself rules of the game for this life, and I have followed them. The surprises of this *Kriegspiel* seem inexhaustible; and I fear that this may well be the only one of my works that anyone will dare acknowledge as having some value. On the question of whether I have made good use of such lessons, I will leave it to others to decide.

Guy Debord, *Panegyric*

CHAPTER 32

Death Instinct

1984–5

Monday 5 May 1984 was a typical start to the week for Gérard Lebovici. It began, as was usually the case, with a flurry of activity in his offices at 11 bis rue Kepler, a not particularly distinguished but nevertheless expensive side-street a stone's throw away from his central headquarters at Artmedia on the prestigious avenue Georges-V. Lebovici was busy with paperwork, but not flustered; he had just come back three days early from a short holiday in the south of France, claiming that he could not bear to be away from his work and that holidays made him tired.

At 1.00 p.m. Lebovici went off to lunch with the film producer Serge Siritzki at the restaurant of the Hôtel Georges-V. Siritzki recalls that he was in a good mood, bubbling with enthusiasm for the latest Alain Resnais film, *L'Amour à mort*, which was just about to start shooting, and flushed with the success of *Emmanuelle 4*, in which he had a substantial financial stake.

Not long after Lebovici's return to the office, there was a phone call for him. Lebovici hardly ever answered any calls directly but took the call when his secretary said, 'It's from Sabrina.' This was Sabrina Mesrine, the twenty-three-year-old daughter of Jacques Mesrine, who Guy Debord had described as 'unstable' and 'dangerous'.

In the years since his shooting at the hands of the police, Jacques Mesrine, the gangster who had briefly been public enemy number one in France, had come to be regarded as something of a folk-hero and was admired for his reckless, swaggering combativeness not only by Debord and Lebovici but also by whole swathes of Left-leaning former radicals.

Mesrine epitomised for many of the 68 generation the daredevil poetic bandit, whose main concern was not money but simply to wrongfoot the law. He was described as an 'intellectual gangster' on account of his articulate and combative style in interviews and 'Monsieur tout-le-monde' ('Mister everybody') because of his skills as a master of disguise. He especially prided himself on his ability to appear inconspicuous and everyday (it is no small coincidence that Mesrine's son is in fact now a professional conjurer, practising skills apparently acquired from his father).[1] The romantic view of

Mesrine was scarcely contradicted, in the eyes of his fans, by the fact that he was also an extremely violent and dangerous man who was a racist (he had been a member of the Right-wing French Algerian terrorist organisation, the OAS) and who had shot two men dead in Quebec. He had also left Jacques Tillier, a journalist who got too close, for dead in a cave in the forest of Senlis in 1979. Mesrine's legacy was more violence: not long afterwards in Castres a schoolkid who had mercilessly killed a teacher had been found in possession of *L'Instinct de mort*, the book which Lebovici had described as 'for the French people of our age, the perfect symbol of liberty'.[2]

In recent years Lebovici had adopted Sabrina as his own child, treating her as his daughter, supplying her with cash gifts and enjoying the dubious prestige of being the patron of the daughter of France's most notorious gangster. Both Guy Debord and Lebovici had particularly admired the way Mesrine had been able to manipulate the media and saw his mysterious death at the hands of the police as vindication of the power of 'the spectacle' to occlude real events with false detail. The Mesrine affair was indeed opened up for legal re-examination in the spring of 2000, after a decade of appeals by Sabrina.

Although it was well known that Lebovici kept dangerous company, there seemed to be no cause for alarm at his disappearance that afternoon. Lebovici liked to disappear from view from time to time; he enjoyed call girls, casinos, gambling clubs and drinking parties and, in the company of Debord, he would deliberately absent himself from his routine for days at a time, reappearing when least expected. On receiving the telephone call, which may or may not have been from Sabrina, he cancelled all his appointments for the afternoon, dismissed his chauffeur and rang his wife Floriana to tell her that he would be late for dinner that evening. He left the building at 6.25 p.m., driving towards Charles de Gaulle Étoile in his Renault 30 TX which, rare for those days, had a radio-telephone.

Floriana waited all night for him to come back, finally contacting the police in the small hours of the following day. At first it was feared that he had been kidnapped, but the absence of any contact with the kidnappers made this theory hard to sustain over the coming hours. Floriana was quizzed on his contacts, political or otherwise. Her agony of waiting, however, was soon over. In the early evening of 7 May, in the course of his routine patrol, a car park attendant, a North African named Lakhdar Ben Khaled, was appalled to find the body of a man slumped over the steering wheel of a Renault 30 which had been lined up against a wall near one of the exits. According to the police pathologist it had been a professional and methodical piece of work: Lebovici had been shot in the back of the neck as precisely as 'at a shooting gallery in a fairground'.[3]

'Blood-soaked marionettes'

There were few clues for the police to go on. The .22 calibre rifle indicated that it was a professional job, a contract killing, as did the methodical form of assassination. A passerby recalled seeing Lebovici's car with three men inside entering the car park at 6.45. There was also a scrap of paper found on Lebovici's body with the name François and a scribbled rendezvous at 6.45 on rue Vernet.

The first line of enquiry was inevitably to do with Jacques Mesrine. The name François suggested François Besse, Mesrine's accomplice who had escaped with him from the jail of La Santé in 1978 and gone on to rob banks and a casino in Deauville. It was known that François was aggrieved at Lebovici's recent republication of Mesrine's memoirs and it was thought that he may have been trying to extort money from Lebovici. It was also known that Sabrina and her partner Hervé Pallud, film-maker and father of Sabrina's child, were angry with Lebovici over his refusal to back a film that they had made about Jacques Mesrine.

The second line of enquiry focused on Lebovici's secretive private life, and in particular his taste for low life, call girls and all-night poker sessions with notorious underworld figures. The police pieced together a theory that one of Lebovici's gangster contacts had asked him to use his various enterprises to launder money made from a trade in bootleg and pornographic videos. This theory was given substance by the fact that two days before Lebovici's death a major trafficking ring in videos had been smashed and fifteen or so traffickers arrested. Lebovici could have been targeted by the gangsters, based in Pigalle, as a suspect police informer or for refusing to help them.

It emerged that Lebovici had also been dabbling in the sex shop trade, a popular way of laundering money. In certain Parisian circles suspicion fell upon a notorious film producer, 'A', whose films, it was well known, were no more than a pretext for laundering money made through other more illicit means. 'A' was in the public eye, someone who dined at Le Fouquet's on the Champs-Élysées and mingled with celebrities and politicians. He was also known for the swift cruelty of his decisions and those who knew him well avoided business with him. Lebovici, if he had crossed 'A', ought to have known this too and had paid the price in full for his naïvety.

'A' was also said to be in league with 'B', owner of one of the most important video companies in Paris (who was now mysteriously said to be on the run in Spain), and a certain 'C', another player in the murky world of cinema finance. All were investigated by the police and as far as possible placed under surveillance, but no truly incriminating evidence emerged.

As the police set about developing theories, the French press had already made up its own mind about the murder of the publisher, naming the mysterious Guy Debord, associate of terrorists, advocate of far-Left violence and Lebovici's 'invisible guru' as the prime suspect in this sordid and shocking affair.

On 11 March in *Le Journal du dimanche*, the best-selling Sunday newspaper in France, the journalist Jacques Tillier, who had survived Jacques Mesrine's attack, led the way with an article in which Debord was described as 'belonging to the shadows. "The Devil". A gimcrack Mephisto for a real tragedy: that of the bewitching of a man[. . .]. Guy Debord, the invisible guru, will perhaps explain to the police the mystery of Gérard Lebovici, and the secret of his power over the key man in French cinema.'

The newspapers began to bristle with theories. The tabloid end of the market, *VSD* and *Paris-Match*, all but accused Debord of murder, describing him as a vengeful and murderous manipulator who, once crossed by his disciples, had no hesitation in summoning up the dark forces of far-Left terrorism to exterminate them. Publications ranging from the mainstream *Le Figaro* to the Communist-run *L'Humanité* added their tuppence worth: the fact that there was no recently published photo of Debord meant that he was trying to avoid the public gaze. That he had never had a job in his life meant that he was an agent financed by Moscow. That he was married to Alice Becker-Ho showed his role in a plot involving Communist China and shady Hong Kong antiques dealers. That he maintained an active interest in Italian politics proved that he was connected to the Red Brigades. Spy, crook and terrorist, Debord was 'the pope of Situationism', who had drawn Lebovici into his murky world and who had taught its deadly creed of Situationist subversion. The journal *Minute* claimed to have the number of Debord's bank account in Moscow and, linking the murder with the Red Brigades via Lebovici's connections with Giangiacomo Feltrinelli, Jean-Louis Baudet, the publisher of *Éditions Afrique la documentation* (who aided Red Brigade offensives launched from France and who had now disappeared) and Gianfranco Sanguinetti, asked, 'Who pulls the strings of these blood-soaked marionettes?'[4]

Words and bullets

Debord was shocked by Lebovici's death, terrified by this sudden hostile attention and even more alarmed to find the press stalking him in Arles, where he heard about the murder, and then on the rue du Bac where he stayed in Paris on his arrival in the capital on 10 March. Along with Gérard Guégan (who claims that Debord was no more suspect than anyone else, but that his fear made him turn the incident into a drama of tragic proportions)[5] and other known radicals, Debord was questioned by police on 10 and 11 March. The senior officer in charge of the investigation, Jacques Genthial, was surprised by Debord's complacent and apparently indifferent manner, but had no grounds to implicate him in the murder.

To his intimates Debord expressed the view that he was convinced that the killing of Lebovici was also an attack on him and that he was determined therefore not to show any fear. Indeed, if anything, Debord was pleased with how he could now put his own sulphurous reputation to good effect. He claimed in private that the press reports about him could have been a lot worse, and that if they had really got their facts right they could have damaged him beyond repair. As it was, their wild inaccuracy made them worse than useless in any real campaign that might have been staged against him. Debord also delighted in terrorising a young photographer in Arles who had been trying to get a picture of him by taking his own photographs of the man and sending them to the cringing snapper's address. Fearing for his own life at the hands of the notorious terrorist, whose reputation was not much better than that of Carlos the Jackal, he stopped trying to stalk Debord. On a more serious note, Debord wrote to Jean-François Martos to thank him for his help in compiling a dossier of malicious press reports about him, reported that the press were 'besieging him but up to now had not managed to get anything' and began planning a counter-attack on the forces of the media spectacle which were now ranged against him.[6]

Lebovici was meanwhile buried in a private ceremony held on 13 March in the Montparnasse cemetery. Only Floriana and Gérard's sister Nicole attended. Debord was not invited, but it was a poem from Jorge Manrique, translated by Debord, which Floriana had engraved on the tombstone. The poem was a homage to friendship:

> What a friend for his friends!
>   For his kith and kin, what a Lord!
>   What an enemy for the enemy!
> What a leader for the bold and faithful!
>   What judgement for the wise!
> For the merry such wit!
>   What great feeling!
>   Benign to his dependants,
>   Fierce with the wicked!
> What a Lion!

The only other details on the tombstone were as spare and curt as any of Debord's biographical notes: 'Gérard Lebovici, born 25th August 1932, assassinated 5th March 1984.'

Debord made no public comment on the murder and was discreet within his own inner circle. He was disgusted that producer and film-maker Jean Aurel had thought of making a film about the affair. He sensed as well that his own life might be in danger. An article called 'Les mots et les balles' ('Words and bullets') had appeared in *Le Nouvel observateur* of

28 December 1984, by an ally and supporter, Claude Roy, which pointed out that the death of Lebovici could also be an excuse by his enemies to destroy Guy Debord.

In the meantime Floriana Lebovici, who had been completely devastated by the killing, tried to keep control of the elements of Lebovici's business life she could master. On the recommendation of her lawyer she appointed Gérard Voitey, a rising young star in the legal world, to take control of the accounts (Georges Kiejman also became involved shortly afterwards). She also hired a private detective to try and work out what had happened. Debord wrote to the young widow on 25 April formally to annul the contract, expressing almost tangentially his regret at the 'horrible assassination'.[7]

At the same time comrades in France and around the world, outraged at the accusations levelled against Debord, rallied to his support. This came in the form of a flurry of pamphlets, distributed in Paris and elsewhere, which claimed to reveal the truth about the killing of Lebovici. One of the clearest and most authoritative pamphlets was 'Ils ont tué Lebovici' ('They have killed Lebovici'), written by 'Le Parti de la vérité' ('The Party of Truth'), which made the claim that the murder had been organised by the state and the French security services. A comparison was made with the case of Toni Negri, the Italian political scientist who in 1979 had been charged with leadership of the Red Brigades and the murder of Aldo Moro. Negri had escaped to France in 1983, where he was appointed to a teaching position at the Université de Paris VIII (Saint-Denis) and was defended in print by the likes of Gilles Deleuze. Negri was a classic example of a public revolutionary whose very life had been threatened by the state whose books he sought to subvert.

An equally lurid account of the murder was published in London, where hitherto the affair had been treated with comic disdain as an incomprehensible vendetta on the French far Left. (In an article, superciliously headlined 'Murder Most French', Frank Johnson, future editor of the *Spectator*, sneered at the participants in the drama and described Champ Libre as the 'publisher of off-beat marginal books'.) The London pamphlet was entitled 'The Apparent Truth about the Assassination of G. Lebovici' and was published anonymously by the Tocsin Press. It gave a reasonably knowledgeable account of Lebovici's links with Mesrine and implicated a certain 'neo-Nazi', Xavier Raufer, in the organisation of the killing. Raufer, who also used the name Christian de Bongain, was alleged to have been incited to attack Lebovici on the grounds that he was working against the state by forging such close links with the criminal underworld and possibly the Red Brigades. It was no accident either that Raufer/Bongain was also a member of Occident, the Right-wing organisation which had played a role in the events of May 68. At the time of writing, Raufer has risen to become a professor at Université de Paris II (Assas) and a leading media commentator specialising on 'urban violence' and 'terrorism'. He makes no secret of his far-Right views or his past.

Guy Debord's own theories about the murder were less charged with baroque detail, and more concerned with what he saw as an attempt by the government, the security services or freelance agents working in tandem to destroy Lebovici and himself. In truth, he knew no more about the killers than the investigating police team. In two letters to Paolo Salvadori, written some months after the affair, he outlined his views on the murder, speculating on both the motives and who the killers might have been. 'General complicity has been so well proved in all the press, as you said,' wrote Debord in the first letter, 'that there is no need to demonstrate that the assassination was encouraged and willed on all sides. It is an execution by the established order. There is obviously a para-state intervention. It could be purely an action committed by the state, but all the same not in the same way as Moro: the government people and the police seemed divided on this affair. Those who did not take the decision themselves are without doubt going to resign themselves to silence.'[8] Debord continued to isolate two of Lebovici's weakest points. Firstly, he was involved in complicated and dangerous business in the cinema world, where a great deal of money was at stake for investors who were outside the law. Secondly, the relationship with Sabrina Mesrine was one which placed him in a vulnerable and threatening position. Most important however was the fact that the revolutionary movement of 1968 was now the target of 'historical vengeance'.

In the second letter to Salvadori, Debord was clearer still about what he meant by this latter term. He dismissed the notion that Lebovici had been killed because he was suspected of preparing with Debord a revolutionary scandal, a 'coup de Strasbourg', in the world of the cinema, but he also noted that many did see their collaboration as a sort of ongoing 'Situationist plot' which was an ever-present threat to the financial security of Lebovici's business dealings. Debord also dismissed rumours circulating about the future ownership of Champ Libre, which some suggested Lebovici was going to give to Debord as a present, like the Studio Cujas, and which would have aroused considerable jealousies amongst any of those who thought they had a claim upon the publishing house. These jealousies were however based on a fundamental misunderstanding of Debord and Lebovici's strategy: Champ Libre, said Debord, was never conceived of as an offensive manoeuvre but as a base for operations. Thus, despite its marginalised position, it was as impregnable as 'a besieged fortress'.

The key to the riddle, as Debord saw it, was not how the murder had been carried out, but what use it could be put to. It was this aspect of the case which the papers had misunderstood: 'The press [. . .] contented themselves with ridiculous counter-truths and old banalities. Just think for a moment what the consequences might have been of a more resolute and methodical research. Terrible!' This was also, he said, the stumbling block for the police who had completely failed to realise that this form of assassination was not an end in itself but part of an ongoing war between radicals and agencies whose identity was always shifting but whose allegiance was to 'social order'.[9]

'I have spent thirty-two years surrounded by a variety of dangers,' he wrote, 'and you know that I have taken very little account of all of them. In contrast this is the first time that I have ever been injured.' He explained that in the course of the summer he had taken 'experimental risks' at Champot, exposing himself to open view for a potential assassin, to see whether he was or was not a target for those who had killed Lebovici, 'who know they are in great danger while I am alive'. Nothing happened. The riddle could not be resolved. This was a 'bitter moment' for Debord who claimed to have understood easily and immediately the motives and the personnel behind the killing of Aldo Moro, but not his friend Lebovici. Still thinking tactically, Debord closed the letter by asking Salvadori to do nothing until there had been 'an ulterior change in the situation'.

Melancholy and mourning

Although the tone in Debord's letters of the period strove towards an icy objectivity, and all his speculations were described in the strategic language of war, the death of Lebovici had left him personally shattered. On 17 April the 'Programme Guy Debord' played for the last time at the Studio Cujas and Debord announced that none of his films would ever again be seen in public as a gesture of protest at the killing of his friend.

In the immediate aftermath Debord also did his uncharacteristic best to act in a practical way. His first concern was with Floriana, her family and with Champ Libre, which Debord urged Floriana to maintain as best as she could. In the spring of 1984 Champ Libre was renamed Éditions Gérard Lebovici in homage to Lebovici and benefited from a new deal with the powerful publishing empire Gallimard which would help with distibution. Although Debord and Alice now spent most of their time in Arles, Debord was still a frequent visitor to Paris, where he would pay his respects to Floriana and pay particular attention to her two sons, Lorenzo Valentin and Nicolas. Both of Lebovici's sons worshipped Debord, who was displaying extremely rare signs of a reciprocal affection.

In November of 1984, under Debord's instructions, Éditions Gérard Lebovici published *Gérard Lebovici: Tout sur le personnage* ('Gérard Lebovici: All about the person'). This was a provocative collection of correspondence from Champ Libre, composed by Debord and Lebovici, leading up to the assassination, as well as an anthology of some of the most hostile or savage of the press articles that had been written after the assassination. The tone was combative: in the introduction, denouncing the calumnies which had been heaped upon Lebovici, Debord quoted Dante: 'It is not with arguments that one can respond to such bestiality, but with a knife.'[10]

The mood in the Debord household however was generally reflective rather than violent. Certainly the death of his closest friend and ally forced Debord to turn further inwards and to retreat even more from what he saw as an irremediably damaged cultural and political world, one in which the spectacle was now all-conquering and all-powerful. The details of life, such as friendship, were all the more important. In the summer of 1984 Debord and Alice came to know Patrick Mosconi, a young future writer of screenplays and 'polars' ('romans policiers' or detective novels) whose disgust at the killing of Lebovici had led him to erect a monument to the publisher in the centre of the Désert de Retz, the abandoned spot which had been so dear to Debord, Bernstein and treasured intimates such as Juan Goytisolo some twenty-five years earlier. Having learned of the gesture, Alice and Guy invited Mosconi to accompany them on a pilgrimage to the spot, and a new friendship and love affair began.[11]

It was still a painful time however. Emmanuel Loi, a young academic and writer who was an occasional member of the Debord entourage at the time, described how the death of Lebovici 'snuffed out his vitality and acted as a warning shot' for Debord. 'The philosophy of combat,' said Loi, 'was insidiously replaced by a pathology of despair.'[12]

CHAPTER 33

Reflections on Violence

1985–7

Exhausted, depleted and at times despairing, Debord lacked neither courage nor a sense of justified grievance over the killing of his friend. From the summer onwards, he brooded in Arles on a book which would in some way form part of a counter-offensive against the forces which he saw ranged against him and restore the initiative to his critical work.

Most importantly, the killing of Lebovici marked a new and deadly turning point in Debord's activity. The war which he had launched against society so long ago was no longer a series of manoeuvres which, faithful to Hegelian and Marxist philosophy, conceived of history as a game and aimed at moving history forward by the concerted application of negative thought and activity. Rather the war now seemed to be moving towards a fatal defeat. Henceforth Debord's strategical positions would be determined by the fact that he saw himself in real danger of assassination by agents of 'the spectacle' whose identity and presence he found almost impossible to determine. He wrote guardedly to Jean-François Martos, implying that it was in the world of cinema itself, the very heart of the spectacle, that Lebovici's killers might be found, partly corroborating police theories that the mysterious producer 'A' had personally arranged the shooting.[1] Other theories came and went, but one thing was clear: the assault which had been made upon him had to be resisted.

In February 1985, when the assassination of Lebovici had been half-forgotten by the media and the general public, Debord published *Considérations sur l'assassinat de Gérard Lebovici* ('Considerations on the assassination of Gérard Lebovici'). This was essentially a refutation of the various media lies which had proliferated in the wake of the murder. This refutation also had a legal application and Debord's lawyer Thierry Levy had little problem securing considerable damages in court from *Le Journal du dimanche* and the hated 'Stalinists' of *Minute* and *L'Humanité* who were sued for libel.

Strangely, the text had little of the wounded and fierce polemicist about it, but was rather distinguished by the classical lucidity of the prose. In recent years, Debord had composed very few texts (the 1980 translations of Jorge Manrique and the accompanying postscript were indeed his most recent literary venture), but this excursion into print marked him out as a stylist of the highest degree. *Considérations* was also an intimate and touching text: Debord described the ties of friendship that drew him to Lebovici, the house at Champot, the festive laughter of parties and impromptu gatherings. He also evoked Arles and the grand house at Saint-Pierre-du-Mont in Normandy of Alice's brother, a dealer in antiques, which had become another place of retreat. He spoke with contempt of the *paparazzi* and the *renseignements généraux* (the French intelligence services) who had been tracking him for decades, mocking their clumsy attempts to connect him with organised crime or international terrorism. He did not however protest his innocence in the face of the spectacular society: 'These journalists, each of them representing in the most servile way the most surprising discoveries of someone else, without denying them a certain collective verve, have described me, without the qualification of a single fact, as a *Maître à penser*, nihilist, pseudo-philosopher, pope, solitary, mentor, hypnotic seducer, blood-soaked marionette, self-obsessed fanatic, devil, *éminence grise*, damned soul, professor of radicalism, guru, tuppence ha'penny revolutionary, agent of subversion and destabilisation in the service of Soviet imperialism, gimcrack Mephisto, troublemaker, extravagant, sulphurous, enigmatic, bad angel, ideologue, mysterious, sadistic madman, total cynic, dregs of non-thought, sorcerer, redoubtable destabiliser, angry, theoretician.'[2]

There was also another text, contained within *Considérations* which revealed the real relationship between Lebovici and Debord. Most crucially, Lebovici was portrayed as an honourable, elegant, aristocratic figure who scorned money, mediocre prestige and the ceaseless chatter of the media world he lived in. Far from being the 'double agent' or Jekyll and Hyde figure the press made him out to be, Lebovici's behaviour was entirely consistent with his (and Debord's) belief that present conditions in the society and era they lived in had reduced most people to a degree of servility which was both disgusting and squalid. The only appropriate response to such a world was lordly contempt. The relation between the two men was therefore based upon the Renaissance model of a complicit opposition between Lebovici the Prince and Debord as the Philosopher-Sage. Recalling Machiavelli, Graciàn and Castiglione, Debord described their friendship in political and poetic terms. Most importantly this was a model of friendship and behaviour which was not only rare in the era of spectacular relations but, because it was based on the most classical notions of friendship and intimacy, stood in direct opposition to the twentieth century. 'This century does not like truth, generosity, grandeur,' wrote Debord in *Considérations*. 'Thus it did not like Gérard Lebovici, who attracted still a little more hateful envy on account of his freedom of mind and his culture. It is Gérard Lebovici who was doing me the honour of visiting me at home. Yes, Lebovici did have ties in the Haute-Loire. I am pleased to think that he has always felt at home there.'[3]

The most stinging attacks in the book were reserved for the spectacle as a totality, from the heart of which the real assault on Debord and Lebovici had been launched. At the same time Debord recognised with painful lucidity that the time of the Situationist International had passed and that the historic moment when the owl of Minerva might take to flight would not come again in his lifetime. He argued, however, that the lingering force of the Situationist International was based precisely on the fact that it had never surrendered or made any concession to the spectacular demands of the age.

Above all Debord sought to emphasise his separation from the age in which he lived, an age in which all authentic taste and meaning had disappeared and real human values were in exile:

> That everything ends in success, concessions and the poor are recompensed from the success, is what is contradicted by the history of hundreds of attempts at revolution. This cannot be said in any case of the Situationist International. It knew how to combat its own fame, as it said it would: this practice is almost without precedent. It did not want to become for anyone a commandment, and it did not want to preserve itself in a position of intellectual authority in future days. We had nothing but time. When I speak about myself, and I have rarely spoken on this subject, a certain cutting tone, which is indeed fitting, is not often approved, and this is not too surprising. There are others who would not have recourse to this: because they would seek to preserve appearances, and because they have no content. But it is a fine thing to have contributed to wrecking the world. What other success could we have deserved?
>
> I do think that I am as 'enigmatic' as one likes to make out. I even think that I am easy to understand. Not long ago, at the beginning of a passion, she with whom I had spoken of a few brief exiles that we had each known, said to me, in a tone of generous brusqueness which is so characteristic of Spain, 'But you, you have spent your whole life in exile.'
>
> So I have had the pleasure as others had the pains of submission. Gérard Lebovici has been killed.[4]

Secrets everywhere

Considérations was in many ways Debord's first real book since *The Society of the Spectacle*, and certainly matched it in its lucidity and the clarity and accuracy of its critical analysis of a society where the 'real has become false'. Debord was concerned however that he did not retreat from real activity into literature and to this end he renewed his friendship with Jaime

Semprun, one of the early and most determined activists in the Champ Libre adventure.

Jaime was the son of the distinguished Spanish novelist Jorge Semprun (later Minister for Culture in Felipe Gonzalez's Socialist government in the late 1980s) who had a reputation in France and Spain as a fearless polemicist and whose own experience of civil war and deportation (he had spent two years in Buchenwald) had shaped his view of the world and literature. Semprun had been courted by Lebovici as he was starting up Champ Libre, but then quickly ousted as Lebovici steered the publishing house in a specifically anti-literary direction.

Jaime had inherited his father's Left-wing convictions, his talent and his flair. In 1974 he had published with Champ Libre a book called *La Guerre sociale au Portugal* ('The Social War in Portugal') which Debord had much admired for its description of the revolutionary movement in Portugal as an endless festival (the fact that the festival was to be short-lived did not dampen Debord's enthusiasm for Semprun's argument). In 1984, with the former Situationist Christian Sébastiani, still one of the most dedicated and virulent ex-Situs, Semprun established a journal which sought to inherit the Situationist tradition of radical dissent, *L'Encyclopédie des nuisances* ('The Encyclopedia of Nuisances').

Debord contributed two short pieces to the journal, persuaded by Semprun that this would mark a return to the practice of critical analysis in the spirit of the Situationist International. In the first of these pieces, the anonymously signed article 'Abat-faim', Debord went on the offensive against the way in which modern society had organised itself so that the most basic human need, hunger, had become itself the basis of a series of illusions which separated individuals from themselves. More precisely, Debord complained that the word 'hunger' had lost all its meaning in a society where appetite was satisfied by substitute foods, such as fast food and other cheap forms of nourishment. The way in which these foods were delivered to the consumer, in McDonald's and other fake palaces of modernism, was the greatest illusion of all, convincing the consumer that he had been satisfied without providing him with either food or nourishment.

This was hardly an original view and in the world where Live Aid had provoked intense debate on the Left about the ethics of hunger and the media exploitation of that hunger, it was hardly likely to cause a stir. What was interesting about the piece was the extent to which Debord moved on from the theses of *The Society of the Spectacle* concerning the 'techniques of the religious illusion' to develop the notion of the production and consumption of food as a state secret. It was these hidden processes, he further argued, that were at the origins of the mysterious and incurable diseases – cancers, viruses – which appeared to be such an intractable part of life at the end of the twentieth century: 'It is not to make us live in a sybaritic manner that half the planet must die in famine; it is to make us live in mud [. . .]. Not only medicine but also food itself, like so many other things, has become a state secret [. . .]. This is the syndrome of the fatal malady of the twentieth century: the society of classes and specialisations, through a constant omnipresent effort, acquires an immunisation against all pleasure. The collapse of immunitary defences against all the poisons that this produces will only be therefore more total.'[5]

The same theme was developed in an article in November 1986 called 'Ab irato' ('With a movement of anger') in which Debord railed against a society in which doctors sought to maximise public attention for their treatments. He cited the example of a mother who had subjected her dying child to an expensive and painful operation at the hands of surgeons whose only concern was publicity. 'It seems that dying is simply not enough,' he growled.[6]

It was no coincidence that as he wrote these pieces Debord was becoming aware of his own mortality. The death of Lebovici had been the first and most brutal lesson. But Debord was now also physically unwell for longer and longer periods. He found himself more susceptible to flu and insomnia than he had ever been before, and was suffering ever more powerful and intense attacks of gout. He resolutely refused to curb his appetites, however, seeking poetic and political justification for his alcoholism and blaming the corrupt and decomposing world around for any poisonous effects that alcohol might bring him. The Chernobyl disaster only served to confirm his perception that it was not he but the world which was slowly being poisoned. The death of a friend from cirrhosis of the liver in 1986 was also, Debord remarked in a letter, the inevitable consequence of drinking cheap and poorly produced beer.

The Game of War

On 15 October 1986 the Librairie Gérard Lebovici opened its doors on rue Saint-Sulpice. The idea, originating from Debord and Floriana, was to offer Champ Libre for public display. In part homage to Gérard Lebovici, and partly as a way of avoiding the vulgarity of media publicity, the shop window also offered occasional exhibitions of such Situationist heroes as Raoul Haussmann and Arthur Cravan. Less predictable was the way in which the shop was now becoming something of a cult site in Paris, attracting Situphiles who lingered in the bookshop hoping to glimpse the legendary, sulphurous revolutionary Guy Debord.

Lebovici's business affairs were now firmly in the hands of Gérard Voitey, the young notary who had stepped into the breach in the wake of the assassination. Voitey, who was a fan of the non-intellectual pleasures of rugby and Elvis Presley, was captivated by his new friends. He always travelled with a chauffeur, dined in the best restaurants and had a pronounced love of ostentation and luxury, and found that many of these tastes were shared by his new 'extremist' friends. Voitey was also developing a fascination for Lebovici, modelling himself physically and intellectually on the renegade producer's style. Floriana had confided to Voitey that Lebovici's plan had been to disentangle himself from the cinema world and, by buying up smaller publishing houses, create his own literary empire. Voitey started to put his own version of this plan into action, establishing in early 1987 Éditions Quai Voltaire, specialising in authors such as Paul Bowles or the elegant essayist, novelist and wit Roger Stéphane.

Debord was concerned both with what he saw as the fragmentation of the Champ Libre set-up and, equally pressingly, with how the Situationist International seemed now to be slipping into history. This process was accelerated in 1985 with the publication by Gérard Bérreby, a young Tunisian Jew enamoured with the energy and fury of the SI, of *Documents relatifs à la fondation de l'internationale situationniste*. This collection of texts, assembled, edited and introduced by Bérreby, was offered in homage to Lebovici, but it also reminded the reader of how total and ambitious the plans of the SI had been.

Reading the conference reports from Cosio, Alba, Munich and Amsterdam, it seemed to Debord that all this activity had happened in another age, another world. Despite the inevitable melancholy that this reading evoked, Debord was also concerned to ensure that the SI's role in history was recorded by those who had access to its original motives and aims, rather than the blurred account of events which was predictably produced in the spectacular form of media reports or academic theses. To this end he set Jean-François Martos the task of writing *Histoire de L'Internationale Situationniste* ('History of the Situationist International'), a book which, according to Debord, had the 'historic mission' of presenting the SI to posterity.

In February 1987 Éditions Gérard Lebovici published its most curious and unsellable publication to date. This was *Le Jeu de la guerre, relevé des positions successives de toutes les forces au cours d'une partie* ('The Game of War, taking into account successive positions of all forces during a game'). The edition was signed by Guy Debord and Alice Becker-Ho (with thanks to Nicolas Lebovici, who had spent many hours playing the game with the couple) and was presented enigmatically as pure if complicated entertainment.

For those who had been reading Debord since the 1960s, studied the auto-dissolution of the Situationist International and followed the career of Champ Libre, the book seemed to reveal the underlying strategy which lay behind many of Debord's most dangerous and puzzling moves. 'In the *Game of War*,' explained the text, 'there are numerous bad dispositions and manoeuvres, but none of the best manouevres on which one can decide, at least as long as there remains a certain equilibrium of forces and positions, is assured of being good.'

This instability, in other words, was the shaping force of the tactics of adversaries in 'the game of war'. Debord had conducted all of his attacks on the spectacular society as essentially negative actions, counter-offensives which were meant to draw the enemy out to an exposed position. This was also how Debord, the philosopher, explained the function of the negative in the Hegelian dialectic, and also how he saw this theoretical construct as being applied and tested upon the battlefield.

The most crucial aspect of the work of negative action, for Debord the game-player, however, was its ability to undermine all known fixed positions: 'The permanent interaction of tactics and strategy can bring about surprises and reversals – sometimes at the last instant.'

CHAPTER 34

Bitter Victory

1988–91

The house in Arles was abandoned in the autumn of 1987. Debord and Alice settled in Paris, in a huge apartment on the third floor of a grand building on the rue du Bac in the 7th *arrondissement*. This was an extremely well-to-do part of Paris, with none of the passages, alleys and labyrinths which Debord had thought so essential to his conception of the city. The only connection with Debord's earlier life was that the apartment was almost adjacent to the square des Missions Étrangères, a site of great psychogeographical importance for the early Situationists, but which now evoked a stern form of melancholy. The apartment was filled with beautiful furniture, paintings and antiques, whilst Debord dedicated himself to the pleasures of food and drink, spending whole days planning elaborate meals and choosing fine wines. There was, however, an aristocratic sense of detachment in his manner, and those closest to him at the time described him as despairing or cynical, often all at once. Anita Blanc, Gérard Lebovici's cousin who had been working with Floriana Lebovici since 1985, found herself briefly an intimate of Debord and Alice. She was invited to dinners, always with herself as sole guest, and would talk for hours with Debord through long afternoons of drinking, when Debord would do nothing but play with the black cat he had made his inseparable companion. Anita noted that, despite his still bright eyes and witty conversation, Debord had returned again and again to the same theme: that of the warrior at rest, whose arms had been laid down for a final time. Anita described him as an aristocrat who had decided to detach himself from life, his century, his time.[1]

There was clearly now a sense of defeat in Debord's thought and demeanour. It was as if, as he remarked himself, his destiny had run its course; the flight of Hegel's owl of Minerva, the bird who had taken wing at nightfall in pursuit of philosophy and whose journey was a metaphor for Debord's life, was now over. 'In the midwinter nights of 1988, in the square des Missions Étrangères, an owl would obstinately repeat his calls, fooled perhaps by the unseasonable weather,' Debord wrote in *Panegyric*. 'And this usual run of encounters with the bird of Minerva, its air of surprise and indignation, did not in the least seem to constitute an allusion to the imprudent conduct or the various aberrations of my life. I have never understood in what way it could have been different, nor how it could have been justified.'[2]

Spectacular domination

The impulse to make a final comment and analysis of the world was also what drove Debord to compose *Commentaires sur la société du spectacle* ('Commentaries on the Society of the Spectacle') to which he devoted the early part of 1988, and which was published at the end of the year.

The central argument of this book was that few moments in recent history had been as falsified as the revolutionary moment of 1968. In the twenty years since May 68, according to Debord, the French Left had organised itself around the demands made upon French society by the middle classes and not the proletariat and had, thereby, installed a nexus of social 'rights' (women's rights, workers' rights and so on) as its guiding theory. The basic principles of the capitalist order, however, were left intact and, in fact, had been reinforced by 'spectacular forms of domination' and 'generalised secrecy' since 1968. This is how the 'society of the spectacle', originally defined by Debord in his famous book of that name in 1967, had, by the late 1980s, hardened into what he termed the 'integrated spectacle'. The term 'integrated' was used to describe the combination of spectacular forces which presented a unified whole. This phenomenon, Debord further insisted, although it originated in the coming together of state, media and capital in France and Italy (*pace* Bernard Tapie or Silvio Berlusconi), was also occurring everywhere in the world and thus signalling the end of the true political history of the twentieth century.

Critical reaction to the book was equivocal: Debord was still considered by a large section of the Parisian literary public to be either an anachronism or the shadowy apologist for, or even sponsor of, terrorism. This was the essential debate of the television arts programme *Apostrophes* which reviewed the book,[3] whilst others saw in Debord the incorrigible and implacable enemy of society, a heroic negativity which served as a critical corrective in an age where politics and art had become interchangeable ciphers of non-meaning.

The most influential of the latter tendency was Philippe Sollers, the novelist and former editor of *Tel Quel*, the journal which in the 1960s had traversed Maoism, psychoanalysis and post-structuralism, claiming itself as the last of the avant-gardes. Above all *Tel Quel* was conceived by Sollers as a laboratory for ideas which would challenge the modernist consensus that art, literature and politics were interchangeable forms of expression which had common ground in real experience; whether they wrote on Georges

Bataille, one of the foremost 'acknowledged heroes' of the group, the Marquis de Sade, Hegel or developed pseudo-scientific theories of the text and the subject, the contributors to *Tel Quel* were united in their faith in the primacy of textual drama over real experience. The events of 1968, it was generally agreed within the *Tel Quel* inner circle, were a 'catastrophe', a judgement made largely on the spurious grounds that 'the irruption of the political signifier into everyday life' (this was how 'Telqueliens' described the spontaneous events of May) had failed to make any impact beyond the theoretical.[4]

Neither the theories of *Tel Quel*, nor the fame and power of its contributors, could have been further removed from the obscure universe of the Situationist International. Debord had always treated the group with contempt and derision, not merely because their revolution was confined to textual theory, but also because the now famous products of the *Tel Quel* group were precisely the sort of mediocre intellectuals whose place in the 'integrated spectacle' was preserved by their espousal of fake revolutionary language.

When he first read *Commentaries on the Society of the Spectacle*, Philippe Sollers, who was now in charge of the journal *L'Infini* and, as an editor at Gallimard, was an important power-broker on the French literary scene, declared himself 'turned upside down' by the lucidity of Debord's prose and the precison of his critical analysis of a society which is dominated and controlled by secrets. Debord's book was now customarily at Sollers' side when he drank and dined at La Closerie des Lilas, the Montparnasse café formerly favoured by Hemingway, Lenin, Trotsky and Joyce, and which is still the favoured haunt of Parisian prime movers in politics and art; copies were pressed on those who had not read Debord. In the pages of *Le Monde*, Sollers described Debord as 'the most improbable author of the century'. In his other works, Sollers began to cite Debord almost incessantly, with all the fervour of a new convert, describing him in print and in conversation as 'the writer who has most clearly understood what it means, what it meant, to be alive at the end of the twentieth century, who has understood how to escape it and how the conditions have changed to make escape almost impossible. To read Debord is not only essential to understanding critical thinking after Marx, but it is also the only way to understand the present, and the future which is emerging from it before our eyes as a spectacle we cannot touch, participate in or control.'[5]

Lower quarters

As Debord's reputation was being fêted in the most exalted Parisian company, his own life and activities followed a well-worn pattern. Mostly in the company of Alice, but sometimes with new companions such as the writer Morgan Sportès or the painter Merri Jolivet, he would walk some fifteen minutes from the rue du Bac and plunge into the heart of Saint-Germain-des-Prés, the much-loved and familiar territory which, although radically changed from its 1950s heyday, was still a comfortably louche environment in which to spend the day drinking.

The new headquarters was a bar called Chez Julienne on the rue Dauphine, a scruffy dive populated by students, would-be and genuine bohemians, drinkers and drifters. Next door to the bar was the bookshop Actualités, still owned by Pierre Sciais, and where a whole bookcase was now devoted to Letterism, Situationism and Guy Debord. In the dusty gloom of Chez Julienne, however, Debord was still thinking, planning and above all drinking, mostly wine but also consuming a fair amount of the owner Andréa's collection of bottled beers (Chez Julienne was closed in 1996: I think, certainly from the musty taste of the beer, that I must have drunk one of the final bottles as Andréa was selling off the last of her stock). He made friends with a would-be writer, Agnès Pavy, who wrote occasionally for the journal Politis but who was also an enthusiastic drinker (Debord was even more impressed by her ex-husband François who was a seriously demanding champion boozer whose special skill was never to display any signs of drunkenness). Agnès was fascinated by Debord's learning and by his contempt for the world around him. He particularly hated the newspaper Libération, the favoured reading of most soixante-huitards. She describes him dressed like a peasant from the Auvergne, drinking slowly but steadily, always in the company of Alice, talking about a hundred different subjects, but each one finely analysed before being finally discarded.[6]

Some who came across Debord during this period saw him, in contrast, as something of a shambolic figure, now almost entirely given over to alcohol. His old enemy Gérard Guégan was pleased to be told by someone who had run into Debord in Chez Julienne that he cut a pathetic figure, dressed like an unemployed schoolteacher, moving salt cellars and peanuts across the counter to illustrate some point of strategy and his theories on the Gulf War.[7]

Other new friends were however seduced by Debord's style. Morgan Sportès first fell into conversation with Alice and Debord drinking in a café in the afternoon. He was impressed not only by Debord's capacity for drink but also by what he called Debord's 'dandyism'. Sportès described Debord as 'a man from another century'. Invited to dine with Guy and Alice after a week of drinking together along the rue de Buci, rue de Seine and rue Dauphine, Sportès noticed that the huge apartment on the rue du Bac was very ordered and very austere. Debord never answered the telephone, touched money or did anything around the house. When not drinking in his favoured cafés, he talked art, politics, literature and philosophy (Sportès recalled a particularly virulent attack on Proust). Debord's 'dandyism' was expressed, thought Sportès, in his contempt and indifference to the society he lived in: 'In this, he was a revolutionary with style.'[8]

Debord's indifference extended to those who sought to use his ideas for their own ends. When Alain de Benoist, the philosopher and intellectual leader of the Right-wing discussion group La nouvelle droite ('The New Right'), established Debord's theories on the society of the spectacle as recommended reading, which justified their own theses on the inexorable slide of Western culture away from its European apogee, Debord's reaction was one of silence. This aloof position was maintained even when, in 1988, shortly after de Benoist had posited Debord as a Right-wing thinker, the ubiquitous Pierre Guillaume, now a leading negationist publisher and defender of the wildest anti-Holocaust propaganda, annexed Debord's theories and put his former comrade in arms in a pantheon of free-thinkers which included Robert Faurisson, Paul Rasinnier, Roger Garaudy and Rudolf Hess.[9]

Museums

The Situationists, once the stuff of legend in radical circles outside France, were now in the process of becoming a cultural myth as heroes of the artistic avant-gardes of the century. The process was accelerated in the first instance by an exhibition which travelled from the ICA in London to the Beaubourg in Paris and to the Institute of Contemporary Arts in Boston. The exhibition was organised by Peter Wollen, Mark Francis and Hervé Passy, and advice was given from Elisabeth Sussman, Thomas Y. Levin and Greil Marcus, figures who were now taking a literary or academic interest in the Situationists. The works on display, as might be expected, were produced during the artistic period of the SI, and it brought together for the first time work by Constant, Jacqueline de Jong, Asger Jorn, Giuseppe Pinot-Gallizio, Jorgen Nash and other 'excluded' artists. Debord's only contribution was a selection of theoretical texts, a collage dating from 1954 and the painting of the slogan 'Abolition du travail aliéné' ('Abolition of alienated work'), which he had produced for the exhibition *Destruktion af RSG-6* in 1963.

Critical reaction to the exhibition was generally positive, despite mutterings from diehard pro-Situs about the apparent contradiction of placing the Situationists in a museum. In France, the USA and the UK it seemed that the Situationists were finally being placed in a context which recognised that what they had sought was not merely to develop art as a revolutionary technique, but that the revolution of everyday life was a totality which implied the abolition of art. This was the central question which most serious commentators were forced to address. (Brian Sewell of the *Evening Standard* held a dissident view: 'Far from vigorous, intelligent and substantial,' he wrote of the SI, 'its subversive ideas were spiteful, silly, morbid and pretentious, and we suffer from them still. The exhibition ends in a sludgily painted chamber, the air mephitic with a stink that induces violent hay fever; the catalogue is bound in sandpaper. "That," said the vendor with Situationist malevolence, "is meant to ruin your other books."')[10]

The Situationists' prestige in the Anglo-Saxon world was further enhanced with the publication in the same year of the book *Lipstick Traces* by the American writer Greil Marcus. Marcus had begun his career as a rock critic, writing for *Rolling Stone* and *Creem* and modelling his style on his friend and hero Lester Bangs, the prototypical 'gonzo' rock journalist who consumed at least as many class A drugs as his subjects. Marcus was also a shrewd, perceptive and subtle writer who saw rock and pop music as offering a way into understanding the secret springs of a nation or a culture's psyche. Not just Dylan, but also Elvis, Johnny Ray or the Shangri-Las were, in this sense, poets who had a visceral, if unconscious, sense of the different levels of complexity which made up a culture's position in history.[11] In *Lipstick Traces*, Marcus set out to understand what it was that made him hear in the Sex Pistols' *Anarchy in the UK* 'a voice which denied all social facts, and in that denial affirmed that everything was possible'.[12]

Marcus was not able to find a complete and satisfying answer, but rather traced a 'secret history of the twentieth century' by marking and delineating the work of all those artists and movements in the century who had sought an art of negation, who had said 'no' to the world as it was and turned away from the century's false promises. He read Dadaists, Surrealists, Letterists and Situationists, each time focusing upon Guy Debord as an almost heroic figure who, as a revolutionary, artist and strategist, had the 'instant route to total change, the reversible connecting factor'.[13] The book was a *tour de force*, an intelligent and passionate engagement with the negative forces working through twentieth-century culture which tore away at received notions of how to read anti-art. It was immediately hailed on both sides of the Atlantic as a classic which, as Terry Eagleton put it in the *New York Times*, understood that for the Situationists 'the metapolitics involves issues of desire, everyday life, the importance of microscopic gesture, which mainstream leftist politics has often enough breezily edited. But it carries with it by the same token an anti-sociality that is impatient with institutions as such. It is hard to dismantle particular institutions without dreaming for a euphoric moment of what it might be like to be free of institutions altogether.'[14]

Back in Paris, safely ensconced in Chez Julienne or the neighbouring headquarters Le Vin des rues, Debord expressed complete indifference to the impact his work and ideas were now making on the outside world. There was a minor stir caused in the Debord circle when an unfortunate journalist for *Village Voice* had confused the London Institute of Contemporary Arts

(ICA) with the Central Intelligence Agency (CIA) and described Debord as working for the latter: what clearer example could there be of deliberate and guided 'confusionism'? When the exhibition came to the Beaubourg Debord was invited to a private viewing but declined the invitation. 'He could not have cared less,' said Alice. 'This was not what he wanted, it could not be in any way satisfying to be in a book or museum. It was the opposite of life.'

A funeral oration

Panégyrique ('Panegyric') was published in August 1989. Although a slim volume of less than ninety pages it was one of Debord's most complex and ambitious works so far, not least because it set out to present the story of his life.

This was not, however, in any sense a straightforward autobiography, but rather an intimate, poetic and occluded account of events which was shaped by the disciplined strictures, laid down by Lautréamont, to which Debord had remained faithful throughout his anti-career, and which demanded that all forms of writing, or art, should be dictated by subjective experience rather than cold fact.

The book was divided into seven short chapters which dealt, in sequence, with Debord's origins, his youth in Paris, drinking, travel, politics, war and a final summing up in which Debord quoted Jonathan Swift, who wrote in his *History of the Four Last Years of the Queen*, 'Neither shall I mingle panegyrick or satire with an history intended to inform posterity, as well as to instruct those of the present age, who may be ignorant or misled; since facts truly related are the best applauses, or most lasting reproaches.'

As an intimate history of his life, *Panegyric* did not intend either to inform or instruct, but rather to present his work and his activity to the world in the form of a 'potlatch', the gift which could not be returned. The style of the book was brilliant, lucid and hard; it was modelled on the great French moralist of the seventeenth century, Jacques-Bénigne Bossuet, but differed from him in its intention to lead the reader astray rather than teach him anything. There were references to Shakespeare, Thucydides, Calderón, Clausewitz, De Quincey, and no sense at all that this was a text which had been written in the twentieth century. This aesthetic decision was also a political one: 'Those who wish to write quickly a piece about nothing that no one will read through even once, whether in a newspaper or a book, extol with much conviction the style of the spoken language because they find it much more modern, direct, facile,' wrote Debord. 'They themselves do not know how to speak. Neither do their readers, the language actually spoken under modern conditions of life being socially reduced to its indirect presentation through the suffrage of the media, and including six or eight turns of phrase repeated at every moment and fewer than two hundred words, most of them neologisms, with the whole thing submitted to replacement by one third every six months. . . . The gypsies rightly contend that one is never compelled to tell the truth, except in one's own language; in the enemy's language, the lie must reign. Another advantage: by referring to the vast corpus of classical texts that have appeared in French throughout the five centuries before my birth, but especially in the last two, it will always be easy to translate me adequately into any future idiom, even when French has become a dead language.'[15]

It was important also to remember that this was a *détournement* of the panegyric in the original Greek sense of a eulogious oration, meant to praise a city or a man who has contributed to the formation of the highest Hellenic ideals, who has shaped history. This notion was turned upside down by Debord, who was here speaking to an audience which did not yet exist and, in a final ironic display of grandeur and bravado, placing himself against time and history by presenting his own funeral oration.

CHAPTER 35

This Bad Reputation

1992–4

The funeral oration that was *Panégyrique* was matched by the publication in the same year of Jean-François Martos' book *Histoire de l'Internationale Situationniste*. This book, elegant, arch, uncompromisingly committed, had been written under Debord's direction and presented an elegiac account of the story of the Situationists and, most poignantly, their relationship to their time. The book was divided into five chapters, each with a heading in Latin, which took the reader from the origins of the Letterist International to the auto-dissolution of the SI. Documents, arguments and incidents were analysed in the finest detail, but there was deliberately no description of the people or personalities who had made the Situationists. Everything was presented as cold, impersonal fact. Most importantly perhaps, despite the fierce statement of intent at the end of the book, that between those who understood Situationist ideas and those who were agents of the 'spectacle' 'hostilities continued', it was also for Debord and his retinue a historical book that marked the end of Situationist theory as a set of ideas which could make an impact on their era.

Real life was also inflicting wounds upon Debord. On 19 February 1990 Floriana Lebovici died. She was forty-nine years old and, almost destroyed by the death of her husband, she was finally killed by cancer. On her deathbed she asked her sons, Lorenzo Valentin and Nicolas Lebovici, never to sell Éditions Gérard Lebovici. This had been Lebovici's own wish and it was now the boys' responsibility either to take control of the business or to wind it up.

Although he did not yet want to show his hand, Debord was clearly perturbed by this turn of events, fearing that in the hands of Floriana's two sons the enterprise would fall into disarray. Shortly after Floriana's funeral Debord approached Gérard Voitey and suggested that he buy the business out. His proposal was that Voitey could become the new Lebovici and the old relationship of 'prince and bandit' could be restored. This appealed to Voitey, who was intoxicated by his dealings with Debord and affected much of the manner of 'le roi Lebo'. To the surprise and shock of Lorenzo and

Nicolas, in the now familiar Debordien style, the first blows were struck without warning or precedent. The first blow was that Debord suddenly refused all contact with the boys, a move which was hurtful enough in the circumstances of their mother's death but made worse by the way in which they had fixed such filial affection upon Debord. The second blow was a classic piece of disinformation, meant to force the naïve and damaged boys' hand. It came in the form of a public announcement in the publishing magazine *Livres Hebdo* which declared that Gérard Voitey was buying up Éditions Lebovici and had already taken over the majority stakeholding in the business. This was not only untrue but actionable and, to Voitey and Debord's undisguised bafflement, the two boys showed their mettle by placing the affair in the hands of solicitors, opening an extremely bitter legal battle which Debord and Voitey would lose.[1]

Even those who had known Debord well, or even loved him, through the years when he displayed the greatest cruelty to his friends were dismayed by this turn of events, which revealed Debord and Voitey as manipulative, underhand and greedy. Certainly, as legal proceedings went ahead, Debord showed little compassion for the boys who had lost their mother and father and regarded him as an older, wiser friend.

Debord's behaviour now was characterised by an icy melancholy. In the autumn of 1992 Suzanne Jamet, who worked for the press service at Gallimard, travelled down to Champot to see Debord, who after protracted negotiations (and accusations from former comrades of betrayal) was now a Gallimard author. The deal with Gallimard had been brokered by Philippe Sollers. Debord refused point blank to meet him. Having so viciously attacked Gallimard in the 1960s, Debord had now dined with Antoine Gallimard himself and found himself considered a respected master of classical French prose.

Jamet was in Champot to discuss the distribution and publicity for Debord's complete works, all of which were about to be published by Gallimard. She arrived at the isolated farmhouse at around 9 a.m. to find Debord waiting for her in a large gloomy room which looked little changed in a hundred years. Debord gave no word of greeting but for five minutes or so drank steadily from a bottle of red wine by his side. 'I really don't know what you are doing here,' he said finally to the young woman, who was thoroughly disconcerted by this performance. The later conviviality and invitation to stay with the Debords at other times did nothing to dispel Jamet's original impression that Debord 'no longer felt that he was connected to his era, no longer felt that he was connected to anything. It was as if he was the only one who could see that everything was leading to catastrophe.'[2]

'The Time of AIDS'

Debord was also by now in an increasingly poor physical condition. His insomnia had become so acute that days and nights would blur into one long exhausting and depressing continuum. Worse still was the inflammatory pain of gout, a condition which now gripped him so severely that he could sometimes barely get in or out of a car. He suffered also from vertigo and suspected that he was developing the first symptoms of peripheral neuritis, a disease of the nerve ends, common in alcoholics, which burns away all feeling in the extremities. Most of these ailments could have been alleviated by a reduction in Debord's alcoholic intake, but this was of course never an option.

Instead Debord sought advice from Michel Bounan, a doctor with radical sympathies who, with a view to publication, had sent the manuscript of his book *Le Temps du SIDA* ('The Time of AIDS') to Floriana Lebovici as she lay dying. The text was left unread until Bounan, impatient at the slow progress on his book, wrote to Guy Debord.

Debord was delighted with *The Time of AIDS*, which he considered a masterpiece of contemporary critical analysis. Bounan's argument in this book, finally published by Gérard Bérreby in 1990, is that the phenomenon of the AIDS virus, and other modern diseases, is linked to the 'infection' which is the 'integrated spectacle'.[3] Bounan's argument was that AIDS was not only a catastrophic epidemic but also a media-controlled event which determined the limits of behaviour under the modern conditions of existence. He compared the way in which the Church in the Middle Ages had evoked the spectre of the Black Plague as a form of social control; the 'spectacular uses' to which AIDS was now being put by the global media performed exactly the same role.

However, in a move which at least for some of Bounan's supporters paralleled the suppression of Situationist theses in earlier times, *The Time of AIDS* was refused an English publication by the publisher Verso. Verso justified this decision on the grounds that the book was a tissue of 'charlatanism and mysticism'.[4] In the meantime, Bounan produced a pamphlet denouncing his critics.[5]

Bounan's suggested homeopathic treatments for Debord were similar to the therapies he advocated in *The Time of AIDS* as alleviatory measures for the HIV virus. Not even Bounan suggested that these treatments offered a cure.

In Paris, Debord's days were spent between Chez Julienne and the plethora of bars and cafés around and between rue de Buci and rue de Seine, or, when overwhelmed by pain, depression or illness, in the apartment on the rue du Bac. Debord saw no one from any of the active periods of the Situationist International. Meanwhile, his reputation as a writer and thinker had never been more exalted: his books were essential reading, wrote Philippe Sollers and a host of lesser luminaries, for all those who wished to understand the century they were living in. For a new generation, who did not remember 1968 but who saw the revolutions of 1989 as revealing the fragility of both democratic and totalitarian systems which reinforce their status via the strategic deployment of 'spectacular forces', Guy Debord and the Situationist International were avatars of a revolutionary spirit which understood the future as well as the present. For the first time since 1968, Situationist-inspired graffiti was a common sight on the walls of the Left Bank, whilst Debord himself was the object of veneration amongst the younger generation of *Libération* and *Les Inrockuptibles*.

In Champot wine and whisky measured out the days with Alice. There were now few visitors and the house was quiet. Most of the villagers thought that it was unoccupied most of the time. In *Panegyric*, Debord had quoted André Masséna, Marshal of France and a hero of the Napoleonic campaigns in Italy, as saying, at the age of fifty-seven, that 'command wears one out'.[6] It was clear that Debord already considered his work to be finished, as he continued, almost with a shrug, 'You don't live twice in this profession, no more so than on this earth. Time does not wait. One does not defend Genoa twice; no one has twice raised Paris to revolt.'[7]

The dangerous classes

Debord published his first and only original work for Galllimard in November 1993. 'Cette mauvaise réputation . . .' ('This Bad Reputation . . .') was however his poorest and least complete work yet, no more really than an assemblage of quotations from the press along the lines of *Considerations on the Assassination of Gérard Lebovici*. It lacked the sense of engagement and polemical bite, inspired by a genuine sense of disgust, which made *Considerations* a book worth reading and indeed placing alongside the best of Debord's critical Situationist texts. His latest book was characterised by a dull and wearied tone and a predictable assembly of enemies, including the inimitable Sollers who had done so much to court Debord, by proxy of course, and broker the deal with Gallimard on the most favourable terms. In truth the book's only real merit was that it functioned quite effectively as a sharp reminder to Gallimard that Debord, for all the claims made for him, was not quite ready to become a classic.

This much was also indicated in the book's title, which came from a lengthier quotation from the Sophist philosopher Gorgias of Leontini ('I have tried to annul the injustice of this bad reputation and the ignorance of opinion'), whose fame rested upon his propositions that nothing is real, reality is unknowable, the knowable is inexpressible. A long and lucid section of 'This Bad Reputation . . .', the only real piece of critical writing in the book, explored the contemporary world in these terms, which in the use of the term 'simulation' evoked another contemporary master of despair, Jean Baudrillard (Baudrillard, although he deplores the fashion for Debord since his death does not disagree that there is a similarity in their work).[8] 'Everywhere speculation has, in the end, become the sovereign aspect of all property,' wrote Debord. 'It auto-regulates itself, more or less according to the local preponderance around the stock markets, states, Mafia: all federated in a sort of democracy of the élites of speculation. The rest is misery. Everywhere, excess simulation has exploded like Chernobyl, and everywhere death spreads as fast and massively as disorder. Nothing works any more, and nothing is believed any more.'

Gallimard published the first book produced by Alice Becker-Ho. This was an unusual text called *Les Princes du jargon*, first published by Éditions Gérard Lebovici in 1990 (it was the publication of this book which, according to Agnès Pavy, had started the row between Debord and the Lebovici sons), which set out to chart the slang of the so-called 'dangerous classes'. This was a term also used by Debord in *Panegyric* to describe the drifters, alcoholics, drug addicts, runaways, delinquents, 'the milieu of demolition experts' of his youth who, in Chez Moineau and other dives across the Left Bank, had represented for him the possibility of freedom. For Alice, 'the dangerous classes' were medieval brigands, travellers, all those who refused to be assimilated into society and whose own language was formed by a subjective impulse to reject pre-ordained codes of communication, 'the language of the enemy'.

Alice's book was rigorously anti-academic and she scorned those who had tried to build a career out of devising linguistic systems from the language of subversion. The term 'the dangerous classes' gave a clue as to how Debord and Alice saw their work and their relation to the society around them. The phrase had been used by Louis Chevalier – much admired by Debord for his book *L'Assassinat de Paris* – in a book called *Classes laborieuses et classes dangereuses à Paris pendant la première moitié du XIXe siècle* ('Working classes and dangerous classes in Paris during the first half of the nineteenth century').[9] This book was the culmination of a series of lectures at the Collège de France in which Chevalier had mapped and analysed the relationship between the city of Paris and the subversive classes it contained. The central argument of Chevalier's lectures was that Paris was defined by its 'negative' criminal elements as much as it was by the demands of capital or commerce. 'Guy talked a lot about the dangerous classes,' explained Alice, 'groups like the gypsies of Arles, or revolutionary workers or thieves, who were classes who made their own laws, who could not be controlled, and who knew that they were opposed to everything.

Even when there were no Situationists left, it was still important for us to be outside the reach of the enemy.'

A testament

The press were not kind to 'Cette mauvaise réputation . . .', describing it variously as a 'flop', a 'disappointment' or simply a rehash of old feuds and enmities. The deal with Gallimard had given rise to rumours that Guy Debord, the notorious and dangerous man of action, might suddenly reveal himself to be a writer of genius. Instead, this book revealed him as a rancorous old bore.[10] Meanwhile, it was decided in Champot to make a television film. The journalist Brigitte Cornand was employed to film parts of Paris and to research film extracts in the Institut national de l'audiovisuel in Paris (this time the extracts were paid for by Canal Plus, the television channel which had commissioned the Soirée Guy Debord).

The illnesses which plagued Debord were now rendering him incapable of any normal functions for large parts of his time. Jean-Jacques Pauvert, the publisher of Bataille and the Marquis de Sade who had been pursuing Debord as an author prior to the Gallimard deal, visited Guy and Alice in the early part of 1994 and noticed that his friend could not get up to greet him. They saw each other again shortly afterwards in Venice. He was then someone who did not pay attention to the slightest worry,' said Pauvert. 'He was always charming. There, I found him changed, sombre, preoccupied.'[11] Another meeting with Pauvert, like many others with friends that summer, was cancelled because 'Guy was not in a fit state to meet anyone'.

Work continued however. Brigitte Cornand was a skilful and stylish journalist who had cut her teeth on the Parisian underground scene, writing in the 1980s for the magazine *Actuel* which had reinvented itself from a hippie past into a Parisian version of *The Face* or *I-D*. She had also produced in 1992 a documentary on the SI for Canal Plus called *Cette Situation doit changer* ('This situation must change') which pleased Debord with its audacious plagiarism. Cornand's film was a witty and powerful compendium of statements about the SI and its history, which included films of Isidore Isou, Gil Wolman's *L'Anticoncept*, detourned films by René Viénet, extracts from *The Society of the Spectacle* and *Panegyric*, a speech by Lacenaire and a photomontage of leading intellectuals such as Philippe Sollers and Marguerite Duras interspersed with hard-core porno footage of a couple fucking in frightening gynaecological detail.

Above all the film affirmed the presence of the SI on the present-day cultural landscape of masters of subversion whose revolutionary theses had not yet been swept away by time or history. In a further provocative gesture, Cornand had also written to Debord to claim cheekily that she had 'detourned' the master of *détournement*. This had further delighted

Debord who invited the journalist to meet him, whereupon she found herself suddenly an intimate and a member of the inner circle. Cornand noted that Debord always wore a scarf which he claimed had been given to him by Gérard Lebovici.[12]

Days and months passed in Champot, drinking, arguing over the shots for the film and the soundtrack. Cornand's visits would last days or weeks, and there was always, despite the obvious vicissitudes of illness, laughter, alcohol and good food in the house. The accordionist Lino Léonardi, whose work was greatly admired by Debord, was employed to play the music that he had composed for *Le Testament* of François Villon, the poem which Villon had supposedly composed as his last act on earth. Despite this clear point of reference, Brigitte Cornand claims to have had no inkling that Debord was contemplating suicide. 'I didn't know he was so ill. While he was alive I felt this heavy feeling of desolation, but after the event it was terrible! . . . And I saw nothing. I understood nothing.'

CHAPTER 36

The Prince of Division

1994

In truth, the preparations had been made long before. The decision had been taken at least a year before the moment which would make Debord once again the master of the game. 'Guy did not have to die,' said Alice, 'it was a clear choice he made. He refused to be defeated by illness, or the world which was making him a famous man of letters. He wished simply not to be present when that happened.'

The signals were there for those who could read them. Throughout the course of that final year projects, books, letters were being assembled in a way which clearly anticipated an end to activity. Not least of Debord's intentions was to ensure that Alice would be financially secure after his death – the deal with Gallimard now had a clear and explicit purpose in Debord's strategic planning. The most important volume published that year was Debord's *Oeuvres cinématographiques complètes* ('Complete Cinematic Works') which was published by Gallimard and which seemed to mark Debord's entry into the pantheon of cinematic artists. It was however an obvious ironic, even sarcastic, gesture, if not a sign of defeat, from a man whose life and career had been dedicated to destroying 'the civilisation of the image'.

In the early part of the year, much to Guy's delight, Alice had herself published with Gallimard her second volume on underworld slang, *L'Essence du jargon*. Alice herself, with a heavy heart, continued to look after the house, look after Guy and think about their life together as something which was already moving into the past. She began to compose poetry, fragile, elegiac pieces which revealed a complicity and intimate understanding of Debord's emotional life. She called him 'The Prince of Division', acknowledging his Mephisthophelean aspect whilst knowing that a part of herself would leave with him when the time came. 'I am frightened of the night, I am frightened of the day which follows, frightened of love, frightened of life without him,' she wrote in a poem.[1]

The autumn in the Auvergne had been especially wet that year and the incessant rain and mist made Champot, more than ever, seem at a far distant remove from the world. Guy and Alice were visited in October by Ricard Paseyro, a Parisian friend of Uruguayan extraction who had spent time in several European prisons for political agitation and who shared with Guy a love of Golden Age Spanish poetry. Paseyro recalled that, on his arrival at the house, Guy had put down his glass, but was too ill to get up and greet him. There was, as ever, a lighthearted conversation and the familiar exquisite courtesy which Guy conferred upon his friends.[2]

Paseyro had brought with him Georges Monti, the owner of the publishing house Le Temps Qu'il Fait who had published Debord's translations of Jorge Manrique. They discussed together a new book, a collection of Debord's contracts with Lebovici and others, which would bring into the open the true workings behind the so-called mystery of the notoriously enigmatic Guy Debord. There were to be no more secrets, at least no secrets which might reveal Debord's truest aims. Thus Debord insisted that for the cover of the book he wanted a picture of 'le bateleur', the mountebank or magician in the tarot pack. There was no occult significance to this: the tarot or *il taroccho*, dear to the gypsies Debord and Alice admired, is still played as a game in France and northern Italy. The art of the game of tarot is to conceal rather than reveal.

Some days after Monti's visit Debord wrote to the publisher to say that he had decided to publish these documents on the principle of 'sólo vivimos dos días' ('we only have two days to live'). He also insisted that the tarot card of the 'bateleur' be used as a final statement about his work: 'It seems to me that this card would add, without having to suggest it in too positive a manner, something which could be seen as a certain mastery of manipulation, and which would opportunely recall all its mysterious qualities.'[3]

Darkness fell early on 30 November in Champot where, as the afternoon moved into evening, Guy Debord put a single bullet through his heart.

AFTERWORD

Spectators of Suicide

As in the Game of Chance
When the dice is thrown
The game is done.
It is already too late.

Alice Becker-Ho, *Comme aux jeux de hasard*

Everything happened very quickly on the evening of 4 October 1994. It was shortly after nine o'clock when two young philosophy students from the Universtiy of Nanterre, scene of so much agitation in the 1960s, left their squat in the Paris suburbs and stole two guns from a police compound on the outskirts of Paris before hijacking a taxi and ordering the terrified driver to head for place de la Nation, a busy and bleak intersection at the eastern edge of the city. At Nation, the pair, laughing and in a party mood, shot dead two policemen, Laurence Gérard and Thierry Maymard, who had been pursuing them, as well as the taxi driver, Amadou Diallo. In the confusion they were able somehow to evade the police and hijack another car, this time a Renault Cinq. As they veered towards one of the main roads out of Paris through the Bois de Vincennes, a police motorcycle skidded in front of them barring their exit. Another policeman, Guy Jacob, was shot dead before police were able to shoot back, immediately killing the boy, twenty-two-year-old Audry Maupin. It was still only 9.30. Everything had happened in half an hour.

The girl, nineteen-year-old Florence Rey, beautiful, blonde and insolent, refused to speak to police or reporters. At first the papers described the couple as a latter-day Bonnie and Clyde, perhaps inspired by Luc Besson's film *Nikita* or Oliver Stone's *Natural Born Killers*, both then showing on the Champs-Élysées. *Paris-Match*, in grim parody of *Hello!*, devoted a three-page photo spread to the killers' apartment – half-eaten bowls of taboulé, cinema posters, maps of Paris, a hunting licence and an empty bottle of Jack Daniel's.

But then details emerged of Rey's fascination with Surrealism and radical politics. Extracts from her writings for the self-styled 'Organisation of

Revolutionary Propaganda' were published which referred to 'the spectacle of daily life' and other Situationist terms. *Le Figaro* described the pair as 'Enragés' and made much of the fact that they were both students at Nanterre, the hotbed of violent dissent in 1968. *Le Nouvel observateur* talked of 'textes situationnistes'. *France 2* went further and described them as 'great admirers of Guy Debord'. There was excited speculation about a third accomplice, a 'Situationist film-maker' (apparently a certain Stéphane Viollet), who, with a grant from the Ministry of Culture, had made an underground film and was now on the run. This film, *De la politique*, depicting the assassination of a policeman was, it was rumoured, passed clandestinely around Paris as a kind of hard-Left snuff movie. Meanwhile, Florence defiantly turned her back on the examining court (presided over by Hervé Stephan, who would later be in charge of the inquest into the spectacular death of Princess Diana) and denounced the whole charade as 'spectacle'. The press made much of scraps of paper found in the squat, apparently part of a game of chance invented by Maupin and Rey, on which were written 'Killers', 'A gun in the hand so that everything becomes clear' and 'No Future!' 'We are all going to die,' wrote Florence in one of her tracts. 'Why live for others. This is not our world.'[1]

It was not long before Florence Rey became a heroine.[2] Patrick Besson, writer and champion of the socially excluded and dispossessed, quickly published a book, *Sonnet pour Florence Rey*, a text in praise of 'social revolt'. Gérard Guégan, who shortly after Debord's death wrote a pamphlet attacking Debord as a failure and manipulator, joined in the fray, claiming that he had lived briefly in the same building as the family of Florence Rey who, in 'the autumn of 1995 was claimed by neo-Debordists, who never fuck and who have never shot a gun, as a Situationist revenger'.[3] Sociologists and criminologists wrung their hands on television and despaired of French youth. Rappers from the *cités*, the council estates of Paris, Marseilles and Lyons, fell in love with the sexy and deadly 'cop-killer' who hated the French state as much as they did and who turned her back on its representative authorities. Debate raged in the pages of *Libération*, *Les Inrockuptibles* and *Le Monde* as to whether this was a genuine act of revolt or a pointless psychopathic murder. In the same pages, journalists with a nostalgia for 1968 and the revolutionary avant-gardes of the early part of the century remembered Germaine Berton, the Anarchist 'exterminating angel' who in 1924 had shot one of the leaders of the Right-wing league Action Française. She had been much admired by the Surrealists for having acted out André Breton's dictum that the truest Surrealist act was to go down to the street and to shoot randomly at passers-by.

When the events happened, Debord had already planned his suicide and, in Champot, in pain and with difficulty, was putting the final touches to his film *Guy Debord, son art et son temps*, the film commissioned for the Soirée Guy Debord on Canal Plus. The opening scenes of the film were a televised studio debate from 1988 on *Commentaries on the Society of the Spectacle*. 'Debord makes the spectacle his Satan,' argued one of the panellists. 'But what I criticise most of all in Monsieur Debord's work is that he justifies violence. And that is unacceptable.'

Debord had selected this extract to begin his film for a clear reason. He saw this deliberate misrepresentation of his work as an example of the way in which the seamless global language of the 'integrated spectacle', which endlessly falsifies the world so that nothing makes sense, absorbs dissident voices so that they can no longer be heard.

The revolutions of 1989, Debord argued elsewhere in the film, were a further part of this process. All that really happened that year, he said, was that fake Communism was replaced by the fake freedoms of consumerist capitalism. No one had really gained anything. The spectacle alone had triumphed, consigning real critical thought, with Marx and Hegel, to the dustbin of history. The result of this was what Debord called 'the world which cannot be verified'. I recalled Debord's description during a trip to Bucharest in 1996 with Gavin Bowd to interview Nicu Ceauşescu, the late dictator's alcoholic son, for the *Sunday Telegraph*. Nicu had died as we were flying over to Romania and on our arrival we found ourselves attending his funeral. This turned out to be a neat demonstration of Debord's notion of the non-verifiable world, as Nicu was mourned by millions in the East as a saint whilst, at precisely the same moment, he was being reviled in the West as a genocidal murderer, rapist and 'a surreal monster'.

The concept of the spectacle implies of course that someone had put the spectacle in place. In 1967, it had been enough for Debord to argue in *The Society of the Spectacle* that the spectacle was organised by those governments who enshrined capitalist economics as their defining faith. By 1994 the world had become more complex. Most crucially, the world was now dominated not by governments but by images. International media corporations were phantom states shadowing the world, with real political power everywhere more distant and invisible. In another key scene in the film *Guy Debord, son art et son temps* a group of African immigrant girls are reading Zola's *Au Bonheur des dames* with a white middle-class teacher in the Parisian suburbs. When they are asked what century they are living in, they reply in all seriousness that they do not know. This scene has no metaphorical importance, but stands as a literal representation of the fact that, like all of us in the society of the spectacle, the girls are condemned to a perpetual present which they cannot understand or alter.

If Debord himself is still read in the twenty-first century it will be because of this insight. His analysis of the way in which the eradication of history has been taking place in front of our eyes and beyond our control is, I think, the clearest and most penetrating diagnosis of the causes and the nature of the most extreme forms of contemporary alienation. It follows from this logic that it is no accident that the texts of a nihilist assassin like Florence Rey can read like Situationist theory. In the society of the spectacle, where time and place have become irrelevant, there is literally nowhere for the alienated individual to go, nowhere to hide. The crisis point is reached when, as it was for Rey and Maupin in the Nanterre squat, as it is for countless spectators of their own lives across the globe, the limited choices of individuals are revealed to them in a blinding moment of lucidity. 'It appears like lightning, which we know only when it strikes,' wrote Debord. Situationist theory does not advocate modern, mindless violence but it understands it perfectly. Suicide or revolution.

This stark opposition is best described in the short Situationist text, *Le Décor et les spectateurs du suicide* ('The décor and spectators of suicide'), written in 1966 in the wake of the supreme 'potlatch' of the Watts riots. In this text Debord described how the central function of modern life is to accumulate empty gifts which because they are meaningless are also deadly. 'Recently in France,' he wrote, 'a certain Bernard Durin killed himself – apparently without reason. He was thirty-seven years old and had been a model employee for the last fifteen of them. Everyone who knew agreed that "he had everything one needs to be happy". He had a ten-year-old daughter, Agnès, who got on well at school. A charming wife. A good job at IBM. A salary of F2,500 a month. An attractively furnished modern apartment. A 404. A television, a washing machine and even an aquarium. . . . That was his life: electronics, skyscraper housing estates, cars, refrigerators and televisions. It was also his death.'

Before his own eyes Guy Debord had seen himself become a classic and a commodity. Like the hated enemies Althusser, Foucault and Lacan, he was now a subject for academic scrutiny on both sides of the Atlantic. Philippe Sollers described him as a prophet of the post-modern age; Régis Debray admired his unsettling but sophisticated radicalism; Gallimard reprinted his works in paperback. The best-selling weekly in France, *Les Inrockuptibles*, named its listing pages for Paris nightlife 'Guide d'Abord (La société du spectacle)' in a final insulting pun.

Debord had also become that most disgusting form of modern phonomena, 'a celebrity'. In recent times, he had his celebrity status grotesquely underlined by acquiring his own 'stalker'. The goonish author of cheap detective novels, Bertrand Delcour had, much to Guy and Alice's irritation, followed them around Debord's favoured Left Bank haunts for a month; the results of Delcour's activities were published in the novel *Blocus Solus* which features a character called Guy Bordeux, the suicidal leader of the notorious 'Simultationist International'. The Florence Rey affair had confirmed this revolting celebrity status even more vividly, whilst the loose and accusatory use of the term 'Situationist' in media reports of the murder only furthered Debord's perception that since the death of Lebovici there had been a concerted campaign by 'spectacular forces' to harass and destroy him. Guy Debord would not however leave final victory to the 'spectacle'.

The first screening of *Guy Debord, son art et son temps* took place at the headquarters of Canal Plus in Paris on 15 December two weeks after Debord's death. The atmosphere was festive, more of a wake than a funeral, and the invited audience of publishers, journalists, former Situationists and enemies received the film, almost unanimously, as a great work. The first public screening took place on Canal Plus on the evening of 9 January, with the film as the centrepiece of the Soirée Guy Debord planned by Debord and Brigitte Cornand. The film was shown alongside *The Society of the Spectacle*, *Refutation* and, most enigmatically, *Latcho Drom*, a film by Tony Gatlif, a friend who had initiated Guy and Alice into the gypsy world and who had embodied for them the principle of 'never using the language of the enemy'.

Guy Debord, son art et son temps had been conceived by Debord as 'anti-televisual'. It is accordingly largely composed of images borrowed from the spectacular society which make up a fresco of unrelenting bleakness: the heart of old Paris dies within a lifetime; forests are attacked by fire and acid rain; high-rise blocks are demolished; teachers are attacked by their pupils in decaying suburban schools; the Aral Sea is turned into a desert and Chernobyl poisons the Ukraine; a Somali mob lynches a woman as UN peacekeepers look on; in the name of bringing us the truth, television shows live coverage of a South American child drowning in mud. The film was prefaced with a quotation from Lautréamont's *Poésies*: 'I write my thoughts with order, with an unconfused design. If they are true, the first to come will be a consequence of the others. That is the real order.' It followed from this logic, a logic which had consistently dictated the rules of Debord's war against the spectacular society, that his first and only appearance on television was in the form of a suicide note. 'Faithful to his word,' commented Patrick Mosconi, describing this event in his notes to the posthumous second edition of *Panegyric*, 'Guy Debord was not there.'

One of the hardest things I have ever had to do was to ask Alice Debord about the death of her husband. As we sat around the table in Alice's apartment in the Marais, with my wife Carmel and Jean-Louis Rançon, and, over wine, cognac and whiskey, endlessly evoked Guy Debord, it seemed pointless to ask why he had killed himself. To anybody who knew Debord it was obvious: illness, pride, a refusal to give in to circumstance, a beautifully negative gesture which was both aesthetic and political, all played a part in his self-destruction. The stories and rumours which had circulated around Paris, linking him with Gérard Voitey and Roger Stéphane, Alice concluded, were no more than ridiculous fictions.

It was much harder for me to ask Alice about the concrete details of death, how she found the body, how she must have suffered then and during the days and weeks afterwards, how she had borne the all too human cost of his action.

She lit another cigarillo and was quiet for a moment as, now slightly drunk on cognac, I put the question to her. Throughout the evening Alice had been saying that I had to write this book for myself and that nothing was taboo, neither sex nor death. But how did she feel then? How did she feel now? These were not abstract questions, nothing to do with Hegelian philosophy or war games. Debord himself, quoting Pascal, knew this when he wrote 'the last act is always bloody'.

'I think it was beautiful,' she said. She recalled the days and years they had spent together, the people they had known and shared, how he enjoyed making her jealous with other lovers, and she pretended it didn't matter, the great adventure and game of their life. The end had not really been so hard, apart from the final moment, of course. And afterwards, when she had to survive and learn to live again. But she did survive, and now she could even enjoy her friends, talk and laugh with all the lightness which previously came from Guy and Alice together. 'There is grief and sadness, but they can be beautiful also. I really loved Guy and I think, I know, that he loved me, and when someone goes away for ever then it is an incredibly painful moment. But it is an intense moment. Guy loved intense moments, always intense moments.' There was a pause. 'It was magnificent. His death was the most beautiful gift he could have given me.'

The funeral on 5 December was a simple cremation in Saint-Étienne, the nearest big town to Champot. And then a few days later, Alice and a few friends went down to the Île du Square du Vert Galant. By poetic accident this spot, which extends into the Seine like the bow of a ship, was also where, on 11 March 1314, Jacques de Mulay, the great master of the Order of the Temple, and Guy, Commander of the Templars of Normandy, had been burned alive for heresy and sedition.

With a toast to Guy, Alice cast his ashes into the Seine.

Notes

Chapter 1: The Lost Domain

1   Jean-Michel Mension, *La Tribu* (Paris: Éditions Allia, 1998), p.47.
2   *Panegyric*, p.12.
3   Ibid., p.12.
4   Léon Trotsky, 'Louis-Ferdinand Céline et la littérature', *Cahiers de la Herne* (Baros: Gallimard, 1987), p.151.
5   Maurice Saillet, 'Notes pour une d'Isidore Ducasse et de ses écrits' in *Oeuvres Complètes de Lautréamont* (Paris: Gallimard, 1960), pp.21–2.
6   Ibid., p.32.
7   Ibid., p.29.
8   *Panegyric*, p.37.
9   Lautréamont, *Chants de Maldoror* (Paris, 1890), p.108.
10   Interview with Patrick Labaste, quoted in Christophe Bourseiller, *Vie et Mort de Guy Debord* (Paris: Plon, 1999), p.25.
11   *Panegyric*, p.34.

Chapter 2: 'Umor' and the Suicide Solution

1   *Panegyric*, p.21.
2   For an account of the relation between André Breton and Jacques Vaché see Jean Prasteau, 'Jacques Vaché: l'inspirateur foudroyé du surréalisme', *Le Figaro* (14 April 1986). Debord himself would have encountered Vaché in any number of Surrealist texts by Breton, as well as Vaché's own text *Lettres de guerre*, published by Louis Aragon and André Breton in the journal *Littérature* in 1920–1.
3   Reprinted in Maurice Nadeau, *Histoire du Surréalisme* (Paris: Seuil, 1964), p.112.
4   André Breton, *Anthologie de l'humeur noir* (Paris: Gallimard, 1940), p.365.
5   Maurice Nadeau, op. cit., p.163.
6   A reliable account of Cravan's life can be found in Roger Shattuck, *The Banquet Years* (London: Faber and Faber, 1955), pp.220–1, 271–2. Ref-

erences to Cravan are scattered throughout Breton's writings, which is where Debord would have first read about him.

7   Arthur Rimbaud, *Une Saison en enfer* (Paris, 1874), p.34.

Chapter 3: The Demolition Expert

1   The term 'Letterist' is the word chosen by the Letterists themselves to translate the French term 'Lettriste' into English. See for example the pamphlet 'If you believe you have genius . . .', reprinted in Jean-Michel Mension, *La Tribu* (Paris: Éditions Allia, 1998), p.49.
2   *Panegyric*, p.16.
3   Interview with Isidore Isou, Paris, 26 April 1999.
4   Two interesting accounts of Isou's participation in the Cannes Film Festival were given by Jean-Michel Mension and Isou himself in *Les Nuits magnétiques*, a documentary history of the Situationist International broadcast on FM Paris 7, 8, 9 and 10 May 1996.
5   Isidore Isou, 'Le manifeste du cinéma discrépant' (Paris: Gallimard, 1952), p.3.
6   *Les Nuits magnétiques*, op. cit., interview with Marc O.
7   Isidore Isou, *L'Agrégation d'un nom et d'un messie* (Paris: Gallimard, 1947). A reading of this text and Isou's early poetry can be found in Andrew Hussey, 'La Divinité d'Isou': The Making of a Name and a Messiah', *Forum for Modern Language Studies* (Oxford University Press, 2000), vol. xxxvi, no. 2, pp.132–43.
8   Isou, *L'Agrégation d'un nom et d'un messie*, pp.241–2.
9   Interview with Isidore Isou, Paris, 26 April 1999.
10 Giuseppe Ungaretti, *Sentimento del tempo* (Rome: Vallechi Editore, 1996), p.32.
11 Isou, *L'Agrégation d'un nom et d'un messie*, p.434.
12 'Lettre à Isidore Isou', *Correspondance de Champ Libre*, vol. II, Paris, 1978, p.143.
13 'Prolegomena for all future cinema', *Ion*, 1952, p.56.
14 *Panegyric*, p.17.

Chapter 4: Like a Pack of Bastard Dogs

1   See Willemijn Stokvis, 'CoBra y el Stedelijk', in *Grupo CoBra, Obras de la colección del Stedelijk Museum de Amsterdam* (Madrid: Fundación La Caixa, 1996), p.11. See also Willemijn Stokvis, *CoBra* (Amsterdam: Librero/Poligrafa, 1994).
2   Jean-Michel Mension, *La Tribu* (Paris: Éditions Allia, 1998), p.46.

3 Ed van der Elsken, *Parijs, Fotos 1950–1954* (Amsterdam: Van Gennep, 1993), unpaginated.

4 Ibid.

5 Jean-Michel Mension, op. cit., pp. 104–5.

6 Isidore Isou, *Front de la jeunesse* (Paris, 1950), reprinted in Jean-Louis Brau, *Cours, camarade, le vieux monde est derrière toi! Histoire du mouvement révolutionnaire étudiant en Europe* (Paris: Albin Michel, 1968), appendix.

7 Ibid.

8 Ibid.

9 Ed van der Elsken, op. cit., 1993.

10 Interview with Ralph Rumney, Manosque, 12 June 1998.

Chapter 5: Howling in Favour of Sade

1 *Panegyric*, p.25.

2 The text of this has been reprinted as Gil Wolman, *L'Anticoncept* (Paris: Éditions Allia, 1994).

3 *In girum imus nocte et consumimur igni*, p. 27.

4 'Prolegomena to Any Future Cinema', *Ion*, 1951, p.41.

5 Georges Bataille, 'Le jeu lugubre', *Oeuvres Complètes*, I (Paris: Gallimard, 1970), pp.147–9.

6 'Hurlements en faveur de Sade', reprinted in *Les Lèvres nues*, 7 December 1955, Brussels, pp. 18–23.

7 Ibid., p.20.

8 Ibid., p.21.

9 Raymond Queneau, 'Sade, mon prochain?', *Nouvelle Critique* 34, 1952, p.23.

10 Jules Janin, *Oeuvres Complètes*, I (Paris, 1963), p.123.

11 André Breton, *Premier Manifeste du surréalisme* (Paris: Gallimard, 1924), p.14.

12 Jean-Michel Mension, *La Tribu* (Paris: Éditions Allia, 1998), p.29.

13 Jean-Michel Mension, *Les Nuit magnétiques*.

14 *Documents rélatifs à la fondation de l'internationale situationniste*, ed. Gérard Bérreby (Paris: Allia, 1985), p.147.

15 Ibid., p.134.

16 Interview with Isidore Isou, Paris, 26 April 1999.

17 Bérreby, *Documents*, op. cit., p.154.

Chapter 6: Playtime

1 An account of this is given in Stephen Barber, *Weapons of Liberation*

(London: Faber and Faber, 1996), pp.18–19.

2 Jean-Michel Mension, *La Tribu* (Paris: Éditions Allia, 1998) p.48.

3 Malcolm Lowry, 'Letter to Jonathan Cape', reprinted in Gordon Bowker, *Pursued by Furies. A Life of Malcolm Lowry* (London: HarperCollins, 1994), p.448.

4 Interview with Ralph Rumney, Manosque, 8 August 2000.

5 Ibid.

6 Johan Huizinga, *Homo Ludens, essai sur la fonction sociale du jeu* (Paris: Gallimard, 1951), pp.34–45; 124.

7 Reprinted in Jean-Michel Mension, op. cit., p.49.

8 Ibid., p.121.

9 Ibid., p.125.

Chapter 7: Who is 'Potlatch'?

1 *Potlatch*, p.11.

2 *Potlatch*, pp.13–14.

3 Ibid., pp.14–15.

4 *Potlatch*, pp.11–12.

5 *Potlatch*, p.87.

6 *Potlatch*, p.57.

7 Ibid., p.95.

8 Ibid., pp.50–1.

9 Georges Clutesi, *Potlatch* (British Columbia: Gary's Publishing, 1969), p.156.

10 See Georges Bataille, 'La Somme athéologique', I, II, *Oeuvres Complètes*, Tomes V, VI, and 'La Part Maudite', *Oeuvres Complètes*, Tome VII (Paris: Gallimard, 1976).

11 This anecdote is recounted in Michel Surya, *Georges Bataille, La Mort à l'oeuvre* (Paris: Gallimard, 1978), pp. 244–7.

12 Jean-Michel Mension, *La Tribu* (Paris: Éditions Allia, 1998), p.87.

13 See Georges Bataille, 'Théorie du 'potlatch', *Oeuvres Complètes*, Tome VII, pp.71–3. Bataille had also by this stage published an article on Isidore Isou which had been well received in Letterist circles. See Georges Bataille, 'La divinité d'Isou' *Oeuvres Complètes*, Tome XI, p.379 (Paris: Gallimard, 1976).

14 'Les cathares avait raison', *Potlatch 1954–57*, pp.36–43.

Chapter 8: Paris without Spectacle

1 'Introduction à une critique de la géographie urbaine', *Les Lèvres nues*, September 1955, p.11.

2   *Potlatch*, p.17.
3   Ibid., p.89.
4   Ibid., p.91.
5   Jean-Michel Mension, *Les Nuits magnétiques*.
6   Ibid.
7   *Internationale situationniste*, I, 1957, p.12.
8   *Potlatch* 12, p.34.
9   'Formulaire pour un urbanisme nouveau', *Internationale situationniste*, 1, pp.24–9. The origins of Chtcheglov's use of the term 'hacienda' are still obscure, even to many Letterists and Situationists who cited this piece as a turning point in the development of 'psychogeography'.
10 Jean-Michel Mension, *La Tribu* (Paris: Éditions Allia, 1998), p.56.
11 *Potlatch* 3, p.4.
12 *Potlatch* 6, p.5.
13 *Potlatch* 9, p.7.
14 Jean-Michel Mension, op.cit., p.56.
15 *Panegyric*, p.34.
16 Jean-Michel Mension, op.cit., p.56.

Chapter 9: The Wreckers of Civilisation

1   *Potlatch* 9, p.10.
2   *Les Lèvres nues* 4, Brussels, 1955, p.12.
3   Ibid., 8, front cover.
4   Ibid., pp.10–14.
5   Ibid., p.11.
6   Ibid., p.11.
7   Constant, *Pour une architecture de situation* (Paris, 1953).
8   'Manifestes de CoBra', 1949, reprinted in *Documents relatifs à la fondation de l'Internationale situationniste*, ed. Gérard Bérreby (Paris: Allia, 1985), p.12.
9   Juan Goytisolo, *Forbidden Territory*, trans. Peter Bush (San Francisco: North Point Press, 1990), p.123.
10 Christophe Bourseiller, *Vie et mort de Guy Debord* (Paris: Plon, 1999), p.106.
11 Ibid., p.106.
12 'Guy Debord et le mal', unpublished typescript, 1957, Situationist Archive, Institute of Social History, Amsterdam.
13 An account of the early work of this group is given in 'Il Giardino d'Albisola', Umberto Gambetta, *Studies and Archives of Western European Avant-Gardes* (Genoa: Sandro Ricaldone, 1997).
14 Accounts of Michèle Bernstein, Ralph Rumney, Piero Simondo,

interviews and conversations, Salisbury, Manosque, Turin, 1997–9. See also the film by Monica Repetto, *Dérive Gallizio* (Alba: Fondazione Ferrero, 2000), which includes interviews with Ralph Rumney, Piero Simondo and Giorgio Gallizio.

15 'Intervista a Piero Simondo, Jorn, L'arte e la scienza, il laboratorio . . .', Umberto Gambetta, op. cit.

16 G. E. Debord, 'Rapport sur la construction des situations et sur les conditions de l'organisation et de l'action de la tendance situationniste internationale', Cosio, July 1957, reprinted in *Documents relatifs à la fondation de l'Internationale situationniste*, Paris, 1985, pp.245–50.

Chapter 10: The Art of the Future

1 Interview with Ralph Rumney, Manosque, 9 August 2000.

2 'Rapport sur la construction des situations et sur les conditions de l'organisation et de l'action de la tendance situationniste internationale', in *Documents relatifs à la fondation de l'Internationale situationniste*, ed. Gérard Bérreby, (Paris: Allia, 1985), pp.609–19.

3 Guy Debord, *Correspondance*, volume 1, juin 1957–août 1960, ed. Alice Debord (Paris: Fayard, 1999), p.23.

4 Interview with Ralph Rumney, Manosque, 8 August 2000.

5 'Fin de Copenhague', in Bérreby, op. cit., pp.550–95.

6 *The Naked City: illustration de l'hypothèse des plaques tournantes en psychogéographie*, screenprint 33 x 47.5cm.

Chapter 11: A Civil War in France

1 *Potlatch*, pp.269–70.

2 'Introduction', *Mémoires*, reprinted by Jean-Jacques Pauvert aux Belles Lettres, Paris, 1963, unpaginated.

3 An account of this period is given in Gavin Bowd, *The Outsiders, Alexander Trocchi and Kenneth White* (Kirkcaldy: Akros, 1998), pp.9–14.

4 Guy Debord, *Correspondance*, volume 1, juin 1957–août 1960, ed. Alice Debord (Paris: Fayard, 1999) p.121, 233.

5 Asger Jorn, 'Les situationnistes et l'automation', *IS*, 1, pp.22–5.

6 Ibid., pp.15–20.

7 Ibid., pp.20–21.

8 Ibid., pp.13–14. Translated by Ralph Rumney.

9 Ibid., p.28.

10 Interview with Ralph Rumney, Manosque, 12 June 1998.

11 Interviews with Ralph Rumney, Manosque, 1998 and 2000. See also

Ted Morgan, *William Burroughs, Literary Outlaw* (London: The Bodley Head, 1983).

12 *Potlatch*, pp.196–7.
13 These ideas are developed most clearly by Henri Lefebvre in his book, *La Somme et le reste* (Paris: La Nef de Paris, 1959).
14 'Une guerre civile en France', *IS* 1, p.32.

Chapter 12: Scandals and Supreme Tricks

1 Reprinted in *IS* 2, p.12.
2 Ibid., p.3.
3 For an account of this encounter see Philippe Sollers, 'Solitude de Bataille', *Les Temps Modernes* 602, 1999, pp.246–63.
4 Interview with Philippe Sollers, Paris, 11 February 1996.
5 Interview with Henri Lefebvre conducted by Kristin Ross, 1983, reprinted in *October* 79, 1997.
6 Reprinted in *Archives situationnistes, Volume 1, Documents traduits 1958–1970* (Paris: Contre-Moule/Parallèles Éditeurs, 1997), p.11.
7 A comic strip documenting this event produced by SPUR is reproduced in *Archives situationnistes*, p.49.
8 Ibid., pp.150–2.
9 Ibid., p.150.
10 *IS* 2, pp.27–30.
11 David Harvey, 'Afterword', in Henri Lefebvre, *The Production of Space*, trans. Donald Nicholson-Smith (Oxford: Blackwell, 1998), p.428. For an account of Lefebvre's remarkable life see also Rémi Hess, *Henri Lefebvre et l'aventure du siècle* (Paris: Editions A. M. Métailié, 1988).
12 Henri Lefebvre, *Critique de la vie quotidienne* I (Paris: Grasset, 1947).
13 Henri Lefebvre, *La Somme et le reste*, reprinted in *IS* 4, p.10.
14 *October* 79, 1997.
15 *IS* 2, pp.32–4.
16 Ibid., p.33.
17 Ibid., p.35.

Chapter 13: Psychogeographers at Work

1 *Panegyric*, p.36.
2 Ibid., p.36.
3 Guy Debord, *Correspondance*, volume 1, juin 1957–août 1960, ed. Alice Debord (Paris: Fayard, 1999), p.155.
4 *Panegyric*, p.35.

5   Interview with Jacqueline de Jong, Amsterdam, 20 June 2000.
6   Interview with Constant, Amsterdam, 21 June 2000.
7   *IS* I, p.16.
8   *Documents relatifs à la fondation de l'Internationale situationniste*, ed. Gérard Bérreby (Paris: Allia, 1985), p.616.
9   *IS* 2, pp. 31–2.
10 A good account of Fourier's ideas is given in Peter Marshall, *Demanding the Impossible* (London: HarperCollins, 1992), pp.150–1.
11 For an account of 'New Babylon' see Constant, *New Babylon, Art et Utopie, textes situationnistes* (Paris: Cercle d'Art, 1997) and Mark Wrigley, *Constant's New Babylon, The Hyper-Architecture of Desire* (Rotterdam: Centre for Contemporary Art, 1998).

Chapter 14: Socialism and Barbarism

1   Quoted in Greil Marcus, *Lipstick Traces* (Cambridge, Mass: Harvard University Press, 1989), pp.353–8.
2   *IS* 5, p.14.
3   This episode is recounted in Guy Atkins, *Asger Jorn* (London: Methuen, 1964), and reprinted in Iwona Blazwick, ed., *An Endless Adventure, an Endless Passion, an Endless Banquet: A Situationist Scrapbook* (London: ICA/Verso, 1989), p.59.
4   *October* 79, 1997.
5   An account of the drawing up of this manifesto and intellectual reaction to it can be found in Mark Polizzotti, *Revolution of the Mind: The Life of André Breton* (London: Bloomsbury, 1995), pp.601–2.
6   Pierre Guillaume, 'Guy Debord', *La Vieille Taupe, Organe de critique et d'orientation postmessianique*, I (Paris, 1996). For a discussion of Debord's status amongst 'negationist' or Right-wing 'revisionist' thinkers see also Philippe Sollers, 'Debord', *Magazine Littéraire, une inventaire de la pensée moderne 1966–96*, hors-série, 1996, pp.12–15.
7   Roger Garaudy, *Les Mythes fondateurs de la politique israélienne* (Paris: Samiszdat/ Roger Garaudy/ Librairie Roumaine de Paris, 1996), pp.151–69.
8   Debord was originally quoted by Guillaume in *Annales d'histoire révisionniste* (Paris: La Vieille Taupe, 1989). An account of the outcome of Garaudy's trial can be found in *Le Monde*, 2 March 1998, p.25.

Chapter 15: No Dialogue With Cunts

1   'Perspectives de modifications conscientes dans la vie quotidienne', *IS* 8, pp. 20–7.

2   Interview with Constant, Amsterdam, 21 June 2000.
3   *IS* 8, p.33.
4   Ibid., pp. 23–6.
5   'I can only think of Debord with anger', letter to the author from Jörgen Nash, 1 July 2000.
6   Guy Debord, 'Les thèses de Hambourg en Septembre 1961 (Note pour servir à l'histoire de l'internationale situationniste)', Annexe 3, in *Internationale situationniste 1958–1968* (Paris: Arthème Fayard, 1997).
7   'Nicht Hinauslehnen', reprinted in *Archives situationnistes, Volume 1, Documents traduits en 1958–1970* (Paris: Contre-Moule/Parallèles Éditeurs, 1997), pp.82–3.
8   Interview with Jacqueline de Jong, Amsterdam, 20 June 2000.
9   Ibid.
10 Ibid.

Chapter 16: Gangland and Philosophy

1   The first and only public account of this incident is given in Natasha Walter, 'Nicholas Walter, Obituary', *Independent*, 13 March 2000.
2   Guy Debord, 'Les situationnistes et les nouvelles formes d'action dans la politique ou l'art', in *Destruktion af RSG-6*, Galerie Exi, Odense, 1963.
3   *IS* 10, pp.73–4.
4   *IS* 9, pp.21–2.
5   Ibid., pp.22–3.
6   Ibid., p.37.
7   Greil Marcus, *Lipstick Traces* (Cambridge, Mass.: Harvard University Press, 1989), p.487.
8   See Guy Debord, *Correspondance*, volume 1, juin 1957–août 1960, ed. Alice Debord (Paris: Fayard 1999), p.35.
9   Andrew Hussey, 'The self-concealing situation', *TLS*, 21 August 1999, p.29.

Chapter 17: The Situationist International Anti-Public Relations Service

1   *IS* 8, p.60.
2   Ibid., p.48.
3   Greil Marcus, *Lipstick Traces* (Cambridge, Mass.: Harvard University Press, 1989), pp.385–8.
4   'Le cinéma après Alain Resnais', *IS* 3, pp.8–10.

5   Friedrich Nietzsche, *The Birth of Tragedy in the Spirit of Music*, trans. Walter Kaufman (New York: Random House, 1992), pp.57–8.
6   Friedrich Nietzsche, fragment numéro 6 (360), *Oeuvres philosophiques complètes* (Paris: Gallimard, 1970).
7   'Maintenant, l'IS', *IS* 9, pp.3–5.
8   Ibid., p.5.
9   *IS* 10, pp.70–1.
10 Christophe Bourseiller, *Vie et mort de Guy Debord* (Paris: Plon, 1999), p.154.

Chapter 18: Exit, Far Left, the Mysterious Mr K

1   Christophe Bourseiller, *Vie et mort de Guy Debord* (Paris: Plon, 1999), p.214.
2   The relation between Perec and the Situationists is described in David Bellos, *Georges Perec, a Life in Words* (London: HarperCollins, 1994), pp.280–1.
3   'Le déclin et la chute de l'économie spectaculaire marchande', *IS* 10, pp.3–11.
4   *De la misère en milieu étudiant, considérée sous ses aspects économique, politique, psychologique, sexuel et notamment intellectuel et de quelques moyens pour y remédier*, par des membres de l'Internationale situationniste et des étudiants de Strasbourg (Paris: Champ Libre, 1996), p.9.
5   Ibid., p.3.
6   The clearest account of the events in Strasbourg is given in Pascal Dumontier, *Les Situationnistes et Mai 68* (Paris: Éditions Ivrea, 1995). See also Andrew Hussey, 'Abolish Everything!', *London Review of Books*, 2 September 1999, pp.29–32.
7   Dumontier, op. cit., p.90.
8   Ibid., p.92.

Chapter 19: Heatwave

1   Olivier Todd, 'Strasbourg en Situation', *Le nouvel observateur*, 21 December 1996.
2   Dominique Jamet, 'La prise de pouvoir des "situationnistes" à Strasbourg', *Le Figaro littéraire*, 1 December 1966.
3   Interview with Brigid Berlin, New York City, 1 March 1996.
4   Christophe Bourseiller, *Vie et mort de Guy Debord* (Paris: Plon, 1999), p.241.
5   Conversation with Ralph Rumney, Manosque, 9 August 2000.

6 The English Section of the Situationist International, 'The revolution of modern art, the modern art of revolution', reprinted in *King Mob Echo* (Edinburgh: Dark Star, 2000), pp.59–71.

7 It should be noted that, according to Donald Nicholson-Smith, there was in fact no 'English section' of the Situationist International at this time, with all fully fledged Situationists belonging to the Paris-based group (Letter to the author from Donald Nicholson-Smith, 1999).

8 Jonathon Green, *Days in the Life: Voices from the English Underground* (London: Heinemann, 1988), pp.249–50.

9 Ibid., p.250.

10 Ibid., p.251.

11 Interview in Jon Savage, *England's Dreaming: The Sex Pistols and Punk Rock* (London: Faber and Faber, 1991), p.30.

12 Conversation with Jamie Reid, The Haçienda, Manchester, 26 January 1996. See also Jamie Reid and Jon Savage, *Up they Rise! The Incomplete Works of Jamie Reid* (London: Faber and Faber, 1987), pp.40–4.

13 Conversation with Anthony Wilson, The Haçienda, Manchester, 30 October 1995. See also Mark E. Smith, Anthony Wilson, Jon King, Stewart Home, 'Situationist Fall-out: Punk Rock, New Wave and the End of the World', *The Hacienda Must Be Built: On the Legacy of Situationist Revolt*, eds Gavin Bowd and Andrew Hussey (Manchester: Aura, 1996), unpaginated.

14 T. J. Clark, 'Introduction' to op. cit., Anselm Jappe, *Guy Debord* (Marseilles: Via Valeriano, 1995) p.ix.

15 Raoul Vaneigem, *Traité de savoir-vivre à l'usage des jeunes générations* (Paris: Gallimard, 1967), p.276.

16 Ibid., p.276.

17 Edmund Buchet, *Les auteurs de ma vie* (Paris: Buchet-Chastel, 1969), p.53.

18 *The Society of the Spectacle*, p.12.

19 Ibid., p.19.

20 Ibid., p.10.

21 Pierre Henri Simon, *Le Monde*, 14 February 1968.

22 Robert Kanters, 'Des iconoclastes parmi nous', *Le Figaro littéraire*, 25 December 1967.

23 François Châtelet, 'La dernière internationale', *Le nouvel observateur*, 3 January 1968.

24 *L'internationale situationniste, protagonistes, chronologie, bibliographie (avec un index des noms insultés)*, (Paris: Champ Libre, 1972), p.60.

Chapter 20: Days of Rage

1 David Caute, *The Year of the Barricades '68* (London: Paladin, 1988), p.78.
2 Ibid., pp.85–6.
3 Eric Hobsbawm, *Revolutionaries* (London: Abacus, 1990), p.123.
4 'Le déclin et la chute de l'économie spectaculaire marchande', *IS* 10, pp.3–11.
5 Christophe Bourseiller, *Vie et mort de Guy Debord* (Paris: Plon, 1999), p.261.
6 Ibid., p.262.
7 David Caute, op. cit., p.83.

Chapter 21: Paris Awakes!

1 David Caute, *The Year of the Barricades '68* (London: Paladin, 1988), p.191.
2 Ibid., p.190.
3 Christophe Bourseiller, *Vie et mort de Guy Debord* (Paris: Plon, 1999), p.269.
4 'La rage au ventre', in *Enragés et situationnistes dans le mouvement des occupations* (Paris: Gallimard, 1968), pp.260–1.
5 David Caute, op. cit., p.190.
6 Conversation with Jean-Marie Bienvenu, Manosque, 10 August 2000.
7 These slogans and graffiti are reproduced in *Enragés et situationnistes dans le mouvement des occupations* (Paris: Gallimard, 1968).
8 Ibid., pp.301–3.
9 Ibid., p.275.
10 Interview with Jacqueline de Jong, Amsterdam, 20 June 2000.
11 Interview with Isidore Isou, Paris, 26 April 1999.

Chapter 22: In Time of War

1 Jamie Reid and Jon Savage, *Up they Rise! The Incomplete Works of Jamie Reid* (London: Faber and Faber, 1987), p.42.
2 *Enragés et situationnistes dans le mouvement des occupations* (Paris: Gallimard, 1968), p.212.
3 Pierre Viansson-Ponté, 'La révolution de mai continue d'exploser dans

les vitrines des librairies', *Le Monde*, 25 January 1969.

4   Jean-Louis Brau, *Cours, camarade, le vieux monde est derrière toi! Histoire du mouvement révolutionnaire étudiant en Europe* (Paris: Albin Michel, 1968), and Éliane Brau, *Le situationnisme ou la nouvelle internationale* (Paris: Nouvelles Éditions Debresse, 1968).
5   'Les démarcheurs abusifs', *IS* 12, p.91.
6   'Situationnistes en mauvaise situation', *La Révolution prolétarienne*, December 1968.
7   'Est récupéré qui veut bien', *IS* 12, p.97.
8   Bernard Pivot, 'Prix Sainte-Beuve sans bévue', *Le Figaro littéraire*, 16 December 1968.
9   Annexe to *Internationale Situationniste* (Amsterdam: Van Gennep, 1970).
10 *Panegyric*, p.3.
11 Ibid., p.25.

Chapter 23: Is the Reichstag Burning?

1   'Les ouvriers d'Italie et la révolte de Reggio de Calabre', *Section Italienne de l'internationale situationniste* (Paris: Contre-Moule, 1988), pp.125–35.
2   'Le retour de Charles Fourier', *IS* 12, p.97.
3   Christophe Bourseiller, *Vie et mort de Guy Debord* (Paris: Plon, 1999), p.291.
4   Ibid., p.300.
5   'Le commencement d'une époque', *IS* 12, pp.3–34.
6   Ibid.
7   Ibid., p.53.
8   *Section Italienne de l'internationale situationniste* (Paris: Contre-Moule, 1988), p.43.
9   An account of this period is given in Alessandro Silj, *Mai più senza fucile* (Florence: Vallechi Editore, 1977). See also *Ma l'amour mio non muore: origini documenti strategie della 'cultura alternativa' e dell 'underground' in Italia* (Rome: Castelvecchi, 1996).

Chapter 24: Without Dead Time

1   *Panegyric*, p.35.
2   Christophe Bourseiller, *Vie et mort de Guy Debord* (Paris: Plon, 1999), p.305.
3   This correspondence is held in the Situationist archive, Institute of Social History, Amsterdam.

4　'Lettre de démission', in *La véritable scission dans l'Internationale, circulaire public de l'Internationale situationniste*, unpublished translation by John McHale (Paris: Champ Libre, 1972).

5　Letter from Raoul Vaneigem to the author, 18 September 1999.

6　Alessandro Silj, *Mai più senza fucile* (Florence: Vallechi Editore, 1977), p.34.

7　*Section Italienne de l'internationale situationniste* (Paris: Contre-Moule, 1988), pp.134–7.

8　'I gruppuscoli rifiutavano il "modello Feltrinelli", *L'Espresso*, 18 March 1971.

9　*Corriere d'Informazione*, 21 March 1971.

10　Denis Lahaye, 'Un mouvement précurseur. L'Internationale Situationniste et "l'utopie concrète"', *Le Monde*, 1 October 1971.

11　'Spectacular', *TLS*, 19 February 1971.

12　*Actuel*, no. 3, December 1970.

Chapter 25: Fall-Out

1　Richard Gombin, *Les Origines du gauchisme* (Paris: Éditions du Seuil, 1971).

2　Jean-Jacques Raspaud and Jean-Pierre Voyer, *L'Internationale situationniste, protagonistes, chronologie, bibliographie, avec un index des noms insultés* (Paris: Champ Libre, 1972).

3　Internal documents of the Situationist International, Situationist Archive, Institute of Social History, Amsterdam.

4　*Le Monde*, 15 January 1972.

5　*La véritable scission dans l'Internationale, circulaire public de l'Internationale situationniste* (Paris: Champ Libre, 1972). The following quotations from this text are from an unpublished translation by John McHale.

6　A useful definition of Hegel's use of the key term *Aufhebung*, its use in *The Phenomenology of Mind*, and an explanation of the difficulty of its translation can be found in Charles Taylor, *Hegel* (London: Cambridge University Press, 1975), p.119. See also 'Translator's introduction' and 'Translator's note', Jacques Derrida, *Writing and Difference*, trans. Alan Bass (Chicago: University of Chicago Press, 1978), p.xix, p.335.

7　Interview with Gérard Guégan, Paris, 22 April 2000.

Chapter 26: Prince and Bandit

1　Interview with Gérard Guégan, Paris, 22 April 2000.

2   *Panegyric*, pp.44–5.
3   *The Society of the Spectacle*, p.125.
4   Ibid., p.38.
5   *Panegyric*, p.47.
6   Christophe Bourseiller, *Vie et mort de Guy Debord* (Paris: Plon, 1999), p.329.
7   Ibid., pp.347–8.
8   François Bott, 'La société du spectacle . . . en film. Le western théorique de Guy Debord', *Le Monde*, 9 May 1974.
9   Thomas Y. Levin, 'Dismantling the Spectacle: The Cinema of Guy Debord', in *On the Passage of a Few People through a Brief Moment of Time: The Situationist International 1957–1972*, ed. Elizabeth Sussman (Cambridge, Mass.: Boston/MIT Press, 1989).
10 Mark Polizzotti, op. cit., p.367.
11 'De l'architecture sauvage', in *Le Jardin d'Albisola* (Turin: Edizioni d'arte Fratelli Pozzo, 1974).
12 Ibid.

Chapter 27: The Courtier

1   'De l'architecture sauvage', unpaginated.
2   Baldassare Castiglione, *The Book of the Courtier*, trans. by Sir Thomas Hoby (London: Dent, 1975), p.151.
3   François Bott, 'Les Situationnistes et l'Économie cannibale', *Les Temps modernes*, 1974, p.2175.
4   Interview with Gérard Guégan, Paris, 22 April 2000.
5   An account of these events is given in Ralph Rumney, *Le Consul* (Paris: Allia, 1998), pp.94–7. Also interview with Ralph Rumney, Manosque, 12 January 1999.

Chapter 28: The Last Chance to Save Capitalism

1   *Panegyric*, p.37.
2   *The Society of the Spectacle*, p.13.
3   *Panegyric*, p.47.
4   Alessandro Silj, *Mai più senza fucile* (Florence: Vallechi Editore, 1977), pp. 31–7. For accounts of the background to Italian politics see also David Caute, *The Year of the Barricades '68* (London: Paladin, 1988), pp. 53–77; Anon., 'Nota alla seconda edizione' in *Ma l'amor mio non muore: origini documenti strategie della 'cultura alternativa' e dell' 'underground' in Italia* (Rome: Castevecchi, 1996), pp.2–5. Peter Marshall, *Demanding the Impossible* (London: HarperCollins, 1992), pp.446–53.

5   *Il Giorno*, 13 August 1975.
6   *Europeo*, 18 September 1975.
7   *Il resto di Carlino*, 11 September 1975.
8   *Panegyric*, p.47.
9   *Le Monde*, 24 February 1975.
10 Christophe Bourseiller, *Vie et mort de Guy Debord* (Paris: Plon, 1999), p.351.

Chapter 29: Fortresses, Firebombs and Films

1   *Panegyric*, pp.48–51.
2   *Le jeu de la guerre*, p.32.
3   Carl von Clausewitz, *On War*, trans. J. J. Graham (London: Wordsworth, 1997), p.296.
4   Reprinted in *Anarchy in the UK: The Angry Brigade*, English Psychogeography Series, ed. Tom Vague (Edinburgh: AK Press, 2000), p.51.
5   Jonathon Green, *Days in the Life: Voices from the English Underground* (London: Heinemann, 1988), p.351.
6   Heathcote Williams, *International Times*, 1977, reprinted in op. cit., *Anarchy in the UK: The Angry Brigade*, op. cit., p.25.
7   Jonathon Green, *All Dressed Up: The Sixties and the Counterculture* (London: Pimlico, 1999), pp.282–3.
8   Christophe Bourseiller, *Vie et mort de Guy Debord* (Paris: Plon, 1999), p.353.
9   *In girum imus nocte et consumimur igni*, p.61.

Chapter 30: Terrorism and the State

1   Gianfranco Sanguinetti, *On Terrorism and the State*, trans. Lucy Forsyth and Michel Prigent (London: Chronos, 1982).
2   Guy Debord, *Preface to the Fourth Italian Edition of The Society of the Spectacle*, trans. Michel Prigent and Lucy Forsyth (London: Chronos, 1983), p.18.
3   See Éditions Champ Libre, *Correspondance*, vol.2 (Paris: Éditions Ivrea, 1996), pp.15–27.
4   Ibid., p.109.
5   Ibid., p.84.
6   Ibid., p.86.
7   Christophe Bourseiller, *Vie et mort de Guy Debord* (Paris: Plon, 1999), p.357.

8 Francisco Umbral, *Y Tierno Galván ascendió a los cielos* (Madrid: Seix Barral, 1990), pp.13–15.
9 *Panegyric*, p.48.
10 *Panegyric*, p.48.
11 Bourseiller, op. cit., p.362.

Chapter 31: The World is Illusion

1 Lucy Forsyth, 'The Supersession of the SI' in *The Hacienda Must Be Built: On the Legacy of Situationist Revolt*, eds Gavin Bowd and Andrew Hussey (Manchester: AURA, 1996), pp.26–40.
2 Ibid., p.28.
3 Christophe Bourseiller, *Vie et mort de Guy Debord* (Paris: Plon, 1999), p.365.
4 Ibid., pp.72–3.
5 *Panegyric*, p.77.
6 Pascal Bonitzer, 'Graal filibuste', *Les Cahiers du cinéma*, July 1981.
7 Hélène Hazera, 'Un peuple sans images', *Libération*, 3 June 1981.
8 Gérard Guégan, 'Ni droite, ni gauche', *Les Nouvelles littéraires*, 4 June 1981.
9 Louis Marcorelles, 'Pavane pour amours déçues', *Le Monde*, 10–11 May 1981.
10 Vincent Rogard, 'Pour gogos en quête de gourou', *Télérama*, 13 June 1981.
11 *Panegyric*, p.17.
12 Bourseiller, op. cit., p.366.
13 Conversation with Cécile Guilbert, Paris, 2 May 2000.

Chapter 32: Death Instinct

1 See interview with Bruno Mesrine by Patricia Tourancheau, 'Il l'a échappé belle', *Libération*, 27 July 1998.
2 Gérard Lebovici, 'Note de l'Éditeur', in Jacques Mesrine, *L'Instinct de mort* (Paris: Éditions Ivrea, 1995).
3 This version of events is based on the account given in Pierre Assouline, 'Enquête sur un éditeur assassiné', *Lire*, May 1988, pp.45–55. See also 'Meutre en sous-sol', *L'Express*, 16–22 March 1984, for information about details of the shooting. Other important press coverage of the shooting is reprinted in *Gérard Lebovici, tout sur le personnage* (Paris: Éditions Champ Libre, 1984).
4 Serge de Breketch, *Minute*, 17 March 1984.

5   Conversation with Gérard Guégan, Paris, 22 April 2000.
6   See Jean-François Martos, *Correspondance avec Guy Debord* (Paris: Le fin mot de l'Histoire, 1998), pp.72–80. This book was withdrawn from sale in Paris after a court injunction launched by Alice Debord. There are also, tantalisingly, three letters dating from the period just after Lebovici's death which have not yet been made public. See op. cit., p.73.
7   Letter from Guy Debord to Floriana Lebovici, reprinted in *Des Contrats* (Cognac: Le Temps Qu'il Fait, 1995), p.63.
8   Jean-François Martos, *Correspondance avec Guy Debord*, p.190.
9   Ibid., pp.191–6.
10 'Note des éditeurs', *Gérard Lebovici, Tout sur le personnage* (Paris: Éditions Champ Libre, 1984).
11 Conversation with Patrick Mosconi, Paris, 11 November 1999.
12 Emmanuel Loi, 'Les lois de l'hospitalité chez Guy Debord', *Lignes*, 31 May 1997.

Chapter 33: Reflections on Violence

1   Jean-François Martos, *Correspondance avec Guy Debord* (Paris: Le fin mot de l'Histoire, 1998), pp.70–1.
2   *Considérations sur l'assassinat de Gérard Lebovici*, pp.87–8.
3   Ibid., p.74.
4   Ibid., p.92
5   *L'Encyclopédie des nuisances*, no. 5, November 1985.
6   Ibid., no. 9, November 1986.

Chapter 34: Bitter Victory

1   Christophe Bourseiller, *Vie et mort de Guy Debord* (Paris: Plon, 1999), pp.410–4.
2   *Panegyric*, p.51.
3   This debate is 'detourned' by Debord as the opening sequence of the film *Guy Debord, son art et son temps* (1995).
4   Useful accounts of the history of *Tel Quel* can be found in Philippe Forest, *Histoire de Tel Quel* (Paris: Éditions du Seuil, 1995), and Patrick ffrench, *The Time of Theory: A History of Tel Quel 1960–1983* (Oxford: Oxford University Press, 1995).
5   Interview with Philippe Sollers, Paris, 11 February 1996.
6   Bourseiller, op. cit., pp.404–5.
7   Conversation with Gérard Guégan, Paris, 21 April 2000.

8 Bourseiller, op. cit., pp.392–4, 400, 411, 413.
9 See, for example, the extracts from Debord's writing quoted in *Annales d'histoire révisionniste*, no. 5, Paris, 1988.
10 Brian Sewell, 'Creating a stink', *Evening Standard*, 13 July 1989.
11 Conversation with Greil Marcus, Manchester, 20 March 1996.
12 Greil Marcus, *Lipstick Traces* (Cambridge, Mass: Harvard University Press, 1989), p.2.
13 Ibid., pp.363–4.
14 Terry Eagleton, 'Rotten, Vicious and Surrealist', *New York Times*, 10 October 1990.
15 *Panegyric*, p.10.

Chapter 35: This Bad Reputation

1 An account of this affair is given in Christophe Bourseiller, *Vie et mort de Guy Debord* (Paris: Plon, 1999), pp.402–5. Lorenzo Valentin absolutely refuses to talk about Guy Debord and has 'consigned him to the past' (Letter to the author from Lorenzo Valentin, 12 October 1999).
2 Bourseiller, op. cit., pp.410–11.
3 Michel Bounan, *Le Temps du SIDA* (Paris: Éditions Allia, 1990).
4 The reader's report (by Donald Nicholson-Smith) has been placed in the 'Bounan Archive' in the Institute of Social History, Amsterdam.
5 Michel Bounan, *Incitation à l'autodéfense* (Paris: Éditions Allia, 1995)
6 *Panegyric*, p.70.
7 Ibid., p.71.
8 Conversation with Jean Baudrillard, Paris, 21 March 2000.
9 Louis Chevalier, *Classes laborieuses et classes dangereuses à Paris pendant la première moitié du XIXe siècle, avec 13 plans et graphiques en dépliant* (Paris: Plon, 1958).
10 See, for example, Oliver Wicker, 'Le grand flop de Guy Debord', *Globe-Hebdo*, 3 November 1993, and Jérôme Garcin, 'Journal Debord', *L'Événement du jeudi*, 11 November 1993.
11 Bourseiller, op. cit., p.418.
12 Ibid., pp.418–20.

Chapter 36: The Prince of Division

1 Alice Becker-Ho, 'Peur', *D'azur au triangle vidé de sable* (Cognac: Le temps qu'il fait, 1998), p.45.
2 Conversation with Irinée D. Lastelle, Manosque, 26 July 2000. See

also Ricardo Paseyro, 'Ma dernière rencontre avec Guy Debord', *Le Figaro*, 10–11 December 1994.

3 'Lettre de Guy Debord à Georges Monti', 27 novembre 1994, *Des Contrats*, p.65.

Afterword: Spectators of Suicide

1 *Paris-Match*, 12 October 1994, pp.25–9.
2 See, for example, Arnaud Viviant, 'Il faut sauver le soldat Rey', *Les Inrockuptibles*, 7–13 October 1998, p.12.
3 Gérard Guégan, *Markus Wolf avait une soeur, je l'ai aimée* (Paris: Grasset, 1997), pp.17–18.

Bibliography

Since the death of Guy Debord, the literature on his work and the activities of the Situationist International has become a veritable academic industry. This bibliography does not in any way claim to be definitive and the articles, essay and studies of Debord I have selected reflect only my personal taste and interests. There are, in any case, two bibliographies available in English and French which can lay claim to extensive coverage. These books are: (for resources in English) Simon Ford, *The Realization and Suppression of the Situationist International; An Annotated Bibliography 1972–1992* (Edinburgh: AK Press, 1995), and (for resources in French) Shigenobu Gonzalvez, *Guy Debord, ou la beauté du négatif* (Paris: Mille et une nuits, 1995).

I have also made extensive use of the Situationist archives held in the Institute of Social History in Amsterdam, the best and most complete collection of Situationist material in Europe, although it is a shame to have to report that in recent times certain documents have disappeared or been defaced. Other important archives which have informed this study are at Bibliothèque de Documentation Internationale Contemporaine (Nanterre), Bibliothèque Nationale de Paris, Bibliothèque du cinéma André Malraux (Paris), Biblioteca Nacional (Madrid), Fondació Antoni Tàpies (Barcelona), New York Public Library, Princeton University Library, Library of the Stedelijk Museum (Amsterdam), Boston University Library, John Rylands Library (Manchester). All interviews in the text are with the author unless otherwise stated. Readers still curious about Guy Debord and the Situationists are also referred to the archives of the Fondazione Feltrinelli in Milan.

You could of course also do worse than buy a book at either Un Regard Moderne (rue Gît-le-coeur) or Actualités (rue Dauphine) and take it to read in a bar on the rue de Buci. That is, after all, where the game began and what it was all about.

Works of Guy Debord

1952–7

'Prolégomènes à tout cinéma futur' and 'Hurlements en faveur de Sade' in *Ion* (Paris, 1952)

Internationale Lettriste, nos 1–4 (1952–4)

Potlatch 1954–57 (Paris: Gérard Lebovici, 1985) and *Guy Debord présente Potlatch* (Paris: Gallimard, 1996)

Les Lèvres nues (Brussels: 1954–8), reprinted by Éditions Allia, Paris, 1995

'Le Labyrinthe éducatif', internal document of the Letterist International (1956)

Guide psychogéographique de Paris: Discours sur les passions de l'amour, Copenhagen: Le Bauhaus Imaginiste (1957)

The Naked City: Illustration de l'hypothèse des plaques tournantes en psychogéographique in Asger Jorn, *Pour la forme* (Paris: Internationale situationniste, 1958)

(with Asger Jorn), *Fin de Copenhague*, Copenhagen: Le Bauhaus Imaginiste, 1957)

Rapport sur la construction des situations et sur les conditions de l'organisation et de l'action de la tendance situationniste internationale (Paris, 1957)

'Remarques sur le concept d'art expérimental', internal SI document (1957)

1957–72

Internationale Situationniste, nos 1–12 (1958–69), reprinted *as Internationale Situationniste 1958–1969* (Amsterdam: Van Gennep, 1970); (Paris: Champ Libre, 1975; Paris: Arthème Fayard, 1997). Debord signed eight articles in *Internationale Situationniste* but many more as well as the overall direction of the journal can be attributed to him.

'Dix ans d'art expérimental: Jorn et son rôle dans l'invention théorique', in *Museum Journaal* 4 (Otterloo, 1958). Reprinted in Luc Mercier, ed., *Archives Situationnistes*, vol. 1 (Paris: Contre-Moules/Parallèles, 1997)

(with Asger Jorn), *Mémoires* (Copenhagen: Internationale Situationniste, 1959), reprinted with introductory note by Guy Debord (Paris: Jean-Jacques Pauvert aux Belles Lettres,1993)

(with P. Canjuers, otherwise known as Daniel Blanchard), *Préliminaires pour une définition de l'unité du programme révolutionnaire* (Paris, 1960)

'Les Situationnistes et les nouvelles formes d'action dans la politique et dans l'art', in *Destruktion af RSG-6: En kollectiv manifestation af Situationisk Internationale* (Odense, Denmark: Galerie EXI, 1963), 15–18

Contre le cinéma (Aarhus, Denmark: Institut Scandinave de Vandalisme Comparé, 1964)

'Le Déclin et la chute de l'économie spectaculaire-marchande' (Paris: Internationale situationniste, 1965)

'Le Point d'explosion de l'idéologie en Chine' (Paris: Internationale situationniste, 1966)

La société du spectacle (Paris: Buchet/Chastel, 1967).

(with Gianfranco Sanguinetti), *La véritable scission dans l'Internationale* (Paris: Champ Libre, 1972)

1972–84

'De l'architecture sauvage', in *Le Jardin d'Albisola* (Turin: Edizione d'Arte Fratelli Pozzo, 1974)

(with Gianfranco Sanguinetti) 'Censor', *Rapporto veridico sulle ultime opportunità di salvare il capitalismo in Italia* (Milan: Ugo Mursia, 1975), reprinted as *Véridique Rapport sur les dernières chances de sauver le capitalisme en Italie* (Paris: Champ Libre, 1976)

Oeuvres cinématographiques complètes 1952–78 (Paris: Champ Libre, 1978)

Préface à la quatrième édition italienne de la société du spectacle (Paris: Champ Libre, 1979)

Stances sur la mort de son père, translation of Jorge Manrique, *Coplas de Don Jorge Manrique por la muerte de su padre* (1477), afterword by Guy Debord (Paris: Champ Libre, 1980)

'Aux Libertaires', introduction to *Appels de la prison de Ségovie* (Paris: Champ Libre, 1980)

1984–94

Considérations sur l'assassinat de Gérard Lebovici (Paris: Gérard Lebovici, 1985; Paris: Gallimard, 1993)

(with Alice Becker-Ho, *Le 'jeu de la guerre', relevé des positions successives de toutes les forces au cour d'une partie* (Paris: Gérard Lebovici, 1987)

Commentaires sur la société du spectacle (Paris: Gérard Lebovici, 1987; Paris: Gallimard, 1992)

Panégyrique, vol. 1 (Paris: Gérard Lebovici, 1989; Paris: Gallimard, 1993)

'*Cette mauvaise réputation . . .*' (Paris: Gallimard, 1993)

Posthumous publications

Des Contrats (Cognac: Le Temps Qu'Il Fait, 1995)

Panégyrique, vol. 2 (Paris: Arthème Fayard, 1997)

In girum imus nocte et consumimur igni (Paris: Gallimard, 1999)

Correspondance, vol. 1, ed. Alice Debord (Paris: Arthème Fayard, 1999)

Filmography

Hurlements en faveur de Sade, Films Lettristes, Paris, 1952

Sur le passage de quelques personnes à travers une assez courte unité de temps, Dansk-Fransk Experimentalfilmskompagni, Paris, 1961

Critique de la séparation, Dansk-Fransk Experimentalfilmkompagni, Paris, 1961

La société du spectacle, Simar Films, Paris, 1973

Réfutation de tous les jugements, tant élogieux qu'hostiles, qui ont été jusqu'ici portés sur le film 'La société du spectacle', Simar Films, Paris, 1975

In girum imus nocte et consumimur igni, Simar Films, Paris, 1978

Guy Debord, son art et son temps, Canal Plus Television, Paris, 1995

Recorded work

Pour en finir avec le travail, Chansons du prolétariat révolutionnaire, EPM Musique 1998, SACEM 984582

Main works by Guy Debord in English translation

Situationist International Anthology, trans. Ken Knabb (Berkeley: Bureau of Public Secrets, 1995)

Leaving the 20th Century, The Incomplete Work of the Situationist International, trans. Christopher Gray (London: Rebel Press, 1998)

The Society of the Spectacle, trans. Donald Nicholson-Smith (New York: Zone Books, 1994)

(with Gianfranco Sanguinetti) *The Veritable Split in the International* (London: Piranha, 1974)

Comments on the Society of the Spectacle, trans. Malcolm Imrie (London: Verso, 1990)

In girum imus nocte et consumimur igni: A Film, trans. Lucy Forsyth (London: Pelagian Press, 1991)

Panegyric, vol. 1, trans. James Brook (London: Verso, 1991)

Selected further reading on Guy Debord, Letterism and the Situationist International

Giorgio Agamben, *I Situazionisti* (Rome: La Talpa di Biblioteca, 1991)

——'Le cinéma de Guy Debord', in *Image et mémoire* (Paris: Hoebeke, 1998)

Libero Andreotti and Xavier Costa, eds, *Situacionistes: Art, política, urbanisme/Situationists: Art, Politics, Urbanism* (Barcelona: Museu d'Art Contemporani/ACTAR, 1996)

Jean-Marie Apostolidès, *Les Tombeaux de Guy Debord* (Paris: Exils Éditeurs, 1998)

Mirella Bandini, *L'Estetico, il politico: Da Cobra all'Internazionale Situazionista 1948–1957* (Rome: Officina Edizioni, 1977)

——'Per loro la società è uno spettacolo', *L'Espresso*, no. 22, Rome, 1975

Jean Barrot, *What is Situationism?* (London: Unpopular Books, 1987)

Gérard Bérreby, *Documents relatifs à la fondation de l'Internationale situationniste* (Paris: Allia, 1985)

Christophe Bourseiller, *Vie et mort de Guy Debord* (Paris: Plon, 1999)

Gavin Bowd and Andrew Hussey, *The Hacienda Must Be Built: On the Legacy of Situationist Revolt* (Manchester: Manchester University Modern Literature Group/Aura, 1996)

Éliane Brau, *Le Situationnisme ou la nouvelle internationale* (Paris: Nouvelle Éditions Debresse, 1968)

Jean-Louis Brau, *Cours, camarade, le vieux monde est derrière toi! Histoire du mouvement révolutionnaire en Europe* (Paris: Albin Michel, 1968)

François Châtelet, 'La dernière internationale', *Le Nouvel observateur*, 3 January 1968

Timothy Clark and Donald Nicholson-Smith, 'Why Art Can't Kill the Situationist International', *October 79* (1997), pp.15–31

Francesca Comissio, 'Prémisse', in *Autour de la création de l'Internationale Situationniste* (Manosqe: Éditions Sulliver, 2000)

Constant, *New Babylon: Art et Utopie, textes situationnistes* (Paris: Cercle d'Art, 2000)

Margaret Crawford, 'The Hacienda Must Be Built', *Design Book Review* 24 (1992), pp.38–42

Frédérique Devaux, *Le Cinéma lettriste* (Paris: Paris Expérimental, 1992)

——*Entretiens avec Isidore Isou* (Paris: La Bartavelle, 1992)

——*Traité de bave et de l'eternité d'Isidore Isou* (Crisnée, Belgium: Yellow Now, 1994)

Pascal Dumontier, *Les Situationnistes et mai 68: Théorie et pratique de la révolution 1966–1972* (Paris: Gérard Lebovici, 1990)

Jean-Michel Frodon, 'Un cinéma sans spectacle', *Le Monde*, 3 December 1994

Rochard Gombin, *Les Origines du gauchisme* (Paris: Éditions du Seuil, 1971)

Dominique Grass, *Contribution à une critique de la société du spectacle* (Mémoire de maîtrise, Université de Franche-Comté, 1999)

Gérard Guégan, *Debord est mort, le Che aussi. Et alors? Embrasse ton amour sans lâcher ton fusil* (Paris: Cahiers des saisons, 1994)

Cécile Guilbert, *Pour Guy Debord* (Paris: Gallimard, 1996)

——*Le Musée Nationale* (Paris: Gallimard, 2000)

Pierre Guillaume, 'Debord', *La Vieille Taupe* (Paris:1995), pp.63–109

Andrew Hussey, '"La Divinité d'Isou": The making of a name and a messiah', *Forum for Modern Language Studies*, vol. XXXVI (Oxford University Press, 2000), pp. 132–43

——'La guerre de l'art: L'art de la guerre. Les exilés situationnistes et pré-situationnistes' in *Autour de la création de l'internationale situationniste*, exhibition catalogue, Éditions Sulliver, Manosque, 2000

——'Abolish everything!', *London Review of Books*, 2 September 1999, pp.29–32

——'The Self-Concealing Situation', *Times Literary Supplement*, 27 August 1999, p.29

——'Saint Guy de Paris', *Times Literary Supplement*, 4 October 1996, p.8

——'From Being to Nothingness', *Independent on Sunday Review*, 10 December 1995, pp.16–22

——'Esprit de Mort', *Harper's Magazine*, September 1995, pp.18–19

——'Au Revoir cruel monde', *Modern Review*, April 1995, p.27

Isidore Isou, *L'Agrégation d'un nom et d'un messie* (Paris: Gallimard, 1947)

——*Esthétique du cinéma* (Paris: Ur, 1953)

——*L'Héritier du Château* (Paris: Éditions Balland, 1976)

——*Contre le cinéma situationniste néo-nazi* (Paris: GB/NV/MB 1979)

David Jacobs and Christopher Winks, *At Dusk: The Situationist Movement in Historical Perspective* (Berkely: Perspectives, 1975)

Dominique Jamet, 'Une opposition aux situationnistes s'est constituée à Strasbourg', *Alsace*, 3 November 1966

——'La prise de pouvoir des situationnistes à Strasbourg', *Le Figaro Littéraire*, 1 December 1966

——'De nombreuse personnalités prennent positions contre les situationnistes', *Le Figaro*, 8 December 1966

Anselm Jappe, 'La lenta dissipazione del pensiero critico', *Il Manifesto*, 3 December 1994

——*Guy Debord* (Marseilles: Via Valeriano, 1995)

Merri Jolivet, 'Nous avons fait ensemble un grand voyage sur place', *Libération*, 6 December 1994

Thierry Jousse, 'Guy Debord: stratégie de la disparition', *Cahiers du cinéma* 487 (1995), pp.41–3

Robert Kanters, 'Des Iconoclastes parmi nous', *Le Figaro Littéraire*, 25 December 1967

Vincent Kaufmann, 'Angels of Purity', *October 79* (1997), pp.49–68

Georges Lavaudant, 'Déjà sa pensée nous aveugle', *Libération*, 6 December 1994

Walter Lewino, *L'Imagination au pouvoir* (Paris: Le Terrain vague, 1968)

Greil Marcus, 'The Cowboy Philosopher', *Artforum* 24 (1986), pp.85–91

Greil Marcus, *Lipstick Traces: A Secret History of the Twentieth Century* (Cambridge, Mass.: Harvard University Press, 1989)

Gianfranco Marelli, *L'amère victoire du situationnisme* (Arles: Éditions Sulliver, 1998)

——*La dernière internationale* (Arles: Éditions Sulliver, 2000)

Francis Marmande, 'Guy Debord, esthète de la subversion', *Le Monde*, 3 December 1994

Jean-François Martos, *Histoire de l'Internationale Situationniste* (Paris: Ivrea, 1995)

——*Correspondance avec Guy Debord* (Paris, Le fin mot de l'histoire, 1998)

Jean-Michel Mension, *La Tribu* (Paris: Allia, 1998)

Robert Ohrt, *Phantom Avantgarde: Eine Geschichte der Situationistischen Internationale und der modernen kunst* (Hamburg: Editions Nautilius, 1990)

Mario Perniola, 'Arte e revoluzione', *Tempo Presente*, December 1966

Franco Pierini, 'I partiti non hanno più niente da dirci', *L'Europeo*, December 1966

J. J. Raspaud, J. P. Voyer, *L'Internationale situationniste. Protoganistes, chronologie, bibliographie* (Paris: Champ Libre, 1971)

Ralph Rumney, *Le Consul* (Paris: Allia, 1999)

——*Pourvu que ça dure* (Manosque: Bureau des inspections banalytiques, 1998)

Simon Sadler, *The Situationist City* (Cambridge, Mass.: MIT Press, 1998)

Gianfranco Sanguinetti (Letter), 'Che situazione', *Panoroma*, Milan, 13 June 1978

Frédéric Schiffter, *Guy Debord l'Atrabilaire* (Biarritz: Éditions de la Distance, 1997)

Pierre Henri Simon, review of *La Société du spectacle* and *Traité de savoir-vivre*, *Le Monde*, 14 February 1968

Philippe Sollers (interview), 'Avez-vous lu Guy Debord?', *L'Humanité*, 5 November 1992

——'Considérations sur la mort de Guy Debord', *Libération*, 6 December 1994

——*La Guerre du Goût* (Paris: Gallimard, 1997)

Arnold Spire, 'Son oeuvre ultime', *L'Humanité*, 2 December 1994

George Steiner, review of *La Société du spectacle*, *Sunday Times*, 21 July 1968

Elisabeth Sussman, ed., *On the Passage of a Few People Through a Rather Brief Moment in Time 1957–1972* (Cambridge, Mass.: MIT Press, 1989)

Olivier Todd, 'Strasbourg en situation', *Le nouvel observateur*, 21 December, 1966

Gilles Tordjmann and Arnaud Viviant, 'La société du spectacle', *Libération*, 2 December 1994

Raoul Vaneigem, *Traité de savoir-vivre à l'usage des jeunes générations* (Paris: Gallimard, 1967)

Fred and Judy Vermorel, *Sex Pistols: The Inside Story* (New York: Music Sales Corporation, 1987)

René Viénet, *Enragés et situationnistes dans le mouvement des occupations* (Paris: Gallimard, 1968)

Edouard Waintrop, 'Guy Debord arrête ici son véritable histoire', *Libération*, 2 December 1994

Natacha Wolinksi, 'Guy Debord s'est sabordé', *Information*, 2 December 1994

Gil J. Wolman, *L'Anticoncept* (Paris: Allia, 1994)

Alan Woods, *The Map is not the Territory* (Manchester: Manchester University Press, 2001)

Other works consulted

Guy Atkins, *Asger Jorn* (London: Methuen, 1964)

Jean Baudrillard, *L'Échange impossible* (Paris: Galilée, 2000)

Alice Becker-Ho, *Les Princes de jargon* (Paris: Gallimard, 1993)

——*D'azur au triangle vidé de sable* (Cognac: Le Temps qu'il fait, 1998)

——*Paroles de Gitans* (Paris: Albin Michel, 2000)

——*Au Pays du sommeil paradoxal* (Cognac: Le Temps qu'il fait, 2000)

Michèle Bernstein, *Tous les Chevaux du roi* (Paris: Buchet-Chastel, 1960)

——*La Nuit* (Paris: Buchet-Chastel, 1961)

Michel Bounan, *Le Temps du SIDA* (Paris: Allia, 1991)

——*L'incitation à l'autodéfense* (Paris: Allia, 1995)

Gavin Bowd, *The Outsiders: Alexander Trocchi and Kenneth White* (Kirkcaldy: Akros, 1998)

——*L'Interminable enterrement* (Paris: Digraphe, 1999)

Gordon Carr, *The Angry Brigade* (London: Gollancz, 1975)

David Caute, *The Year of the Barricades* (London: Hamish Hamilton, 1988)

T. J. Clark, *The Painting of Modern Life, Paris in the Art of Manet and his Followers* (London: Thames & Hudson, 1985)

Norman Cohn, *The Pursuit of the Millennium: Revolutionary Millenarians and Mystical Anarchists of the Middle Ages* (London: Oxford University Press, 1957)

Daniel Cohn-Bendit, *Obsolete Communism, the Left-Wing Alternative* (London: Penguin, 1968)

Colin Crouch, *The Student Revolt* (London: Bodley Head, 1970)

English Section of the Situationist International, *King Mob Echo* (Edinburgh: Dark Star, 2000)

Patrick ffrench, *The Time of Theory: The History of Tel Quel 1960–1982* (London: Oxford University Press, 1995)

Philippe Forest, *Histoire de Tel Quel 1960–1982* (Paris: Éditions du Seuil, 1995)

Juan Goytisolo, *En los reinos de taifa* (Barcelona: Seix Barral, 1986)

Jonathon Green, *Days in the Life – Voices from the English Underground* (London: Heinemann, 1988)

Gérard Guégan, *Markus Wolf avait une soeur, je l'ai aimée* (Paris: Grasset, 1997)

Michel Guet, Maxi-Tour, *Toute ressemblance avec un pays ayant existé* (Franche-Comté: Lettres de Change, 1997)

Chantal Guillaume, *Le Bon Ledoux du Jura* (Besançon: Bureau des inspections banalytiques, 2000)

Hervé Hamon and Patrick Rotman, *Générations*, vols 1 and 2 (Paris: Éditions de la Découverte, 1992)

Sophie Herszkowicz, *Pétition à l'Académie des Beaux Arts pour les étudiants que l'on empêche de dessiner* (Arles: Éditions Sulliver, 1997)

Christopher Hibbert, *King Mob* (London: Reader's Union, 1959)

Stewart Home, *The Assault on Culture* (Edinburgh: AK Press, 1991)

Johan Huizinga, *Homo Ludens* (Paris: Gallimard, 1951)

Karl Korsch, *Karl Marx* (Paris: Champ Libre, 1971)

Philippe Labro, *Ce n'est qu'un début* (Paris: Denoel, 1968)

Irinée D. Lastelle, *Le Scarabée – Seuil nucléaire et dissolution* (Arles: Éditions Sulliver, 1997)

Gérard Lebovici, *Tout sur le personnage* (Paris: Champ Libre, 1984)

——*Correspondance* (including letters from Guy Debord), vols 1 and 2 (Paris: Éditions Ivrea, 1996)

Henri Lefebvre, *Introduction à la critique de la vie quotidienne* (Paris: Grasset, 1947)

——*Critique de la vie quotidienne* (Paris: L'Arche, 1958)

——*Le Temps des mépris* (Paris: Stock, 1975)

Milano/Derive Approdi, *. . . ma l'amor mio no muore, origini documenti strategie dell 'cultura alternativa' e dell 'underground' in Italia* (Rome: Castelvecchi, 1996)

Jean Maitron, *Histoire du mouvement en France* (Paris: Francis Maspéro, 1951)

——*Le Mouvement anarchiste en France* (Paris: Francis Maspéro, 1975)

Jacques Mesrine, *L'Instinct de mort* (Paris: Champ Libre, 1984)

Lewis Mumford, *The City in History* (New York: Harcourt Brace, 1961)

Gabriel Pomerand, *Saint Ghetto des prêts* (Paris: OLB, 1951)

Jamie Reid, *Up they Rise: The Incomplete Works of Jamie Reid* (London: Faber and Faber, 1987)

Jon Savage, *England's Dreaming, Sex Pistols and Punk Rock* (London: Faber and Faber, 1991)

Roger Shattuck, 'Paris Letter', in *Accent: A Quarterly of New Literature* (Urbana, 1948)

Alessandro Silj, *Mai più senza fucile* (Florence: Vallecchi, 1977)

La Société du Mensonge Ébranlée, *Rien n'est permis, tout est vrai* (Lyons: Publications des Associés autonomes, 1998)

Alexander Trocchi, *Cain's Book* (New York: Grove Press, 1960)

Tom Vague, *Anarchy in the UK: The Angry Brigade* (Edinburgh: AK Press, 1997)

Ed van der Elsken, *Parijs! Foto's 1950–1954* (Amsterdam: Van Gennep, 1984)

Index